American Catholic Identities
A Documentary History
Christopher J. Kauffman, General Editor

Keeping Faith

European and Asian Catholic Immigrants

Jeffrey M. Burns

Ellen Skerrett

Joseph M. White

Editors

ORBIS BOOKS

Maryknoll, New York 10545

Copyright © 2000 by Jeffrey M. Burns, Ellen Skerrett, and Joseph M. White.

Published by Orbis Books, Maryknoll, New York, U.S.A.

Manufactured in the United States of America

For document no. 91, which is from *America*, all rights are reserved. For subscription information, call 1-800-627-9533 or visit www.americapress.org.

Library of Congress Cataloging-in-Publication Data

Keeping faith : European and Asian Catholic immigrants / Jeffrey M. Burns, Ellen Skerrett, Joseph M. White, editors.
    p.   cm. — (American Catholic identities)
    Includes bibliographical references.
    ISBN 1-57075-317-2 (hardcover) — ISBN 1-57075-297-4 (pbk.)
    1. Immigrants—Religious life—United States—History—19th century—Sources. 2. European American Catholics—History—19th century—Sources. 3. Catholic Church—United States—History—19th century—Sources. 4. United States—Emigration and immigration—Religious aspects—Catholic Church—History—19th century—Sources. 5. Immigrants—Religious life—United States—History—20th century—Sources. 6. European American Catholics—History—20th century—Sources. 7. Asian American Catholics—History—20th century—Sources. 8. Catholic Church—United States—History—20th century—Sources. 9. United States—Emigration and immigration—Religious aspects—Catholic Church—History—20th century—Sources. I. Burns, Jeffrey M. II. Skerrett, Ellen. III. White, Joseph Michael. IV. Series

BX1407.I45 K44 2000
282'.73 – dc21
                                             00–039984

To our spouses

Sabina
John
Rebecca

For their love and support

CONTENTS

Part 2
PHOTO ESSAY:
BUILDING THE IMMIGRANT CHURCH

Part 3
DIVERSIFYING THE IMMIGRANT CHURCH

Part 4
AFTER 1924:
THE PERSISTENCE AND TRANSCENDENCE
OF ETHNICITY

Part 5
ASIAN IMMIGRANTS

Part 6
NEW MODELS AND CONCERNS

FOREWORD

Christopher J. Kauffman

To comment that this work is "comprehensive" is not only to collapse into the rhetoric of cliché but also to mask the reality by an abstract understatement. No published work, and certainly no documentary history book, includes the number of immigrant groups that *Keeping the Faith* includes. The structure of the book is also unique: chronology blends with the stories of particular ethnic groups and with specific topics such as birth control, as in the section titled "The Transcendence of Ethnicity." There is a fine balance between, on the one hand, episcopal and clerical commentaries on ethnic groups and, on the other hand, the comments "from below" that highlight the experiences of a particular ethnic group.

At first glance the sectional divisions according to particular ethnic groups appear to be artificial boundaries separating the experience of one ethnic group from all the others during a specific period when several groups experienced industrialization, periodic economic depressions, and the movement toward class divisions. However, the many immigrant groups included in the volume preclude a topical arrangement, and where it is feasible the editors do integrate the experiences on topics and themes — for example, the German and Irish during the Americanist crisis and the various elements relating to parish developments. So the boundaries are actually congenial with organic developments, despite the general separation according to the group rather than the topic. The advantage of the division by ethnic group is that the reader is treated to three-dimensional portraits of many ethnic groups — the documents on groups such as the Austrians, Czechs, Lithuanians, and Slovaks form a mural of Eastern European life in the United States. Multiregional stories come to life in several sets of documents, such as those regarding the Polish and Italian communities in cities and towns in the East, Southwest, and Far West.

With nearly one-third of the book devoted to documents on the many Asian-American peoples, parishes, and schools in the United States, the originality of this documentary history of immigrant communities becomes quite evident. As Jeffrey Burns notes in his introduction, Asian Catholic immigrants range from Filipinos who came from a predominantly Catholic country to Japanese who converted in the contexts of parish language schools on the West Coast. While the European immigrants were bearers of the Judeo-

Christian cultural heritage, most of the immigrants from Asia were influenced by Confucian, Taoist, Buddhist, and animist religious strands in their cultures.

An article by theologian Peter Phan in *The U.S. Catholic Historian* (vol. 18, winter 2000) is abundant with insight into the complexity of Vietnamese Catholic life in the United States. That article and the brief introduction to document 129 below help illuminate several documents included here on tensions and conflicts in the diocese of San Jose. Phan explores social inculturation of the Vietnamese Catholics into American society, as well as their religious inculturation in a post–Vatican II world, developments that require negotiations between the Vietnamese Catholics and their American neighbors as well as between the former and Catholics of other ethnic traditions. These negotiations are further complicated by the pluralism in church and society.

Two distinctive patterns emerge in this documentary history: first, the dominance of the ethnic parish from St. Peter's German parish in early nineteenth-century Baltimore to the personal parish for the Vietnamese in San Jose in 1989; and, second, the creation of ethnic organizations to strengthen the groups' power and effectiveness in dealing with social and religious challenges. The persistence of nativist responses, the discriminatory practices in various social, economic, and political spheres, and the significance of generations among immigrant groups are strands woven into these patterns affecting ethnic life in the United States. These strands are symbolic of the need for ethnic groups, both in the past and today, to define and redefine their identities in order to deal effectively with the insider groups.

It must come as no surprise that each of the three editors has published works in parish history with an emphasis on the ethnic dimension. They have wrought an eminently useful collection of documents laced with clear and insightful introductions. Burns, Skerrett, and White have mined rich veins of documents, adding luster to religious immigrant history. Undergraduates and graduate students, as well as their professors, can easily integrate many of these documents into their courses, their theses, and their publications.

ACKNOWLEDGMENTS

In putting together this book, we were dependent on a vast number of persons and institutions. We want to thank most heartily the following people, who either suggested documents or supplied us with documents. We are grateful to you all. Stuart MacKenzie, Sister Catherine Ann Curry, P.B.V.M., and Rev. John Reilly of the Archives of the Archdiocese of San Francisco. Diana Zimmermann and Mary Elizabeth Brown of the Center for Migration Studies, Staten Island, New York. Betty Vetere of the Maryknoll Mission Archives. Sister Marguerita Smith, O.P., of the Archives of the Archdiocese of New York. Joseph Casino of the Philadelphia Archdiocesan Historical Research Center. Joseph Coen of the Archives of the Diocese of Brooklyn. Rev. Conrad M. Borntrager, O.S.M., of the Servite Provincial Archives, Chicago. Carol J. Callahan, director of advancement, Woodlands Academy of the Sacred Heart, Lake Forest, Illinois. Steve Dailey, Milwaukee County Historical Society. Denise Eggers, assistant archivist, St. Paul College, Washington, D.C. David Gibson, United States Catholic Conference. Jean M. Glockler, Holy Family Preservation Society, Chicago. Brother Michael J. Grace, S.J., archivist, Loyola University of Chicago. James L. Hansen, State Historical Society of Wisconsin. Sister Anita Therese Hayes, B.V.M., archivist, Sisters of Charity of the Blessed Virgin Mary, Dubuque, Iowa. Robert Johnson-Lally, archivist and records manager, Archdiocese of Boston. John J. Treanor, vice chancellor of archives and records, and Julie A. Satzik, assistant research archivist, Archdiocese of Chicago's Joseph Cardinal Bernardin Archives and Records Center. Philip M. Runkel, assistant archivist, Department of Special Collections and University Archives, Marquette University, Milwaukee. Paul Lane, Photo Source, Evanston, Illinois. Joseph M. McAuley, assistant to the literary editor, *America* magazine. Diane Novosel, president, Society for the Preservation of the Murals of St. Nicholas Croatian Catholic Church. Sister Margaret Phelan, R.S.C.J., assistant archivist, Society of the Sacred Heart National Archives, U.S.A., St. Louis, Missouri. Christine Taylor, Archives of the Archdiocese of Seattle. Monsignor Francis Weber, Archival Center, Archdiocese of Los Angeles. Cecil White, St. Patrick's Seminary Library, Menlo Park, California. Sister M. Gemma, C.S.F.N., Archives of the Sisters of the Holy Family of Nazareth, Des Plaines, Illinois. Sister Mary Michael Gecewicz, C.S.F.N., Archives of the Sisters of the Holy Family of Nazareth, Philadelphia. Jay P. Dolan and Philip Gleason, University of Notre Dame. Genevieve Ng. Anita

Specht. Michael Dalton. Dominic Fasso. Monsignor John Strynkowski. Pat Allen. Rachel Bundang. Angela Yung-mi Pak. Albert Acena. Madeline Duntley. M. Mark Stolarik. Sister Mercedes Voytko, SS.C.M. Edward J. Casey. Dianne Casper. Kenneth R. Desautels. Charles and Frances Purcell Fanning. Suellen Hoy. Joseph J. O'Shaughnessy. Joan Radtke. Steve Rosswurm. Helen A. Sclair. Michael C. Skerrett. Sister Loretta Rybacki. Nancy Rybacki. Sabina Burns. Rebecca L. White. Sister Angelyn Dries, O.S.F. Timothy Matovina. Rev. William Wolkovich-Valkavičius. Msgr. James F. Connelly. Robert L. Reid. John T. Strachan. P. J. Skerrett.

We thank those who granted permission to publish their documents.

We are grateful to Christopher J. Kauffman and William R. Burrows for all their advice and encouragement.

Finally we thank the unnamed technicians — known to God — who service the many photocopy machines used in the course of collecting materials for this project.

GENERAL INTRODUCTION

Jeffrey M. Burns, Ellen Skerrett, and Joseph M. White

The Catholic Church in the United States is and has been an immigrant church. From the earliest arrivals of the English in colonial Maryland to the most recent immigrants from the Philippines and Vietnam, Catholic immigrants have sought to live out their faith in what has often been a hostile environment. In meeting the needs of immigrants, the Catholic Church faced serious challenges. First, the church had to establish itself sufficiently to make certain that it could provide Catholics with the basic ministries of worship and sacraments. Second, it had to accommodate the languages and cultures of wave after wave of immigrants. The accommodation of immigrants became the central theme of U.S. Catholic life into the 1920s, as it continues to be at the end of the twentieth century. This accommodation generated tremendous conflicts as immigrant groups vied to have their vision and experience of Catholic life respected. As a result, the church that developed was not a monolithic institution, though it has often been perceived as such. Rather it was a mix of various cultures. Though the American church became "the immigrant church," in fact, it consisted of many immigrant churches.

The massive immigration of the nineteenth century clearly altered the face of U.S. Catholicism, but the Catholic community's transition from one predominant ethnic group to a diversity of groups began in the late eighteenth century. Until then, most Catholics in the new republic were of English stock and resided in rural Maryland, where they upheld a genteel tradition of accommodating to the prevailing Protestant and slaveholding culture.[1] In the 1790s, French priests driven from their homeland by the French Revolution arrived in the United States to take up ministry to American Catholics. By their superior education and refinement, these émigrés reinforced a genteel image of Catholicism. Beginning around 1815 immigration from Ireland and Germany to the United States began to increase, rising notably at midcentury

---

1. See Thomas W. Spalding, *The Premier See: A History of the Archdiocese of Baltimore, 1789–1989* (Baltimore: Johns Hopkins University Press, 1989).

when major agricultural crises in Ireland and in parts of German-speaking Europe sent some two million immigrants to the United States. Accordingly, by 1860, the Catholic Church in the United States had become the nation's single largest religious body, with over three million members. By then, bishops and clergy of the majority Irish within the American Catholic community had taken firm charge of the church's overall direction, creating what many ensuing immigrant groups referred to as the "Irish Catholic Church in America."

In dealing with the church's English-speaking majority, German Catholics led the way in pioneering what became the basic approach to accommodating immigrants — the national parish. As early as 1787, German Catholics in Philadelphia established the first such parish, Holy Trinity, where they could hear sermons, sing hymns, and celebrate devotions in their native language and preserve these traditions for their children. The national parish also provided a buffer to the hostile American environment and the aggressive Americanizing tendencies among some of the church's Irish leaders. The national parish, then, became the central institution in immigrant communities for the preservation of faith and culture, but it also served as a means of adjustment and assimilation to American life.

With the national parish already established as the model of ministering to immigrants, the Catholic Church welcomed more groups from 1870 to 1924. While arrivals from Germany and Ireland continued, immigration of such major European groups as Italians and Poles increased dramatically. So did immigration from Mexico and French-speaking Canada. Each group brought different religious cultures and had varied expectations of the church as they established themselves in the United States. Accordingly, each group responded differently to the model of the national parish. By 1920, the six major groups, Irish, Germans, Italians, Poles, French Canadians, and Mexican Americans, according to Jay P. Dolan, accounted for 75 percent of the Catholic population. In addition to these numerically large groups, some twenty-two other ethnic groups arrived, with four — Slovaks, Lithuanians, Ukrainians, and Czechs — being the largest.[2] The Catholic Church, then, was no longer marked by the numerical dominance of Irish and Germans as in the era before 1870, but these two groups continued to dominate national church leadership.

With the arrival of so many Catholic immigrants, church leaders debated for more than a century the question of whether a significant portion of immigrants "lost" their religious faith when they came to the United States. Some reports suggested that Catholic immigrants had indeed abandoned religious faith as they assimilated to American life. The St. Raphael Societies' memorial of 1891 (see document 30) and the Polish "I Polacchi" memorial of 1920

---

2. Jay P. Dolan, *American Catholic Experience: A History from Colonial Times to the Present* (Garden City, N.Y.: Doubleday, 1985), 156.

(see document 67), both claiming that millions of immigrants left the church, demanded more attentive, more sympathetic ministry to immigrant groups. In practical terms such memorials proposed the creation of more national parishes and the appointment of bishops from and for the different ethnic groups. These proposals received an unenthusiastic reception from the predominantly Irish-American hierarchy, who expected the rapid assimilation of immigrants to the English language and American ways. In 1925, as the era of mass immigration closed, Rev. Gerald Shaughnessy, S.M., a future bishop, furnished an answer to the ongoing question in his assessment of Catholic immigration, *Has the Immigrant Kept the Faith?* According to Shaughnessy, the church in the United States was remarkably successful in this regard: "The conclusion that presents itself is that the vast Catholic immigration into the United States throughout the past century has been successfully assimilated and retained by the American Church."[3]

We have titled this volume *Keeping Faith* not only to reflect the institutional concern of preserving the immigrants' faith but also to highlight the immigrants' active participation in establishing and defining the faith in the new land. In other words, immigrants were not merely passive recipients of pastoral care. Countless laymen and laywomen collaborated with immigrant priests and men and women religious to build and support churches, sponsor parochial schools, form devotional societies, and in myriad other ways lay the foundation for the Catholic Church in the United States. Rev. Francis C. Kelley, founder of the Catholic Church Extension Society and a future bishop, captured this reality in a 1915 address:

> It is not so much a question as to what the Church did for them [the immigrants] as what they did for the Church. The blessings of religion, of course, are inestimable; but these people knew what the blessings were and took very good care that they should have them. Wherever there were twenty-five Irish families the Church appeared, and no thanks to anyone but God and those twenty-five families. Wherever the same number of Germans settled the case was the same. It took a few more Poles, possibly, but the church they built made up for the greater number that it took to build it.[4]

In reality, of course, the Poles were just as eager if not more so to establish and maintain their own parishes. Despite Kelley's positive views, immigrant church-building could also be the source of problems — immigrants who raised money and built their own churches considered the churches their own and resented the intervention of outsiders, even when those outsiders happened to be bishops.

---

3. Gerald Shaughnessy, *Has the Immigrant Kept the Faith?* (New York: Macmillan, 1925), 214.
4. Bishop Francis C. Kelley, "The Church and the Immigrant," *Catholic Mind* 13, no. 17 (8 September 1915): 472.

The immigrants were keeping faith not only with the Catholic Church but also with the traditions of their homelands. As historian Mack Walker once observed of the Germans, "They did not come to establish something new, they came to reestablish something old."[5] Such was true of most immigrant groups. When the nation's first Polish immigrants settled at Panna Maria, Texas, in 1854, they brought with them the bell and great cross from their village church in Poland, which they incorporated into their new church in Texas. The immigrants' connections to their mother country and their resistance to assimilation to America often resulted in severe conflict within the American church, whose leaders often understood its role to be the Americanization of new immigrants. Bishop Edmund M. Dunne of Peoria asserted in 1923, on the eve of immigrant restriction:

> Certain well-defined principles have from the very beginning guided the Church in dealing with those of her members who sought for larger opportunities in the new land...These principles might be thus briefly summarized: (1) The immigrant must be kept faithful to his religion; (2) Through his own language as long as necessary; (3) He must at the same time be made a good American citizen.[6]

Not all groups had a similar understanding of the church's role.

The documents selected here (and in a later volume) reflect the richness of immigrant Catholicism as well as the problems and frustrations immigrants encountered. The selection is not limited to European groups but includes Catholic immigrants from Asia and Latin America, who represent the fastest-growing segment of the Catholic population today. (Latinos, it should be noted, are treated in a separate volume in this series.) Asian immigration has escalated since the Immigration Reform Act of 1965. What is striking about Asian Catholics is how similar their struggles are to those of previous immigrant groups. They too want ministry in their own language and their traditions respected. They too have created their own distinctive communities to assist in keeping the faith. Once again the church is an immigrant church, one that reflects the dynamism of accommodating new groups as the new groups grope for their own voice and place within the U.S. Catholic Church.

We have divided our study into six parts. Part 1, "Establishing the Immigrant Church," presents the Irish and Germans, the two largest Catholic immigrant groups in the nineteenth century. The Irish, after a struggle with

---

5. Mack Walker, *Germany and the Emigration, 1816–1885* (Cambridge, Mass.: Harvard University Press, 1954), 69.

6. Edmund M. Dunne, "The Church and the Immigrant," in C. E. McGuire, ed., *Catholic Builders of the Nation* (Boston: Continental Press, 1923), 4.

French leaders in the U.S. church, established their dominant role in its leadership. In turn, the Germans arrived in substantial numbers to challenge Irish dominance and achieve significant influence particularly in the Midwest.

Part 2, "Photo Essay: Building the Immigrant Church," combines photographs and documents to address a chief feature of the immigrant church — church-building. Church edifices were powerful statements of the immigrants' faith and devotion and proclaimed the Catholic presence in the larger community.

Part 3, "Diversifying the Immigrant Church," examines the many groups — Poles, Italians, French Canadians, and eastern Europeans — that came at the end of the nineteenth century and dramatically diversified the makeup of the U.S. Catholic Church. The varied styles and traditions of these groups were often sources of enormous tension and conflict with church leaders.

Part 4 examines the repercussions of the restrictive Immigration Act of 1924, which imposed national quotas discriminating against new immigration from traditionally Catholic countries. With fewer immigrants arriving, the church entered a period of consolidating the efforts of the previous century, though characteristics of the immigrant church persisted. By the 1980s, however, some national parishes established in the nineteenth century were no longer necessary and were closed. The closings generated strong protests from ethnic communities, often to the surprise of diocesan officials.

Part 5 focuses on various Asian immigrant groups, which have become increasingly important since the Immigration Act of 1965 opened a new era of mass immigration. The distinctive Chinese, Japanese, Filipino, Vietnamese, and Korean Catholic experiences are explored here.

In part 6, the documents reflect "new models and concerns." In recent years, the old Americanization model of assimilation has given way to the model of "cultural pluralism." Equally significant, a large number of recent immigrants are refugees, which presents the U.S. church with serious pastoral concerns.

To assemble this book, we read through seemingly countless ethnic and immigrant histories. What struck us was how few of these studies paid any attention to immigrants' religious experience — something we believe is essential to understanding immigrant communities. Historical studies of Catholicism in the United States were not much better. The scholarly study of immigrants' role in the history of the Catholic Church in the United States is by and large a recent phenomenon. Until the 1970s, historians of Catholicism gave scant attention to the religious experience of immigrant Catholics. The deans of the Catholic history profession in the United States, Monsignors Peter Guilday and John Tracy Ellis of the Catholic University of America, both paid fleeting attention to immigrant groups. Rev. Thomas T. McAvoy, C.S.C., in his general history,[7] paid more attention to immigrant concerns, but even he limited his attention to Germans and Irish — no mention is made of Italians, Polish, or other eastern European groups. In Ellis's 1969 revision of his classic *American Catholicism*, he observed, "One of the weakest areas in the literature on American Catholicism is immigration history."[8]

The trend to examine Catholic immigrants developed slowly. Following Shaughnessy's 1925 study, there were several pioneering efforts to examine Catholic immigrant life published in the 1930s and 1940s, including Lambert Schrott on German Catholics in the colonies,[9] Mary Gilbert Kelly on Catholic colonization projects,[10] and Emmet Rothan on antebellum German Catholic immigrants.[11] At the Catholic University of America, John Tracy Ellis directed two significant dissertations on aspects of Catholic immigrant issues, Joan Bland's 1951 history of the Catholic Total Abstinence Union that addresses Irish religious and social life,[12] and Colman Barry's 1953 work on German-American Catholics. Barry's work was one of the first significant studies of Catholic issues related to a specific immigrant group, reflecting his belief that "the Catholic Church in the United States has been in large measure an immigrant institution."[13] Despite his presentation of conflict between German Catholics and the church's Irish leaders, Barry's study concludes on a positive note concerning the church's role of assimilating immigrants: "The Catholic Church in the United States proved to be an effective 'melting pot' for immigrants."[14] Also in the 1950s, one of the first dissertations to focus on the national parish appeared — Vincent J. Fecher's study of German national parishes in Philadelphia and Baltimore.[15] Of all these studies, only Barry's continues to be a standard text in U.S. Catholic historiography.

In 1968, Philip Gleason published the first significant advance in the historiography of immigrant groups in more than a decade with *The Conservative Reformers: German-American Catholics and the Social Order*.[16] He described

---

7. Thomas T. McAvoy, C.S.C., *A History of the Catholic Church in the United States* (Notre Dame, Ind.: University of Notre Dame Press, 1969).

8. John Tracy Ellis, *American Catholicism*, 2d ed. (Chicago: University of Chicago Press, 1969), 301.

9. Lambert Schrott, *Pioneer German Catholics in the American Colonies, 1738–1784* (New York: United States Catholic Historical Society, 1933).

10. Mary Gilbert Kelly, *Catholic Immigrant Colonization Projects in the United States, 1815–1860* (New York: United States Catholic Historical Society, 1939).

11. Emmet Rothan, *The German Catholic Immigrant in the United States (1830–1860)* (Washington, D.C.: Catholic University of America Press, 1946).

12. Joan Bland, *Hibernian Crusade: The Story of the Catholic Total Abstinence Union* (Washington, D.C.: Catholic University of America Press, 1951).

13. Colman Barry, *The Catholic Church and German Americans* (Milwaukee: Bruce, 1953), 3.

14. Ibid., viii.

15. Vincent J. Fecher, *A Study of the Movement for German National Parishes in Philadelphia and Baltimore, 1787–1802* (Rome: Universita Gregoriana, 1955).

16. Philip Gleason, *The Conservative Reformers: German-American Catholics and the Social Order* (Notre Dame, Ind.: University of Notre Dame Press, 1968).

this work as "a case study in the assimilation of a Catholic immigrant group."[17] In it he presented the evolution and adaptation of the German Catholic Central Verein to the American social order. Gleason's work was a breakthrough as the first serious intellectual history of a Catholic immigrant group.

The following year Rudolph J. Vecoli, in his seminal article "Prelates and Peasants: Italian Immigrants and the Catholic Church,"[18] challenged the "Americanist" approach of most mainstream American Catholic historians. Vecoli notes:

> It is a curious fact that the historians of the "Church of the Immigrants" have neglected the study of many of the peoples who today constitute major elements in the American Catholic population. One may speculate that this was a consequence of the apologetic perspective which long dominated American Catholic historiography. The American character of the Church, not its foreign origins, provided the central theme of Catholic historical writing.[19]

Vecoli called for a new look at the many different immigrant groups, especially a reconsideration of Italian Catholics, who needed to be examined on their own terms rather than with preconceived notions as to what constitutes a "good" American Catholic.

The major breakthrough in Catholic immigrant history came with Jay P. Dolan's 1975 monograph, *The Immigrant Church: New York's Irish and German Catholics, 1815–1865*. In this study, Dolan constructed a classic social and urban history which redirected the focus of Catholic studies. His approach, variously described as history from the "bottom up" or with a "view from the pew," aimed to present Catholicism as experienced by ordinary Catholic immigrants. Early in the study Dolan reflects, "The church the immigrant knew was not an abstract entity; it was localized and represented in the neighborhood parish church. Built of wood or stone, it occupied space in the neighborhood, people could see it, touch it, and enter inside it to pray or simply to get out of the cold."[20] This approach was a clear break from the standard ecclesiastical and episcopal histories that so dominated American Catholic historiography. It was Dolan who popularized the term "immigrant church" and initiated a new era of Catholic immigrant historiography.

The publication of *The Immigrant Church* coincided with the publication of three other important immigrant and religious histories in 1975. Each dealt with what Vecoli had dubbed the "neglected groups" of Catholic immigrants:

---

17. Ibid., vii.
18. Rudolph J. Vecoli, "Prelates and Peasants: Italian Immigrants and the Catholic Church," *Journal of Social History* 2, no. 3 (spring 1969): 217–68.
19. Ibid., 219.
20. Jay P. Dolan, *The Immigrant Church: New York's Irish and German Catholics, 1815–1865* (Baltimore: Johns Hopkins University Press, 1975), 4.

Silvano M. Tomasi on Italians in New York; Josef J. Barton on Italians, Rumanians, and Slovaks in Cleveland; and Victor Greene on Lithuanians and Poles.[21] These studies represented an advance not only in Catholic studies but in immigrant studies as well. In 1978, Timothy L. Smith's seminal article in the *American Historical Review* on the close relationship of religion and ethnicity reinforced the new direction in immigrant and religious history.[22] The time was ripe for a "new" Catholic history.

The decade following Dolan's *The Immigrant Church* witnessed a flurry of new Catholic immigrant studies. In addition to Victor Greene's work, scholarly studies of Poles appeared, including T. Lindsay Baker on Silesian Poles in Texas,[23] Joseph J. Parot on Chicago Poles,[24] and Lawrence D. Orton on Detroit Poles.[25] In 1978, Arno Press published *The Other Catholics*,[26] a significant collection of essays on "neglected" immigrant groups, including Czechs, Italians, Poles, Slavs, Greeks, Ruthenians, and Slovaks. Other major monographs included in-depth studies by Lawrence J. McCaffrey on the Irish[27] and James W. Sanders on Catholic schools.[28]

The establishment of the Cushwa Center for the Study of American Catholicism with Jay P. Dolan as director ensured institutional support for the new approach. The center published two histories related to Catholic immigrant life as part of the Notre Dame Studies in American Catholicism: Anthony J. Kuzniewski's study of the Kruszka brothers and the Polish church war in Wisconsin[29] and Charles Shanabruch's study of Catholic immigrant groups in Chicago.[30]

---

21. Silvano M. Tomasi, *Piety and Power: The Role of the Italian Parishes in the New York Metropolitan Area, 1880–1930* (New York: Center for Migration Studies, 1975); Josef J. Barton, *Peasants and Strangers: Italians, Rumanians, and Slovaks in an American City, 1890–1950* (Cambridge, Mass.: Harvard University Press, 1975); Victor Greene, *For God and Country: The Rise of Polish and Lithuanian Ethnic Consciousness in America* (Madison, Wis.: State Historical Society, 1975).

22. Timothy L. Smith, "Religion and Ethnicity in America," *American Historical Review,* 83 (December 1978): 1155–85.

23. T. Lindsay Baker, *The First Polish Americans: Silesian Settlement in Texas* (College Station, Tex.: Texas A. & M. University Press, 1979).

24. Joseph J. Parot, *Polish Catholics in Chicago, 1850–1920* (DeKalb: Northern Illinois University Press, 1981).

25. Lawrence D. Orton, *Polish Detroit and the Kolasinski Affair* (Detroit: Wayne State University Press, 1981).

26. Keith P. Dyrud, Michael Novak, and Rudolph J. Vecoli, eds., *The Other Catholics* (New York: Arno Press, 1978).

27. Lawrence J. McCaffrey, *The Irish Diaspora in America* (Washington, D.C.: Catholic University of America Press, 1984); the revised edition has been retitled *The Irish Catholic Diaspora in America* (Washington, D.C.: Catholic University of America Press, 1997).

28. James W. Sanders, *The Education of an Urban Minority: Catholics in Chicago, 1833–1965* (New York: Oxford University Press, 1977).

29. Anthony J. Kuzniewski, *Faith and Fatherland: The Polish Church War in Wisconsin, 1896–1918* (Notre Dame, Ind.: University of Notre Dame Press, 1980).

30. Charles Shanabruch, *Chicago's Catholics: The Evolution of an American Identity* (Notre Dame, Ind.: University of Notre Dame Press, 1981).

The Center for Migration Studies (CMS), established on Staten Island at the former Scalabrinian seminary in 1964, also supported research and writing on immigrant groups. In 1975, CMS published Richard Linkh's study of the Americanization policies of the U.S. Catholic Church.[31] Over the next quarter-century a steady stream of immigrant studies would come from CMS.

In 1985 a significant study addressed the Italian immigrant experience — Robert A. Orsi's *The Madonna of 115th Street: Faith and Community in Italian Harlem, 1880–1950*. This innovative social history, according to the author, is "a study of religion in the streets."[32] His focus is one Italian *festa* held annually in Harlem, which he studies using anthropological methodologies to describe personal relationships within the family, community, and church. The book's success has been phenomenal, and it has become a standard in college courses on American religion and on American Catholicism.

In the 1980s, several authors produced works aiming at a synthesis of the Catholic immigrant story. Jay P. Dolan used the story of the immigrant church as the linchpin of his general history of Catholicism in the United States, *The American Catholic Experience*.[33] Though not intended as a monograph on Catholic immigrants, it remains the most thorough synthesis of that subject to date. Two studies that followed shortly after Dolan's work are useful histories of Catholic immigrants — one by Dolores Liptak, R.S.M., and the other by James S. Olson.[34]

The new research on Catholic immigrants also began to filter into more general histories, such as diocesan histories,[35] regional studies,[36] the history of Catholic schools,[37] and histories of religious orders.[38] Specific studies of immigrant groups also continued to appear in the 1980s and 1990s.[39]

---

31. Richard Linkh, *American Catholicism and European Immigrants (1900–1924)* (Staten Island, N.Y.: Center for Migration Studies, 1975).

32. Robert A. Orsi, *The Madonna of 115th Street: Faith and Community in Italian Harlem, 1880–1950* (New Haven, Conn.: Yale University Press, 1985), xiii.

33. Dolan, *American Catholic Experience*.

34. Dolores Liptak, R.S.M., *Immigrants and Their Church* (New York: Macmillan, 1989); James S. Olson, *Catholic Immigrants in America* (Chicago: Nelson-Hall, 1987).

35. See Leslie Tentler, *Seasons of Grace: A History of the Catholic Archdiocese of Detroit* (Detroit: Wayne State University Press, 1990); James B. Earley, *Envisioning Faith: The Pictorial History of the Diocese of Scranton* (Scranton, Pa.: n.p., 1993).

36. Dolores Liptak, R.S.M., *European Immigrants and the Catholic Church in Connecticut, 1870–1920* (New York: Center for Migration Studies, 1987); Jay P. Dolan, ed., *The American Catholic Parish: A History from 1850 to the Present*, 2 vols. (Mahwah, N.J.: Paulist Press, 1987).

37. JoEllen M. Vinyard, *For Faith and Fortune: The Education of Catholic Immigrants in Detroit, 1805–1925* (Urbana: University of Illinois Press, 1998); Timothy Walch, *Parish School: American Catholic Parochial Education from Colonial Times to the Present* (New York: Crossroads, 1996).

38. Joel Rippinger, O.S.B., *The Benedictine Order in the United States: An Interpretive History* (Collegeville, Minn.: Liturgical Press, 1990); Patricia Byrne, C.S.J., "Sisters of St. Joseph: The Americanization of a French Tradition," *U.S. Catholic Historian* 5 (summer/fall 1986): 241–72; Carol K. Coburn and Martha Smith, *Spirited Lives: How Nuns Shaped Catholic Culture and American Life* (Chapel Hill: University of North Carolina Press, 1999).

39. Mary Elizabeth Brown, *Churches, Communities, and Children: Italian Immigrants in the Archdiocese of New York, 1880–1945* (New York: CMS, 1995); idem, *From Italian Villages to Green-*

The scholarly study of Asian Catholic immigrants is a virgin field. While numerous studies dealing with Asian immigrants have been published, few consider the Catholic dimension. Even studies dealing with the predominantly Catholic Filipino immigrants rarely discuss religious experience. This omission may be due in part to the fact that a significant number of Asian immigrants have arrived only since 1965. The National Catholic Educational Association has published a collection of essays on Asian Catholic immigrants, *A Catholic Response to the Asian Presence,* which contains a useful bibliography.[40] Several studies treat Asian Catholic immigrants, but none extensively.[41] The *U.S. Catholic Historian* has advanced the study of Asian Catholic immigrants by devoting an entire issue to the topic, as it has done with other immigrant groups.

Despite few publications on Asian Catholics, the study of Catholic immigrants has come a long way since 1975. Indicative of the maturity of the field is the series of fine essays published on each European Catholic ethnic group in *The Encyclopedia of American Catholic History,* published in 1997.[42] The essays reflect the influence of recent scholarship on each group.

The study of all Catholic ethnic groups, past and present, will no doubt continue and lead to an increased understanding of the immigrant experience that has shaped and reshaped the Catholic community in the United States.

---

wich Village: Our Lady of Pompeii, 1892–1992 (New York: CMS, 1992); June G. Alexander, *The Immigrant Church and Community: Pittsburgh's Slovak Catholics and Lutherans, 1880–1915* (Pittsburgh: University of Pittsburgh Press, 1987); M. Mark Stolarik, *Growing up on the South Side: Three Generations of Slovaks in Bethlehem, Pennsylvania, 1880–1976* (Lewisburg, Pa.: Bucknell University Press, 1985); idem, *Immigration and Urbanization: The Slovak Experience, 1870–1918* (New York: AMS Press, 1989); Stephen J. Shaw, *The Catholic Parish as a Way-Station of Ethnicity and Americanization: Chicago's Germans and Italians, 1903–1939* (Brooklyn: Carlson, 1991); Stephen M. DiGiovanni, *Archbishop Corrigan and the Italian Immigrants* (Huntington, Ind.: Our Sunday Visitor Press, 1994); William Wolkovich-Valkavicius, *Lithuanian Religious Life in America: A Compendium of 150 Roman Catholic Parishes and Institutions,* 3 vols. (Norwood, Mass.: n.p., 1991, 1996, 1999); James S. Pula, *Polish Americans: An Ethnic Community* (New York: Twayne Publishers, 1995); Mary Louise Sullivan, M.S.C., *Mother Cabrini: "Italian Immigrant of the Century"* (New York: Center for Migration Studies, 1992); Austin Morini, O.S.M., *The Foundation of the Order of the Servants of Mary in the United States of America (1870–1883),* trans. Conrad M. Borntrager, O.S.M. (Rome: Edizioni Marianum, 1993); and Peter R. D'Agostino, "Missionaries in Babylon: The Adaptation of Italian Priests to Chicago's Church, 1870–1940" (Ph.D. diss., University of Chicago, 1993).

40. Suzanne E. Hall, S.N.D.deN., Ruth Narita Doyle and Peter Tran, C.Ss.R., eds., *A Catholic Response to the Asian Presence* (Washington, D.C.: National Catholic Educational Association, 1990).

41. See Jeffrey M. Burns, "Building the Best: A History of Catholic Parish Life in the Pacific States," in Dolan, ed., *American Catholic Parish,* 2:7–135; Angelyn Dries, O.S.F., *The Missionary Movement in American Catholic History* (Maryknoll, N.Y.: Orbis Books, 1998); and Madeline Duntley, "Japanese and Filipino Together: The Transethnic Vision of Our Lady Queen of Martyrs Parish," *U.S. Catholic Historian* 18 (winter 2000): 76–101.

42. Michael J. Glazier and Thomas J. Shelley, eds., *The Encyclopedia of American Catholic History* (Collegeville, Minn.: Liturgical Press, 1997).

Part 1

ESTABLISHING
THE IMMIGRANT CHURCH

Introduction

On 25 March 1634, two small ships, the *Ark* and the *Dove,* landed at St. Clement's Island in the Potomac River. The ships carried about two hundred English people to found a new colony — Maryland. The proprietor of the colony, Cecil Calvert, Lord Baltimore, a Catholic, saw it not only as a financial investment but also as a place where English Catholics could settle and freely practice their faith. A minority of Maryland's founders were Catholics. From their arrival these Catholics began to develop ways of adapting to a culture that was predominantly Protestant and often hostile — a course of adaptation that American Catholics carried on for generations.

Another dimension of Catholics' ongoing adaptation to the American scene was to welcome new groups of immigrants. This began in the eighteenth century as Catholics of English background in Maryland and Pennsylvania came to terms with German Catholic immigrants settling in Pennsylvania. In due course, Germans formed a Catholic church for themselves in Philadelphia in 1787, thereby establishing an influential model of U.S. Catholic life — the national parish (see document 21).

Through the colonial era, diversity expanded with the arrival of Irish immigrants, who, as English speakers, received ministry from English Jesuit priests. In the wake of the French Revolution (1789), some refugees arrived from France and the French West Indies. Though small in number, the French influx included some highly educated priests who left a favorable impression on American Protestants, but their ministry to the growing number of Irish Catholics was not always successful. Reacting against French clergy, many Irish sought ministry only from Irish priests. These French-Irish differences are addressed in several documents.

The arrival of nearly one million Irish immigrants in the thirty years leading to the Great Famine (1845–50) transformed the U.S. Catholic Church. As the number of Catholic dioceses grew, bishops were increasingly drawn

1

from Irish clergy. And Irish clergy, either immigrants or trained in the United States, gradually increased. With the Great Famine, Ireland lost a million people to death but more to migration. Between 1845 and 1855, more than one million Irish entered the United States, most of them Catholics. The influx reinforced the Irish hegemony in the American Catholic community.

Irish immigrants posed major challenges to Americans and to the church's leadership. Though most had been tenant farmers on small holdings in Ireland, few Irish arriving in America sought to make a living on the land. The Irish settled primarily in the cities, forging large communities there; often they formed the poorest segment of society. Their lack of education and skills gave credence to Americans' perception of them as crude and unruly. Heavy alcohol consumption by some reinforced their poverty and the unfavorable impression of their behavior. In response, the Irish, both clergy and laity, supported movements for total abstinence from alcohol. In addition, church leaders found that Irish immigrants had little formal understanding of their faith, and many followed superstitious practices. Clergy launched vigorous efforts to conform the Irish to a pattern of regular religious observance with Sunday Mass, reception of sacraments, and nonliturgical devotions and prayers.

After the Irish, the second largest group of Catholics arriving until the late nineteenth century was German speakers — mostly from German states that would unite to form the German Empire in 1870. Through the nineteenth century, Germans left their homeland for varied reasons. Population growth diminished economic opportunities; industrialization displaced artisans' work and cottage industries; and religious persecutions alienated Catholics. Moreover, famine afflicted some German-speaking areas in the periods 1817–20 and 1846–50. It is difficult to estimate numbers of German Catholic immigrants, since they did not come from a single state but from several that had both Protestant and Catholic populations. The famine of the late 1840s and its aftermath brought nearly a million Germans to the country, many of them Catholics.

When German Catholics began arriving in the United States in substantial numbers in the 1830s, churches for English-speaking Catholics did not attract them. They demanded the ministry of German priests. Soon Germans, in response to lay initiative, were forming German churches. They adapted models of communal government from their homeland to their national parishes as reflected in their insistence on lay trustees, a practice that sometimes brought them into conflict with Irish bishops. Germans' adherence to their churches was strong. For them, the parish was the place where, in the words of Bishop John Martin Henni, "language saves faith." The Germans' religious faith, language, and rich culture were all integrally united in their identity.

Catholic immigrants, whether Irish or German, revealed tremendous energy in building parishes and institutions during this "bricks and mortar" era. In a nation without state support of churches or church institutions, immigrants willingly sacrificed from meager earnings for the construction of great monuments in wood, brick, or stone that symbolized their faith.

In the closing years of the nineteenth century, competing visions of Catholic life increasingly divided Irish and German Catholics. For Germans the preservation of their ethnic parishes and institutions appeared threatened if they were not accorded equal canonical status with equivalent institutions for Irish Americans. Some German Catholic leaders sought a greater representation of Germans among the U.S. bishops and appointment of German vicars general for dioceses with a substantial German population. Germans also were uneasy if not hostile to the rhetoric of some U.S. bishops, the Americanists, who promoted the rapid assimilation of immigrants to the English language and American ways, an assimilation that would make the Catholic Church appear less foreign and more a part of American life. The documents address reactions to these accumulating complexities of differing positions within the Catholic community by the end of the nineteenth century.

Throughout the nineteenth century some Americans were attracted to virulently anti-Catholic movements and organizations. Groups such as the American or Know-Nothing Party and the American Protective Association attacked Catholics, asserting that they could not be good citizens of the United States because of their loyalty to the pope, the ruler of a substantial state on the Italian peninsula for much of the century. Catholics, it was held, should be proscribed from political participation. While Catholics vigorously opposed these pernicious attacks, the question of how best to adapt to American culture remained.

The French and Irish

The increase of immigration to the United States at the beginning of the nineteenth century dramatically changed the contours of Catholicism in the nation. Following the French Revolution in 1789, a number of French priests fled the intense anticlericalism of the revolution. With their excellent training and the dearth of priests in the United States, several found their way into positions of leadership. The Irish Catholics, ever-increasing in numbers, did not always welcome their ministry. The following three documents suggest that the tensions that the American church confronted throughout the nineteenth century were already present early in the century. Two questions recur in all three documents: What makes a "good American"? Which ethnic group is best suited to adapt to America?

1. Archbishop Ambrose Maréchal's Views on the Irish, 1818

In this document, French-born Ambrose Maréchal, third archbishop of Baltimore (1817–28), reflects on the growing immigration and the scarcity of priests. More important, Maréchal's report highlights his impatience with the trustee conflicts in Charleston, South Carolina, and Norfolk, Virginia, inspired by largely Irish congregations.[1] The following report was translated by Rev. Urban J. Stang.

...[It] is almost impossible to believe what large number of Europeans come to this country. It is estimated that during the present year about two hundred immigrants per day came to our shores from Europe. Among these there were very many Catholics...

[Since there are few native clergy, the American church must rely on priests from Europe.] According to Americans, English priests are more pleasing to the citizens in these regions,...There are only four English priests in my diocese;...besides the four...priests, I have no other, nor can I obtain others. The Belgian, French and German priests have shown themselves to be the best of missionaries...Some indeed do not pronounce English perfectly; but they do announce the word of God in a manner that is not displeasing to Americans...The Irish, who are moved by the spirit of God and imbued with truly ecclesiastical habits, serve religion fruitfully. For they are prompt in their work, speakers of no mean ability, and outstanding in their zeal for souls. Indeed, it gives me great joy that many of this race are in my diocese; I would certainly gladly receive many more like them with open arms. But alas, so many priests who have come hither from Ireland, are addicted to the vice of drunkenness, and I cannot place them in charge of souls until after a mature and thorough examination. For when they have once obtained faculties from us, it is hard to say what harm they would bring down upon the Church of God, if they should fall back into the vice of drunkenness. Nor would there be much remedy left to us by which we could put an end to their scandals. For if we should take away their faculties or attempt to do so, they would shake off the yoke completely and trouble the American Church with unbelievable seditions. They can do nothing among the faithful who are Americans, English, or belong to any of the European nationalities. They indeed flee from them. But it is truly surprising how much authority these drunkard priests exercise among the lowest classes of their own race. For since these consider drunkenness only a slight imperfection, they strenuously defend their profligate pastors, associate with them, and enter into and remain with them in schism. The lamentable fact is proved clearly in the history of all the dissensions that have occurred in the Church in North America...It was not

---

1. For a description of this conflict, see Thomas W. Spalding, *The Premier See: A History of the Archdiocese of Baltimore, 1789–1989* (Baltimore: Johns Hopkins University Press, 1989). For a general discussion of the trustee conflict, see Patrick Carey, *People, Priests, and Prelates: Ecclesiastical Democracy and the Tensions of Trusteeism* (Notre Dame, Ind.: University of Notre Dame Press, 1987).

the Americans, nor the English, nor the immigrants who came from other countries in Europe who disturbed or are disturbing the peace at Charleston, Norfolk, Philadelphia, etc., etc.; but it was those priests from Ireland, who were given over to drunkenness or ambition, together with their accomplices, whom they win over to their side by means of innumerable artifices. Most recently they tried...to persuade these ignorant people that the Bishops of Boston, Bardstown, and myself intended secretly to establish a French hierarchy in these provinces and to expel Irish priests...But indeed 1. Ten Irish priests received faculties from me...2. The greatest part of the clergy who are now studying theology in the Seminary in Baltimore, are Irish...

John Tracy Ellis, ed., *Documents of American Catholic History* (Milwaukee: Bruce, 1956), 214, 215–17. Printed with permission of the estate of John Tracy Ellis.

2. Bishop John Dubois and the New York Irish, 1827

The French-born priest John Dubois had fled the French Revolution in 1791 to come to the United States, where he had a distinguished career that included founding Mount Saint Mary's College and Seminary at Emmitsburg, Maryland. His appointment in 1826 as third bishop of New York disgruntled the Irish there, who preferred Father John Power, an Irishman who had served as administrator of the diocese for twenty-one months prior to Dubois's arrival. In Dubois's initial pastoral letter he addresses their concerns forthrightly. Already present is the desire of a specific immigrant group to have a bishop of their own. By the end of the nineteenth century the Irish would be on the opposite side, listening to pleas for German and Polish bishops. They would concur with Dubois's concern, "Is each nation to have a Bishop of its own?"

...The next objection [to being named bishop of New York] has been drawn from our foreign birth; but America has shown lately that a foreigner who has devoted himself to her service, is no longer considered as an alien. If We were not long ago American by our oath of allegiance, our habits, our gratitude and affection; thirty-five years spent in America, in the toils of the mission and of public education, would surely give Us the right to exclaim, *We are American too!* But We are all Catholics. Are not all distinctions of birth and country lost in this common profession? Were the Apostles natives of the countries, to which they were sent to preach the Gospel, and over which they received Episcopal jurisdiction? Is St. Patrick less the patron and protector of Ireland for having been born in Gaul? In this city there are American, Irish, English, French, Spanish and German Catholics: Is each nation to have a Bishop of its own? When formerly We watched over the couch of our sick American, Irish, and German brethren; when, for thirty-five years, We rode nights and days to afford them the sweet comforts of religion, did they ever inquire where we were born? Why, then, put that question now...? And who are those who object to our foreign birth? Are they not in the same sense, foreigners themselves? for, the question was not Why an American had not been appointed, but why it was not an Irishman? as if all old national distinctions could exist amongst us from the moment in which we were engrafted on the American stock, as if We did not cease to be Irishmen, Frenchmen, and Germans, as soon as, by our oath of allegiance, we had shaken off all foreign political ties, to become children of the great American family. Whence, then, this old national jealousy? Did you suppose We would have less affection, feel less interest for the Irish, who are the greatest number of our diocesans?...[T]he long sufferings endured by the Irish, for the sake of their faith, their unexampled fidelity under every species of trials and persecution, entitle them to the respect, veneration and affection of every Catholic, and much more of every Bishop...

> Peter Guilday, *The Life and Times of John England, First Bishop of Charleston* (New York: America Press, 1927), 1:448–49.

3. Bishop John England's Views on French Leadership, 1835

Irish-born John England was named the first bishop of Charleston, South Carolina, in 1820, in part to lessen the tensions between the Irish and the French. England set out to adapt the Catholic Church to the republican values prevalent in the United States. He established a constitution for his diocese, allowing for lay participation in decision making that reflected structures in the U.S. Constitution. He was also a strong advocate of episcopal collegiality through regularly convening councils of bishops. In the following document he clearly states his preference for the Irish over the French in terms of who should direct the church in the United States.

I am daily more and more convinced, that the genius of this nation and the administration of the French are not easily reconciled. Besides this, one of the strongest topics of prejudice against our Religion is that it is a foreign Religion, and it is not American, that it is the Religion of strangers, of aliens, etc. The Irish are easily amalgamated with the Americans. Their principles, their dispositions, their politics, their notions of government, their language and their appearance become American very quickly, and they praise and prefer America to their oppressors at home. The French can never become American. Their language, manners, love of *la belle France,* their dress, air, carriage, notions, and mode of speaking of their religion, all, all are foreign. An American then says: "It might be very good, but 'tis foreign aristocracy." Trivial as this might seem, it has impeded the progress of our Religion here. And the French generally refer to France as the standard of perfection. The French clergy are generally good men and love Religion, but they make the Catholic Religion thus appear as exotic, and cannot understand why it should be made to appear assimilated to American principles...

> Peter Guilday, *The Life and Times of John England, First Bishop of Charleston* (New York: America Press, 1927), 1:481–82.

The Irish

4. St. Patrick's Day Parade, Chicago, 1888

*In cities and towns across the United States, St. Patrick's Day parades consti-
tuted a visible reminder of the Irish Catholic presence in America. The order
of marchers, published in the daily newspapers, revealed the complexity of the
Irish experience: Catholic fraternal and charitable groups followed military companies and members of the secret Clan-Na-Gael, organizations that supported
the violent overthrow of British rule in Ireland. Ironically, the traditional starting
place for Chicago's St. Patrick's Day parade achieved international notoriety as
the scene of the 4 May 1886 Haymarket "massacre" when a bomb exploded
during a meeting of workers. In a telegram to Charles Stewart Parnell, president of the Irish National Land League and chairman of the Irish Parliamentary
Party, Patrick Egan assured him that "not a single Irishman was among the Anarchists at Chicago, while most of those who fell defending public order were
of our nationality." Although St. Patrick's Day parades were predominantly male
events, they usually began with Mass in a cathedral or an Irish parish and featured stops at schools and convent academies founded by women religious.
Chicago's St. Patrick's Day parade, begun in 1843, ended in 1901 because of
the increase in deaths from pneumonia following the annual event. The parade
was reestablished downtown by Mayor Richard J. Daley in 1956.*

... The customary procession in honor of the day was not large, but it was
orderly, bright with flags, gay with music, and well managed. Col. Thomas J.
Ford was Grand Marshal of the day, and his aides were numerous and well
able to keep the procession in hand. The only hitch was in getting the several
divisions in marching order, as Haymarket square, the starting-place, was so
jammed with people that evolutions of any kind were difficult. Shortly after 2
o'clock the word was given and the advance guard took its way north on Desplaines street, the procession starting from the exact spot made historic by the
bursting of the Anarchist bomb. "St. Patrick's Day in the Morning" was the
air to which the line first set its step. From Desplaines it turned into Indiana
[Grand Ave.]. The route was as follows: On Indiana to State, to Washington,
to Dearborn, to Monroe, to LaSalle, to Jackson, to Fifth ave. [Wells St.], to
Harrison, to Blue Island avenue, to Twelfth [Roosevelt Rd.], to Loomis, to
Taylor, to Halsted, to Adams, to Desplaines [the site of St. Patrick's Church].
The Mayor reviewed the procession from the piazza of the Academy of the
Sacred Heart, No. 485 [1258] West Taylor street. The advance guard reached
the academy at 4:20. Immediately Mayor Roche, with the Reverend Mother
Superior Niederkorn and Mme. Garesché and Mme. Jones, appeared upon the
piazza. Upon the balcony above sat Miss Shea. She impersonated Erin and
was dressed in white satin and spangles, and wore a crown of green. Draped
over the balcony was the American flag and at her side was a harp draped in
green. Three little girls, dressed in white, ran down to the curb and presented
Marshal Ford with a handsome bouquet of lilies. The Marshal and his aides

doffed their hats, the Mayor removed his Derby, and the procession moved on. It took fifteen minutes to pass and was composed as follows:

Platoon of police under Lieut. Cook and Sergt. O'Connor, 26 strong.
Grand Marshal Thomas J. Ford and aides.
Reed's Drum Corps.
First Regiment Hibernian Rifles, composed of:
Company E, Capt. Cunneen, 28 strong.
Company G, Capt. Quinlan, 24 strong.
Company B, Capt. Carroll, 30 strong.
Company D, Capt. Lynch, 48 strong.
Company H, Capt. O'Reilly, 35 strong.
Company F, Capt. O'Connor, 24 strong.
National Fife and Drum Corps.
Clan-Na-Gael Guards, Capt. Buckley, 35 strong.
Holy Name Zouave Cadets.
St. Stanislaus Cadets.
President John Foley and Vice-President Michael Fitzgerald, Irish-American Council, in carriage.
Officers and members Hibernian Benevolent Society in carriages.
Father Mathew Fife and Drum Corps.
Father Mathew Cadets.
Father Mathew T[otal] A[bstinence] B[enevolent] Society.
Bolger's Band.
Division No. 4, A[ncient] O[rder] H[ibernians].
Finerty Fife and Drum Corps.
Division No. 26, A.O.H.
Beck's American Band.
Division No. 23, A.O.H.
Division No. 6, A.O.H.
Independent Fife and Drum Corps.
Division No. 2, A.O.H.
Lemont Band.
Divisions Nos. 16, 17, and 5, A.O.H.
Roseland Band.
Pullman Division, A.O.H.
South Chicago Division, A.O.H.
Divisions Nos. 25, 31, 11, 19, and 22, A.O.H.
Second Regiment Drum Corps.
Father Hagan's N. M. T. & B. Society.
Carriages containing officers and members A.O.H. and prominent Irish-American citizens.

"The Green Flag Waved," *Chicago Tribune,* 18 March 1888.

5. Views on Irish Immigration to the United States, 1900

The massive emigration of Irish in the nineteenth century raised the question of whether it was desirable for them to leave their homeland. Church leaders naturally looked at the religious consequences of the Irish uprooting themselves from their native culture to begin a new life in the United States. The social, personal, and religious costs of emigration concerned Bishop John Clancy of Elphin, Ireland, who in 1899 posed a series of questions to Rev. M. J. Henry, director of Our Lady of the Rosary Mission in New York. The following selections include Bishop Clancy's questions with Father Henry's answers.

1. Would it be desirable, if it were possible, to prevent emigration from Ireland?

2. If the Irish people were still to elect to go abroad, what should be done for them before their leaving home (a) from the industrial, (b) from an educational, [and] (c) from a religious point of view to prepare them for life in a foreign country?

3. What are the special dangers to which the Irish people are exposed abroad, and how could these dangers be removed or lessened?

4. What industries are Irish young men and women best fitted for in foreign countries?

5. Are many of the Irish people lost to the faith abroad? How could this evil be prevented?

6. Could anything be done to insure greater security for them on board ship? Would it be desirable to have a special matron placed in charge of the steerage passengers on board?

7. Ought not priests, travelling by sea, be permitted to say Mass on Sundays and Holidays for Irish steerage passengers, these being almost all Catholics?

8. Ought not priests, who are recommended to the Company for this purpose[,] be permitted to visit the steerage portions of the vessel?

9. What should be done to secure the safety of Irish emigrants, more especially of Irish emigrant girls, on landing?

10. In case Irish emigrants have to travel a great distance inland, could provision be made to procure refreshments for them at stopping place[s], as has been frequently done for German emigrants?

Father Henry's reply answers each question:

Mission of Our Lady of the Rosary,
7 State St.,
N.Y. City
Oct. 31st, 1900

Right Rev. and dear Bishop Clancy:

Apologizing for my delay which was unavoidable I hasten to reply as fully yet as briefly as possible to your important queries.

1. Would it be *desirable* to *prevent* emigration from Ireland?

As a general rule, *yes.* Of course there are exceptions. When there is question for example of the re-union of families, as may sometimes happen, two or three members of the family are settled here, they send for the remainder, father or mother, or both as the case may be, then it would prove harsh and cruel to prevent such emigration. But taking into consideration emigration from Ireland as we find it to-day, where young men and young women arrive without any definite ideas of what they are going to do, coming, as they say "to try their luck[,]" then I say it would be a thousand times better for them had they remained at home. The struggle for the common, ordinary means of livelihood, not to mention luxuries, is sharp and bitter. Many fall by the way-side, and I am sorry to have to say become absolute failures. The prospects for young women are brighter, but then as a rule their life too is a grind and a struggle. A few years of close confinement soon steal the bloom from their cheeks and the lustre from their eyes and the music from their hearts, and they become more like bleached, waxen, soulless automatons than the light-hearted, merry colleens that they once were. No! better comparative poverty at home with their innocent amusements, their green fields and pure air than all they may hope to win in this "land of the free and the home of the brave." So that taking it all in all it would be desirable, if it were possible to prevent emigration from Ireland.

2. [a] What should be done for those intending to emigrate from an industrial standpoint?

For young men I would advise them to learn a good trade, whether it be horse shoeing, or carpentry, or bricklaying, or plastering or gardening. Men skilled in these trades always command good wages. Shoemakers, tailors or bakers are below par, because so much of their work is done now by machinery. Coachmen and waiters are also in demand.

With regard to young women, a good knowledge of housekeeping, i.e. cooking, chamberwork and laundry, would insure them first class positions at any time. It is unfortunately the lack of this knowledge that makes their lot here so hard. Milliners, seamstresses, sales-ladies, typewriters, etc. are simply a drug [*sic*] in the market.

[b] From an educational stand-point? Well from my experience it strikes

me that an ordinary education, reading, writing, and arithmetic, combined with a good trade would be about the best equipment for young men electing to emigrate. While they say there is always room at the top, the walks in *professional* life are over-crowded. Lawyers, doctors, stenographers, clerks et omne hoc genus are at a discount.

[c] From a religious stand-point? They should not only be well grounded in christian doctrine, but they should also be prepared to answer the ordinary objections against the Church and her doctrines that are constantly urged against them in this country.

3. What are the special dangers to which Irish people are exposed here?

Well owing to the cosmopolitan character of the people the dangers are many. They may however be summed up under three heads.

1st The drink habit. It would be one of the greatest blessings in the world if a total abstinence wave would sweep over Ireland from the Cliffs of Donegal to the fair hills of Kerry, and from Dublin Bay to Achill Island. The treating habit under the guise of hospitality is still very prevalent, and on the occasion of the "New Arrival" be he relative or friend is brought into full play with what result I need not say. Now if the young men and specially the young women were to take a pledge say *for five years even* before leaving, it would be a tremendous help to them here, where the American people are always on the outlook for steady, sober, self reliant help.

2nd Indifference to religion, and as a consequence a lowering of their standard of morality. From contact with unbelievers, thrown at times by their employment into the company of Atheists and scoffers of all religion; living out with Protestant families you may readily understand how first the Mass is omitted, then the Sacraments neglected and then indifference if not loss of their faith. Here unfortunately is where liberty becomes a license and instead of a blessing proves a curse. This is well exemplified in a letter written by a townsman of mine some thirty years ago. Writing to the "old country" he said, "this is the greatest country in the world, fresh meat three times a day and you needn't give a d — n for the priests."

3rd Mixed Marriages. On the evils of mixed marriages I need not dwell, suffice it, that they have been reprobated by the Church. Now special warnings from the Altar on these subjects would I am sure, be heeded and accomplish much good.

[At this point the numbering of responses again corresponds to Bishop Clancy's questions.]

4th What industries are they best fitted for? As stated already the young men coming as they do are simply unskilled laborers and have to enter into competition with their pick-axe and shovel with other nationalities. — Italians, Poles, etc. to eke out a bare existence. The Italians are more economic, can live on poor fare and consequently can afford to work for less wages than the ordinary Irishman.

5th Are many of the Irish people lost to the faith? While there is a leakage owing to the reasons given above, still I would say there is no wholesale loss. While a good many become indifferent but few apostatize or lose the faith.

6th If it could be arranged it would be desirable to have a special matron placed in charge.

Above all young women should be strictly cautioned not to make acquaintance with strangers on board the steamer, these strangers are often polished rascals and their company is dangerous. The same can be said of some of the women so the fewer friends they make in that direction the better.

7th About saying Mass on Sundays and holydays for the steerage passengers, that would have to be arranged for with the steamship companies.

8th Certainly if the priests are prudent and would not act as if they owned the whole line of steamers.

9th By having just such a mission as the "Mission of Our Lady of the Rosary." What the mission has done and is doing may be gleaned from the enclosed circular issued this year as well as from a souvenir pamphlet both of which I am sending with marked references.

10th Certainly all their wants in that line are provided for.

Now right Rev. and dear Bishop I have tried to answer as briefly yet as satisfactorily as I know how the questions proposed. The question of emigration is indeed a grave one.

It is a pity and a burning shame to see so many young people, the very flower of the flock, leaving their old homesteads and flying as if from a plague the land of their birth; scattered hither and thither the Lord knows where, like chaff before the wind. If you can do anything at all to keep them home do it. The few dollars they make hardly compensate them for all they lose. It is simply "tasting the fruit of the tree of the knowledge of good and evil." But if they come, as I presume they will, then let the priests warn them "in season and out of season" to avoid the use of intoxicating liquors, let them inculcate the vital necessity of attending mass, frequenting the Sacraments and insist upon *self-reliance* and *self-respect*.

Father Henry's views on Irish immigrants were based on his experience as director of the Mission of Our Lady of the Rosary, whose work is described in its promotional brochure cited above and quoted in part below.

Mission of Our Lady of the Rosary

The work of the Mission in detail may be summed up as follows: — 1st. It exercises a moral influence over steamship lines to protect the immigrant on board their vessels. 2d. It watches over, guides and assists at the landing-depot those immigrant girls who intend to proceed by rail or steamboat to destination. 3d. It examines the claims and fitness of the relatives or friends who call for the immigrant. 4th. It provides a Home "free of charge" for those girls whose friends do not call on the day of arrival or who have no friends at all, or who are unable to proceed on their journey. 5th. It tries to locate relatives of those who bring indefinite addresses. 6th. It secures positions in good families for those ready to go to work. 7th. It supplies the good offices of the priest who alone can bring confidence, encouragement and hope to the heart of the Irish exile. Although our Records were burned a few years ago in the fire at Ellis Island, it is safe to calculate that 70,000 Irish girls were guests of the Home since its foundation.

Two representatives of the Mission are always present when the trans-Atlantic liners from English and Irish ports discharge their passengers at the landing-depot. In the sixteen years these lines made 5016 trips to this country, or nearly one arrival every day. A little calculation will show that on an average about 95 Irish people landed at the immigrant depot every day since. During the year ending June 30th, 1899, 21,637 Irish landed at the Barge office — an increase of 4063 over the corresponding period a year ago. Of this number 12,470 were females — mostly young girls. Under the protection of the Mission all these girls either reached their destination in safety or found their friends or secured employment. Sometimes during the year the capacity of the Home was overtaxed. On the 19th of May last 172 Irish girls came to the Home at 9 p.m. The Leo House for German Catholic Immigrants cordially received those whom we could not conveniently accommodate. These statistics speak louder than words of the extent and greatness of the Mission's work.

The Mission is dependent entirely upon charity. From its institution to the present time no money has been asked or expected of the immigrant girl. This is a splendid tribute to the generosity and chivalry of the Irish race in America. Each year on the 1st of October (the month of the Rosary) we bring our claims to the notice of the public. We appeal for funds to carry on the good work during the coming year. Everyone interested in the welfare of the fair daughters of Erin ought to give a subscription to the cause. Every Irish girl in America must not forget the Home that receives her sister and whose friendly threshold she perhaps has crossed. We rely on our good "Collectors" throughout America. Our Lady of the Rosary Society is fast growing in popular favour. Membership, entitling one to many spiritual benefit[s], is only 25 cents a year. The "Collectors" work is to secure as many members as possible. The revenue from this is a powerful aid to the Mission. May we retain our old friends and enlist many new ones!

Archives of the Archdiocese of New York. Dunwoodie, N.Y. Printed with permission.

6. Cardinal James Gibbons on Irish Immigration, 1897

The country's most prominent Catholic leader as archbishop of Baltimore from 1877 to 1921 and the only U.S. cardinal from 1887 to 1910, Cardinal James Gibbons, an Irish ethnic born in the United States, had well-formed views on Irish immigration. In contrast to Father Henry's views formed from a close working relationship with Irish immigrants, Cardinal Gibbons took a broad and indeed favorable view of the Irish experience in the United States. This positive outlook is reflected in the following article published in Ireland in 1897.

Very naturally, I will be asked what advice ought to be given the intending immigrant from Ireland. I might answer by referring to the natural advisers at home and here, as well as to the admirable literature which has grown up about this question in past years...I can only offer a few general suggestions, of a moral and political character, leaving to others the more practical and economic view of this grave problem.

1. The Irish immigrant ought to be a *model of the natural virtues*...He must, therefore, adapt himself to the land in which he seeks a refuge, and he must remember that he owes a debt of gratitude to that country which opens wide its doors to him, and places within easy reach what is today the greatest of civil privileges, American citizenship. He leaves a land where as yet he is debarred, directly or indirectly, from many things that his heart desires, but that his race or religion, or both, prevent him from enjoying. He comes into the chief state of the New World, and in five years he walks a king among men, clothed with the panoply of free citizenship, with the right of suffrage, active and passive, eligible to every office but the highest, from which, however, his children are not disbarred...

2. The American people admire thrift, perseverance, business honor, faith of contracts. Their's is a mighty commercial state; but it is no nation of shopkeepers, if by that be meant a "gross, vulgarian" soul. They love the virtues that adorn the days of peace, but they are surely not deficient in those that befit the strenuous period of war...What if there be excesses or dangers? Every healthy body has its crises, its perils, and states are not free from them. But the recuperative powers of this state are beyond calculation, for deep in the hearts of the vast majority of its citizens are planted religious conscience, belief in one God and His revelation, admiration and practice of virtue, natural and scriptural, charity and forbearance, belief in a future life of rewards and punishments.

3. There is here no public legalized blasphemy, no ostentatious violation of the Sunday rest, no cynical disregard of the claims of virtue, nor will the immigrant see here the idea of God and His guiding Providence relegated to the family or the individual. This nation of over one hundred and one millions reads with gladness and piety the annual formal message of our President, wherein God, Providence, Prayer, Christianity are formally allowed and commended to every citizen. The American heart is, therefore, a religious, nay, a

Christian heart; and in that heart lies the panacea for the crescent ills of our political life.

4. It will not be amiss if I say here a few words on *good citizenship*. The Irish immigrant who arrives on our shores beholds before him a most varied political life, in which ward, town, city, county, state, and nation play each a *role* of absorbing interest. He is already half fitted by his language, domestic political training, and certain innate tendencies or qualities, to enter into this life. He usually does, and with no small share of success, for the Irish race has developed the world over, a rare political capacity, as the history of the English colonies alone will show, or a cursory view of the foreign relations of England in this century.

On this blessed soil of freedom the Irish immigrant needs to cultivate every civic virtue, interest in all public problems, conscientious study of public issues, the sense of union for the common weal, unprejudiced devotion to the growth of the State, incorruptible exercise of the sacred right of the ballot, which is the holy fountain of our political life and well-being, and to poison or trifle with which is to cut at the root of our State. The laws guarantee and promise to protect the free exercise of the right of suffrage...

5. It would not be proper for me to recommend publicly to immigrants any particular part of the United States. But it will not be out of place if they are recommended not to immigrate without some definite knowledge of where they are going, and what they expect to do. This is a dictate of natural prudence...

6. When he can command it, the immigrant ought to bring with him a sum of money as large as his means or circumstances will permit. This would be wise, even in a new colony. It is much more needed in these times, when the great cities are becoming congested, and sudden economic disturbances frighten the world of commerce and business into inactivity. It takes means also to cross the great stretches of the country, to purchase land, stock it, and live until the land is productive...

Perhaps someone will ask what I think of Irish immigration in general. Ought the Irish to stay at home, or ought they emigrate very largely, and especially to the United States? It is a grave problem. Ireland is a very ancient nation, with a very glorious history, and her race of men is pre-eminently adapted to the soil on which they live...

Yet this same history shows us the Irish race as possessed beyond all others with the spirit of the world-wanderer. The earliest reliable utterances of their history bear witness that they were seafaring, adventurous people; and since their conversion to Christianity there can be no doubt that this spirit has been heightened and consecrated by religious ardor for the propagation of Christianity. Willingly or unwillingly, wittingly and unwittingly, they have been a people of missionaries longer than any other race. No other people ever gave themselves *en bloc* to Christian missions as they; and no other people ever suffered for their Catholic faith as they. And when, with the dawn of this century, the remarkable movements began which have today produced some 130,000,000 of English-speaking people, and been the chief element in the renaissance of Catholicism from its Continental tomb, it was the Irish who were the pioneers, they being then almost the only English-speaking Catholics, and devoting themselves the world over to the planting of the Catholic faith, the support of its claims and its missionaries, and the sustenance of the Papal authority...

I would not, therefore, discourage Irish immigration, because there are at stake more than economic considerations. There are at stake the interests of the Catholic religion, which in this land in this age are largely bound up with the interests of the Irish people. God's hand is upon them, going and coming; and I prefer to believe that He who harmonizes the motion of the planets and the flow of the tides, is also First Agent and Prime Mover in those no less mysterious movements by which people pass from one land to another, even as Israel went down out of Egypt into Canaan, or the Wandering Nations came out of the frozen North and overflowed the Roman Empire.

> Cardinal James Gibbons, "Irish Immigration to the United States," in *A Retrospect of Fifty Years* (Baltimore, 1916), I:275–83; the article first appeared in the *Irish Ecclesiastical Record* 1, 4th ser. (February 1897): 97–109.

7. Bishop Bernard McQuaid's Approval of the Ancient Order of Hibernians, 1894

Irish immigrants brought to the United States the Ancient Order of Hibernians (AOH), a fraternal organization founded in 1565. At the time of its founding, when the Catholic Mass was proscribed by law in Ireland, the Hibernians functioned as a secret organization with one duty of its members: to stand watch while itinerant priests said Mass for their persecuted congregations. As penal laws diminished in the nineteenth century, Hibernians were involved in aiding the plight of tenant farmers. The AOH was first established in the United States at New York City in 1836. As the organization spread to other Irish communities in the country, it became associated with some groups that Catholic bishops condemned for their secret oaths or violent activities. In the following selection, Bishop Bernard McQuaid of Rochester, New York, reviews the history of the church's approach to the AOH and his approval, given in 1894, for its activities in his diocese.

The Ancient Order of Hibernians of America receives the privilege of this public service and a certain recognition by church authorities in this diocese of Rochester for the first time.

It is proper to state on this occasion the ground of objections in the past and the reasons for the change.

Ecclesiastics like myself who remember the early history of this organization, when such prelates as Archbishop Hughes of New York and Archbishop

Wood of Philadelphia reprobated and condemned the order, and for good reason, have viewed with distrust and fear any countenance shown to its members until the objectionable features of the old society had been discarded.

These features were its binding oath and its affiliation with some secret oath-bound center of authority in Europe, in Scotland, I believe. Attention was chiefly at one time attracted to the Order by its sympathy with the Mollie Maguires of Pennsylvania — a murderous organization that slaughtered its victims by the dozen and consigned to the scaffold its agents, many of whom had committed the crime, for which they died, by virtue of the oath they had taken. The Hibernians of those days were implicated in the crimes of the Mollie Maguires. It is well for the men of this generation to know and remember these facts. I do not believe that the Order as an Order counseled or sanctioned such crimes, but designing men in the Order used it and its dupes for their own nefarious purposes. What took place in the past may take place again. Hence the need of proper provisions and precautions.

Another society, over which the curse of God seems to hang — the Clan-na-gael — sought to make use of the Hibernians for their purposes. Some of the Clan-na-gael worked their way high into the Order. Fortunately for the Hibernians, they have not been led astray or duped. Yet the presence of members, or ex-members of condemned societies, in the Hibernian organization aroused fear in the minds of many who were disposed to aid a seemingly worthy Order, provided it could be done consistently with the always safe teachings of the Church.

For many reasons, it is not expedient, but rather it is highly dangerous, for an American society to be affiliated with a parent society in any of the European countries. We are well rid of Europe, and the less we have to do with it the better. But, when the European society is a secret, oath-bound organization, such as the Free Masons, the Carbonari, the Fenians, the Clan-na-gael, etc., our American societies, organized chiefly for mutual aid and benevolent purposes, become smirched by the wrongdoings of their foreign associates, and the evil grows in magnitude. We do not need these European entanglements in political or social life. If Catholic Irishmen may, with impunity and without reproach, become tools in the hands of foreign oath-bound societies, so may Catholic Germans, Catholic Poles, Catholic Italians, with equal impunity ally themselves to foreign oath-bound secret societies. The people who do not like this country and insist upon keeping up unlawful affiliation with the old countries of Europe, would do well to return to the country from which they came.

It does not follow that a European may not retain a tender love for the land of his birth, where he buried the bones of his ancestors; it does not follow that he may not glory in the noble achievements of the fatherland; but it does mean that he should not tie himself, hand and foot, to the secret governing power of any European organization. The Catholic Church cannot afford to sanction any body of her children who ally themselves with any such European body.

A second important objection to the Ancient Order of Hibernians, as first constituted in this country, was the oath of secrecy, by which its members were bound. Such oaths are never manly, are un-American, lower the taker of them in his own estimation, as well as in that of his fellow-citizens, and are a serious danger to government in a republic, whose free and untrammeled vote at the ballot box is its only safety.

I am pleased to say, from representations made to me by members in the Order competent to speak from knowledge and whose words I am warranted in trusting, that in the Ancient Order of Hibernians of America these two objections no longer exist. The obligations, contained in the Ritual of the Order, are not of the nature of an oath, and are such as one could, with a safe conscience, take, and in no way lessen a man's self-respect or degrade his manhood. I am also informed that this section of the Ancient Order of Hibernians has no connection, directly or indirectly with any society in Europe, but particularly not with a certain one in Scotland. The Scots were canny when they opened their treasury for the receipt of Irish-American money.

It was not my fault that, at the last Plenary Council of Baltimore, these objectionable features in the Ancient Order of Hibernians were not eliminated, and a marked line of distinction drawn between the two parties in the Order. Had it been pleasing to the fathers of the council to give the matter due consideration at that time, the cloud that has hung over the Order would have long passed away. It is to the credit of the right-minded laymen in the Order that they themselves have removed all obstacles in the way of a satisfactory recognition by church authorities.

As loyal children of the church, you will always give heed to her words of warning, confident that she will put no more restraint on your conduct as Christians and citizens than the interests of faith and morals may demand. She wants her children to be men, high-minded, industrious, and sober men. A great future is before the Irish race in this country; it will rest with themselves to realize all that their best friends crave for them. Too often an Irishman's worst enemy is himself. It is a part of the work of this Order to help elevate the character of its individual members.

No one questions the loyalty of the Irishmen to the country of his adoption. There is no war o[r] battles now impending, but the strifes of other kinds will arise from time to time. An Irishman's place will be on the side of law and order. Your constitution demands that its members oppose socialism, anarchy, and what disturbs the public peace.

Yours is not a church society, and you cannot, therefore, expect the same church privileges which are accorded to church societies. But as Catholics, in your individual capacity, you should take pride in upholding the honor of your Church, stand by her in all her struggles, be among the most faithful in the performance of religious duties, win the approval of your pastors by generous co-operation with them in all good works and be slow to find fault and criticize.

Frederick J. Zwierlein, *The Life and Letters of Bishop McQuaid* (Rochester, N.Y., 1925), 2:467–80.

8. Father Theobald Mathew's American Temperance Crusade, 1851

Father Theobald Mathew (1790–1856), a Capuchin friar, had preached the gospel of temperance to Irish peasants in the 1830s and 1840s, with astonishing results. Several million men, women, and children in Ireland "took the pledge" to abstain from alcoholic beverages, and the custom crossed the Atlantic with emigrants of the Great Famine. Father Mathew's American tour from June 1849 through January 1851 received widespread, positive coverage in the press. Indeed, he addressed a meeting of both houses of Congress.

One of the greatest benefactors of the human family that our favored country has ever entertained, is about to leave us and to return to his native land to die, after a life devoted to the poor, the afflicted and the friendless.

Fifteen years ago, the good and Rev. Father Mathew, stimulated by the benevolent desire to increase the comforts, and add to the happiness of the people of Ireland, invited them to join the Temperance army, and with him to abandon the use of all that could intoxicate.

At his invitation, that people, proverbial for their generous hospitality, laid aside long cherished habits. In a few years nearly six million enrolled themselves among his disciples, and afforded a self-sacrificing spectacle to mankind, the like of which has few parallels...

The famine year left the Apostle of Temperance from TWENTY-FIVE TO THIRTY THOUSAND dollars in debt, incurred solely in behalf of suffering humanity...

We have all been witnesses of his zeal, and of his devotion in his sacred calling since his arrival in July, 1849. Regardless of health, forgetful of fatigue, anxious only to reclaim the unfortunate, and to win our youth to the ways of sobriety, his labors have been unceasing. More than half a million of our people have taken the temperance pledge at his hands; everywhere he has gone he has scattered the blessings of peace, of happiness and of good will among men, broadcast over the land.

FELLOW CITIZENS: It is our duty to proclaim to you and to our country, that, now when his mission has terminated, nothing awaits this good and pious man on his return to his home, but increased misfortunes and accumulated sufferings, unless an effort be made to relieve him from his pecuniary responsibilities.

We refer you to the eloquent and feeling letter from Hon. HENRY CLAY to HENRY GRINNELL, Esq., which we are permitted to publish, for the full particulars of the good Father's painful position — a position we have endeavored briefly and truthfully to lay before you...

Those who are willing to contribute to the FATHER MATHEW FUND, are invited to send their donations to HENRY GRINNELL, Esq., New-York, who will act as Treasurer. And friends in other parts of the Union are requested, after having read this Appeal, to adopt prompt measures to collect funds, which they are also invited to forward to the same address, or to any of the undersigned.

NEW-YORK, Tuesday, Sept. 23, 1851

AMBROSE C. KINGSLAND,	GREENE C. BRONSON,
JAMES G. KING,	M. H. GRINNELL,
C. W. LAWRENCE,	E. K. COLLINS,
ROBERT KELLY,	SHEPHERD KNAPP,
SIMEON DRAPER,	JAMES HARPER,
MATTHEW MORGAN,	THO'S O'CONOR,
WM. V. BRADY,	JOHN W. EDMONDS,
TERENCE DONELLY,	CHARLES M. LEUPP,
MARSHAL S. BIDWELL,	ROBERT EMMET,
JONATHAN I. CODDINGTON,	HAMILTON FISH.
C. H. MARSHALL,	

"An Appeal to the American Public, in Behalf of the Very Rev. Father Mathew," *New York Times,* 25 September 1851.

9. Henry Clay on Father Theobald Mathew, 1851

The great American statesman Henry Clay (1777–1852) lent his voice to the fund-raising campaign for the Irish "apostle of temperance." By focusing on Protestants in American temperance movements, historians have left the impression that Irish Catholics were uninterested or uninvolved in campaigns to curb intemperate drinking among immigrants. Yet Father Mathew Societies flourished in the United States through the 1890s, providing models of middle-class behavior as well as leadership in local Irish parishes.

MY DEAR SIR: I have enjoyed the high satisfaction of meeting with FATHER MATHEW, and entertaining him at my house. On his return to the city of New-York from the prosecution of his noble works of humanity and benevolence, in the valley of the Mississippi, he did me the honor to call to see me. During his sojourn in the United States, he has been again stricken with paralysis, which, although it has not affected the expression of his bland and benign countenance, nor materially impaired his articulation, disqualifies him from making those great exertions, to which he was accustomed in earlier life, and in robust health. Nevertheless, his labors, with but little relaxation and repose, have been unremitting, and have been attended with the most encouraging success. Upon descending the Mississippi, he administered, in one of the towns situated on its banks, the pledge to seven hundred persons. He ascended it, after an interval of some months, and stopping at the same town, he had the gratification to find that among the converts there were but three instances of relapse...

During his long and brilliant career in Ireland, among the millions of persons, the victims of intemperance, or in danger of becoming addicted to it, to whom he gave the pledge, he often met in the poorer classes persons in great indigence and want. To some of these he supplied, from his own purse, money to afford them immediate relief, which, though small in particular cases, in the aggregate amounted to a considerable sum...

The consequence is that this great benefactor of mankind, this true friend of the poor, is left in a state of great pecuniary embarrassment; threatened by creditors on his return to Ireland, and exposed, himself in old age, and under the influence of disease and infirmity, to that pinching want, which, in better days, and in more prosperous times, he so generously relieved in others...

This most excellent and extraordinary man is about to depart from among us, after having, it is to be hoped, with the aid of Providence, redeemed near half a million of inhabitants of these States from one of the most debasing of all pernicious habits. Shall he return without any substantial manifestations of the public gratitude towards him? Shall even no effort be made to put him at ease, and to smooth and soften the pillow of his declining years? I think I am not deceived as to the generous hearts of my countrymen, nor as to the warm Irish hearts of his, in believing that, if his actual condition were generally known, thousands would readily, and with the greatest alacrity, rush to his relief. His fame and a just appreciation of his signal merits are secure, and will be transmitted to the admiration of the remotest posterity. He will be regarded as one of the wonders of this remarkable age. But what will that posterity think of the present generation, if he be permitted to pine and languish in poverty and want and suffering, during the remnant of a life which has been worn out by an exclusive devotion to its service? And such a glorious service! What reproaches will not be made for culpable insensibility to the value of the greatest moral reform ever achieved by one man! Shall not we, in the United States, endeavor not to merit any part of them?

Knowing well your public spirit, and your generous impulses, my object in addressing you is to ascertain if something cannot be done for Father Mathew, worthy of him, and worthy of us, before he leaves our shores. On all occasions of munificence we naturally turn our attention to our great cities, and to [New York] as the first of them. We ought to do something, we can do something, in the interior. I am ready, from my limited means, to contribute my mite.

But it is in the large cities, where concert and cooperation are so easy to be brought about, that most can be effected...

Letter of 28 May 1851 from Hon. Henry Clay to Henry Grinnell, quoted in *New York Times*, 25 September 1851.

10. Father Theobald Mathew in Brooklyn, 1851

In contrast to early American Protestant temperance campaigns aimed at men, Irish Catholic women – and children – "took the pledge" to abstain from intoxicating beverages. By the 1870s and 1880s, many parishes had incorporated the ritual for candidates making their first Holy Communion and Confirmation.

FATHER MATHEW. — This gentleman's last sermon in this city, at the Church of St. Charles [Borromeo], Sunday morning, was listened to by a very large audience. Hundreds were unable to obtain entrance into the church, and were compelled to go away without hearing him.

In the afternoon he administered the pledge at St. Paul's Church, Court-street, to a large number of our citizens of both sexes. This being his last visit to Brooklyn, there was an immense number present to gaze for the last time, probably on this earth, upon this great Apostle of Temperance. He has administered the pledge to over 12,000 persons in this city since his arrival among us.

"Brooklyn," *New York Times*, 4 November 1851.

11. Irish Stereotype, 1861

American newspapers routinely chronicled alcohol abuse among Irish immigrants, contributing to the public perception that they were unfit to be citizens. By the 1850s, "Bridget" the domestic servant had become a stock figure in cartoons and on the stage. So pervasive was the stereotype that generations of Irish Catholics refused to christen their daughters after Ireland's most famous female saint.

Disorderly. — Bridget McFadden, a young and blooming maid of 21 years, sat sunning herself on the deck of one of those gallant crafts that sail the murky waters of the raging canal. She was thinking of her sailor-lover, Michael McCarty. The time appointed for him to come had passed, and the moments dragged heavily. As she sat revolving in her mind the thoughts of her lover, she suddenly espied a large crowd collected around a man dressed in sailor's clothes. She was sure it was Michael, and into the crowd she rushed. It was Michael. He was paid his week's earnings on Saturday night, on the strength of which he got drunk and disorderly, and was in the rough hands of an officer when Bridget saw him. With a true devotion she interceded for the release of her lover, and protested against the necessity of lodging him in the station-house, until the whisky was out of him, insisting that she would get it out sooner than the officers. But the policeman was firm, and so too was Biddy.

She rolled up her sleeves, and at the officer she went. All to no avail, however, for another "star" made his appearance, and Bridget and Michael were lodged in the station-house.

Chicago Times, 20 August 1861.

12. Archbishop John Ireland on Total Abstinence, 1882

Irish Catholic attitudes toward alcohol and temperance were far from uniform in the nineteenth century. Irish-born Archbishop John Ireland of St. Paul, Minnesota (1838–1918), a nationally known figure in the Catholic temperance movement, blamed the low status of Irish working men on their love of whiskey and beer. But to Irish saloonkeepers, often pillars of their parish as well as local politicians, Ireland's clarion call for total abstinence fell on deaf ears. Nor did it gain much of a hearing in predominantly German towns and cities where workers were accustomed to "Continental" Sunday celebrations with beer gardens and singing societies.

...It is my privilege to know the men of the Catholic Total Abstinence Union. I have for many years myself labored in your ranks: I have been honored in the past with a seat in your conventions. I know your zeal for the glory of God and for the salvation of souls. I know your motives and the courage with which you follow them out despite misapprehension or censure...

Irish exiles have been from the first days of the Republic landing on the shores of America. The Irish and their descendants number millions to-day among us. What should we not have expected from the Irish in America, when we consider their own powers, physical, moral and intellectual, and the boundless resources of the New World, which were laid open to them! What we should have expected we find wherever they have shunned liquor; we do not find it wherever they have patronized the whisky shop, and alas! as a great portion of them have loved the glass, a great portion of them are failures in America... You who would delight in showing to your fellow-citizens the ideal Irish element, labor to advance the total abstinence cause. This is the work for true Irish patriots, a work which leads to sure and priceless victories and demands no other sacrifice than the dashing from one's lips of the perfidious cup.

The comparative poverty of the Irish people in America is a matter of public notoriety. It is a lamentable fact. They are the hewers of wood and drawers of water. Go where the hardest work is to be done, you find Irish men — burrowing in the mines of Pennsylvania, wasting away their life-blood amid the never-ceasing din of industrial machinery in New England, strewing with their corpses lines of railroads or canals. In large cities the tenement quarters are thronged with them, a family striving to breathe in each room of a building five stories high, crammed with human beings from cellar to roof. This condition of things is deplorable. Forced poverty is hurtful to soul and body.

Mortality attains fearful proportions. In the tenement houses of New York 75 per cent. of all children born, die within a few years after their birth. The report of a Boston Medical Association shows, that while Irish families are far more numerous than those of native New Englanders, yet on account of a greater mortality among Irish children, the New England population would keep pace with the Irish, were not the latter constantly receiving new accessions from emigration. Bad ventilation and alcoholism, adds the report, are impairing fearfully the general sanitary status of the Irish people. No influence for good, social or political, can they have amid this poverty. What room for evils of all sorts, physical and moral! Well, what is it that keeps the Irish people in these low social conditions? The saloon. Thither goes the money earned at the sweat of their brow; thence do men issue, broken down in health and strength, to swell the lists of idlers and paupers. Our disgrace and our misfortune in America is the number of Irish saloon-keepers...It is idle talk to advise the people to secure homes of their own, to leave the crowded cities, to gain by labor and economy a competence for themselves and their families; we must lay the axe to the root of the evil, first teaching them to shun the saloon, which is swallowing up their earnings...

The power for good of the Total Abstinence movement is proven by plain facts. Visit one after the other a parish where a vigorous total abstinence society is maintained, and a parish where the movement is neither commended nor heard of; compare the social and religious condition of the one with those of the other — no further argument will be needed in favor of my thesis.

The need of the hour is a grand tidal wave of total abstinence sweeping over the land...Will it be made with sufficient force to save the people? This is the vital question for the future of Irishmen in America, and, I might add, for the future of religion. Total abstinence is the saving principle. Will the men be found in required number to make it a living power? The answer rests with the priests and laymen of the country[,] with those whose position and influence mark them as leaders of their fellow-men...

> *Address delivered by Rt. Rev. John Ireland, in the Cathedral of St. Paul, Minn., Aug. 2nd, 1882* (Philadelphia: Dan F. Gillin, Printer, 1882).

13. Irish-American Women and Labor, 1936

In a memoir completed three years before her death, Margaret M. Haley (1861–1939), president of the Chicago Teachers' Federation, highlighted the crucial role Catholic fraternal groups played in introducing Irish women into the ranks of labor unions. As a result of their involvement in parish-based groups, Irish-American women were well acquainted with parliamentary procedure — and voting — decades before they were granted the franchise in 1920.

Some one has said that the fraternal beneficiary insurance organizations of women did more to pave the way for women toward public life than did the actual enactment of the Nineteenth Amendment [1920]. Possibly it's true. I made my own entrance into the courts and the newspapers through membership in one of these organizations, the Women's Catholic Order of Foresters.

I was a dimly obscure and entirely uninterested member of one of its units, called courts, when the returned delegate from one of its conventions told me that the High Chief Ranger, a Mrs. Elizabeth Ro[d]gers, had secured her own election for life, "merely as a compliment." I announced at the meeting that I was against anything of the sort. I'd never seen Mrs. Ro[d]gers, I didn't know much about the organization, I knew nothing of its politics, but I knew the principle of election for life was wrong, un-American, autocratic. I said so whenever the topic arose during the year, and the women of the court elected me delegate to the next convention.

With a group of women — Annie Daley, Mary Downes, Mary Finan, and a score of others — who were also opposed to the idea I studied parliamentary law...I don't know why I was chosen to lead the fight. I'd never before attended a convention. I knew nothing whatever of insurance law. I knew something of the theory of politics, but nothing of its practice. I weighed less than a hundred pounds. I was far more interested in a new blue silk dress than I was in any cause. The only qualification I had for the doubtful honor was my willingness to tell Elizabeth Ro[d]gers herself that she was all wrong...

If I had known I'd been expelled from the order I'd have said more, but perhaps I said enough. I was looking down on faces twisted with hatred, faces of women who were under other circumstances good wives and mothers and sisters and daughters and friends and neighbors. But I had touched the raw nerve of their pocketbooks, and they were going to punish me! That was the base of the battle. Mrs. Ro[d]gers had permitted women beyond the age limit to enter the [Catholic Order of Foresters]. In a little while the policy would wreck it, but their heirs would have the amounts of their policies before that time. That was the secret of her power. For that they would have dragged me limb from limb...

Battleground: The Autobiography of Margaret A. Haley, ed. Robert L. Reid (Urbana: University of Illinois Press, 1982), 29–30. Printed with permission of Robert L. Reid.

14. Margaret Haley and the Women's Catholic Order of Foresters, 1900

The transformation of Margaret Haley from a teacher in a public school to a union president began in 1898 when she filed suit against her parish-based fraternal society. Following her victory in court, Haley became business agent of the Chicago Teachers' Federation, representing more than three thousand members. Under her leadership, the CTF fought for teachers' raises and pensions as well as school tax reform and municipal ownership. A funeral Mass for Haley, a devout Catholic all her life, was celebrated in St. Bernard Church in Chicago's Englewood neighborhood on 9 January 1939.

In a ruling announced to-day the branch Appellate court judicially affirms the complaint of Margaret A. Haley against the Women's Catholic Order of Foresters already sustained by the Circuit court. Margaret A. Haley has, for fifteen years, been a teacher in the Chicago public schools, and in April, 1898, she was sent as a delegate from St. Bernard's court, No. 144, Women's Catholic Order of Foresters, to the annual session or convention of the order.

At one of the sessions of the convention during her absence Miss Haley, by the vote of the delegates present, was expelled from membership in the order and her insurance declared forfeited. Miss Haley appealed from the ruling of the annual session, declaring that she had not been allowed a trial in accordance with the laws of the order, and that the session had no jurisdiction to declare her expulsion from the order.

The Circuit court issued an injunction restraining the officers of the order from further proceeding in the matter and declaring the complainant to be "a member of the order in good standing and entitled to all the rights and privileges of a member in good standing." This decree is sustained by the branch Appellate in every particular.

> "Teacher Wins Her Case: Court Rules Margaret A. Haley is Member of Order of Foresters," *Chicago Daily News,* 2 January 1900.

15. Letter to Sister Agatha M. Hurley, B.V.M., 1894

Eleanor Hurley, born in County Cork, Ireland, in 1826, grew up in Dubuque, Iowa, where she joined the Sisters of Charity of the Blessed Virgin Mary. In 1867 she and a group of eight other B.V.M.s established a school for girls at 631 West Maxwell Street in the Chicago neighborhood later immortalized by Jane Addams's Hull-House. By 1894, the B.V.M.s had expanded their mission to include six more parochial schools on the city's North, West, and South Sides. The following letter, sent to Sister Mary Agatha on her golden jubilee, demonstrates the difference Irish women religious made in the lives of working-class Catholic children.

St. Louis University,
St. Louis, Mo.,
Dec. 8th, '94

Dear Sister Agatha,

...When, as a little boy, I knelt, morning after morning at the altar of the dear old chapel I often thought of the wonderful beauty of the lives of your Sisters, and how dear their souls must be to Him, who daily looked down upon them, and who understood, as the tender Jesus alone could understand, the fullness of their sacrifice. It was to me the first whisperings of a vocation[,] and what it was to me, I know the example of you and your Sisters — through the Holy Ghost — has been to many, many others, pointing and leading upward to those high and silent, yet beautiful heights, of religious perfection... And I know, that, as you think of the many boys who served at the old school and who have followed the banner of Ignatius, who have died in harness, or are in the midst of the fray, or only preparing for the coming battles far off; you will breathe a little prayer to day for one who is but the least in Christ.

    Again wishing you most heart-felt congratulations

      I remain,

        Yours in the Sacred Heart,

          Edward P. Sullivan, S.J.

> Archives, Sisters of Charity of the Blessed Virgin Mary, Dubuque, Iowa. Printed with permission.

16. Jane Addams and the Sisters, 1910

Although Irish Catholic immigrant women and their American-born relatives were among the most visible laywomen from the 1850s on, their contributions to education, health, and charitable institutions often received short shrift in the daily press.

The conferring of the honorary degree of Doctor of Laws on the great railroad magnate, James J. Hill, and the honorary degree of Master of Arts on Jane Addams of Chicago Hull-House by Yale University last week has stirred up Professors [Albion] Small and [Paul] Shorey of Chicago University. They think that Yale did not show very high appreciation of values when it gave only a Master's degree to Jane Addams and a Doctor's degree to James J. Hill — that Jane's Hull-House is of more value to humanity than James' whole railroad.

    Now granted that this good woman, Jane Addams, has done much along social lines for the uplifting of the poor and the relieving of the needy, is it not a fact — aye and a fact often lost sight of — that right here in Chicago and indeed in every large city of this continent there are dozens of women in our Catholic Sisterhoods, who silently and unobserved with no trumpet of press or people are doing twenty times more for the poor and afflicted than Miss Addams ever did? Yet, we hear of no honorary degrees being conferred upon those noble women who seek to know only the will of God and care not for the approbation of man...

"The Conferring of Honorary Degrees," *New World,* 2 July 1910.

17. Unitarian Minister Praises Irish Women and Catholic Schools, 1912

In an address before the Free Religious Association in Boston, Unitarian minister Jenkin Lloyd Jones, a supporter of Jane Addams and the Hull-House settlement, discussed the different perceptions of the Catholic Church that existed in the East and the Midwest, especially regarding the role of Irish Catholic women in public schools.

... I believe, if I must put it so, that the Catholic Church is the greatest manufactory of American citizens now organized. First, because to it is entrusted the largest amount of raw material. It has the largest hopper; more material is thrown into that hopper than into any other hopper I know of. And, second, because in this latitude and longitude of the spirit, the Catholic Church is itself being transformed... You tell me that the public schools of Chicago are passing into the hands of the Catholic Church. I look into the statistics of the Chicago public schools and am forced to recognize the fact that perhaps seventy per cent of the lower grammar-grade teachers are Catholic. What an alarming fact! But don't be scared. I know these "schoolma'ams." I know them very well. I work with them. I rejoice in their work, and I tell you if ever the issue comes, you can trust them to "rally round the flag." They take these children from the far-away corners of Europe out of homes untouched by democracy or the spirit of the twentieth century, and infilter into their veins the love of liberty, the joy of democracy, the pride of Abraham Lincoln and George Washington; and above all the English language, and I tell you there is no danger in that material. There is no occasion to be scared... There is something in the Irish blood that seems, when once we get it into America, to run on the masculine side into the police-force and on the feminine side into the school-force. They are the best material to make "schoolma'ams" of that we have in Chicago, and obviously in Chicago they are the best and safest material out of which to make policemen. I don't know how it is in Boston; perhaps you have another experience... I tell you that this United States is not a stranger to the sanctifying power of the Catholic Church that makes patient men and women, that makes noble institutions. I have taken water out of the canteen held to my lips by a Catholic priest on the battle-field. I have seen the Sisters of Charity binding the tattered wounds of bleeding soldiers under the glaring sun of a southern battle-field; and I have witnessed how they trained orphans and fostered the elders...

No, I am not scared of the Catholic Church, and no more do I despair of our democracy, notwithstanding the great tide of turbid and undeveloped life that is poured into the United States daily at Ellis Island and elsewhere. So long as there is a Catholic Church to receive them, so long as there is an institution of religion to labor with them and to prepare them and to ripen them for American citizenship, I will believe we are equal to the job, and that the work should be encouraged. All this I say while remembering and accepting your word for it, that you have some very disagreeable people here in Boston, some people who don't know how to behave themselves...

"The Roman Catholic Church in the United States: Remarks of Jenkin Lloyd Jones before the Free Religious Association of Boston, May 24, 1912," in *Unity*, 1 August 1912, 346–48.

18. Helen Jackson's *Convent Cruelties,* 1923

The publication in 1919 of Helen Jackson's Convent Cruelties *provided a stark reminder that anti-Catholic sentiment regarding women religious was alive and well in American life and thought. The book purported to document Helen Riggle Jackson's "sensational experience" in convents in Detroit, Michigan, and Newport, Kentucky. Reprinted five times by 1923, the tract urged Americans "to agitate suppression of Good Shepherd Convents" and "secure for the inmates their God-given rights to live and enjoy freedom as guaranteed by the American Constitution." The following "testimonial" by George Laubach appeared in the appendix to an edition circulated during the 1920s, when Ku Klux Klan activity was at an all-time high.*

Roman Catholic sweat shops, convent prisons and secret intrigue are daily being brought to our attention. Light on inner deviltry and cruelty in secret chambers of Catholic institutions is frequently revealed. The good old United States is becoming alarmed over these secret hidden facts; never was such public interest taken in this timely question, as at the thrilling present time.

Anti-Roman Catholic Societies are federating and the universal public pulse is stirred as never before. The time is fast approaching when sleeping Protestants will be thoroughly awakened. The life of Helen Jackson within Roman Catholic sweat shops and convent walls is vividly portrayed... Having known her and her christian character for a number of years, I can vouch for the truthfulness of her statements and allegations in regard to Roman Catholic cruelty, and tortures, while incarcerated within their prison walls.

Helen Jackson has a marvelous memory of scenes and describes them with clearness and rapid touch of finish... [S]he has the facts and knows how to present them, and whoever promotes her lectures or the sale of her books, is promoting the cause of liberty and humanity.

Quoted in Helen Jackson, *Convent Cruelties; Or, My Life in a Convent: A Providential Delivery from Rome's Convent Slave Pens; A Sensational Experience* (Toledo, Ohio: privately printed, 1923), 107.

19. Catholic Schools and Irish Female Social and Economic Mobility, 1920

By 1910, the daughters and granddaughters of Irish immigrants increasingly filled the ranks of the American labor force as teachers and principals in public schools and as white-collar workers. Much of this success was due to the pioneering efforts of Irish women religious, who educated young women for the world of work. Building on the success of their convent academies and high schools in the Midwest, the Sinsinawa Dominicans established Rosary College (now Dominican University) in River Forest, Illinois. In his address at the cornerstone laying in 1920, Archbishop George W. Mundelein commented on the unusual attitudes of Irish parents toward the education of their daughters.

The Church has always considered as the principal part of the mission entrusted to her by her Divine Founder to be the duty of Teaching her children. This mission she has carried on throughout the ages from the beginning[,] and in carrying it onward, she has adjusted herself to the customs of the times and the differences of places...

Nearly 75 years have gone by since the first little band of Sisters of Mercy came to Chicago and opened the first little school at the invitation of Bishop [William] Quarter. And though the space of time that has intervened is encompassed in the lifetime of a man, yet that little band has been multiplied a thousand times and more. So that to-day this diocese has a greater army of women Religious of Nuns than any other city in the world. And yet no other city needed them more, for here have come by the hundreds of thousands the children of more than a score of nations, drawn here by the needs of the more than 50,000 factories that are here in this great industrial city. And as a result of their increasing labors we have built up a sterling, stalwart, splendid Catholicity. We have built up a school system that is inferior to none in the world, and I say that in no spirit of boasting, for by their fruits you shall know them, by what they are accomplishing is the way of telling the tale. Naturally our first solicitude was for the little ones: to see to it that the proper foundation was laid in the hearts of the young. In their acquisition of knowledge, the knowledge of God and of His laws must come before their knowledge of the laws of man or even the laws of nature. St. Thomas Aquinas tells us that it is necessary that the first act of man when coming to the use of reason should be a turning towards God. That explains why everywhere we begin by installing the primary grades. That too perhaps explains why in the lower grades in some of our schools, the child receives its religious instruction in the tongue it is most familiar with at the time, the language it has heard daily from the mother's lips and in what it has a more copious and better understood vocabulary than in the language of the land, with which later it becomes better acquainted, as it comes more in contact with those outside the walls of the home.

It was only after these lower grades were firmly established that we took the next step, and here in this city on all sides were begun the smaller high schools, still under the care of the Religious. What was the reason? Simply because we felt that too great a risk would be incurred in permitting the boy or girl just emerging from adolescence with its attendant dangers, with its indiscriminate quest after knowledge, coming from the warmth of our Catholic school, from the close guardianship of the Religious, to be suddenly plunged into the icy bath of a secular Godless high-school, with no hindering hand to prevent them from browsing in fields filled with the poisonous weeds of forbidden knowledge[,] and our high-schools grew and prospered. I do not know whether others have noticed it as much as I have who came from the east where the Catholic high-schools were unfortunately few. But it will always redound to the credit and glory of the Irish immigrants and early settlers here that wherever they could and where they had the schools under proper auspices they always gave their daughters the chance of better education. The father may have been only a laborer in the trenches, the mother without any education, but where the daughter showed signs of ability and a desire to study, they brought any and every sacrifice that she might have intellectual advantages... That may explain the large number of Catholic girls with distinctly Irish names who are teachers in our municipal schools, for once they entered the high-schools under the care of the Sisters, they surmounted every obstacle and readily passed every examination, so that I am told that seventy percent of the teachers in the public schools are graduates of the Sisters schools, and yet our system is not complete.

Due partly to the march of modern progress, partly too, to the economic change of the past few years, woman is coming out of the sheltered place she has occupied until now. Some of us may regret to see it, some of us hail it with joy, yet we cannot fail to read the signs of the times. The day is not far distant when women will take high places in the professions on the rostrum, in the university faculty. Shall our Catholic women be debarred from these opportunities? If not, then we must prepare them under Catholic direction, fill them with Catholic ideals... Again have our Religious come forward at this critical time and offered to advance further in the cause of Religious education to which they have dedicated their lives. Today we really inaugurate that work here; we have laid the corner stone of a great work, a real temple of learning, this time not for children, not for boys or girls, now for the women of our church. This will be the finishing school, the West Point or Annapolis where we prepare the officers who are to lead the battalions of our Catholic women at the proper time. From this institution will come the thinkers, the doers, the leaders of their sex... [Rosary College will not be] confined to the few: neither wealth nor age nor race will be any advantage, neither will they prove a hindrance to entry here.

Some of us perhaps feel that the Sisters are running a great risk in undertaking the erection of [a] building, costing a million dollars at this time, when building operations are so costly, without any sources of income, practically without funds. But they have placed their trust in God and their confidence in the Catholic people of Chicago, and as they are working for the glory of One and the welfare of the other they feel that they will not be deserted by either. And if the great mass of our people will be infected by the enthusiasm of the little band of women who have aided and encouraged the Sisters in their effort, there is no question of the ultimate splendid success of the work. May God then bless and prosper the work we are initiating this day and make it a consolation to the Church and people of Chicago.

> Transcript of Archbishop George Mundelein's address at the cornerstone laying of Rosary College, 20 June 1920, Madaj Collection, 6, 1920, M 236, Archdiocese of Chicago's Joseph Cardinal Bernardin Archives and Records Center. Printed with permission.

20. Protests of Film *The Callahans and Murphys,* 1927

> *Throughout the nineteenth century, Paddy and Bridget had been stock characters in the American theater, depicted mostly as figures of fun, "greenhorns" trying to make their way in an unfamiliar society. No sooner had these stereotypes begun to lose their currency, however, than they resurfaced on the silver screen. Chicago's leading African-American newspaper applauded New York's Irish for protesting their unflattering portrayal in motion pictures.*

New York, Aug. 26. — Police reserves were called out last night to quiet a disturbance created in a W. 42d St. theater when a number of patrons arose and denounced as "an insult to the Irish" a film entitled "The Callahans and Murphys" which was being shown. Threats to wreck the theater and destroy the film were made while other patrons rushed for the exits, and a crowd gathered on the sidewalks. The trouble started during a scene depicting an Irish picnic, with the festivities turning into a free-for-all fight in which bricks and clubs were used.

Wreck Theater

The police reserves were again called out last Thursday night to stop a disturbance resulting from the showing of the film. Electric light bulbs were broken against the screen and chemicals were poured on the floor at Loew's Orpheum theater in E. 36th St.

The attitude of the Irish towards this film is a great contrast to the attitude of other Americans towards such pictures as "The Birth of a Nation" and similar films whose chief themes constitute insults to a large percentage of American citizens. This picture, produced obviously for propaganda purposes, went the rounds of this country with little or no protest. It is now being shown in Poland, after a successful run in other European countries.

The American motion picture market is at all times flooded with pictures whose chief purpose is to burlesque and insult certain American citizens. These films, for theaters, usually go the rounds throughout the North and South and never arouse more than feeble protest.

> "Pictures of Irish Life Bring Protest: Indignant Patrons Wreck Theaters," *Chicago Defender,* 2 September 1927.

The Germans

21. Incorporation of Holy Trinity Church, Philadelphia, 1788

The Catholic community in colonial America, largely English in background, began to diversify with the growing number of German Catholics in the eighteenth century. In 1787, German Catholics of Philadelphia initiated the founding of an ethnic congregation of their own and obtained legal incorporation from the Pennsylvania legislature in 1788. Their founding of Holy Trinity Church launched the first Catholic national parish in the United States. The following "Act of Incorporation" of Holy Trinity Church was typical of an era when state laws provided for members to incorporate and own church property.

Preamble

Sect. I. Whereas the members of the German religious society of Roman Catholics, belonging to the church called the "Holy Trinity," and residing within the city of Philadelphia and the vicinity thereof have represented that they have at a considerable expense, purchased a lot of ground at the northwest corner of Spruce and Sixth Streets, in the said city, and nearly completed a house or church for the public worship of Almighty God, called "the Holy Trinity," and have prayed to be incorporated, and by law enabled to receive such donations and bequests as have or hereafter may be made to their said society, as well as to manage the temporalities of their said church as other religious societies within this commonwealth may or can do, and it being just and reasonable as well as conformable to the spirit of the constitution, that the prayer of their petition be granted. Therefore,

Sect. II. *Be it enacted and it is hereby enacted by the representatives of the Freemen of the Commonwealth of Pennsylvania in General Assembly met & by the authority of the same,* That the German subscribers and (OTHERS) being or who shall hereafter become members of the said religious society of German Roman Catholics, now or hereafter worshipping at the said church, called the Holy Trinity, are and from & immediately after the passing of this act, shall be & they are hereby erected into and declared to be one body politic and corporate, in deed and in law, by the name, stile and title of "The Trustees of the German Religious Society of Roman Catholics of the Holy Trinity Church, in the city of Philadelphia," and that they the said trustees and their successors, to be elected as hereinafter mentioned, by the name aforesaid, shall have perpetual succession, and shall be capable in law to purchase, take, have, hold, receive and enjoy, to them and their successors, in fee simple, for any lesser estate, any lands, tenements, rents, hereditaments or real estate, whose yearly value in the whole shall not exceed the sum of five hundred pounds, by grant, gift, bargain and sale, will, devise or otherwise, and also to purchase, take, hold, possess or enjoy, any monies, goods, chattles or personal estate whatsoever, by gift, grant, will, legacy or bequest, and the same lands, tenements, rents, hereditaments, and real and personal estate, excepting always the said church called the Holy Trinity, and the lot of ground and appurtenances thereto belonging...

Sect. III. *And be it further enacted by the authority aforesaid,* That the first Trustees of the said Corporation shall be and consist of the following persons, viz, the eldest Pastor of the said church for the time being, George Ernst Lechler, senior, James Oellers, Christopher Shorty, senior, Henry Horne, Adam Premir, Anthony Hobky, Jacob Threin and Charles Bauman, all Members of said Corporation and subscribers toward the building of said church. And the future Trustees of the said Congregation shall be, and consist of the eldest Pastor of the said church for the time being, duly appointed, and of eight Lay Members of the congregation, worshipping in and contributors to the said church, to be appointed and elected in the matter hereinafter mentioned.

Sect. IV. *And be it further enacted by the authority aforesaid,* That all and every the Members of the said church, having subscribed to building of the same, or who shall hereafter contribute any sum of money, not less than ten shillings annually, toward the support of the said church, shall meet on Monday immediately next after Whit-Sunday, which will be in the year of our Lord 1 thousand seven hundred & ninety, so on in every year for ever thereafter at such place in the said city, as shall be appointed by the said Trustees, whereof notice shall be given in the said church at the beginning of divine worship on Whit-Sunday in the morning and then & there shall choose by ballot, the said eight Lay Trustees in manner aforesaid, by a majority of those Members qualified to vote as aforesaid, who shall so meet between the hours of one and three of the clock in the afternoon of every such day, and the Trustees so chosen shall be and continue Trustees of the said Corporation, until the next election; and on the Sunday next after every such election, the Trustees so elected, shall be published in the said church, and their names entered in the book, of the said Corporation for that purpose to be kept; and the said eldest Pastor for the time being so appointed, and Members so chosen Trustees as aforesaid, shall be and continue Trustees of the said Corporation until the close of the next election, at which time and place they shall be prepared with and render a just and true account of all the monies by them received and expended for the use and benefit of the said Corporation & Congregation the preceding year, which accounts shall be signed by the eldest Pastor aforesaid for the time being, as well the other Trustees.

Sect. V. *And be it further enacted by the authority aforesaid,* That all and every the person and persons in whome any estate real or personal whatsoever is or shall be, at the time of passing this act vested for the use of the regular Members of the said congregation of German Roman Catholics, now or hereafter worshipping at the said church, called the Holy Trinity, of or for any estate or interest, whatsoever, shall and they are hereby enjoined and required upon the reasonable request & proper costs and charges of the said

Trustees, by good and sufficient conveyances and assurances in the law, to convey and assure, assign, transfer and set over to the said Trustees, by the name aforesaid, and to their successors and assigns for ever, all and every the messuages, lots, lands, tenements, rents, hereditaments & estate, real and personal whatsoever, whereof he or they are or shall be seized or possessed as aforesaid, to have and to hold the same to the said Trustees, their successors and assigns, to and for the use of the Society of German Roman Catholics, now or hereafter worshipping at the said church called the Holy Trinity, forever...

Sect. VI. *And be it further enacted by the authority aforesaid,* That it shall and may be lawful to and for the said Trustees and their successors from time to time, as occasion shall require, to meet together for the purpose of transacting the business of the Society under their care, of the time and place of which meetings due notice shall be given to all the said Trustees at least one day before, at which meetings the eldest Pastor aforesaid being present shall be President, and if five of said Trustees shall attend, they shall form a quorum or board and shall have power by a majority of votes present to make, ordain and establish such rules, orders and regulations for the management of the temporal business, the government of their schools and disposing of the estate of the said corporation, as to them shall seem proper. Provided that such rules, orders and regulations be reasonable in themselves and not repugnant to the Constitution and Laws of this state. And Provided also, That in the disposal or alienation of the estate of the said congregation and corporation the consent and concurrence of the major part of the regular Members of the said church, qualified to vote as aforesaid, shall be first had and obtained.

Enacted into a law at Philadelphia, on Saturday the fourth day of October in the year of our Lord one thousand seven hundred and eighty eight.

PETER ZACHARY LLOYD
Clerk of the General Assembly

Signed by order of the House
THOMAS MIFFLIN, Speaker

An Act to Incorporate the Members of the Religious Society of German Roman Catholics of the Church Called the Holy Trinity in the City of Philadelphia (Philadelphia, ca. 1787), original copy in the Philadelphia Archdiocesan Historical Research Center.

22. The Plan of Boniface Wimmer, O.S.B., for Ministry to German Immigrants, 1845

Boniface Wimmer, a Bavarian Benedictine monk and priest, enthusiastically supported the restoration of Benedictine monasteries suppressed in many parts of Europe during the wave of secularization of church property in the early nineteenth century. As part of the revival of Benedictine monasticism, he sought to reenergize its missionary aspects, especially for the growing German migra-

tion to the United States in the 1840s. His letter to a German diocesan priest, Peter Henry Lemcke, a pastor in western Pennsylvania, outlined his views. In 1846 Wimmer founded the Benedictine monastery at Latrobe, Pennsylvania, that became St. Vincent Archabbey, and he went on to establish a network of Benedictine monasteries in Minnesota, Kansas, New Jersey, North Carolina, Alabama, Illinois, and Colorado.

Every Catholic who cherishes his faith must take a deep interest in missionary labors; but religion as well as patriotism demands that every German Catholic should take a special interest in the missions of America. To us it cannot be a matter of indifference how our countrymen are situated in America. I, for my part, have not been able to read the various and generally sad reports on the desolate condition of Germans beyond the ocean without deep compassion and a desire to do something to alleviate their pitiable condition. Thus, I have given much thought to the question of how they might be practically assisted. It is not difficult to understand what should be done — more German-speaking priests should be found laboring for the spiritual welfare of our countrymen in America. The only question is how to get priests and what kind of priest will do the work most successfully. The answer to the second question will also give the solution for the first. I do not wish to offend anyone, but my opinion is that secular priests are not the best adapted for missionary labors. History shows that the Church has not availed herself of their services to any great extent in missionary undertakings. I do not mean to say that a secular priest cannot labor effectually within a limited territory in America, for there are many who labor successfully even at the present day. But they cannot satisfy themselves. They are in great danger of becoming careless and worldly-minded. I cannot agree with Dr. Salzbacher when he says that the spiritual needs of our countrymen can be provided by perambulating missionaries, who go about like the Wandering Jew from forest to forest, from hut to hut; for unless such a missionary be a *Saint* not much of the spiritual man would remain in him, and even then by such transient visits not much lasting good could be accomplished. The missionary, more than any other priest, stands in need of spiritual renewal from time to time, consolation and advice in trials and difficulties. He must, therefore, have some place where he can find such assistance: this may be given by his bishop but he will find it more securely in a religious community — in the midst of his confreres.

He should also have a home to receive him in his old age or when he is otherwise incapacitated for missionary labors; he should have no worldly cares, otherwise he might neglect or even forget his own and others' spiritual welfare. All this can be had only in a religious community. For this reason, therefore, religious are better adapted to missionary work than secular priests. In a community the experiences of the individual become common property; all have a common interest, stand together and have the same object in view. A vacancy caused by death or otherwise can be filled more readily and having fewer temporal cares, they can devote themselves more exclusively to the spiritual interests of themselves and others. Thus, all other things being equal, a religious priest in a community should be able to work more effectively on the missions than the secular priest who stands alone.

The next question is: What religious Order is most adapted for the American missions, not to convert the native Indians but to provide for the spiritual necessities of German immigrants?

As far as I know the only Religious in the strict sense of the word now found in America are the Jesuits and Redemptorists. The missionaries of the Middle Ages, the Benedictines, Dominicans and Franciscans are not yet represented in the New World, except by a few individuals who do not live in monasteries. The Jesuits devote their energies principally to teaching in colleges; their students are mostly from the higher classes of society and many of them belong to Protestant families. Many Jesuits are also doing excellent work among the Indians, and others have charge of congregations in cities near their colleges. But while they accomplish so much in their sphere of labors, they can do little for Germans, because few of them speak their language. The Redemptorists are doing noble work for our countrymen in the States: in cities and thickly settled country districts they have large congregations, and also do what they can for others as traveling missionaries. Some secular priests likewise go about among scattered Catholics doing good, but they naturally and necessarily concentrate in cities where there is a large Catholic population.

We see, therefore, that much is being done in America; very much, indeed, when we consider the small band of priests and the difficulties under which they labor. But as yet nothing has been done for the stability of the work, no provision has been made for an increase of German-speaking priests, to meet the growing demand for missionary laborers. It is not difficult to see that secular priests, whose labors extend over a district larger than a diocese, can do nothing to secure reinforcements to their own number. But why have the Redemptorists and Jesuits not accomplished more in this line? By his vows neither the Jesuit or Redemptorist is bound to any particular place, but he must always be prepared to leave his present position at the command of his superiors, and may also request if not demand, his removal for weighty reasons. This has many advantages, but for America it seems to me also to have disadvantages. For the successor of the one who has been removed will require a long time to become acquainted with all the circumstances with which his predecessor was familiar, and even the uncertainty as to how long he will remain at any particular place will be an obstacle in his way. Moreover, the fact that Jesuits generally receive only the children of richer families, many of whom are Protestants, into their institutions, because they depend upon them for their sustenance, and that the Redemptorists are by their statutes required to devote themselves to missionary work, and can, therefore, not be expected to take charge of seminaries, gives us no reason to hope that the spiritual wants of Americans, particularly of German-Americans[,] will be provided for by native German-speaking priests. And in case the mission societies of Europe should unexpectedly be rendered incapable of supplying money or reinforcements in priests, the situation would become even more serious. But even supposing that everything remains as it is, we cannot hope to have an efficient supply of priests as long as we have no means of securing a native clergy for the United States of America. For the number of those who are educated at Alt-Oetting or elsewhere in Germany is not in proportion to the continually increasing emigration to America, not to speak of the natural increase of Germans in America itself. Jesuits and Redemptorists are, therefore, doing noble work in America and their number should be increased as much as possible; but they will scarcely be able to remove the chief cause of the deficiency of German-speaking priests. We need not speak of the Dominicans and Franciscans; there are very few German Dominicans, and the present social conditions of America seems not to call for Mendicant Friars.

We now come to the Benedictines, who are not as yet represented in the United States. In my opinion they are the most competent to relieve the great want of priests in America. In support of my opinion I will adduce some facts: but I must again state that I have not the remotest intention of belittling the efforts and successes of other religious Orders; on the contrary, I am desirous of seeing them labor in the same field, side by side with the Benedictines.

History abundantly proves:

1. That we owe the conversion of England, Germany, Denmark, Sweden, Norway, Hungary, and Poland almost exclusively to the Benedictines, and that in the remaining parts of Europe Christendom is deeply indebted to them.

2. That the conversion of these countries was not transient but lasting and permanent.

3. That this feature must be ascribed to the fact that the Benedictines are men of stability; they are not wandering monks; they acquire lands and bring them under cultivation and become thoroughly affiliated to the country and people to which they belong, and receive their recruits from the district in which they have established themselves.

4. That the Benedictine Order by its Rule is so constituted that it can readily adapt itself to all times and circumstances. The contemplative and practical are harmoniously blended; agriculture, manual labor, literature, missionary work, education, were drawn into the circle of activity which St. Benedict placed before his disciples. Hence they soon felt at home in all parts of Europe and the same could be done in America.

When we consider North America as it is today, we can see at a glance that there is no country in the world which offers greater opportunities for the establishment and spread of the Benedictine Order, no country that is so much like our old Europe was. There are found immense forests, large uncultivated tracts of land in the interior, most fertile lands which command but a nominal price; often for miles and miles no village is to be seen, not to speak of cities. In country districts no schools, no churches are to be found. The German colonists are scattered, uncultured, ignorant, hundreds of miles away from the nearest German-speaking priest, for, practically, they can make their homes where they please. There are no good books, no Catholic papers, no holy pictures. The destitute and unfortunate have no one to offer them a hospitable roof, the orphans naturally become the victims of vice and irreligion — in a word, the conditions in America today are like those of Europe 1000 years ago, when the Benedictine Order attained its fullest development and effectiveness by its wonderful adaptability and stability.

Of course, the Benedictine Order would be required to adapt itself again to circumstances and begin anew. To acquire a considerable tract of land in the interior of the country, upon which to found a monastery, would not be very difficult; to bring under cultivation at least a portion of the land and to erect the most necessary buildings would give employment for a few years to the first Benedictine colony, which should consist of at least two or three priests and ten to fifteen brothers skilled in the most necessary trades.

Once the colony is self-supporting, which could be expected in about two years, it should begin to expand so that the increased number of laboring hands might also increase the products and revenues to be derived from the estate. A printing and lithographing establishment would also be very desirable.

Since the Holy Rule prescribes for all, not only manual labor and the chanting of the Divine Office, but also that the monks should devote several hours a day to study, this time could be used by the Fathers to instruct the Brothers thoroughly in arithmetic, German grammar, etc., thereby fitting them to teach school, to give catechetical instruction and in general to assist in teaching children as well as grown persons.

Such a monastery would from the very start be of great advantage to German settlers, at least to those who would live near it. They would have a place where they could depend upon hearing Mass on Sundays and hear a sermon in their own language; they would also have a place where they could always be sure to find a priest at home to hear their confessions, to bless their marriages, to baptize their children and to administer the last sacraments to the sick if called in time.

Occasionally the Superior might send out even the Brothers two by two to hunt up fallen-away Catholics, to instruct children for their First Communion, etc. All subsequent monasteries that might be established from the mother-house would naturally exercise the same influence.

So far, the services rendered by the Benedictines would not be extraordinary; any other priests or religious could do the same, except that they would not likely be able to support themselves without assistance from Europe; whereas a community of Benedictines, when once firmly established[,] would soon become self-sustaining.

But such a monastery if judiciously located would not long remain isolated; all reports from America inform us that the German immigrants are concentrating themselves in places where churches have been erected or where a German-speaking priest has taken up his residence. This would also be found, and to a greater extent, if there were a monastery somewhere with a good school. In a short time a large German population would be found near the monastery, just as in the Middle Ages, villages, towns and cities sprang up near Benedictine abbeys. Then the monks could expect a large number of children for their school, and in the course of time, as the number of priests increases, a college with a good Latin course could be opened. They would not be dependent upon the tuition fee of the students for their support, which they could draw from the farm and the missions (though these would not be a source of much income in the beginning). Thus they could devote their energies to the education of the poorer classes of boys who could pay little or nothing, and since these boys would daily come in contact with the priests and other monks, it could scarcely be otherwise but that many of them would develop a desire of becoming priests or even religious. I am well aware that to many readers these hopes and expectations will appear too sanguine, since all efforts at securing a native American clergy have hitherto failed so signally. But we must remember that the annals of the missions as well as the oral reports of priests who have labored in America, inform us that these efforts were more theoretical than practical, that there was a desire of making such efforts, but they were not really made, and that those which were really made were more or less restricted to English-speaking clergy, and that in general there were neither sufficient means nor sufficient teachers to train a native German-speaking clergy. It is said that the young American is not inclined to devote himself to the sacred ministry because it is so easy for him to secure a wife and home; that the American has nothing in view but to heap up riches of this world; that fathers need their sons on the farms or in the workshops and, therefore, do not care to see them study. But, let me ask, is it not the same here in Europe? Are the rich always pleased when their sons study for the priesthood? Are all Germans in America well-to-do or rich? Are they not as a rule the very poorest and to a certain extent the menials of the rest? Moreover, is the first thought of a boy directed to matrimony? Is it any wonder that he should show no inclination for the priesthood when he sees a priest scarcely once a year; when divine services are held in churches which resemble hovels rather than churches, without pomp and ceremony, when the priest has to divest himself of his priestly dignity, often travels on horse-back, in disguise, looking more like a drummer than a priest, when the boy sees nothing in the life of a priest but sacrifice, labor and fatigue?

But all this would become quite different if boys could come in daily contact with priests, if they received instructions from them, if the priest could appear to advantage, better dressed and better housed than the ordinary settler, if young men could learn from observation to realize and appreciate the advantages of a community life, if they could learn to understand that while the life of a priest requires self-denial and sacrifice, his hopes of a great reward are also well grounded. Yes, I do not doubt but that hundreds, especially of the lower classes, would prefer to spend their lives in well regulated monasteries in suitable and reasonable occupations, than to gain a meager livelihood by incessant hard labor in forest regions. Let us remember that here in Bavaria from the year 740 to the year 788 not less than 40 Benedictine monasteries were founded and the communities were composed almost entirely of natives from the free classes, who had enjoyed the advantages of freedom in the world and could have chosen the married state without difficulty or hindrance. Why should we not reasonably expect the same results in the United States where the conditions are so similar?

But such a monastery in North America would not draw its recruits exclusively from the surrounding country, but also from the great number of boys, who either during the voyage or soon after their arrival in America lose their parents and thereby become helpless and forsaken. An institution, in which such unfortunate children could find a home, would undoubtedly be a great blessing for that country. And where could this be done more easily than in Benedictine monasteries as described above, in which young boys could not only attend school, but also do light work on the farm or in the workshops and according to their talents and vocation become priests or at least educated Christians and good citizens[?] Surely, many of these would gladly join the community as brothers and or priests, and thus repay the monastery for the trouble of educating them.

In this way numerous religious clergy could soon be secured, and then some of the Fathers might be sent out to visit those Catholics who scarcely ever see a priest; occasionally at least they might preach the word of God and bring the consolations of religion even to those who live at a great distance from the monastery; small congregations could be established, and the seminary could soon furnish a goodly number of secular clergy.

But where could the Benedictines be found to establish such a monastery in North America, and where are the necessary means for such an undertaking? The writer is informed that there are several Fathers in the Benedictine Order here in Bavaria who would gladly go upon such a mission, and with regard to Brothers there would be no difficulty whatever; within a few years not less than 200 good men have applied for admission into one of our monasteries. It is a well known fact that of those who are studying for the priesthood many are joining the Redemptorist Order simply because it offers them hope of becoming missionaries in America.

The necessary funds could easily be supplied by the *Ludwig-Missionsverein*. Bavaria annually pays 100,000 florins into the treasury of the Society. Would it be unfair to devote one tenth of this sum to the establishment of monasteries in America, especially since just now hundreds of our own nationality are seeking homes in the United States, and consequently the money contributed would be used to further the interests of Germans in general and our countrymen [Bavarians] in particular? Could a better use of such contributions be made or could anything appeal more loudly to our national patriotism? Is it right that we should continually look after the interests of strangers and forget our own countrymen? Moreover, whatever would be done for the Germans would advance the well-being of the entire Church in America. We must not stifle our feelings of patriotism. The Germans, we hear it often enough, lose their national character in the second or third generation, they also lose their language, because like a little rivulet they disappear in the mighty stream of the Anglo-American population in the States. Is this not humiliating for us Germans? Would this sad condition of affairs continue if here and there a German center were established, to which the stream of emigration from our country could be systematically directed, if German instruction and sermons were given by priests going forth from these centers, if German books, papers and periodicals were distributed among the people, if German boys could receive a German education and training, which would make themselves felt in wider circles?

Let us, therefore, no longer build air castles for our countrymen in America. Let us provide for their religious interests, then their domestic affairs will take care of themselves. Benedictine monasteries of the old style are the best means of checking the downward tendencies of our countrymen in social, political and religious matters. Let Jesuits and Redemptorists labor side by side with the Benedictines; there is room enough for all and plenty of work. If every Religious Order develops a healthy activity within its sphere, the result will be doubly sure and great. North America will no longer depend upon Europe for its spiritual welfare, and the day may come when America will repay us just as England, converted by the Benedictines, repaid the continent of Europe.

The letter originally appeared in the *Postzeitung* of Augsburg, Germany, 8 November 1845, and was reprinted in the appendix to Colman J. Barry, O.S.B., *Worship and Work: St. John's Abbey and University, 1856–1956* (Collegeville, Minn.: Liturgical Press, 1956), 345–51; reprinted in John Tracy Ellis, ed., *Documents of American Catholic History* (Wilmington, Del.: Michael Glazier, 1987), 1:279–88. Printed with permission of the estate of John Tracy Ellis.

23. Views of German Catholic Trustees in Cincinnati, ca. 1850

Cincinnati emerged as the fifth largest city in the United States by 1850, its population constantly augmented with the arrival of thousands of Germans. Cincinnati's Irish-born bishop since 1833, John Baptist Purcell, generally accepted the German Catholics' organizational practices of independent incorporation of their own institutions such as a cemetery, newspaper, and orphan asylum but not parish church property, though he approved the practice of lay

parish trustees or wardens to assist the pastor in administering parish temporal-
ities. The harmony of these governing arrangements sometimes broke down, as
in the case of the Germans' ownership of cemeteries, which was the occasion
of a lengthy pamphlet, excerpted here, revealing the Germans' views on how
church property should be held and administered.

The "Queen of the West" published, in the course of several weeks past, a
number of articles attempting to disgrace the Board of Trustees of the "German Catholic Cemetery Association," and to throw the firebrand of discord
into that otherwise peaceable society. The assailants, conscious of the iniquity
of their cause, did not dare to give their names; but cowardly hurled their poi-
soned arrows against the Board of Trustees, from behind the hiding place of
anonymity. Yet, finding their wicked design frustrated by treating their ma-
licious attacks with silent contempt, they at last procured the signatures of
some obedient servants of the "Right Reverend anonymity;" it will, therefore,
now be proper to repel those unjust charges, and to unmask the demagogues
and traitors.

The undersigned, Committee, by order of the Board of Trustees, do hereby
perform this unpleasant duty as follows:

1. To mention the secret motives of those "pious servants of the Lord."

2. To preface this with a brief history of the foundation of our Cemetery
    Association.

No. 1. As to those secret motives, they can be no secret to those, who have
some knowledge of the designs of our (the Roman Catholic) Reverend and
most Reverend Clergy. Their design is to exclude the Catholic citizen from
all participation in the ownership of Catholic Church and School property.
He is to remain an outlaw in this respect. Although Catholic Congregations
may have raised hundred thousands for the acquisition of Churches, School-
houses or Cemeteries, the property shall not be owned by the Congregation,
the deeds are not to be made to them; but the Bishop of the respective diocese
usurps the ownership of the Church property, acquired by the millions of
drops of sweat of laboring Catholics; to him the property is made over on
the public records; and if any one dares to doubt the propriety or justice of
such proceeding, he will be slandered, branded as a heretic, or, according to
the newly invented term, as a hickory Catholic.

But the Catholic Germans, who came to this, the land of liberty, for the
sake of liberty, do not mind such persecutions, and had the moral courage to
defy these spiritual weapons. They learned by experience in the old country,
the pockets of the Clergy to be rather deep — they there experienced the clerical arrogation in temporal matters — they never intended to escape from the
tyranny of princes, merely for the purpose of submitting to the still more disgraceful yoke of priestcraft. The unjust and rapacious practice of the Catholic

Bishops, to usurp all the property purchased by the hard earned savings of the members of their Congregations, and the fact, that those Right Reverend gentlemen caused exclusively to be entered into their own names, the property acquired by the Congregations, created the first suspicions, and these suspicions were naturally increased on learning the high discreditable conduct of a certain Bishop of Detroit. By comparing the condition of the Catholic Congregations in Germany with those of the United States, a striking difference was found in favor of the former. In Germany, the Congregations manage their own property, independent of the Clergy, the Bishop does not own a particle of the Church property, he has no more claim to the same, than to the property of any private person. The Priest is paid by the congregation and is exclusively confined to his clerical functions. Yet there the Catholic faith and the Catholic religion is in as good, if not a better condition than here. Considering these facts, the question naturally occurs:

"How is it that the Catholics in an oppressed country like Germany, are better protected against the rapacity of Priests than in these free United States?"

"How is it, that in this country, the Bishops can, without let or hindrance, appropriate to themselves all the property acquired by the congregations?"

These questions circulated from mouth to mouth, and soon the answer presented itself. We enjoy in this country freedom of religion — the government does not interfere in ecclesiastical matters — it gives protection to the congregations when demanded, and if then the congregations are so foolish or imbecile as to suffer themselves to be made serfs or slaves, and to have taken from them their last cent by the Clergy, then the foolish, blind, and servile members are to blame; not the government. This answer did not fall upon sterile ground; it contains a striking truth; and on account of the continued arbitrary conduct of the Catholic clergy, and for other well established causes, (referred to, subject No. 2) a great number of Germans determined hereafter not blindly to submit to this course of things...

> The Civil Right of the Catholic People Usurped by the Roman Priests and Bishops, Being a Word in Self Defense against Anonymous and Non-anonymous Attacks upon the Board of Trustees of the St. Peter's Cemetery Association (Cincinnati, 1850). Printed with permission of the Cincinnati Historical Society Library.

24. Regulations for Cincinnati's German Catholic Parishes, 1850

Since the formation of Cincinnati's first German congregation in 1833, Bishop John Baptist Purcell had allowed the growing number of the city's German parishes — eight by 1850 — to follow the German practice of governing the temporal affairs of their churches through elected trustees. At the same time, the bishop retained ownership of church property in trust for the laity. In 1850, the year Cincinnati became an archdiocese with Purcell as its first archbishop, he approved the following regulations for the German parishes' governing arrange-

ments under "wardens" — a title that he preferred over "trustees." The German tradition of laymen, but not laywomen, sharing in parish governance was cited as a characteristic of German Catholics in America in Father Peter Abbelen's memorial presented to the Holy See in 1886 (see document 28).

Those appointed from time to time to have charge over the above mentioned affairs will bear in mind: That all church property as soon as acquired by the church is property belonging to God, and no longer to man, (although still intended for his use) and that therefore the right for administering the same, belong only to those appointed by Jesus Christ to govern his church. They will therefore consider themselves as assisting the Bishop only and not as acting in any other name or by any other authority. Consequently they will discharge their trust with fidelity and in a truly Catholic spirit.

They will further never meddle with things spiritual or with matters appertaining to the divine worship, duties and obligations of the clergy and the like.

1. Each church will have six wardens besides the first pastor. Each member must be 30 years of age, of an exemplary and irreproachable character, sound in faith and views respecting the administration of church property, must have made his Easter duties, and have a seat or pew in the church, so that no one can say anything against him. The first Pastor will be President, and in his absence one of his associates, and if all are absent, or prevented, the wardens may select one pro tem. from among themselves. The President may delegate his office for such time as he may deem fit. Besides him there will be a cashier, first secretary, second ditto if it be deemed necessary.

2. The President discharges all the customary duties of his station. He will further call and preside over all meetings of the congregation, and committee of delegates. He will sign all accounts, bills, bonds if presented for payment, countersign the Bonds, and keep the Bondbook.

3. The first secretary will keep correct minutes of all the proceedings of the wardens, hold a true account of all receipts and expenditures, sign accounts if presented for payment, make a true and complete inventory of all the articles belonging to the church school, and parsonage. At the end of each year, he will present a complete statement of the different receipts and also expenditures for church, schools, salaries made during the past year. Together with the condition of the church regarding its debts, and how much has been paid off, or incurred.

4. The second secretary will have charge of the pew book, and let the pews and seats. He will receive the monies for them, together with the ordinary collections in the church and pay the same to the cashier. Every 3 months he will make a report of the monies received, to the President and first secretary. At the expiration of the year he will make a full report.

5. The cashier will have charge of all monies, give his receipt and sufficient surity for the same. He will pay no monies unless sanctioned by the wardens if possible, but in no case without a previous order from the President or one

appointed by him. When called upon by him, or wardens, he must allow the treasury to be examined.

6. The wardens will be elected for one year commencing with the first Sunday in February. In case of removal, resignation or death, the highest from the remaining list of candidates will supply the place. To avoid dissatisfaction, no one, except him who has charge over the pew books, shall serve more than 2 successive years at any one time. The election of the wardens must be confirmed by the Bishop, who may also remove them when he deems it expedient.

7. On the first Sunday in January, 6 delegates will be appointed by the congregation to nominate 2 candidates for each office, besides six others, of whom the one half will be elected on the 3d Sunday of the same month. No delegate can be a candidate at the same time.

8. The wardens will meet regularly once a month and at other times when called together by the Pastor. They will see that order is preserved during divine service, raise the collections, provide funds to meet the debts, pay the established expenditures, and preserve everything in proper order and repair. They establish the price of the pews and see that the rent is duly collected. All expenditures exceeding $100.00 must first be submitted to the congregation and all amounting to $50.00 and upwards for any one article (Insurance, established salaries, and necessary repairs excepted) must first be made known to the Bishop and receive his express approbation and sanction. They will see that all surplus money is deposited in some safe public institution, where it may be had at any moment, and when if possible, it may not lie useless to the congregation. In no case shall they loan to one another, or to private individuals since it is apt to bring the church into difficulties, and tending only to cast odium and disgrace upon themselves and congregation. On the first Sunday in February, they will present their books in order, and submit the same for examination by the committee of 3 appointed for this purpose, who likewise inspect the Treasury. If the committee finds the report and books correct it will sign the books, if not and they cannot rectify it, they will state it to the vicar general and if he cannot arrange it, a meeting of the congregation will be called to whom they report the difference. The Committee must have the books examined within 2 weeks after their appointment.

9. During the month of March each year, the Vicar General, together with 2 assistant priests appointed by the clergy of the different churches will examine the books containing the receipts, expenditures, and debts of each Church, and report the same to the Bishop and afterwards to the clergy.

10. Since the debt resting on the different churches is already very great, prudence and honesty require, that nothing, which is not really necessary, shall be done by the wardens, in the way of incurring new debts or making any improvements. They will further strive by all means in their power to diminish annually that debt; to facilitate which, they will hold annually 2 collections in each church. If the congregation finds the many different col-

lections too burdensome, the pastor and wardens can agree to suppress or diminish those collections foreign to the church.

11. The church will never become responsible for any debts contracted by individuals or by the societies belonging to the congregation. If any thing is proposed to be done so far for which a collection must be taken up in the church [and] if such article exceeds $50.00 it must first be sanctioned by the Bishop. No donation shall be received, nor anything else of moment made or taken away, against the will of the first pastor or the Archbishop. All donations made to the church belong to the church and the donor can neither take them away, nor exercise any control over them.

12. The organist and sacristan are appointed by the clergy of each church. And upon just grounds, the clergy can dismiss them.

13. The spiritual instruction of the children being entrusted by the Church to the Pastors, it follows that the school teachers are only the assistants of the Pastors, and must therefore be entirely under their control. It belongs therefore to the clergy of right to examine, appoint, and dismiss the teacher; to determine the Books, the course, time and plan of studies, and otherwise watch over, the welfare of the schools. The clergy and wardens determine their salary [and] those of the organist and sacristan. The wardens will provide for all the wants of the schoolhouse, the comfort of the children especially in church, assist on all necessary occasions to keep order, watch over the conduct of the children especially in church, and see that the established tuition fees are duly collected. Whenever it shall be deemed necessary by the clergy to appoint an additional teacher, they must first submit it to the Bishop, at least while the church is in debt. If the clergy and wardens deem it expedient to increase the salary of any teacher, sacristan, or organist, they must in like manner submit it to the decision of the Bishop.

14. If any society or meeting wishes to occupy the church, it must first obtain the express leave of the first Pastor. No layman can be allowed to speak publicly in church, since this would be against her established rules and against the purpose for which the church is.

15. For a meeting of the congregation 30 will be requisite to constitute a quorum. No one can propose more than one candidate for any purpose. Those only can speak and vote who are 21 years of age, have discharged their Easter duties and hold moreover a seat or pew in the church.

16. Every church is liable for, but only for, its own debts.

John B. [Purcell], Archbp . . . of Cinti.
Cincinnati, 25th Nov. 1850

"Regulations for the Administration of the Temporal Affairs of the German Rom. Catholic Churches of Cincinnati to Be Observed until Altered or Recalled by the Archbishop," Purcell Papers, Archives of the Archdiocese of Cincinnati. Printed through courtesy of the Historical Archives of the Chancery, Archdiocese of Cincinnati.

25. Instructions for German Catholic Immigrants, 1869

Jesuit Father Ernst Reiter, who ministered to Germans in Boston, compiled a comprehensive directory of German Catholic clergy, parishes, and religious institutions in the United States in 1869. For German-speaking immigrants arriving in the country, the directory provided a convenient way of locating services in their own language. In the volume's introduction, Father Reiter provided an unfavorable assessment of American life as well as some practical and spiritual advice to immigrants. His advice on spiritual matters is given as follows.

Good Advice for Immigrants

Nowhere can there be found more disappointed, deceived, swindled, and cheated people than in the United States of America where almost everyone, without exception, strives to raise himself as quickly as possible and become rich without concerning himself about the means. And where so frequently brother seeks to take advantage of and to dupe brother, and even the son to dupe the father as a stranger. Where every man is respected and esteemed almost simply and solely according to the money that he has, so that it is a common figure of speech, even among the best Christians: "The man is worth 50,000 or 100,000." And yet another expression: "Every man has his price," that is, is for sale and is bought for more or less money — his honor and good name, his fatherland, his friend and his brother, and, unfortunately, usually the cheapest and easiest, his faith, his soul, and his salvation. Where especially the German so likes to play the common man is more ashamed than any other [immigrant group] of his nationality and mother tongue and cannot become Americanized fast enough and who may also throw off his faith. Such a one almost, without exception, suffers failure. That is good advice worth money. I want to put together here at the very least a few such [pieces of] good advice...

Good Advice for the Well-being of the Soul

  A. Before the Voyage

     1. Part from your parents and relatives in peace if you want to begin in America with happy courage and God's blessing and want to be spared the terrible grief because it is no longer possible to reconcile personally with your gravely offended parents.

     2. Make your peace with God and clean your conscience with a good confession. Through this, you do not run the risk, in case of misfortune on the sea, of falling into the eternal precipice of hell while your body falls into the depths of the sea.

     3. If you have spoken about a pilgrimage or something similar, honor that pledge before you leave.

4. Trust or fear whom? In regard to agents or companions, so that you are not exploited by the former, and what is worse, become hired out or sold to places or persons where awaits the greatest danger for faith and innocence: shield yourself from such companions. Do not let yourself be betrayed or seduced.

5. Take your baptismal certificate, marriage certificate, and a certificate of sodality membership as well as a letter from your priest. With these you can easily identify yourself at the place of your new settlement. And in time of need, which, contrary to expectations, may come to you, you will thus be able to find help from a priest, as well as from fellow Catholics and countrymen, more easily and abundantly.

6. Young persons who began an acquaintance [in Germany] and want to come over here together should get married first; certainly at home, or, in case this is not possible, in Bremen, Hamburg, or Le Havre, where Catholic German mission priests have special faculties [to officiate at weddings]. Otherwise, there is, without doubt, under way on the ship an abominable life of sin.

7. Whoever can not endure mockery, contempt, and ridicule for his faith, remain outside [of America], especially all who are of frivolous and inconstant behavior, for even though they are informed in their faith and zealous in visiting church and receiving the sacraments, they fall from their faith here just as the leaves fall from the trees in autumn.

8. Catholics who grew up in totally Catholic areas should consider a long time about settling in America, for experience teaches that such persons fall, first and last, from the faith because they did not live in community with heretics and unbelievers.

On the Trip

1. If you are in any kind of a position to take a first or second class cabin, do not take your place in between decks because in such places is, especially at night, a disorderly, unclean, and terrible confusion.

2. Young women should not go around with young men and should not stay in the same compartment with their male friends as so often happens. Also guard against the insidious favors and services of the crew, however high in rank. Mostly, it is incomprehensible how a young woman can make such a long, and for her doubly dangerous, trip other than in the company of her parents or even a grown sister.

On Arrival

1. One, especially young people, must especially guard against leaders and guides who impose themselves or ingratiate themselves so that one does not come into a thieves' den or den of vice. Instead, if no near relative or friend stands ready to receive you, turn to the above-named trusted representatives of the Central Verein.

2. One must not stay in an area or place where no German priests, churches, or schools are to be found. Instead, one should take upon oneself what was mentioned in the introduction. Also, do not settle in places where a German priest is placed in an entirely English community, because one such priest may leave soon due to a transfer or death, and then only an English-speaking priest comes in his place. Such places are marked in this book with the letter "E" behind the title of the church . . .

For Life in America

Continually proclaimed from the mouth of the famous missionary and true apostle of the Germans, Father Francis X. Wenninger, S.J., and unforgettably resounding in the ears of all his audience are the words: "America! America! — yes, yes, — America! You are, to me, a dangerous land." There you must indeed find your own way, for body and soul you are in it, so accept a little good advice.

1. As soon as you settle in a community, present yourself to your new priest and show him the baptismal, marriage, sodality, and fraternity certificates you brought with you, and if you received one, the letter of introduction from your previous priest. With these he can become acquainted with you and you with him, as is certainly proper. Unfortunately, this occurs very seldom, and therefore, it comes about, especially in large cities or also even in widely separated communities, that many new parishioners live for a year in their parish without becoming acquainted with the priest, unless they are presented the opportunity to baptize children or perform a wedding. The natural consequence of it is that such become indifferent Christians if they were not already.

2. Equally, join the religious fraternities, sodalities, and organizations established in the parish. Otherwise, you will certainly become lukewarm and negligent in the practice of religion.

3. If, in the parish, as in almost all German communities, one or another Catholic aid society is established to help in sickness and

death, join this as well, and even more so. By doing this, you will not be enticed or blinded by the apparent benevolence of some variety of freemasonry and thereby endanger faith and salvation. Indeed, it is well known to every Catholic that whoever joins the masons incurs excommunication in life and in death, and if he does not separate from the masons, he is deprived of all sacraments including a church funeral. Among Germans one finds especially every kind of freemasonry calling itself "red men" [Improved Order of Red Men] and the Oddfellows (a typical name) and Hurugari. Also the Turners are, according to their own statutes, which the author has read, a society hostile to religion. Also the so-called Temperance Men are, in spite of their apparently good purpose and name, a secret society and enemy of the Church. When a man wants to lure you into some kind of society, ask your priest for advice in all cases, but also obey him...

4. Do not go to work for, and even less into service for, German Protestants or fallen-away Catholics, and do not trust in your good religious knowledge or in your own strength. Mockery and laughter bring more to loss of faith than does torture. Not so dangerous as the Germans is service or work for American Protestants or unbelievers, who, in general, are more liberal and tolerant than others with the exception, however, of Baptists and Methodists, who combine with their strange theology, which makes a mockery of all common sense, a true conversion experience, or more accurately, a topsy-turvy madness.

5. In the United States, the government is not worried about religion, and, therefore, gives not one penny's contribution for church buildings, nor for Catholic schools or the salary for priests and Catholic teachers. So, here there is not other means than through renting the pews (as church seats are called here), through frequent collections in church and home, as well as through high school fees to bring in the necessary money to finance the unavoidable expenses. Thus, be on guard not to take offense at such things or to regard the whole of religion in America as a money thing and in this to find a convenient excuse and justification to quit going to church altogether. There exists also here in this country a particular command from the pope in the sixth precept of church law: "You should pay your contribution to the priest." It is usually this point that is the main annoyance for new immigrants from Germany, where this does not occur. It is otherwise with the Irish.

6. Another stumbling block for German immigrants is often that here in the land of freedom, they find more days of fast and abstinence than in the old fatherland, and they want to discover in it through a peculiar logic a difference of faith. Through this they only prove that they have not learned to distinguish between irreversible lessons of faith and changeable church discipline which conforms in many points to the varied needs and conditions of various lands. In some points it must even be surrendered to the prudence and precaution of the bishop governing his own diocese. Or do you think that a bishop here in America has to turn to your previous bishop in Germany in such matters? And still from the beginning, not a few persist in such foolish beliefs. Others spring quickly over such things to other stumbling blocks when they find out that fewer holy days are offered here than over there [in Germany].

7. Do not put your children in the official state schools, which one should properly call pagan schools, if they do not deserve even worse names for their partly open, partly hidden attack against Catholics. Examples of such schools even exist in Germany in the model-state of Baden.

8. In marriage unions, stick to a Catholic German. The character of the Irish, also so strong and secure in their Catholic faith, is too very different from that of the German to be beneficial in such a heartfelt bond like that of marriage. Fifteen years' residence in a city and in a state where proportionately more Irish live than in any other region of the United States sufficiently convinced the author of this fact. It is an almost invariable defect that the children of such a marriage in language and character become more Irish than German, or nothing of either.

9. Shun the bad habit of some Germans here in this land to anglicize their names and together with their names Americanize greatly. So the author himself found and indeed everyone finds here German families named "Klein" and now written and spoken as "Small;" Stein written and spoken becomes "Stone;" "Weber" is written and spoken as "Weaver;" and so forth...

10. Let no rent be paid to you in your own home by your sons and daughters, as they so often do here as soon as they come out of school and can often earn more in factories, workshops, and stores than is good for them. Indeed, make them immediately independent of father and mother. Play the lord of the house, and

make them lodge themselves elsewhere if you want to maintain discipline and order in the house.

11. With your children, continue to speak German, at least with father and mother in the home, indeed, force them to. Otherwise, they will soon make you, even if it is unpleasant, yield to speaking English, or rather stammering and stuttering. And then comes the inevitable result and experience that your own children laugh in your face just as soon as, and as often as, you open your mouth, and they scorn and even scold you as a dumb Dutchman.

12. Finally, never take shame in your mother-tongue, your nation, and your old fatherland in America. Pfui! That is only peculiar to the Germans, while the Irish, French, and others who are also here still are proud of their mother-tongue and their fatherland. Listen to what a native born American scholar, who himself learned with pleasure although with trouble, the German language, wrote about Germans and their language in his review of the illustrated monthly paper, *Die Alte and Neue Welt,* published by Benziger Brothers in New York and Cincinnati for the magazine *The Catholic World,* July 1869, page 575: "As for our German fellow Catholics, they ought to be proud of possessing in their own rich and grand mother-tongue a magazine which does them so much honor, and ought to give it their universal support... We fear that the children of our German fellow-citizens are too much disposed to forget the glorious fatherland of their parents, which is in them a great folly, to be checked and discouraged in every way. It is not necessary, in order to become good Americans, to disown and forget the country and the literature of one's ancestors. If it is worthwhile for those whose mother-tongue is English to spend years in acquiring a knowledge of the language and literature of Germany, it is surely a great piece of folly for those whose early education has given them the means of attaining this knowledge without any trouble to throw it away as of no value."

Ernst Reiter, S.J., *Schematismus der katholischen deutschen Geistlichkeit in den Vereinigten Staaten Nord Amerika's* (New York, 1869), trans. Anita Specht.

The Germans and Irish

26. Immigrant Catholic Life in New York, 1830s and 1840s

To minister to the growing German-speaking Catholic population, members of the Congregation of the Most Holy Redeemer (Redemptorists) arrived in the United States from Austria in 1832. Their superior or visitator from 1835 to 1841, Father Joseph Prost, C.Ss.R., left a memoir of his experiences ministering to immigrants in urban America during the 1830s and 1840s. The following excerpt describes the common practices of church support in German and Irish parishes in the northeast United States.

Before I begin the story of my travels, however, which I had to make as Visitator, I want to tell of the benefit I got from my stay in New York. I became acquainted with things that I could hardly have learned elsewhere; namely, the system followed in America for assuring church income that will maintain the priest and divine worship, and the system followed to regulate how and by whom churches and their goods are owned in America.

Most church income is derived from sittings and pews in the church itself. During the week, everything in and about the church is free. Far different, however, is it on Sundays or feast days. In order to be able to hear Mass in a suitable place in church on Sunday, a person must have rented a sitting or a pew in the church for a definite period and for a fixed sum; or else on Sunday he must pay some definite sum for a sitting. For the very poor there is some poor place assigned; but if a person does not wish to stand among them, he must pay something to get into the church. This last we never put into practice in our [Redemptorist] churches; the only payment was for sittings. Nothing was asked of those who stood in the aisles. Sittings and pews have their varying prices, according to location. In most churches there is every year, or twice a year, or sometimes even four times a year, an auction of these sittings and pews. Every pew or sitting goes to the highest bidder. In those days there were no real parishes in the United States. Every church was a kind of mission church, and the pastor assigned was called a missionary. The bishop gave his missionary his faculties for baptisms, anointings, weddings, etc.

Where there were many priests assigned, one of them was the rector — for there has to be someone in charge. Every Catholic was free to choose, if there were several churches in the place, the one he favored. Everyone chose the church he liked best. Thus it happened that many a one lived close to a church that he did not attend, but went to one farther away. The reason for his choice would be a favorite preacher, or church music, or other things. The more people came to like a preacher or services in a church, so much the more did attendance increase, and so much the more rose the price of pews and sittings in this church. Besides, there was a collection taken up at Mass after the Offertory.

Out of this income the pastor's salary was paid; out of it also were paid the school teachers, organist, sexton, etc.; likewise the debt on the church, interest on the debt, what was needed for divine worship, and for building maintenance.

If this did not suffice, collections were made from house to house; or the people were asked to subscribe to yearly, half-yearly, or monthly special collections. In the beginning the bishop drew his salary as rector of his cathedral; later on, all churches of the diocese had to contribute to the support of the bishop out of their own income.

This system of church support came to America from England and Ireland. If all priests and bishops had been true apostles, and if all modern Catholics had the spirit of the first Christians, such an arrangement for gathering funds for church, etc., would not have been necessary. But since both priests and people do not possess the original Christian spirit any longer, such an arrangement had to be made. And it is practiced not only by Catholics, but by all sects. The Irish and English were accustomed to this arrangement from childhood; thus they find no difficulty about it in America; on the contrary, they find it necessary and natural. If they are asked, whether they think it unsuitable to have something like this for a Catholic church, they answer: Either we have to try to raise money in this way in order to have our churches, our priests, and our divine worship, or else we have to do without them. If there is anyone who cannot afford it, we shall see to it that he gets his place in church.

I have seen that there must be a certain compulsion: otherwise, many a one will take what he owes God and the church, and spend it in a saloon. In a certain sense, too, this compulsion is only justice: for I have known people who were well off, and who would have done nothing for the Church, if they had not been prodded to it. At the same time, many a poorer person was doing all in his power. And it is not right that these poor people should have to bear all the burden of supporting the church, while other skinflints keep their money in their pocket, or are able to carry it off to the saloon.

In the countries like the United States, where everything — churches, schools, etc., have to be built from nothing, it is necessary that everyone do his duty; and if anyone is allowed to get out of giving what he can, it will be soon felt. Thus also, if a priest in America does not know just how to bring everyone to do his part, he will not get anything done. So too, if a priest in such a country has once roused a great part of the people against him, so that they will no longer contribute anything, there is no other remedy than to replace him. Standards applied in other countries do not fit here. There, churches have no debts; there are foundations or the government itself to provide the living of the priest, maintenance of divine worship, etc. In such cases, it is not felt if even a great many do not contribute; for the free-will offerings will be enough. It is true, that in this money-raising there is many a dark spot, as there is in all human arrangements. But it still remains true that a certain strictness is a necessary part of money raising. Is not this the case also in Catholic countries, in regard to raising of tithes, etc.? And is it not necessary even in Catholic [countries] that the priest try to make the faithful realize that they have a duty to pay their taxes and dues to churches and monasteries? This is all the more necessary in a country where everything is beginning from scratch; everything is just beginning to be built, raised, arranged, and maintained. In many cities property to build a new church can be bought for only a huge sum. Thus the property for the German church in New York, in 1835, cost $6,000.00. And only then does the building begin. A parish that is able to pay out one-fourth of the total cost of property and building, is very fortunate. Three-fourths remain as a debt to be paid, plus the interest, which is at least six per cent (in New York the lowest is seven per cent.)

If interest is not paid, or if the capital sum is not paid off according to the terms of the contract, then steps will be taken in a very business-like way, and there is danger that everything will be lost. In such circumstances, one has every reason to become concerned about the money to be raised for the church by pew rent, etc. I have already said that the Irish are used to this kind of thing from childhood. It is another matter altogether with the Germans. To them it is something entirely new. To make them realize its necessity requires time, patience, eloquence, and a good deal of energy. And still there will be criticism from the unthinking masses, who do not realize that even in Europe they were the ones who had to support all this with their taxes; only with this difference that in Europe, they had to pay it into the hands of state officials; and their taxes in the United States are only one fiftieth of what they had to pay in Europe, and perhaps still less. But at the same time the priest in America must make it plain that what he is after is only what is just, and also that he himself is completely free from self seeking and the wish to make money for himself.

And that was just the way in which the Redemptorists made a good impression in America. Even their enemies acknowledged that they were not trying to get rich, and that when they did have much, they spent much on the church. In our churches I usually saw only one altar, which was quite enough for the two or three priests that were stationed there. The rest of the space was filled with pews. This is required by the crowds of faithful, who otherwise could not have found a place in church. It was also required by the lack of money, for the greater the number of pews, the higher the income. I have already mentioned how costly the building sites are in cities. It was not always possible to buy the most suitable place for a large enough church, school, etc. Lack of money forced the parishes to be satisfied with a small place. In order to provide more room in church for the people, and also to be able to have a school in this confined space, there usually were galleries added along three sides of the church. Churches also were built with a base-ment. The school was usually in this basement; often the sacristy was there too, with a staircase leading from it up behind the altar. Often too the priest's quarters were beneath the church.

In the Jesuit church in Philadelphia, in 1840, I saw they had a school be-neath the church, and also above it under the roof. Necessity had taught them that you need not buy room above or under the church; but that it is still there and can be used, even while the property next door could not be pur-chased at a high price. And since they had to look to the essentials, there often was no regular architectural style to be seen in the buildings. The first priests who came to the United States were Irish. In England and Ireland they had to contend with the same difficulties, and so in their own countries had adopted these same building principles. And that is why one sees that the manner and style of building churches, schools, and rectories came to America from Ireland.

Europeans who come to America and see these churches, often express themselves very critically to the effect that American Catholics do not under-stand how to build churches, etc. Criticism is easy and costs nothing. These people often only want to show their learning. But they have not learned enough to realize that before you criticize, you should try to understand the circumstances of the case. By such criticism they show their zeal, but it is only a zeal for architecture, no[t] zeal for the salvation of their neighbor. Let us take two priests: one builds a church in the proper church style without galleries, so it will not look like a theatre, etc. Naturally, fewer people will find place there. The other, however, builds a church on the so-called Irish or American style, so all the people, or as many as possible, will have room. He does not look to the style, but to the needs of the Catholics. Which of the two will receive the higher reward from God? If both styles can be united, that of course is the best. But if that cannot be done, and [the] builder chooses that which is more needed, rather than beauty and style, he should not be harshly criticized. How many a priest is glad to have a roof above his head when he says Holy Mass to keep out the rain!

"Memoirs of Rev. Joseph Prost, C.Ss.R.," in "Historical Studies and Notes: Founding the Redemptorist Congregation in the U.S.A., 1832–1843," *Social Justice Review* 64, no. 10 (February 1972): 378–80. Printed with permission.

27. A Missionary's Views on Catholics' Religious Behavior, 1854

In 1853, Father Bede O'Connor, Benedictine monk of the Abbey of Maria Ein-siedeln, Switzerland, arrived with his confreres in southern Indiana to found a monastery that is today St. Meinrad Archabbey. O'Connor, born of Irish parents in London and educated in Switzerland, spoke German and English fluently so that after arriving in America he was soon absorbed in ministry among German, Irish, and American Catholics in communities along the Ohio River in southern

Indiana. His observations, taken from a letter to the dean of Maria Einsiedeln Abbey, describe vividly recent immigrants' religious behavior.

Dear Father Dean!

It gives me great joy that our community is so respectable. May it continue to increase not only in numbers but in solidarity, that we lonesome missionaries may be worthy to experience the blessed increase. From here, it is a fact: the harvest is great, the workers are few. Lack of priests is the reason why so many who call themselves Catholic care so little about their religion. That [condition] the missionary experiences daily[;] when on his mission, he comes in contact with all kinds of people[,] when he must hear how some of these people were baptized Catholics but seem to have forgotten it, who never practice their faith because the church is too far and the priest is often farther away, and besides they are surrounded by Methodists or others and to get along well with them they give up the externals of their religion and are satisfied with the inner consolation that they are Catholic...

Perhaps it would interest your Grace to know how the individuals in America express their Catholicism. Since I have dealt with those various nationalities, their individual expressions make an impression on me.

The Germans are probably as they were in Germany. Though I cannot say I am well acquainted with customs in Germany I can say that here in church they are edifying and stiff. It is not true that they are cold towards religion; one sees that their hearts beat warmly for religion. But their body, their feet stand fast and they hold to the earth. To consider the German during the sermon was for me a special study and I seemed to read two thoughts in their eyes: 1) the preacher is right; one cannot play with the poor souls, I will do better; and then 2) tomorrow I must begin with the mowing; the good weather is coming; my fields could look better. So the German is willing, when a good thing is to be done for the church, to give his share. Whenever something in this line is proposed he says: "Yes, that would be good; that is necessary, that I have thought of for a long time, etc." But when one touches here and there his pocketbook there one sees at once how he thinks three or four times about his land and property, and when he has done that says: "Yes, Father, these are bad times; my corn will not ripen; ten of my hogs have been lost, if I were like so and so I would give so much, but a dollar I'll give anyway."

But the Germans are very exact in the reception of the sacraments and seldom will a German fail to attend Mass on Sundays and to send his children to school on week-days. Another characteristic about the Germans is that they will not in religious matters, allow themselves to be anglicized. I informed the bishops of this, I know Germans in America who are very capable and use English in their every day life but never confess in English and understand hardly half of an English sermon. Of men who write, e.g. articles in English papers — you will hardly believe this — neither would I if I did not have it from experience — who in confession to me must enlarge their confession because at their former confession they could not express themselves in English. So the religious life of the Germans seems intimately joined to their life as Germans and vice versa. But the ones who have left their German nationality have also left their religion. It appears here clearly that the one who denies the character of his country, soon will deny his Creator and his soul. But I will not continue with these thoughts. I only wished to indicate how the good German-American shows his religion outwardly.

And now secondly — the Irish. The Lord increase the room for their elbows. Seeing the Irish in church at the asperges [the sprinkling rite formerly performed before Sunday High Mass], I did not wish to advise each one who is fully master of the muscles that come in contact with his diaphram at the same time. The hands of these good people are on this occasion far above their heads in order to get a drop of holy water and if one succeeds in this he raises his eyes to heaven so that one sees only the white in his eyes while all the rest of the body makes a deep reverence and the thumb of the right hand makes three large crosses on the forehead, the mouth, and the heart. That is the custom of the Irish, large and small. Also the good people at religious services let themselves be lightly touched and they show this touch not only by lifting their eyes to heaven but by stretching out their hands and putting them together again, almost as the priest does at the Dominus Vobiscum, and they bend their bodies from front to back or vice versa. During this they are in a kneeling position; standing, the strong swinging would not work on account of the balance. This and similar actions of the Irish can be misleading to the young and inexperienced priest. Far from me be the thought that these expressions come from hypocrisy. No, not that. But one cannot place any further value on them...

What shall I say — when these externals are over[,] the [Irish] people are not converted from their drinking and quarreling. Further the Irish show their religious spirit and zeal [by] gladly helping the priest in material goods. But this good will does not cover all kinds of needs...

The Irishman is big-hearted and considers as a recognition of his faith that he always gives the priest some money when he gives him a sacrament (the sacrament of penance excepted). At marriage, for example, the priest receives $5, otherwise the couple, friends and relatives would not be considered Catholic, for they reason thus: the one who cannot give the priest $5 is not in a position to marry.

With the same reasoning you can understand that such marriages are good for the poor missionary. I, however, since I came to America have had but three Irish marriages. So my sharing is not very great. But in regard to Baptism it is better, for as often as I baptize a child of Irish parents I receive three, sometimes five or six dollars as a stole fee. These stole fees come in handy because my poor church and community still lack very much.

In this way the Irish show that they want to be Catholic and add to this a great respect for the priest who is considered above all others. Moreover, they have a horror of breaking the command of fasting. Eating meat on Fridays seems to the Irish the same as losing one's faith.

But what pleases me above all else is their religious spirit and with all their faults they are truly good people. To the sick and the dying they show active love. When in such a case it would cost them the whole world and they were 100 miles from a priest it is not too much for them to get the priest to a dying person, relative or not. It is [in] this they outdo the Germans by far although the latter are also very good in this matter. To all this add that the Irish have a great love for the Mother of God and this they show in their speech. Thus you have some details regarding the Irish and their religion who though they might not often receive the sacrament will die for their faith.

You might find this striking but I think the explanation is easy. He is a thoroughly good natured man, a piece of solid marble and when the master strikes him with the chisel something good will result. But God forbid, if the master fails, instead of elevating the people the result will be that they go deeper into the mud. Any instruction to him is wasted and in the striving for daily bread even the religious instruction is skipped. So they grow up and it is not their fault that they do not know better. Their religion is not brought to them; it is as inborn and what they know they have to a great extent taken in with their mother's milk. I learned that when in the cholera time I used the occasion to scare them a little.

> Father Bede O'Connor, O.S.B., Cannelton, Indiana, to the dean of Maria
> Einsiedeln Abbey, Switzerland, 12 July 1854. Printed with permission of
> St. Meinrad Archabbey Archives.

28. German Catholic Grievances in the Abbelen Memorial, 1886

As the American Catholic community's largest non-English-speaking ethnic group during the nineteenth century, German Catholics across the country had many points of contact with the church's largely Irish or Irish-American hierarchy. German Catholics took pride in their parishes and other institutions where their language and culture were preserved. Hence, they believed themselves threatened when their parish churches were not accorded the same canonical status as English-language parishes, as happened in some dioceses. The English-speaking, largely Irish ethnic Americanists among church leaders, such as Archbishop John Ireland of St. Paul and Bishop John Keane of Richmond, articulated their vision of a Catholic Church adapted to American culture. Catholics would thereby no longer have to hear the anti-Catholic accusation that they were foreign in everything. The Americanists' views clashed with those of the Germans. In this context, the vicar-general of the heavily German Archdiocese of Milwaukee, Father Peter Abbelen, offered his views of the unequal treatment of Germans in the American church in the following memorial presented to the

Congregation for the Propagation of the Faith, the Roman congregation having jurisdiction over Catholics in the United States.

Memorial on the German Question in the United States Written by Rev. P. M. Abbelen, Priest of Milwaukee, Approved by Most Rev. Archbishop of Milwaukee, and Submitted to the Congregation de Propaganda Fide in November 1886.

1. The question concerns the relation of non-English to English parishes, and especially the relation of German to Irish parishes in the United States of North America.

2. We ask of the Sacred Congregation de Propaganda Fide that it so define this relation that German parishes shall be entirely independent of Irish parishes, or on a par with them; that rectors of Irish parishes shall not be able to exercise any parochial jurisdiction over Germans enrolled in any German church, or who by right should be thus enrolled, whether they be newcomers from Germany or born in America of German parents.

3. We ask for this equality and independence because in many places they are denied to us. In some places, for example in St. Louis, German churches are called chapels of ease, in other places English churches only are called parish churches, while the others, that is to say, those of Canadians and of Germans, for instance in the Diocese of Albany, are called special churches, and in still other places, for instance in New Orleans, every distinction by name being omitted, German churches have no parochial rights. Finally, in other places, as in Baltimore, by law, that is, according to the diocesan statutes, German rectors have no jurisdiction over those born in America. It is true that in fact the Most Eminent Cardinal, with his great prudence and charity, grants them parochial rights, but this does not prevent Irish rectors from acting against the letter of the law, and meddling in various ways with the rights of Germans.

Nearly everywhere the opinion prevails that Irish rectors are truly and by right the parish priest of all those who were born in America, as if having over them an eminent domain; that German priests are, of course, necessary to take care of the souls of Germans while they speak the German language, but it cannot fail to happen that they shall in the course of time lose their language and learn English, and that the sooner this happens the better; that the ecclesiastical status of the Germans is therefore a transitory one, and that German parishes should not be put on an equal footing with English parishes. There are also some who think that it is contrary to canon law that there should be two independent parishes in the same territory, and for this reason also that the English should be the only parish.

4. There are many and very grave reasons why it would seem this relation of dependence and subordination should be abolished, and entire independence and co-ordination established:

a) Before our Civil Government foreigners, once they have been, as the saying is, "naturalized," are entirely equal among themselves, and even enjoy the same rights as Americans properly so-called, and they may attain to the same honors and offices with the one exception of the office of President; and shall there be a distinction before ecclesiastical law between children of the same mother so that a very great part of them shall be compelled to consider her not so much as a mother, as a step-mother, and to regard themselves as strangers more or less welcome, but not children of the family as dear as the others to the heart of the mother?

b) It may well be inquired, whence do English Catholics derive the right to put themselves before non-English? If you except that very small number of Catholics who are and have been Americans for many generations, nearly all Catholics who use the English tongue are Irish, immigrants from Ireland and their descendants. Now they are no less foreigners and no less American than the Germans and other nationalities, newcomers from Europe. While in the Eastern States the Irish are more numerous and arrived earlier than the Germans, it is not so in the Middle States and still less in the Western States.

For they [the Irish] live among their countrymen of whom many are Protestants, Rationalists, Free Thinkers, Masons, and numbers of other secret societies. All of these leave no stone unturned to pervert Catholics to their irreligious following, nor alas without success, especially where the necessary means are wanting to hold them to the practice of their religion. But the great majority of Germans have resisted and, God helping, will always resist their machinations and temptations. Their works make it clearer than the day that they are Catholics, since their churches, schools, and various charitable institutions are not surpassed in number or size by the others, and not infrequently surpass them. Their religious orders and congregations, both of men and women composed of Germans, occupy certainly no inferior place in works of charity and education. Their domestic life and civic virtues reveal their truly Christian spirit. They are of edification to all by their pious practices, frequent reception of the Sacraments, and the number of their pious sodalities. Equal to others in all things, in certain things they surpass them. For example, the only Normal School for the education of secular teachers is a German one. Only the Germans have daily Catholic papers, and they have five of them. There are more than 30,000 German men from different States united in one so-called "Central" Society [Central Verein]. In almost every parish there are benefit societies. In the matter of education, and especially of parochial schools, no one who is not entirely ignorant of the origin and growth of these schools can deny that the system of parochial schools, which now flourishes, owes its origin to the zeal and perseverance of the Germans. You will hardly ever find a German church without a parochial school annexed, to which nearly all, if not all, parents send their children. There are some who say that the Germans most religiously care for the Christian education of their children.

5. Therefore, it is certainly not clear why Catholic Germans should be kept in a position inferior to that of the Irish. By granting the equal position which we ask, no right of the Irish would be impaired, while an injustice and a disgrace would be removed from the Germans.

6. But various objections are urged against the co-ordination: It is objected (a) — "It is against canon law that two or more independent parishes should be in the same territory." I deny this. Both authors and facts prove the contrary. As to facts: In Austria, in the Orient, in Canada, not rarely parishes, properly so-called, are to be found, independent one of the other, in the same territory. And authors, who are most approved, explicitly teach that this system is not against canon law. The very distinguished Philip de Angelis, in the work *Lessons in Canon Law* etc. (Book III, Title II), discussing the condition "that [a parish] should have a population circumscribed within certain territorial limits within a diocese," so that it is clear that in the idea of a parish is comprised a population dwelling in or inhabiting a certain portion of a territory as commonly occurs in all civil and ecclesiastical jurisdiction, adds in express words: "But this in our case does not prove that in the same territory there may not be more than one parish; since there may be two and even three when the same territory is inhabited by populations of different nationalities and tongues. Thus in the United States of America in the same territory and even in the same town there will be, say a parish of Irish and a parish of Canadians, the one comprising all those of that territory who are Irish or speak the English language; the other comprising all Canadians, that is, those who speak the French tongue, and so on; but each parish comprises all those of the same nationality who dwell there and not those who are settled there, unless they be of the same nation and tongue" (Vol. III, p. 37).

The same argument is to be found in A. Bonal, S.J., *Institutions of Canon Law* (Vol. II, p. 8). And what these most learned authors say about Irish and Canadians are with much greater reason applicable to Irish and Germans in the United States in which there are at least twenty German Catholics for one Canadian.

It is objected (b) — "All this controversy is more theoretical than practical." If the dependence and subordination of which we are speaking existed only in law, and were not practiced in fact, perhaps they might be said to be merely theoretical, although even in such cases they would have no true and just cause for existing. But they are very far from not being reduced to practice. On the contrary, for this very purpose they are asserted, and, as we have already seen, they are supported with fallacious arguments in order that practical consequences may be made to flow therefrom. For example, Irish rectors without the knowledge and even in spite of German rectors may lease pews to Germans, collect money from them for churches, receive their children in their schools and admit them to First Communion, marry them, administer the last Sacraments to them, and bury them, but no means vice versa although the German rector may be perfectly familiar with the English language, and the Irish rector may speak hardly one or two words of German. All can see that this is a disturbance of good order, a cause of quarrels among priests, and takes on a scandalous appearance of sordid avarice. There is [an] end to well-ordered pastoral government and to the effectual care of souls if the faithful can run from one shepherd to the other at pleasure, withdraw themselves from the vigilance and the authority of their own pastor.

It is objected (c) — "The common welfare requires that Catholics shall be one in language and customs. Therefore, when the greater part of them is of English speech, and customs, the lesser part should conform. We are in America, we should be Americans." Certainly, and we wish to be. But the good of the Church above all things requires that each of her parts shall be good, faithful, united in love and reverence toward their common mother, and that they should prove themselves by their faith and morals to be true children of the Church. Now experience teaches that the only means by which Catholic Germans (and other foreigners) shall be able to preserve their Catholic faith and morals is that they shall have their own priests, who shall instruct them in the language and in the traditions of their fatherland. Wherever even Bishops have fallen into that most fatal of errors, I shall not say of heart and will, but of judgment and administration, of seeking to "Americanize" Germans as speedily as possible, refusing them, for instance, permission to build a school or church, committing them to the pastoral care of a priest ignorant of their language; wherever that most sad dictum, "let them learn English," has prevailed or now prevails, there has been and there will be, a truly deplorable falling away from the Church. Witnesses to this fact are the missionaries of the various orders. But even though the Germans should have their own priests and their own churches and schools, if they would be obliged to subordinate themselves to Catholics of another nationality, for instance to the Irish, as they were Catholics of an inferior order of a worse character, they would never bear it with patience. They would feel that an injury had been inflicted upon them by the Church and that they were discredited among other Germans, non-Catholics, and they would be alienated from the Church. In matters political, social, and commercial, the Germans certainly hold no inferior place among American citizens — they are proud of their country, especially now after that celebrated *Kulturkampf* in which the Germans in Europe were made a spectacle to angels and to men. And shall they not be considered worthy here in America to enjoy the same rights as the Irish? Clearly, all those who know the German character, especially their tenacity, constancy, and their love of country, and, on the other hand, consider the dangers with which, as we said above, Catholic Germans are surrounded in the midst of their own countrymen, will surely do nothing, if they have love for souls, to render more difficult the perseverance of the Germans in the Catholic faith.

Moreover, they are entirely in error when they think that German bishops and priests, led by a certain want of sympathy for American institutions, are striving to prevent Germans from ever becoming Americans. This opinion of many is but a pretense and a delusion. Witness the innumerable schools, colleges, and academies, erected by Germans and directed by German priests and religious orders, in which the English language and English culture take, if not a first place, at least an equal place, with the German. Witness the material prosperity and the honorable position of the Germans among their American fellow citizens. All these things could not be if Germans did not adapt themselves to the language and manners of the Americans.

Let the "Americanization" of the Germans be a slow and natural process; let it not be hastened to the prejudice of the religion of the Germans. They will kick against the goad.

It is objected (d) — "But it happens that one or another German family may prefer to belong to the English church, and perhaps with so firm a purpose that if compelled to remain in the German church they may leave altogether. What then?" These cases are rare and will be most rare if Irish priests will not meddle in the affairs of Germans. If, however, there shall be sufficient cause for such a family to change to the English church, for instance, because the younger members of the family are more familiar with the English tongue, than with the German, let them go and let them be formally enrolled in the English parish. But it is by all means to be avoided, that members of the same family should belong to different churches. For instance, the parents to the German and the children to the English. In such cases there is an end of domestic devotions and the vigilance which parents should maintain as to the attendance of their children at divine services and reception of the Sacraments. Children, as long as they remain under parental authority in a parental home[,] should by all means belong to the church of their parents; afterwards, if they have homes of their own, let them be free if they know the English language to pass over to the English church, but once and for all.

In all this controversy, besides a difference of language, we must not by any means make light of the difference and discrepancy of Catholic customs as they are to be found among Germans and Irish. The Irish, on account of the oppression and persecution which they suffered for religion's sake in their own land, love simplicity in divine service, and in all the practice of religion, and do not care much for pomp and splendor. But the Germans, from the liberty which as a rule they have enjoyed in the exercise of their religion from the earliest times, and the traditions of their fathers, love the beauty of the church edifice and the pomp of ceremonies, belfries and bells, organs and sacred music, processions, feast days, sodalities, and the most solemn celebration of First Communion and weddings. These and other like things, although not essential to Catholic faith and life, foster piety and are so dear and sacred to the faithful that not without great danger could they be taken away from them.

Then, again, Germans differ very much from the Irish in the administration of ecclesiastical goods and affairs. For nearly everywhere the former so manage their temporal affairs that the rectors, with a body of laymen, or even laymen alone, properly elected, carry on the administration, while the Irish leave all these things in the hands of the priests. It must be confessed, it sometimes happens among Germans that the laymen meddle too much in such affairs, but this rarely happens; nearly everywhere the temporal affairs in German parishes are administered exceptionally well.

Finally, even manners and social customs of the two nationalities differ exceedingly. Thus it happens that scarcely ever will you find Germans and Irish united in matrimony. All this is here said neither to favor the Germans nor to disparage the Irish. Rather, these things are told by way of a narrative and as matters of fact, that it may be made clear how vastly one differs from the other, these two nationalities which are the principal parts of the Church in the United States, and how necessary it is that each should have its own priests and churches co-ordinate and independent. With the lapse of time, by a certain natural formative process one will become more assimilated to the other. But, God forbid that any one should dare, and most of all, that bishops and priests should endeavor to accelerate this assimilation by suppressing the language and customs of the Germans. The German temperament and a most sad experience demonstrate that their effort is not conducive to edification, but for the destruction and ruin of souls.

Since these things are so, we ask that the Sacred Congregation de Propaganda Fide shall define and decree:

1. That German parishes (and the others, French, Slovenian, etc.) shall be placed on an equal footing with the English (Irish) and shall be entirely independent of them. No distinction whatever either by general law or by episcopal precept to be made between them as to parochial rights and privileges.

2. Also, in the designation of irremovable rectorships, German parishes be under no disadvantage as compared with the Irish, provided the conditions prescribed by the Third Plenary Council, Baltimore, Title II, chapter v, be fulfilled.

3. All immigrants from Europe be assigned to the church of their own language whenever there is one in their place of residence, and be treated as members of that church, and the same hold good for their offspring born in America, as long as they remain under parental authority.

4. As to the descendants of German families who are their own masters and as to more remote generations, if they use the English language as their vernacular, according to the common acceptance of this term, let them be free

to pass over to the English church, provided that the transference be made formally and forever, and that the consent of the rector be given in writing or even by the judgment of the bishop, if perchance, a contest should arise. The same also shall be permitted to the Irish who may be familiar with the German tongue.

5. Let bishops and priests be admonished on the one hand, not by any means to seek to suppress and root out the language, manners, customs, usages and devotional practices of the Germans, unless they shall be contrary to the Decalogue or the precepts, discipline, and rubrics of the Church; and on the other hand, to foster and promote the English language in the education of youth, and particularly in the parochial schools.

6. Let bishops who are ignorant of the German language, and, who govern mixed dioceses, be obliged besides an Irish vicar-general, to nominate a German, or, if they should wish to have but one, to appoint such a one as shall have the knowledge and ready use also of the German language.

7. If, in the course of time, especially when immigration ceases, in any church the use of the English language should be found more necessary than that of the German, the rector, either of his own motion or by the judgment and order of the bishop, shall use the English tongue, and if it should perchance come to pass that on account of the proximity of an English church a new division of territory should be necessary, let the division be made with prudence, justice, and charity.

All and each of these things we ask.

First and second — Because we believe it to be right and just.

Third — Because the greater part of this request follows from No. 1, and the latter part seems to be necessary, to preserve families in the practice of religion.

Fourth — Because in this manner we think that provision is made for the personal liberty of each and the good will of all.

Fifth — In the first part, lest the love of the Germans toward the Church and their confidence and love toward bishops and priests should be endangered; in the other part to promote even the material good of all.

Sixth — For the salvation of souls.

Seventh — Because of the justice of the thing in itself and for the salvation of souls.

Eighth — Because in the condition of our affairs the solution of doubts must be a sufficient and a sure one.

I have read and have approved.

+Michael Heiss
Archbishop of Milwaukee

Colman J. Barry, O.S.B., *The Catholic Church and German Americans* (Milwaukee: Bruce, 1953), 289–96.

29. Reply of Bishops John Ireland and John Keane to the Abbelen Memorial, 1886

Shortly after Father Peter Abbelen arrived in Rome to present his memorial, Bishop John Ireland of St. Paul and Bishop John Keane of Richmond came to the Eternal City to consult with the Congregation of the Propagation of the Faith on the organization and statutes for the proposed Catholic University of America, which the American bishops had voted to establish at their Third Plenary Council of Baltimore in 1884. When Ireland and Keane learned about the memorial and obtained a copy, they composed their own reply, twice as lengthy as Father Abbelen's document. The following excerpt expresses the two Americanist bishops' reaction to the memorial.

Answer to the Abbelen Memorial by Bishop John Ireland of St. Paul
and Bishop John J. Keane of Richmond,
presented to Cardinal Giovanni Simeoni,
prefect of the Congregation de Propaganda Fide,
December 6, 1886

The Congregation of the Propaganda will permit us to present a few observations upon the German Question in the Church in the United States. As we arrived in Rome, upon a mission to treat with the Propaganda concerning the project of the Catholic University, which the hierarchy of the United States desire to establish at Washington, we were very much surprised to find there a German representative, calling himself the delegate of bishops and of German Catholics of America, and asking in their name legislation altogether novel and exceptional, and of which the effects, we are convinced, would be disastrous to the Church in the United States. The American bishops of the English language, and some American bishops even of the German language, have no knowledge of the presence of this representative in Rome, nor of the demands, in their actual form, which he has submitted to the Propaganda. When the knowledge of this secret movement shall have come to them, the bishops of the United States will be exceedingly indignant. We are convinced that they would never forgive us, if we did not hasten to expose the bad faith of this German party, and to communicate to the Propaganda the sentiments which we know to be those of a very great majority of the American Episcopate.

We shall first make some general observations upon the German Catholics in the United States, and then some more particular observations upon the demands presented by Rev. Father Abbelen to the Congregation of the Propaganda:

1. The question under consideration is styled, according to Father Abbelen, "The question in the United States between the German Catholics and Irish Catholics." Presented in these terms, the question cannot be discussed; it has no existence. The only question that can be considered is this: "The ques-

tion between the English language, which is the language of the United States, and the German language, which emigrants from Germany have brought to the United States." Why the Germans so often give this question another form, as if to indicate that there is a conflict of races in America between Germans and the Irish, we do not know. But neither the truth nor justice of the case permits us to accept what they seek to impose upon us. There is in the United States no Irish Church, nor are there any Irish parishes; no efforts are made in the United States to establish an Irish Church, or Irish parishes. What we find in the United States, instead of Irish parishes, are parishes of the English language, which are composed either of Catholics who are not at all of the Irish race, or of Catholics whose ancestors may have been Irish, but who today are, from every point of view, Americans, and they do not wish to be considered Irish; or again they may be composed of Catholics born in Ireland, or the immediate descendants of Irish emigrants. Our parishes of the English language are never called Irish parishes. The English-speaking bishops and priests, of which a large number are in no respect of the Irish race, have the interests of the Church in the United States too much at heart not to endeavor to eliminate from religious affairs Irish nationalism, and to impress them, as far as the circumstances of time, place, and sound principles will permit, with an elevated and Catholic character, against which no element, in a very heterogeneous population, could raise any objection. For the rest, let it be said to their praise, the Irish Catholics, even the recent emigrants, do not interpose any serious obstacle to these desires of their religious superiors. Whatever may be their attachment to the land of their birth, they hasten, on arriving in America, to adopt American ideas and manners, and they understand that, in regard to matters of religion, intermingled as they are with other Catholics, speaking like them the English language, but not like them of the Irish race, they must, for the general good, lay aside their national spirit. The sole question, then, which can be considered, in what regards the English-speaking bishops and priests in America, is this — the question between the English language and the German language.

2. The Congregation of the Propaganda will permit us to state here, what is already well known, that the German language is far from being the only foreign language in use among Catholics in the United States. The French Canadians, Poles, Bohemians, Dutch are very numerous, and it is well to remark that, according to the present rate of emigration to the United States, it will not require many years for some of these nationalities to be more largely represented there than the German nationality. The concessions made to the Germans will, in the course of time, be claimed by the French, Bohemians, and Poles for their languages, and the Church in the United States will be little more than *moles informis et indigesto* — without unity, without life, without authority. We have already had an intimation of what is threatening us. Last year, in a general reunion of Bohemian Catholic societies, the complaint

was made, in language little respectful either to Rome or to the American hierarchy, that up to this time there had been no Bohemian in the American episcopate. The Canadians, as is well known, are exceedingly turbulent; and their cry, whether in the halls of their societies or in the offices of their papers, is that henceforth a decided regard must be had for their national spirit and language in diocesan administrations. A German bishop, the late Bishop of Green Bay, Mgr. F. Krautbauer, often spoke of the almost innumerable difficulties in the government of this diocese, on account of the preponderance there of French and Slav elements. On account of our heterogeneous population in the United States, we cannot have too much fear of legislation, however unexceptional, in favor of a particular nationality, or of the language of this nationality, and our wishes cannot bring about the time too soon when, without any detriment to our souls, there will be among us more unity of spirit and more unity of language.

3. We are bound to notice the fact that not all German Catholics or Catholics of German origin have the same ideas upon the question which is now engaging our attention. There exists what we may call the active party, whose object seems to be to preserve intact the German spirit among German emigrants and their descendants, and to prevent them from changing their language to the English language, and to give a preponderant position to German influence in the Church in America. This is the party of which Father Abbelen is now the representative at Rome. It is not for us to judge of the motive which is inspiring the action of this party; we merely wish to mark its line of conduct, and to point out the grievous results. This party is posing, in its public declarations in the United States and in its appeals to Rome, as the German people of America. This pretension is very far from the fact. There are a great number of Germans in America who entertain ideas altogether different. They oppose the establishment of a permanent Germany in America; they approve of the use of the German language in so far as is useful or necessary for the welfare of souls, but they refuse to carry this usage to an extreme, merely for the sake of German patriotism, and they openly declare their conviction that in America *coeteris paribus,* the English language, as the language of the country, deserves the preference, and that religion is better served when this preference is accorded to it. We can cite in the episcopate Mgr. [Martin] Marty, Vicar Apostolic of Dakota, and among the lower clergy, Mgr. Batz, domestic prelate of the Holy Father and Vicar-General of Milwaukee. Many priests of German origin, and many laymen especially, share the sentiments of these venerable personages. The number of adherents of this moderate party, which may be called the German American party, is increasing from day to day, according as the Germans have the time to Americanize themselves...

8. We believe we have said sufficient for the Congregation to understand that to the German question, as it has been presented by Fr. Abbelen and Mgr. Heiss, there is also a non-German side, which, in all justice, should not fail to

be heard. We have said enough to show that in a country with a population as heterogeneous as ours, a legislation in favor of a particular nationality is a most dangerous thing, and should be granted only in an extreme case, and after the bishops of that same country have had the time to present the views which their experience of the difficulties of the ministry have enabled them to form. We will now submit several brief observations upon the special demands made by Fr. Abbelen:

a) They demand that the German parishes have, in every respect, the same rights as English-speaking parishes. We have no thought of disputing the justice of this demand. It is evident to us that there must be perfect equality among the parishes of every foreign language and the parishes of the English language. No privileges; equality for all; this is our doctrine and our practice.

But what astonishes us is that the demand should have been made as if there existed in the United States a state of things different from what this demand seeks to establish. We know a great number of American dioceses, and in all these dioceses, the same rights are scrupulously accorded to the German parishes that are accorded to others. Fr. Abbelen mentions St. Louis, New Orleans, Albany, and Baltimore. That is, after all, but four dioceses in seventy. We have heard, it is true, that there was some difficulty upon this subject in St. Louis and in New Orleans; not that they wished to mark the German churches as inferior, but because the decree [on clandestine marriage], *Tametsi,* having been promulgated in these places, it was feared that it [the decree's effect] would suffer by recognizing several parishes in the same territory. As to Baltimore, we know that Fr. Abbelen is mistaken. For in the acts of the synod of 1876, we find: *"Quando uterque (parens) gente Germanus sit, rector Germanorum necessario erit adeundus ad sacramenta matrimonii vel baptismi suscipienda."* The Bishop of Richmond was a priest in the diocese of Baltimore for several years, and he is certain that German pastors enjoy the same rights of the former. We, therefore, object to the demand for a general legislation, made at Rome on this subject, because such a demand supposes a general state of affairs in America which does not exist, and the existence of which we would regret. If there is some local difficulty, let redress be sought from the local authorities, and if that should not prove satisfactory, let an appeal be taken for this particular locality; but let there be no general appeal, nor any general legislation.

b) They ask that in the establishment of *pastores inamovabiles,* German priests be placed on the same footing as English priests. We answer: The bishops of America have no other thought as to this subject, and any legislation in [this] regard would be useless. We cannot but believe that these two demands have been made for no other object than to present with them to the Propaganda certain complaints, more or less imaginary, which the Germans have been wishing for some time to bring against the non-German clergy, and thus to follow up with other demands which we will now mention:

c) They demand that all German emigrants, and their children, as long as they are under the control of their parents, be regarded as subjects of German parishes.

The demand in this form contains nothing that does not already exist in the United States. A formal approbation of this demand by the Propaganda would, however, give rise [to] difficulties. The demand being approved, the German pastors would not only reserve for themselves the right to baptize and to solemnize matrimony, but they would prevent their parishioners from ever sending their children to English Catholic schools, or from ever renting a pew in English churches. Great injustice would be caused by such claims.

Catholics, either English or German, believe that they have the right to send their children to any school, provided it is Catholic. The English Catholic sometimes desires his child to be instructed in German or French, and sends him to a school where these languages are taught. A German believes that his child can be taught German sufficiently at home, and he sends him to a school where these languages are taught. Moreover, it is custom everywhere that the parishioner of one church may, if he wishes, rent a pew in another church, hear Mass and go to confession where he chooses. Why impose upon Germans restrictions which the English do not recognize? Let German and English parishes be equal in every respect but let there be no privileges for German parishes. It must also be said that in certain localities there are very few restrictions for Catholics in the choice of their parishes. This liberty the ecclesiastical authorities consider necessary, in order to make the practice of his duties easy to every Catholic. If a family, living in the immediate jurisdiction of a church, rents a pew in another church, it may call upon the pastor of the latter for all the offices of religion. In this case, that cannot be refused to Germans what is accorded to the English, and what some Germans would claim. There must always be equality, but not privileges; let each bishop dispose of all these matters as he may think best for his own defense.

d) They demand that if the descendants of Germans wish to join English churches after they have adopted the English language, they be required to obtain formal permission of the German pastor, or of the bishop. This is an affair of too little importance to become the subject of general legislation. Let each bishop arrange such matters for his particular diocese. For the rest, it is sufficiently difficult to keep Catholics to their duty, without charging them with other annoying and useless regulations. The object of the demand is to make Americanization of German descendants more difficult, to permit the German pastor to decide when the time for such change has come, to interpose objections, should he wish to do so.

e) They demand that the Propaganda instruct English bishops and priests not to attempt, in any manner, to suppress the use of the German language, or to discourage German manners and customs. We answer: To give such an instruction would suppose that a serious injustice is being practiced in regard to the Germans. We deny this. To give such an instruction were to accord to the Germans a protection both special and odious, and to condemn and dishonor the bishops of the English tongue in America.

f) They demand that for mixed parishes the bishop appoint priests understanding English and German. We have already answered this demand, in showing the rule which the bishops in America follow in regard to mixed parishes.

g) They demand, finally, that when the bishop does not understand German, he be obliged to appoint a German vicar-general, at the same time with an Irish vicar-general. We answer: However desirable it may be supposed to be in particular cases to have a German vicar-general, a general rule upon this subject could not be made without serious injury. What would they do, for instance, in the diocese of St. Paul, where, according to the wishes of everybody, the vicar-general is a Frenchman? Must a German be appointed there? Then the Irish, Bohemians, Poles, and Dutch would want a vicar-general, and there would be six of them in a single diocese. What is to be done in the diocese of Richmond, where the only vicar-general is a Belgian? Let Rome order a German vicar-general, and an exceptional position would thereby be given to the Germans, which would so puff them up as to make the position of the English Catholics, whether clergy or lay, intolerable. And what rule would there be for German bishops, who, almost always in mixed dioceses, have only a German vicar-general? And, what is more, in America the vicar-general is of little importance, because the bishop attends directly to the diocesan administration. To impose upon the bishop a particular man, or a man of a particular race, would reduce to the smallest limits the liberty of the bishop in the administration of his diocese, and we have no fear that the Propaganda will encourage any such idea.

We have presented the foregoing observations to the Propaganda merely for the purpose of showing that the Catholics of English tongue deserve to be heard, and to obtain such delay in the consideration of all these questions as may enable the bishops of the United States to become acquainted with what is going on at Rome, and to allow them to communicate their ideas to the Propaganda. However wise the decision may be which the Propaganda may make at present in regard to this subject, the American bishops will take offense, because they will perceive in these rules the success of the secret movements of a party. The bishops have, until now, believed that unity existed among them; that the members of the hierarchy had confidence in one another; that the questions affecting the interests of religion in their country could be discussed, at least in the first instance, between themselves in peace and fraternal love. With the most profound regret they will learn that they are mistaken, and that while all seemed calm around them, a tempest was rising and about to break forth. But, at least, we pray that the Congregation may not approve these sinister intrigues, and that before any decision is made it remand all these questions to the bishops of the United States.

The consultation which the Propaganda held some time ago with certain American bishops, related to only one of the questions submitted by Fr. Abbelen, and that one was of the least importance. Our confreres have no knowledge of the document which he has presented. Our prayer to the Congregation, then, is to suspend all deliberation upon this document until the necessary information of what is passing has been transmitted to the American bishops, and their advice has been heard.

> John Ireland, Bishop of St. Paul
> John J. Keane, Bishop of Richmond

To His Eminence
Cardinal Simeoni, Prefect of the
Holy Congregation of the Propaganda
    Rome, Dec. 6, 1886

> Colman J. Barry, O.S.B., *The Catholic Church and German Americans* (Milwaukee: Bruce, 1953), 296–99, 308–12.

30. St. Raphael Societies' Memorial, 1891

Peter Paul Cahensly, a wealthy German Catholic shipping merchant of Limburg an der Lahn, Germany, formed the St. Raphael Society for the protection of German Catholic immigrants in 1871, with a New York affiliate formed in 1883. In view of the societies' work of assisting immigrants before, during, and after their travels in America, the societies' leaders were concerned with issues facing immigrants after settling in the United States. Addressing the often-debated issue of immigrants' loss of the Catholic faith in America, the societies submitted the following memorial to Pope Leo XIII in 1891.

First International Conference of St. Raphael Societies' Memorial to
Pope Leo XIII, February 1891

Most Holy Father,

The presidents, secretaries general, and delegates of the societies under the protection of the Holy Archangel Raphael for the protection of emigrants, encouraged by the benevolence which Your Holiness has shown them, assembled on December 9 of last year at an international conference in Lucerne to deliberate upon means best suited to serve the spiritual and material well-being of their Catholic compatriots who have emigrated to America, the number of which is in excess of 400,000 yearly.

The above mentioned take liberty to place before Your Holiness, with deepest respect, the fact that the numerous emigrants constitute a great strength, and could co-operate eminently in the expansion of the Catholic Church in the several states of America. In this way they could contribute to the moral stature of their new homeland, as well as to the stimulation of religious consciousness in the old European fatherlands.

Only the true Church, of which Your Holiness is the highest shepherd, can obtain these happy results because it is the true source of all progress and civilization.

But in order that European Catholics, in their adopted country, preserve and transmit to their children their faith and its inherent benefits, the undersigned have the honor to submit to Your Holiness the conditions, which in the light of experience and in the nature of things, appear to be indispensable for that purpose in the countries of immigration. The losses which the Church has suffered in the United States of North America number more than ten million souls.

1. It seems necessary to unite the emigrant groups of each nationality in separate parishes, congregations, or missions wherever their numbers and means make such a practice possible.

2. It seems necessary to entrust the administration of these parishes to priests of the same nationality to which the faithful belong. The sweetest and dearest memories of their homeland would be recalled every minute, and they would love all the more the holy Church which procures these benefits for them.

3. In areas settled by emigrants of several nationalities who are numerous enough to organize separate national parishes, it is desirable as far as possible, that a pastor be chosen to guide them who understands the diverse languages of these groups. This priest should be strictly obliged to give catechetical instruction to each of the groups in its own language.

4. It will be especially necessary to establish parochial schools wherever Christian public schools are not available, and these schools should be separate, as far as possible, for each nationality. The curriculum of these schools should always include the mother tongue as well as the language and history of the adopted country.

5. It seems necessary to grant to priests devoting themselves to the emigrants all rights, privileges, and prerogatives enjoyed by the priests of the country. This arrangement, which is only just, would have the result that zealous, pious, and apostolic priests of all nationalities will be attracted to immigrant work.

6. It seems desirable to establish and encourage societies of various kinds, confraternities, charitable organizations, mutual aid and protective associations, etc. By these means Catholics would be systematically organized and saved from the dangerous sects of Freemasons and organizations affiliated with it.

7. It seems very desirable that the Catholics of each nationality, wherever it is deemed possible, have in the episcopacy of the country where they immigrate, several bishops who are of the same origin. It seems that in this way

the organization of the Church would be perfect, for in the assemblies of the bishops, every immigrant race would be represented, and its interests and needs would be protected.

8. Finally the undersigned wish to point out that for the attainment of the objectives which they have enumerated, it would be very desirable, and this they vigorously urge, that the Holy See foster and protect in the emigration countries: (a) special seminaries and apostolic schools for training missionaries for emigrants; (b) St. Raphael societies for the protection of emigrants, and that it recommend to the Most Rev. Bishops that they establish such societies in the emigration countries where they do not exist, and that the Holy See place them under the protection of a Cardinal Protector.

The undersigned hope for the happiest and most immediate results from this organization and these measures. Emigration missionaries trained under the direction of a distinguished Italian Bishop have already gone to America. Others, members of neighboring nations, are waiting, before entering, upon their important and holy calling, for the Supreme Shepherd of the Church, by a decree of his wisdom, to guarantee the free exercise of their mission. If the Holy See will lend its indispensable co-operation, wonderful results should result. The poor emigrants will find on American soil their priests, their parishes, their schools, their societies, their language, and thus cannot fail to extend the boundaries of the Kingdom of Jesus Christ on earth.

In giving solemn testimony of their loyal devotion to the Apostolic See, the undersigned humbly beg Your Holiness to grant paternal approbation to the proposals which they have proposed for the salvation of souls and the glory of our holy mother, the Church, in the different American nations. With the most loyal devotion, Your most devoted, humble, and obedient sons:

[The names of the boards of directors of the German, Austrian, Belgian, and Swiss St. Raphael Societies then follow.]

Colman J. Barry, O.S.B., *The Catholic Church and German Americans* (Milwaukee: Bruce, 1953), 313–15.

31. The Cahensly Memorial, 1891

Later in 1891 Peter Paul Cahensly again expressed his concerns for the immigrants' loss of faith. Using statistics that were open to question, he addressed his memorial to Cardinal Mariano Rampolla, the Vatican secretary of state.

Memorial presented to Cardinal Mariano Rampolla,
Secretary of State to Pope Leo XIII,
by Peter Paul Cahensly and Marchese Giovanni Battista Volpe-Landi

Your Eminence,

We obediently submit some considerations in respect to emigration to America. This important question involves interests of great consequence from the social as well as religious point of view. A continuously rising flood carries people of different countries to America, and will be more so in the future. Statistical figures indicate that in the year 1889, 439,400 Catholics emigrated to America from Europe. Of these, 178,000 went to North America[,] which in addition received thousands of immigrants from Canada, Mexico, Brazil, and other South American countries. Calculations, based on most reliable information, indicate that the Catholic immigrants and their descendants should have increased the Catholic population of North America to twenty-six million. The actual number of Catholics in that great country is hardly higher than ten million. Accordingly, Catholicism in that American republic up to the present has suffered a loss of sixteen million souls. The following are the main reasons for this decrease in the Catholic ranks:

1. The lack of adequate protection for emigrants at the time of their departure from their native country, during the journey, and upon their arrival in America.

2. The lack of priests and parishes for different nationalities among immigrants.

3. The frequently exorbitant financial sacrifices which are asked from the faithful.

4. The public schools.

5. The lack of societies, Catholic and national unions, mutual aid and protection, etc., for laboring classes.

6. The lack of representatives of different nationalities of immigrants in the hierarchy.

> Colman J. Barry, *The Catholic Church and German Americans* (Milwaukee: Bruce, 1953), 316.

32. Reply of the American Archbishops to the Cahensly Memorial, 1892

The Catholic archbishops of the United States — not the whole body of bishops — met annually between 1890 and 1919 to deliberate on matters facing the American Catholic community. At their meeting for 1892, they took up the challenge of Cahensly's allegations and recommendations and addressed the following letter to Pope Leo XIII.

Most Holy Father,

During the past year a suppliant memorial by Peter Paul Cahensly, presented to the Holy See, embarrassed us, the duly appointed bishops of the Church in the United States of North America, and sorely wounded the heart of Your Holiness, God so disposing, the Holy See did not concur with the petitioners. Although they tried their best, under the impulsion of right motives, to achieve their goal, they expended their energies in this direction to no avail.

It is true that at this moment we are able to contemplate with pleasure neither the elimination of serious errors set forth in the aforesaid petition, nor powerful support for our arguments. Wherefore we, the Archbishops of North America, gathered together in plenary session at New York for the consideration of Church affairs, consider it appropriate on this occasion that the several errors which were set forth in the said petition concerning our pastorate over the people be corrected, that our solicitude for the faith be vindicated, and that the sorrow of Your Holiness be abated and be turned into joy by a statement of the truth.

Maintaining silence upon what does not concern us, or upon what is of slight importance, we shall turn our attention to the most serious part of the aforesaid petition, declared to be devoid of truth: namely, that sixteen million Catholics in the United States have been lost to the Faith.

It is impossible to conceive of a more serious and unfair accusation against the youngest branch of the Church; an inspection of the public records of the Republic of the United States proves beyond any shadow of a doubt that in the past seventy years the total number of immigrants who landed upon our shores did not exceed sixteen million people, who were neither of a single nation nor a single faith; before this period immigration was very slight.

Furthermore, it is worth noting that, unfortunately, the majority of Catholic immigrants belong neither to the closely-knit religious groups of Europe, nor have they all, in their fatherlands, been adequately supplied with the means for the fullest exercise of their religion.

On the contrary, the facts clearly show that the American regions in earlier unhappy times were the refuge of those who cried out most vehemently against crimes of the civil power or infringements of the sacred rights of individuals. This type of man, to whom the institutions of his native land appear fraudulent and criminal, and who is "wiser than the children of light," can most easily exercise influence over those who were raised in good conscience.

To all of these must be added the very great number of immigrants who have died because of severe and sometimes unhealthy climatic conditions, because of arduous labor, because of the lack of necessary subsistence, and particularly because of the activity of cholera and the general prevalence of yellow fever, which spread among the immigrants day and night.

Careful study of official documents on immigration, and diligent examination of the suggestions above noted indicate that the claim set forth in the aforementioned petition was without validity or was at best based upon specious arguments.

From about 1820 to the present, immigrants — Catholics, Protestants, and Jews combined — hardly reached the number claimed. And among the Catholic immigrants a large, if not the greatest number, were those who, in their native lands, were least solicitous about the exercise of their religion.

Is it therefore to be wondered at that a man who paid little if any attention to religious exercises at the time he was driven from his own country should, upon coming to America where he is continually fatigued as the result of heavy daily labor, gradually lose the faith without realizing it because he spends his life among Protestants, depends for his very existence upon them, and lives perhaps fifty miles from the nearest church? This remains among the mysteries of divine wisdom.

No one can deny, and we in all honesty admit, that indulgence toward original immigration resulted in certain losses to the Church, necessitated not by pastoral neglect, but by unfortunate conditions. Furthermore, according to historical evidence, it is equally impossible to deny that at that time there existed no episcopal seminary for the training of priests, and that the Sacred Congregation for the Propagation of the Faith ordered Bishop Carroll not to entrust the holy ministry in America to foreign priests.

Shining examples of the Church testify to the priests who supplied spiritual assistance to the early immigrants, multiplying themselves by their works and zeal, serving widely scattered areas, heroically undergoing the greatest dangers, and finally going forward cheerfully to their deaths for the salvation of the faithful.

Illustrious examples in point were Bishop-elect Grässel, Bishop Gartland, Bishop Barron, and innumerable priests who gave up their lives working for their brethren afflicted by the plague. Other examples were almost all the bishops of America who crossed the Atlantic to procure priests who might bring the consolation of the faith to the throngs of immigrants, and from whom our times can never withhold commendation.

Now that churches are built and workers are plentiful in the vineyard of the Lord, the things which unfortunately occurred, not from lack of zeal, but because of the peculiar conditions surrounding a growing Church, are no longer to be feared. Fifty years ago doubtless the harvest was great, but the laborers were few. Only the one Archiepiscopal See of Baltimore had been erected in the United States; sixteen episcopal seats were set up, one with 528 priests, 512 churches, and thirty-three Catholic schools, so that a single diocese sometimes included an area almost as large as all of France.

And now, fifty years later, the aspect of affairs is definitely altered. The Catholic Church in the United States has grown marvelously; it now numbers eighty-eight consecrated bishops, almost 9,000 priests, 9,500 churches, and 303,000 students.

To these figures should be added, wherever they have been established, the seminaries for priests in which students from various areas are instructed in knowledge and the virtues in order that they may bring spiritual aid to the faithful.

What is of the greatest importance is that, as a result of all this it has become the especial care of the episcopate to supervise the allotment of functions, and to see to the increase of religion in the lands of America. Would that the future might be forecast in terms of these developments which, with God's help, have taken place in so short a period. On the other hand, consideration of the declining significance of the Protestant sects resulting from the competition engendered by division justifies, perhaps, the hope of an even greater expansion of the Catholic religion.

Faithfully obedient to the commands of Your Holiness, and guided by your advice, we are doing our utmost to bring our lands together in the Faith and in political order so that soon our country may acquire the name of a Catholic nation, as envisioned by Christopher Columbus[,] whose memory we have formally commemorated with festivities during these recent days.

In the meantime, humbly prostrate at the feet of Your Holiness, we again profess obedience, and from our hearts beg the Apostolic Blessing upon us and upon the faithful people entrusted to our care.

Colman J. Barry, *The Catholic Church and German Americans* (Milwaukee: Bruce, 1953), 317–19.

Anti-Catholicism

33. Samuel F. B. Morse, Imminent Dangers to the Free Institutions of the United States, 1834

Since the colonial era, hostility to Catholicism has been a staple of American culture. During the early part of the nineteenth century, as Catholic immigration from Ireland and Germany increased and the church's institutional presence grew more visible, anti-Catholic feelings became more virulent. Physical violence against Catholic churches and institutions erupted in several places. But the rhetorical violence of anti-Catholic literature was even more widespread – an example being Maria Monk's Awful Disclosures of the Hotel Dieu Nunnery of Montreal, *a scurrilous bestseller published in 1836. Among the common attacks on the church was the accusation that observant Catholics could not be loyal Americans because their adherence to the pope interfered with the free exercise of citizenship. Hence the Catholic Church's image of authoritarian control of its members clashed with the republicanism of the United States. The intense anti-immigrant and anti-Catholic feeling culminated in the 1850s with the rise of the American or Know-Nothing Party. The following text is from Samuel F. B. Morse's attack* Imminent Dangers to the Free Institutions of the United States through Foreign Immigration *(1834), in which Morse alerts his fellow Americans to the dangers of increasing Catholic immigration. He singles out for special chastisement the Leopoldine Foundation, an Austrian-based Catholic mission organization that funded Catholic institution-founding and paid the travel expenses of Catholic missionaries among the immigrants. Its activities were similar to the Protestant home missions societies formed in the same era.*

...And who are the members of the Roman Catholic Communion? What proportion are natives of this land, nurtured under our own institutions, and well versed in the nature of American liberty? Is it not notorious that the greater part are *Foreigners* from the various Catholic countries of Europe? Emigration has of later years been specially promoted among this class of Foreigners, and they have been in the proportion of three to one of all other emigrants arriving on our shores; they are from Ireland, Germany, Poland, and Belgium. From about the period of the formation of the Leopold Society, Catholic emigration increased in an amazing degree. Colonies of Emigrants, selected, perhaps, with a view to occupy particular places, (for, be it remembered, every portion of this country is as perfectly known at Vienna and Rome as in any part of our own country,) have been constantly arriving... We have lately been told by the captain of a lately arrived *Austrian vessel*... that a desire is suddenly manifested among the poorer class of the Belgian population, to emigrate to America. They are mostly, if not all, Roman Catholics...

They obey their priests as demigods, from the habit of their whole lives; they have been taught from infancy that their priests are infallible in the greatest matters, and can they, by new importation to this country, be suddenly imbued with the knowledge that in civil matters their priests may err...? Who will teach them this? Will their priests? Let common sense answer this question. Must not the priests, as a matter almost of *certainty*, control the opinions of their ignorant flock in civil as well as religious matters, and do they not do it?...

I have set forth in a very brief and imperfect manner the evil, the great and increasing evil, that threatens our free institutions from foreign *interference*. Have I not shown that there is real cause for alarm? Let me recapitulate the facts in the case, and see if any one of them can be denied; and if not, I submit it to the calm decision of every American, whether he can still sleep in fancied security, while incendiaries are at work; and whether he is ready quietly to surrender his liberty, civil and religious, into the hands of foreign powers.

1. It is a fact, that in this age the subject of civil and religious liberty agitates in the most intense manner the various European governments.

2. It is a fact, that the influence of American free institutions in subverting European despotic institutions is greater now than it has ever been, from the fact of the greater maturity, and the long-tried character, of the American form of government.

3. It is a fact, that Popery is opposed in its very nature to Democratic Republicanism; and it is, therefore, as a political system, as well as religious, opposed to civil and religious liberty, and consequently to our form of government.

4. It is a fact, that this truth, respecting the intrinsic character of Popery, had lately been clearly and demonstratively proved in public lectures, by one of the Austrian Cabinet, a devoted Roman Catholic...

5. It is a fact, that this member of the Austrian Cabinet, in his lectures, designated and proscribed this country by name, as the *"great nursery of destructive principles; as the Revolutionary school for France and the rest of Europe,"* whose contagious example of Democratic liberty had given, and would still give, trouble to the rest of the world, unless the evil were abated.

6. It is a fact, that very shortly after the delivery of these lectures, a Society was organized in the Austrian capital, called the St. Leopold Foundation, for the purpose "of promoting the greater activity of Catholic Missions in America."

7. It is a fact, that this Society, is under the patronage of the Emperor of Austria,...that it is an extensive combination, embodying the civil, as well as ecclesiastical *officers*, not only of the *whole Austrian Empire*, but of the neighboring Despotic States, — that it is actively at work, collecting moneys, and sending agents to this country, to carry into effect its designs.

8. It is a fact, that the agents of these foreign despots, are for the most part, *Jesuits*.

9. It is a fact, that the effects of this society are already apparent in the otherwise unaccountable increase of Roman Catholic cathedrals, churches, colleges, convents, nunneries, &c., in every part of the country; in the sudden increase of Catholic emigrations; in the increased clannishness of the Roman Catholics, and the boldness with which their leaders are experimenting on the character of the American people.

10. It is a fact, that an unaccountable disposition to riotous conduct has manifested itself within a few years, when exciting topics are publicly discussed, wholly at variance with the former peaceful, deliberative character of our people.

11. It is a fact, that a species of police unknown to our laws, has repeatedly been put in requisition to keep the peace among a certain class of foreigners, who are Roman Catholics, viz., Priest-police.

12. It is a fact, that Roman Catholic Priests have interfered to influence our elections.

13. It is a fact, that politicians on both sides have propitiated these priests, to obtain the votes of their people.

14. It is a fact, that numerous Societies of Roman Catholics, particularly among the Irish foreigners, are organized in various parts of the country, under various names, and ostensibly for certain benevolent objects; that these societies are united together by correspondence, all of which may be innocent and praiseworthy, but viewed in connection with the recent aspect of affairs are at least suspicious.

15. It is a fact, that an attempt has been made to organize a military corps of Irishmen in New York, to be called the O'Connell guards; thus commencing a military organization of foreigners.

16. It is a fact, that the greater part of the foreigners in our population is composed of Roman Catholics.

> Peter Guilday, *The Life and Times of John England* (New York: America Press, 1927), 2:200–204.

34. Orestes Brownson on Native Americanism, 1854, 1856

Vermont-born Orestes Brownson (1803–76), who converted to Catholicism in 1844, is considered by many to be the outstanding American Catholic intellectual of the nineteenth century. Brownson wrote a series of controversial articles in the mid-1850s for his journal, Brownson's Quarterly Review, *which argued that foreign-born Catholics needed to adapt to American culture. While condemning the anti-Catholic Know-Nothing Party, he argued that legitimate native Americanism was simply pride in one's nationality. The problem with American Catholicism was that it was too closely identified with the Irish. Brownson's aggressively assimilationist and Americanist approach did not find favor with many Irish Catholics, including Archbishop John Hughes of New York.*

There is, say what you will, such a thing as American nationality. It is true, that the population of the United States is composed of English, Irish, German, French, Scotch, Dutch, Welch, Norwegians, Africans, and Asiatics, to say nothing of the aborigines; but the population of English origin and descent are the predominating class... They were for the United States as a nation first in the field, the original germ of the great American people, and they constitute at least three fourths of the white population of the country. They are the original source of American nationality, the founders of American institutions, and it is through their heart that flows the grand and fertilizing current of American life. It is idle to deny it... Individuals of other races have done their duty, and deserved well of the country, but only by assimilating themselves to the Anglo-Americans and becoming animated by their spirit... There is, therefore, no use for any other nationality to strive to preserve itself on our soil...

[The American nationality] feels it has the right to say, in all not repugnant to the moral law, "it is for you to conform to us, not for us to conform to you. We did not force you to come here; we do not force you to remain. If you do not like us as we are, you may return whence you came"...

"Native Americanism," *Brownson's Quarterly Review* (July 1854): 335–37.

... We insist, indeed, on the duty of all Catholic citizens, whether natural born or naturalized, to be, or to make themselves, thorough-going Americans; but to be American is to understand and love American institutions, to understand and love the American mission, to understand and love American liberty, to understand and love American principles and interests, and to use with free and manly spirit the advantages of American citizenship to advance the cause of religion and civilization. Those who will not be Americans in this sense, we disown, we hold to be "outside barbarians," and not within the pale of the American order. They have no business here, and the sooner they leave us the better... But whoever does his best to be in this sense an American, whoever is devoted to true American interests, and is fired with a noble ambition to promote the glory of America, we embrace as a countryman, wherever he was born or reared; we hold him to be our fellow-laborer, and to him we make our appeal...

"Mission of America," *Brownson's Quarterly Review* (October 1856): 443–44.

... The grounds taken by our non-Catholic countrymen against Catholicity are three: 1. It [i.e., Catholicism] is foreign and opposed to our nationality. [The second and third are that Catholicism is antiliberal, and anti-industrial.]

Now we all know that this first objection is very strong in the non-Catholic American mind, and that it is strengthened by the fact that the great body of Catholics here are immigrants and their children. The American not a Catholic regards the Church as un-American, and to him she comes in and spreads here only in conjunction with a foreign nationality. For large masses of the American people Catholicity is simply the *Irish* religion, and to become a Catholic is regarded as the same thing as to become an Irishman. Of the fact there is no doubt, and that, humanly speaking, it operates unfavorably to the reception of our holy religion by our countrymen, there can be just as little, because it adds to their prejudice against the Church the no less strong prejudice against a foreign nationality. Nothing is therefore more prudent than for one in our position thus to show that he preserves his Americanism...

[Brownson goes on to lament the prejudice against the Irish, but acknowledges that it is a reality in the United States.] We are grieved and mortified that it is so, but so it is, and the Catholic American must not be required to shoulder the national prejudice, but must be permitted in all freedom to distinguish for his countrymen between Catholicity as Catholicity, and Catholicity as identified with the Irish or any other foreign nationality. Why should he beat his head against a granite wall? ...

...The more prominent we make the Irish nationality, and the more we identify it with Catholicity, the more do we confirm the prejudices of the American people against our religion. What we want, so far as our non-Catholic countrymen are concerned, is, that our religion be presented to them free from all association with any foreign nationality whatsoever...

Here is the difficulty in this country with the great body of our Catholics. Catholicity is their old national religion. They embrace, cherish and defend it as the religion of their fathers, and identify it so closely with their own nationality, that they hardly conceive the possibility of the one without the other, and are therefore exceedingly apt in Americanizing to lose their Catholicity. Hence the question has two grave aspects, the one affecting non-Catholic Americans, and the other the Catholic immigrants themselves. It is necessary to convince the former that they can, so to speak, *Catholicize* without ceasing to be Americans, and to enable the latter to Americanize without ceasing to be Catholics.

"The Know Nothings," *Brownson's Quarterly Review* (October 1854): 469–72.

35. The Oath of the American Protective Association, 1893

In 1887, the anti-Catholic American Protective Association (APA) was founded in Iowa and quickly spread nationally. By 1896, the APA claimed about one million members throughout the country. The following document is the "secret oath" of the APA, 31 October 1893.

I do most solemnly promise and swear that I will always, to the utmost of my ability, labor, plead and wage a continuous warfare against ignorance and fanaticism; that I will use my utmost power to strike the shackles and chains of blind obedience to the Roman Catholic church from the hampered and bound consciences of a priest-ridden and church-oppressed people;...that I will use my influence to promote the interest of all Protestants everywhere in the world that I may be; that I will not employ a Roman Catholic in any capacity if I can procure the services of a Protestant.

I furthermore promise and swear that I will not aid in building or maintaining, by my resources, any Roman Catholic church or institution of their sect or creed whatsoever, but will do all in my power to retard and break down the power of the Pope, in this country or any other;...

I furthermore promise and swear that I will not countenance the nomination, in any caucus or convention, of a Roman Catholic for any office in the gift of the American people, and that I will not vote for, or counsel others to vote for, any Roman Catholic, but will vote only for a Protestant, so far as may lie in my power...that I will at all times endeavor to place the political positions of this government in the hands of Protestants, to the entire exclusion of the Roman Catholic church, of the members thereof, and the mandate of the Pope.

To all of which I do most solemnly promise and swear, so help me God. Amen.

John Tracy Ellis, ed., *Documents of American Catholic History* (Milwaukee: Bruce, 1956), 500–501. Printed with permission of the estate of John Tracy Ellis.

Part 2

PHOTO ESSAY: BUILDING THE IMMIGRANT CHURCH

Introduction

Brick-and-mortar Catholicism has been an enduring feature of the immigrant church in America from the 1790s to the present day. Wherever they settled, Catholics of very diverse economic and ethnic backgrounds devoted scarce resources to constructing houses of worship that compared favorably — and often surpassed (especially in numbers) — those of their Protestant and Jewish neighbors. It was no accident that Catholic churches became landmarks in towns and cities across the United States. These powerful symbols of faith and identity proclaimed in a visible way that Catholic immigrants were creating a place for themselves in America.

That historians have paid so little attention to the process of church-building is ironic because, as the documents that follow make abundantly clear, commentators in the nineteenth and early twentieth centuries found Catholic churches and ritual fascinating. Newspapers devoted column inch after column inch to cornerstone layings and dedications, describing in detail the ornately carved altars and statues, stained glass windows, and pipe organs. Whether the house of worship was located in New York City or in a frontier town on the shores of Lake Michigan, the message was the same: Catholic immigrants were building edifices that enhanced civic life by their size and beauty. Moreover, in terms of material culture, Catholic churches challenged conventional wisdom about class and refinement. As one critic noted wryly in 1862, "it is greatly to be regretted, that cultivated Americans, who enjoy the luxury of art abroad, should be content with white-washed walls at home." Seen in this light, brick-and-mortar Catholicism enabled immigrants to put themselves on an equal footing with native-born Americans. And it worked! Indeed, the same newspapers that decried Catholic newcomers as threats to democracy and the fabric of urban life routinely praised solemn ceremonies of consecration and feast day processions as models of order, decorum, and stability.

Yet the contrast between the conditions under which poor immigrants lived and worked and the churches in which they worshiped scandalized many Americans, including some Catholic priests and bishops. One of the most outspoken critics of brick-and-mortar Catholicism was Bishop John Lancaster Spalding of Peoria. In 1880, referring to the dismal failure of the Irish in America, he compared the magnificent churches financed by immigrants to the pyramids of Egypt, built by slaves, and argued that the construction of urban Catholic churches represented "the absence of home and a future for God's people."

Luxury or necessity? As the following documents and photographs illustrate, Catholic churches contributed to the development of towns and cities, just as they had in Europe and Asia. In the 1850s, artists such as James T. Palmatary and George J. Robertson captured the relationship between church and turf in their oversized "bird's-eye views" of new American cities. While the Catholic steeples provided incontrovertible proof that immigrants definitely left their mark on the urban landscape, until quite recently, historians have failed to explore the complex process of church-building. And, as Kathleen Neils Conzen, a historian at the University of Chicago, reminds us, it has been a great loss. In returning to St. John's Cathedral in Milwaukee years after doing her dissertation on Germans, Conzen stepped inside the 1853 edifice and suddenly realized that she was seeing "not just a building but a declaration of war, a church unmistakably in the German Baroque tradition, a Counter-Reformation symbol of assertive Catholicism triumphant, erected by a Swiss bishop in a Yankee-Yorker city with strong German Lutheran and free-thinking, as well as Catholic, elements."[1]

All too often, historians have used parishes and Catholic churches as a convenient framework to discuss larger issues of ethnicity, assimilation, and race relations. Perhaps unintentionally, the bricks and mortar fade into the background, diminishing the importance and significance of sacred space. Yet there are positive signs that this attitude is changing. In his recent book *Urban Exodus: Why the Jews Left Boston and the Catholics Stayed*, Gerald Gamm argues that "an institution like a church or a school or a state capitol or a ballpark does not just matter for those who identify with the institution. It matters for everyone in the neighborhood."[2]

The following photographs and documents reveal the complexity of brick-and-mortar Catholicism as well as its public expression in sacramental celebrations, processions, and festivals. We hope readers will begin to understand how and why this experience paid dividends, as immigrants in the pew believed. To understand and evaluate the legacy of this church-building competition, first with Protestants and Jews, and then with other Catholic ethnics, we also need

---

1. Kathleen Neils Conzen, "Forum: The Place of Religion in Urban and Community Studies," *Religion and American Culture* 6, no. 2 (summer 1996): 108.

2. Gerald Gamm, *Urban Exodus: Why the Jews Left Boston and the Catholics Stayed* (Cambridge, Mass.: Harvard University Press, 1999), 29.

to know in greater detail what it meant for immigrants to create a church of their own and decorate it with funds raised through door-to-door collections and parish bazaars. And as the names on stained glass windows attest, we need to know much, much more about women domestics and schoolteachers who contributed financially to erect these places of beauty in their lives and in their neighborhoods. Finally, in the spirit of *Keeping Faith,* we hope this chapter will provide perspective in the debate over historic preservation of Catholic churches at a time of large-scale closings and consolidations.

Brick-and-Mortar Catholicism

36. Bishop John Carroll Blesses a Boston Church, 1803

That church-building conferred benefits on a Catholic minority became evident in the campaign to erect Holy Cross Church on Franklin Place (now 214 Devonshire Street). Charles Bulfinch (1763–1844), Boston's first city planner, who had designed the state house on Beacon Hill in 1798, drew up plans for Massachusetts's first Catholic church. He also contributed financially to the subscription list headed by President John Adams. Ground for Holy Cross was broken on St. Patrick's Day, 17 March 1800, and construction on the $20,000 brick edifice continued over the next three years. On dedication day, "the exterior of the church was illuminated so that the entire front was resplendent with light, and the gilded cross surmounting the edifice stood out with the glow of a thousand lamps."

Yesterday the Roman Catholic Church, lately erected in this town, was consecrated by the Right Reverend Bishop CARROL [*sic*], with the appropriate ceremonies. A very respectable and crowded auditory were assembled on the occasion — and many persons were excluded by the want of room. The edifice is strikingly neat, and convenient. Over the altar is placed a large picture of the crucifixion of our Saviour, painted by MR. HENRY SARGENT, of this town.

New England Palladium, 30 September 1803.

37. Bishop Benedict J. Fenwick on Holy Cross Cathedral, Boston, 1829

One of the earliest commentators on brick-and-mortar Catholicism in the United States was Benedict Joseph Fenwick, S.J., second bishop of Boston from 1825 until 1846. Raised to the status of a cathedral in 1808, Holy Cross soon became too small to accommodate all the Catholics living in Boston. In his memoir, Fenwick recounted plans for enlarging the church on Franklin Street.

The next object ... was to enlarge the [church] ... to give greater extent to the sanctuary for the admission of the Candidates to the ministry of the Church, as well as of the children serving at the altar — a measure the more necessary

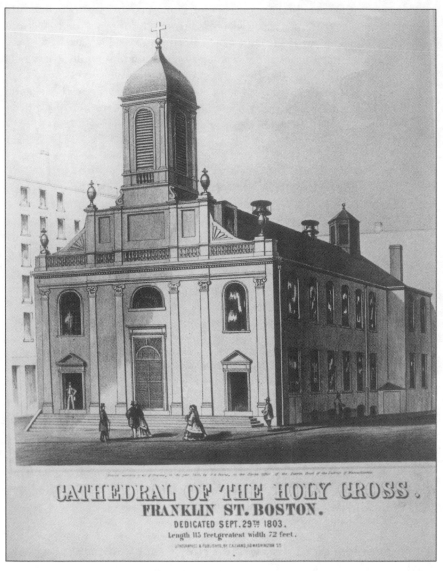

CATHEDRAL OF THE HOLY CROSS.
FRANKLIN ST. BOSTON.
DEDICATED SEPT. 29TH 1803.
Length 115 feet, greatest width 72 feet.

1. Holy Cross Church, Boston. A remarkable example of Protestant and Catholic co-operation when it was built in 1803, Holy Cross was financed in part by donations from such well-known Americans as President John Quincy Adams. Boston's foremost architect, Charles Bulfinch, designed the Italianate structure, acclaimed by Irish and German Catholics as "elegant...[uniting] decency and ornament with economy." Despite its enlargement in 1829, however, Holy Cross Cathedral did not become one of Boston's cherished landmarks. Papal Nuncio Gaetano Bedini declared it "a sorrowful contrast to the rest of the splendid city," and the structure was demolished in 1860. Archives of the Archdiocese of Boston. Reproduced with permission.

to be adopted, as the Church of the HOLY CROSS had become the Cathedral of the Diocese, and in its original construction, had not been designed for that purpose...The work was commenced in the summer of 1827, and completed the following year. As the Cathedral now stands, it is one of the largest and most beautiful Churches in Boston and is capable of containing three thousand persons, having three Altars, and three spacious galleries. Its central situation in the City and the respectability of its neighbourhood will always insure it a preference among Catholics, even when other churches come to be hereafter erected.

> Quoted in *Memoirs to Serve for the Future: Ecclesiastical History of the Diocese of Boston,* ed. Joseph M. McCarthy (Yonkers, N.Y.: U.S. Catholic Historical Society, 1978). Reprinted with permission.

38. Bishop John England's Appeal for St. Mary's, Charleston, South Carolina, 1838

After St. Mary's Church on Hasell Street in Charleston, the "mother parish of the Carolinas," was destroyed by fire in 1838, Bishop John England solicited contributions from Catholics throughout the United States. Contrary to the bishop's predictions that Irish and French Catholics in Charleston would have to lower their expectations, the new St. Mary's was an elegant example of Greek Revival architecture, the most popular style in America in the early nineteenth century. The cornerstone of St. Mary's was laid on 15 August 1838 – a feast day cherished as "Lady's Day" in Ireland – and it was formally dedicated on 9 June 1839.

BELOVED BRETHREN: —

You are already aware of the awful dispensation of Divine Providence by which nearly one third of the city of Charleston has within a few years been reduced to ashes; the principal destruction having taken place toward the termination of the last month, leaving a melancholy token of ruin and of desolation to point out the former abode of industry, of wealth, of decoration and of happiness. You know that in the late conflagration, about one thousand of our stores and dwellings have been consumed within a few hours; and extensive suffering and despondency have come upon families whose prospects were, on the very day previous, as cheering and flattering as their enjoyment appeared to be secure...

The Roman Catholics of this city, are, as a body, the least wealthy of its religious denominations...

From the numbers of the Catholics in this city, and the manner in which they are separated, as well as from their situation in life, the larger portion of them having little power to dispose of their own time, even on the Sundays; it is absolutely necessary to have three churches; two in the city and one in the outlets. About thirty years since a brick edifice of moderate dimensions had been erected and was used as the only place of our worship. It was sur-

2. St. Mary's on Hasell Street, Charleston, South Carolina. Founded in 1789 in an old Methodist meeting house, St. Mary's represented "the first established site of Catholicity in the Carolinas and Georgia." The new brick church, opened in 1806, was completely destroyed in the great fire of 1838. Against a rising tide of nativism, St. Mary's parishioners commissioned Christopher Kane to build the elegant Greek Revival edifice that stands today at 89 Hasell Street. In adopting the most popular style of architecture in America, Irish and French immigrants focused positive, public attention on Charleston's Catholic minority. (So too did their Jewish neighbors across the street: Kahal Kadosh Beth Elohim [1841] and St. Mary's are mirror images of each other!) Frances Purcell Fanning. Reproduced with permission.

rounded by a cemetery, where the remains of those who originally worshipped in the church are deposited. This church, latterly known as St. Mary's, had lately undergone a thorough repair and been fitted up in such a manner as gave the prospect of many years of service with very few demands for its preservation... The congregation and their friends had subscribed to pay the amount of the expenses, and had defrayed all except [$2,000]. In one night, the church and its organ were destroyed, notwithstanding every exertion to save them... You have given food to the hungry amongst us, — you have given drink to the thirsty, you have clothed the naked, you have sheltered the houseless and consoled the afflicted. We now intreat you, to afford us an opportunity of worshipping according to the dictates of our consciences, at those altars before which our fathers and their progenitors bowed in adoration of the heavenly Father, of his beloved son Jesus Christ, and of the Holy Ghost...

Some of our brethren of other religious denominations have also been deprived of their places of worship, but their friends and their associates have with a creditable liberality come to their aid. Their edifices will rise from the ashes, more durable in their structure, more commodious in their arrangement, more decorated in beauty. Our expectations are more limited; we must be content with less. But even for procuring what is merely necessary, we must be dependent upon the generosity of our friends, of the charitable [and] of the benevolent and of the liberal...

(Signed) +JOHN, Bishop of Charleston.
Charleston, S.C. May 28, 1838

"To the Charitable and Benevolent Citizens of the United States," *Boston Pilot,* 16 June 1838.

39. Consecration of St. John's Cathedral, Milwaukee, 1853

During his U.S. tour, 1853–54, Archbishop Gaetano Bedini, papal nuncio to Brazil, consecrated St. John's Cathedral in Milwaukee on 30 June 1853. At this and similar ceremonial events on his tour, he got a firsthand look at the growing strength and influence of the Catholic Church in America. Although some criticized his visit, Bedini informed Rome that "the Protestants here, with very few exceptions, are kind enough and free from the cruel and tenacious hostility which characterizes those in the more populated cities, like Philadelphia and New York."

Sunday, July 31, 1853

... The Christian,... tho' he can never equal by his poor effort, the vastness of God's handiwork, yet he builds the finest edifice of which he is capable — he raises his altar — he adorns it with the highest art, with sculpture and painting and silver and gold... The Christian house may be lowly — as the houses of the Roman patriots are said to have been in comparison with their public

3. Bird's-eye view of Milwaukee, 1854. Artist George J. Robertson's bird's-eye view of Milwaukee faithfully depicted the steeple of St. John's Cathedral, the largest and most impressive structure in the new city when it was dedicated in 1853. Lithographs produced by German immigrant artisans and sold by subscription to residents and businessmen — and investors abroad — provided visible proof that Catholic churches, schools, and convents contributed to America's urban development. Credit: Milwaukee County Historical Society. Reproduced with permission.

buildings — but that place, where he meets his God more particularly, must be the best he can build: he would feel ashamed to have his own parlor more beautiful than the Temple where he sings praises to his Maker. — Perhaps if we could compare the dwellings of people with the shrine at which they worship the difference might tell the strength of their religion...

About 7 o'clock A.M. Monsignor Bedini, Archbishop of Thebes, and Papal Nuncio to Brazil, assisted by Dr. [Joseph] Salzman as Deacon, and Father Donohue, as Sub-deacon, began the ceremony of the consecration of St. John's Cathedral, by walking in procession with the clergy of the diocese three times around the building, and sprinkling its walls with holy water; the dews of heaven also descended gently on the building. Each time they came to the door, they asked that the doors "be lifted up for the King of Glory to enter:" after obtaining admission, the consecrator made the sign of the cross on the threshold, and by an exorcism, he commanded all evil spirits and "Phantasms" to behold that sign and flee away thus saying "Peace to this house!" The consecration began with the Hymn "Veni Creator," the invocation of the holy spirit — when advancing to the middle of the church, they all knelt down and chanted the "Litany of the Saints," then rising, the Archbishop made the sign of the Cross three times in the air, and mixed salt, ashes, and wine together, to keep in remembrance that Christ is the true Vine, that we are dust and ashes and that the faithful are the salt of the earth. He then went to the corner of

the building and crossing diagonally to the other corner making in his way the
letters of the Greek and Latin Alphabet, upon spots of ashes on the floor, with
his staff, the whole of which put together formed a Cross — which signified
that the Orient and the Occident were joined in one by the Christian Religion. He then goes up in front of the altar saying, "I will go up to the altar of
my God; to God who giveth joy to my youth;" signing the altar with the sign
of the cross, he returns to the door on the inside of which he makes the sign
of the cross, also on the door step, then returning to the sanctuary they go up
to the altar, and after praying, sing the beautiful Anthem, "Asperges me," com-
passing the altar about seven times, and sprinkling it with holy water. Then
proceeding to the body of the Cathedral he goes round and sprinkles the walls
three times in like manner, and the same on the floor in the form of a cross,
and from the centre throws some towards the four quarters of the world. They
then knelt down and prayed and having made the sign of the cross in the air
and chanted part of the preface of the Mass returned again to the altar and
prayed again. Then going into the side Chapel, where the bones of the Martyrs, taken from the old church, had been watched all night previous, they
walked out in procession, four Priests carrying on a kind of bier the relics
on their shoulders, while attendants fumed them with incense — proceeding
outside the church with the Priests of the diocese following, they carry them
round, singing songs of triumph, then return within and set the relics down
before the Altar; the consecrator and singers then go to the door and return
chanting all the way to the sanctuary, and going up to the marble table, among
clouds from burning incense they place caskets containing the relics on each
side of the tabernacle — and having done some masonry which I could not
see, they kneel and pray again, and with the Altar enveloped with the smoke
of the incense, placed the relics of the Martyred Saints in the Sarcophagus,
with songs of praise — this seemed to me the most solemn and imposing of
the whole ceremony, and occupied a long time...

The Consecrator, assistants, &c., went next to the body of the Church,
to the twelve pillars — which signify the twelve Apostles — and mounting up
anointed the crosses thereon with blessed oil, and signing them with the sign
of the cross, he repeated over each one in a clear, strong voice: "Sanctificatur,
Consecratur, templum hoc: In nomine Patris, et Filii, et Spiritus Sancti; in
honorum Dei, et Gloriosae Virginis Mariae, at que omnium Sanctorum, ad
nomen et memoriam Sancti, Johanus, Pax tibi!" The singers at each repetition
making the vaulted roof ring with Hallelujah to God and the Lamb.

About this time the doors were opened and the people rushed in and filled
the body of the church; the seats being reserved for the Ladies; and the Consecration being finished shortly after, the Archbishop and the Clergy retired
into the side chapel to prepare for the celebration of the first Mass in the
temple now sanctified, hallowed, and fitted, for that holy sacrifice.

I may remark here that from morning till night the best of order was maintained, and everything was done in the manner befitting such an occasion...

After a short space the Celebrant, the Archbishop of Thebes [Bedini], Archbishops Hughes of N.Y., Purcell of Cincinnati, and Kenrick of St. Louis, the Right Reverend Bishops O'Connor, of Pittsburg[h], LeFevre, of Detroit, Vandevelde [Van de Velde] of Chicago, and the much loved Bishop of the Diocese; with Drs. Salzman, Norris, Paulhuber, and Ives; and some sixty or seventy Priests took their seats in the sanctuary; immediately on their entry, a tremendous burst of music filled the Cathedral, and the celebration of Pontifical High Mass commenced. I will not attempt to describe the Music, but I presume it was of the first order; neither will I attempt to describe the holy sacrifice which followed...In relation to the *place,* I would say one thing; that altho' upon the humblest Altar that Religion rears, and beside which poverty ministers, the same sacrifice is offered, the same graces may be obtained; tho' no place is too mean for supplication or for praise, yet so long as we are mortal, so long as poetry is a relic of the human mind, so long, also, will the magnificence of the room, the sculptured Altar, the paintings, the solemn beauty of the music, the rich vestments of the Priests, and the colored light from the stained glass — like fragments of the rainbow, sprinkled over the whole — raise emotions in the soul, which the baldness of the lecture room must ever fail to do...

[Archbishop John Hughes] said it might seem far fetched to connect an event of to day, with that which took place eighteen centuries ago, but what had taken place on this last day of July [1853] on the banks of Lake Michigan, the consecration with solemn pomp and rite, of this magnificent temple to the worship of God, where less than thirty years ago, perhaps on this very spot, the savage Indian threaded the mazes of the war-dance — was but the fulfilment of the prophecy contained in the text [John 11:47], that the death of Christ was not partial, but for all the children of God.

He congratulated the Right Rev. Bishop of Milwaukee [John Martin Henni], who in his brief Apostleship, inspired by his patron St. John — had done so much in this large and new field, and...congratulated the Architect [Victor Schulte], and the workmen, and the faithful generally, that they had here a place to bring their children to Holy Baptisms, to give them to God in their youth; and that the youth of both sexes, attached to each other by mutual affection, could come here to enter the holy state of matrimony and receive a benediction on their union.

He then spoke of the ubiquity and universality of the Catholic Church; that it knew no geography, no politics; of its unity, not of place or time, but of its truth, and its unity of teaching that truth...

He spoke of the divinity of her government; of her sacraments, as so many channels to salvation, by which the erring may return or come to God...

Here I confess, that in the listener I forgot the reporter, and must fail in giving the reader any idea of the power, simplicity and breadth, which were the chief characteristics of the Archbishop's Sermon. His eloquence moves along like a cloud, large, calm and dignified; with the sunlight beaming on it, for about his mouth resides one of the sweetest expressions compatible with the manly nose and forehead he possesses.

In the evening Vespers was sung; after which, Archbishop Purcell gave a most eloquent and beautiful sermon on the "Real Presence," full of thought, full of illustration from Nature, and full of argument; which I would only mar and destroy by attempting to report. Altogether the day was an important one, and I could not help thinking, that when this beautiful city of Milwaukee will have grown perhaps to fifty times its present size — when our children's children will have been forgotten — its then inhabitants looking on this building — may say, "this was the flood-mark here, of the Religion of Jesus Christ in 1853."

> "Consecration of St. John's Cathedral, Milwaukee," *Milwaukee Daily Sentinel,*
> 2 August 1853.

40. Archbishop Gaetano Bedini on the Legacy of Brick-and-Mortar Catholicism, 1855

During his American tour, Archbishop Gaetano Bedini completely revised his opinion about the wisdom of contracting huge debts to build cathedrals and parish churches. Bedini informed the Sacred Congregation of the Propagation of the Faith in Rome that, far from draining the scarce resources of Catholic immigrants, church-building actually improved the public perception of Catholicism in the United States. Not only did Catholic churches compare favorably with Protestant houses of worship, but they also challenged conventional notions about the poor.

...Everyone knows that within a few years the Catholic Religion has made remarkable progress in the United States, and if at first, the Church or a Catholic community was considered a rarity in that vast land, now it can be said that it not only occupies a considerable position; but that, even when compared to the individual Churches and Sects of the Dissidents, it far surpasses them in number...

It is only natural that as the Protestants lose their esteem for the Protestant doctrine, their esteem for Catholic doctrines increases. In fact, a Bishop and a Catholic priest are usually welcomed and well respected, and the self-styled Protestant Bishops are eager for the esteem and favor which they receive. Frequently, the generous assistance of rich Protestants helps to build Catholic institutions. In the higher class, the one more distinguished by education or easier circumstances or culture, Catholicism has found favor and respect. However, since they are accustomed to see it professed by the Irish, who are

4. Constantino Brumidi's crucifixion mural, St. Stephen's Church, New York City. During a visit to Rome in 1850, Archbishop John Hughes commissioned Constantino Brumidi (1805–80) to decorate the interior of St. Stephen's Church, designed by James Renwick. But before the artist could emigrate, he was arrested and sentenced to jail as a republican revolutionary. Brumidi left Rome after receiving a "full and unconditional pardon" by Pope Pius IX and arrived in New York on 18 September 1852. According to Dr. Barbara A. Wolanin, Brumidi's Raphaelesque frescoes in the Capitol and his work in St. Stephen's established his reputation "as the artist of the most important ecclesiastical and political monuments then being constructed" in the United States. Reproduced with permission of pastor of St. Stephen's Parish, New York.

all destined to be servants or to have the most laborious and miserable jobs because of their poor living conditions, which they preserve in a most miserable and at times revolting aspect, they form the idea of Catholicism as the Religion of the poor, a religion which can be pitied and helped by them, but because of their snobbishness and supposed social dignity never professed by them. The Southern and Western provinces and Baltimore would be exceptions to this. The latter, because it is the cradle of Catholicism and was founded by Lord Baltimore, who was a Catholic and was able to keep in his domain rich and outstanding families, who have always been Catholic. The former, because the people coming from French or Spanish colonies always knew Catholicism as the State religion from the beginning, and even now it is almost predominant.

...Churches, institutions and even conversions are multiplying like lightening...I think much must be attributed to the increasing prosperity of the Catholic people, who by building religious houses and by more intense worship have put themselves more in evidence than before, and this activity has rekindled their zeal. Another reason for this increase is the natural birth rate, which in general is considered extraordinary among some portions of the American populace, and even more extraordinary in lower Canada. Many families have ten or twelve sons. But the basic reason for this increase is the immigration of the Irish and the Germans, which never stops and which brings thousands and thousands of immigrants to that continent every year...The immigration from Europe, especially that of the Irish[,] is the important fact which makes Catholicism great in America...[But h]ow many Catholic immigrants have lost the Faith!...[T]he real reason is that many of them find it impossible or [are] without any means to practice their religion and to have the benefit of instruction and the Sacraments. The Dioceses are so vast and the population so spread out; the Churches are scarce and the priests even scarcer. On the other hand the Protestants are ready with their many Churches and centers, with their flattery and their fatal lure of esteem, prosperity and wealth...I noticed that the Bishops are deeply disturbed over the building of new cathedrals, which they have either begun or are in the process of building. These are vital thoughts for them. The huge development of the cities does not allow the Catholics to have modest churches. The majesty, the convenience of external worship, is now a dire necessity lest the Catholics suffer in comparison with the Protestants, who have many beautiful and appealing churches. Furthermore, these cathedrals may stop the preconceived ideas of the rich and influential, who think that poverty is the exclusive prerogative of Catholics. It is very interesting to note that Americans usually associate poverty with disgrace. They cannot recognize poverty, even voluntary poverty, as a virtue. The United States is so rich in resources and so dedicated to material prosperity that poverty is always considered as an indication of the most reproachable laziness; and everything that gives the impression of poverty is thought of as nothing and shameful to be associated with.

In addition to cathedrals, the American Catholics need more seminaries and secondary churches, schools, orphanages, hospitals and the like. They get these from charity, collections, and I might add, even by financial speculation...I must also add that the Catholic people have a wonderful sense of responsibility. They pay their pew rents and give to the collections...

The only income, at least the principal income[,] of the Bishops is the pew rent of the churches...The pews are for the exclusive use at all functions and at any hour for those who rent them. However, they are only rented for the High Masses and the related sermons. At the other hours Masses and sermons are alternated, and again and again the churches are filled. I would dare say though that some of them take excessive care to rent the pews to those who offer more, and the pews fill almost the entire church so that only a small space remains for those who wish to assist standing up. Therefore the idea of side altars has almost disappeared. In building a new church, they first calculate how many pews it will hold and from this they can determine beforehand the yearly income. It is true that even if they had side altars, they would not have enough priests to celebrate the required Masses. But even without these side altars, which recall to mind the devotion to the saints, their devotions, if I might be permitted to observe, are too monotonous and very similar to those of the Protestants. But it seems that this system is being corrected. The new churches have two altars along side the main altar in the front of the Church. One of these side altars is always dedicated to the Blessed Mother.

I knew that they received a special income for extraordinary ceremonies because no one at all is permitted to enter the church without an admission ticket, for which they must pay more than one scudo (about one dollar). This system was particularly used when I consecrated churches and Bishops, and I could not help but show my surprise and voice my disapproval. The ceremonies seemed to become theatrical shows. Yet, I saw that all the Bishops want this system and they showed me the necessity of keeping this fine means for reducing the debt of each church. They assured me that every Catholic worthy of the name thinks nothing of this system and is happy to be a part of it. Furthermore, the system prevents the troublemakers or those who would deride or abuse the ceremonies from entering. Finally, they assured me that at other times during the day the same church is open to everyone, that they may attend the other religious functions gratuitously. I must admit that these explanations seemed plausible but they never completely convinced me, and I always was reluctant to fully accept their reasoning...

I must confess that when I was with the Nunciature in Vienna, I saw many American Bishops coming for help to reduce the debts on their churches. At that time I had a bad opinion of them for undertaking such excessive debts and I believed that it was advisable to recommend that they undertake no debts out of proportion to their resources. But when I had the chance to visit them in America, I changed my mind entirely. Since the greater part of them were in places, which were just starting to grow, much depended on how well they could establish the Church and how rapidly they could occupy the land and build Catholic institutions in the principal spots. Speed is most important, speaking both economically and morally. When the value of the land rises they have then an undeniable advantage. It assures them that the Catholic body will be more in evidence and it prevents the excessive gathering of Protestants, whose preponderance is assured everywhere else; and therefore they are assured of greater prosperity.

The city and Diocese of Milwaukee suggested these thoughts to me. Fifteen years ago it was a simple mission of a few savages, situated on the banks of wonderful Lake Michigan. Now it is a town of 24,000 inhabitants. The Bishop's great wisdom in buying lands and building institutions has made the condition of the Catholics (who number about 10,000) superior to the condition of the Protestants... If at times it would seem advisable to recommend that the Bishops not burden themselves with debts for their churches, it would be much better to encourage them, or at least not to frighten them, because their business acumen raises the Protestant opinion of Catholics, in the sense that it remedies the supposition that all the Catholics are poor (and everybody knows well the consideration poor people have in America) and this helps the public to esteem Catholicism and facilitates more conversions.

Boston, for example, might be called the most aristocratic city in America and even pretends that it is the Athens of the United States. It must be admitted that it is deserving of that name. Well, the lack of even a mediocre cathedral discourages not only the sympathies but even the consideration of the Protestants and prevents Catholics of high social position from competing with the Protestants of that city. It seems to me that the Bishop is frightened about incurring more debt. However, having seen the vivid desire of the Catholics (who number 60,000 in a population of 150,000) and the assurance of his priests, who promised to take up collections, I was forced to encourage him in this undertaking with my first donation of one hundred scudi ($100), which was followed at once by a greater offering of his priests...

"The Report of Gaetano Bedini, Archbishop of Thebes, to His Eminence Cardinal Fransoni upon the Nuncio's Return from the United States of America," in Rev. James F. Connelly, *The Visit of Archbishop Gaetano Bedini to the United States of America (June, 1853 – February, 1854),* Analecta Gregoriana 109 (Rome: Libreria Editrice Dell'Università Gregoriana, 1960), 195–224. Printed with permission of Msgr. James F. Connelly.

41. Bishop John J. Hogan on Church-Building in Chillicothe, Missouri, 1859

As difficult as it was to create sacred space in new American cities, the experience often paled in comparison with country parishes. In addition to living at great distances from one another, members of farming communities had to import stained glass windows and other objects of refinement from city manufacturers. Moreover, as country pastors soon discovered, the demands of farm life generally precluded daily worship and devotions that became a distinguishing feature of urban parishes by the 1850s. In the following document, Bishop John Joseph Hogan recalls the challenge of building a church for Irish immigrants who had settled in the northwest corner of Missouri, about two hundred miles from St. Louis.

I NOW turned my attention to the erection of the church at Chillicothe, for which I had got a site some time previous. The building was to be frame, seventy feet long, twenty five feet wide, eighteen feet story, with bell tower, sacristies, altar, communion rail, pews, confessional, choir gallery, and stained glass windows. I let the contract for the foundation to a man who made strong preferential claim for the job because he was a Catholic...[and] he was from Chicago, where, as he stated, he was well known, and had built much elegant masonry. The foundation wall, which was to have usual depth in the ground, was to be twenty inches above ground. It was to be built of good rubble masonry, with dressed stone along the front of the building, and hammered stone along the sides and end. Soon the stone was on the ground, of good quality, prepared according to contract, and the work was to be commenced at once. It was well known, as a matter spoken of, that I intended to be absent for some time on a missionary tour through the neighboring counties. The contractor aware of my intention, requested me to pay him in advance for the work. He said he was out of money, that the stone was on the ground ready, that it would be laid in the wall in a few days, and that upon my return I would find the work done and to my entire satisfaction. I paid him in full, and set out forthwith on my journey. When I had left, he sold the cut and hammered stone to be used in another building, and then built the foundation of the church of the cheapest stone he could find. Afterwards, skipping from town, he sought pastures new, hoping no doubt, in a world full of fools, soon to find another verdant young clergyman. Arriving home, I went to inspect the work and found that I could kick it to pieces with the heel of my boot. I soon, however, had the rotten stone and crumbling wall rebuilt with better material, and by an honester mechanic. The superstructure was of green oak framing timbers, joists, studding, rafters, sheathing, cut to order at a neighboring saw-mill. The weather-boarding, shingles, flooring, doors, frames, altar and pew boards, and boards for finishing, also nails and hardware, were bought in St. Louis, shipped by boat to Brunswick, and thence by a smaller boat that plied on the Grand River, to Chillicothe landing.

5. St. Thomas Aquinas, Archbald, Pennsylvania. Irish miners and their families built St. Thomas Aquinas parish against the backdrop of the culm pile in Archbald, Pennsylvania. A classic illustration of Catholic sacred space in industrial America, this photo depicts the original frame church (1858), on the left, and the brick Romanesque edifice, designed by Philadelphia architect Edwin Forrest Durang. With its ornate murals and stained glass windows, St. Thomas Aquinas quickly became a landmark in the community following its dedication on the feast of the Assumption, 15 August 1875. Rev. Thomas J. Comerford, pastor from 1892 to 1924, was a staunch supporter of the United Mine Workers Union and baptized its president, John Mitchell. Edward J. Casey Collection, Archbald, Pennsylvania. Reproduced with permission.

Chillicothe and the Fine Arts

The stained glass windows were made in St. Louis at Miller's Stained Glass factory, thence were shipped by boat to Hannibal, thence by rail to Shelbina, the western terminus at the time of the Hannibal and St. Joseph Railroad, and thence by wagon to Chillicothe, where they arrived safe, not a square inch of glass broken. Alas, the windows which were really beautiful, were not suffered to shower their rainbow tints very long over the secluded little sanctuary. A rather too warm sermon from the fervid young missionary, against forbidden secret societies, brought the gentlemen of grips and signs to visit his chapel at the midnight hour, and to belabor with barbarous sticks and guns, the artistic little gems, brought like pearls from afar, that were willing to live on and shine for God, even in the depths of the wilderness. Chillicothe's first little Catholic church had to humble itself to the level of its surroundings. Henceforth its windows were to be of vulgar glass. By great efforts, and by collections made near and far, the little church was completed. The church lot, too, was fenced, and all was paid for, so far as I knew. It was a strong tie for the hearts of Catholic people, to stop there and settle, as many of them did from that day forward.

> Bishop John Joseph Hogan, "Church Building at Chillicothe," in *On the Mission in Missouri, 1857–1868* (1892; reprint, Glorieta, N.Mex.: Rio Grande Press, 1976), 54–56. Reprinted with permission of John Strachan.

42. Proposals for a Jesuit College, 1857

The success of Catholic immigrants in creating churches and schools was not lost on contemporary observers. The Chicago Tribune, *a widely respected abolitionist newspaper, decried the increasing presence of Catholics in the city and urged Protestant readers to withhold financial contributions. But as the walls of Holy Family Church and, later, St. Ignatius College rose, the newspaper changed its tune, declaring these institutions to be "ornaments" that enriched the city's reputation for architecture.*

We see that [the *Chicago Daily Times*] manifests no little anxiety for the erection of a Jesuit Church and University at the corner of Twelfth Street and [Blue] Island Avenue, and that it calls loudly upon Protestants who own real estate in that vicinity to be liberal in their contributions for the furtherance of the enterprise. As it is clearly within the province of a public journal to urge its readers to give to any project toward which it may be favorably inclined, so it is within editorial line of duty to urge the withholding of benefactions, when asked for a dangerous or unworthy purpose. The *Times* chooses to assist in the spread of Jesuitism; and, hence it pleads that it may have the contributions of the liberal. The *TRIBUNE* regards Jesuitism as eminently anti-Republican and anti-American; it begs Protestants to think twice before they aid in any way the founding of Jesuit institutions in this city. We do this not in a spirit of intolerance, but upon the warrant of facts which show that the Society of Jesus is the most virulent and relentless enemy of the Protestant faith and Democratic government. Jesuitism is the embodiment of despotism in religion and politics — so dangerous in its aims and ambition that it is scarcely allowed in countries where Catholicism is the belief of nine-tenths of the people. Jesuitism is the same now as when it was suppressed in Catholic France and Spain. It has not abated an iota of its lofty pretensions, nor has it been dispossessed of the least of its propensity for mischief. That Protestants who hold to a purer and better faith, should be influenced to aid in establishing it here, where it has already proved its anti-democratic tendencies, is preposterous, be the plea upon which that aid is asked, ten times more specious than it is. It is sufficient that they give it the protection of our institutions and laws. We trust that no Protestant will be caught with the bait though it is artfully gilded. Jesuitism can take care of itself, without Protestant money.

> "Proposals for a Jesuit College," *Chicago Daily Tribune,* 25 May 1857.

43. Our Roman Catholic Brethren, 1868

At the same time that Thomas Nast's cartoons depicted Irish immigrants as a threat to American democracy, mainstream publications featured articles that reflected admiration — if not praise — for Catholic churches and ritual. Protestant observers singled out the size of urban congregations; the beauty of church interiors; the deportment of worshipers; and the presence of children as obvious signs of the growth and development of the Catholic Church in the United States.

ONE thing can be said of our Roman Catholic brethren, and especially of our Roman Catholic sisters, without exciting controversy, — they begin early in the morning. St. Stephen's, the largest Catholic church in New York, which will hold five thousand persons and seat four thousand, was filled to overflowing every morning of last November at five o'clock. That, however, was an extraordinary occasion. The first mass, as housekeepers are well aware, usually takes place at six o'clock, summer and winter; and it was this that I attended on Sunday morning, December 8, 1867, one of the coldest mornings of that remarkably cold month... At ten minutes to six, when I stood in front of the spacious St. Stephen's Church in Twenty-Eighth Street, there seemed to be no one going in; and, the vestibule being unlighted, I was confirmed in the impression that early mass did not take place on such cold mornings. To be quite sure of the fact, however, I did just go up the steps and push at the door. It yielded to pressure, and its opening disclosed a vast interior, dimly lighted at the altar end, where knelt or sat, scattered about one or two in a pew, about a hundred women and ten men, all well muffled up in hoods, shawls, and overcoats, and breathing visibly. There was just light enough to see the new blue ceiling and its silver stars; but the sexton was busy lighting the gas, and got on with his work about as fast as the church filled. That church extends through the block, and has two fronts. As six o'clock approached, female figures in increasing numbers crept silently in by several doors, all making the usual courtesy, and all kneeling as soon as they reached a pew. At last the lower part of the church was pretty well filled, and there were some people in the galleries; in all, about one thousand women and about one hundred men. Nearly all the women were servant-girls, and all of them were dressed properly and abundantly for such a morning. There was not a squalid or miserable-looking person present. Most of the men appeared to be grooms and coachmen. Among these occupants of the kitchen, the nursery, and the stable there were a few persons from the parlor...

There is a difference between Catholics and Protestants in this matter of praying. When a Protestant prays in public, he is apt to hide his face, and bend low in an awkward, uncomfortable attitude; and, when he would pray in private, he retires into some secret place, where, if any one should catch him at it, he would blush like a guilty thing. It is not so with our Roman Catholic brethren. They kneel, it is true, but the body above the knees is bolt upright, and the face is never hidden; and, as if this were not enough, they make certain movements of the hand which distinctly announce their purpose to every beholder...

On this cold morning the priest was not as punctual as the people. The congregation continued to increase till ten minutes past six; after which no sound was heard but the coughing of the chilled worshippers. It was not till seventeen minutes past six that the priest entered, accompanied by two slender, graceful boys, clad in long red robes, and walked to his place, and knelt before the altar. All present, except one poor heathen in the middle aisle, shuffled to their knees with a pleasant noise, and remained kneeling for some time. The silence was complete, and I waited to hear it broken by the sound of the priest's voice. But not a sound came from his lips. He rose, he knelt, he ascended the steps of the altar, he came down again, he turned his back to the people, he turned his face to them, he changed from one side of the altar to the other, he made various gestures with his hands, — but he uttered not an audible word. The two graceful lads in crimson garb moved about him, and performed the usual services, and the people sat, stood, knelt, bowed, and crossed themselves in accordance with the ritual. But still not a word was spoken. At the usual time the collection was taken, to which few gave more than a cent, but to which *every one* gave a cent. A little later, the priest uttered the only words that were audible during the whole service. Standing on the left side of the altar, he said, in an agreeable, educated voice: "The Society of the Holy Rosary will meet this afternoon after vespers. Prayers are requested for the repose of the souls of — "; then followed the names of three persons. The service was continued, and the silence was only broken again by the gong-like bell, which announced by a single stroke the most solemn acts of the mass, and which, toward the close of the service, summoned those to the altar who wished to commune. During the intense stillness which usually followed the sound of the bell, a low, eager whisper of prayer could occasionally be heard, and the whole assembly was lost in devotion. About twenty women and five men knelt round the altar to receive the communion. Soon after this had been administered some of the women began to hurry away, as if fearing the family at home might be ready for breakfast before breakfast would be ready for them. At ten minutes to seven the priest put on his black cap, and withdrew; and soon the congregation was in full retreat. But by this time another congregation was assembling for the seven-o'clock mass; the people were pouring in at every door, and hurrying along all the adjacent streets towards the church. Seven o'clock being a much more convenient time than six, the church is usually filled at that hour; as it is, also, at the nine-o'clock mass. At half past ten the grand mass of the day occurs, and no one who is in the habit of passing a Catholic church on Sunday mornings at that hour needs to be informed that the kneeling suppliants who cannot get in would make a tolerable congregation of themselves.

What an economy is this! The parish of St. Stephen's contains a Catholic population of twenty-five thousand, of whom twenty thousand, perhaps, are old enough and well enough to go to church. As the church will seat four thousand persons, all this multitude can hear mass every Sunday morning. As many as usually desire it can attend the vespers in the afternoon. The church, too, in the intervals of service, and during the week, stands hospitably open, and is usually fulfilling in some way the end of its erection. How different with our churches! There is St. George's, for example, the twin steeples of which are visible to the home-returning son of Gotham as soon as the Sound steamer has brought him past Blackwell's Island. In that stately edifice half a million dollars have been invested, and it is in use only four hours a week. No more... Our Roman Catholic brethren manage these things better. When *they* have invested half a million in a building, they put that building to a use which justifies and returns the expenditure. Even their grand cathedrals are good investments; since, besides being always open, always in use, always cheering and comforting their people, they are splendid illustrations of their religion to every passer-by, to every reader of books, and to every collector of engravings. Such edifices as St. Peter's, the cathedrals of Milan and Cologne, do actually cheer and exalt the solitary priest toiling on the outskirts of civilization. Lonely as he is, insignificant, perhaps despised and shunned, he feels that he has a property in those grandeurs, and that an indissoluble tie connects him with the system which created them, and which will one day erect a gorgeous temple upon the site of the shanty in which now he celebrates the rites of his church in the presence of a few railroad laborers.

While these successive multitudes have been gathering and dispersing something has been going on in the basement of St. Stephen's — a long, low room, extending from street to street, and fitted up for a children's chapel and Sunday-school room... [T]he energetic and truly catholic superintendent of St. Stephen's school, Mr. Thomas E. S. Dwyer, informed me, that, before beginning this school, he visited all the noted Sunday schools in New York, Protestant, Catholic, and Jewish, and endeavored to get from each whatever he found in it suitable to his purpose... At one end of this exceedingly long room is a small, plain altar, with the usual candles and other appurtenances; and on one side of the room, about midway, is a large cabinet organ, with an enclosure about it for the choir of children who chant the responses and psalms of the mass. On the walls between each window are the showy pictures usually found in Catholic institutions... When Mr. Dwyer began this school a few years ago, only two hundred children attended, — a mere handful in a Catholic parish, — but every teacher bound himself to visit each of his pupils once a month, and so endeavor to interest the people in the school. The effect was magical. Children came pouring in, until now the average attendance is two thousand, and there have been in the school at one session three thousand three hundred and forty...

Such are the exercises of a Catholic Sunday school: mass, thirty-five minutes; catechism, about the same time; singing, fifteen minutes; the Gospel of the day read; a prayer of five lines; to which is occasionally added a short address by the pastor...This Sunday school of our Roman Catholic brethren will doubtless improve when its zealous and amiable teachers have better facilities and a better school-room. It has already an excellent feature: this one session of an hour and a half is, at once, church and Sunday school; and nothing more is required of the children during all the rest of the day. There is no afternoon school, and the children are not expected nor advised to hear a second mass. Our Roman Catholic brethren never compel young children, over-schooled during the week, to attend Sunday school from nine to half past ten; to remain in church, understanding nothing of what is said and done there, until past twelve; and then, after dinner, to endure both school and church again, happy if they escape them in the evening...

Our Roman Catholic brethren are acquiring so great an estate in the United States, and acquiring it so rapidly, that it becomes a matter of public concern how they get it, what they do with it, and, especially what they *will* do with it by and by, when it shall have become the largest property held in the country by or for an organization. Other organizations usually live from hand to mouth; but, somehow, the Catholics always contrive to have a little money ahead, to invest for the future. The Catholic Church, seven tenths of whose members are exempt from the income tax because their income is under a thousand dollars a year, is a capitalist...There are spots in the Western country, over which the prairie winds now sweep without obstruction, that will one day be the sites of great cities. Our Roman Catholic brethren mark those spots, and construct maps upon which, not existing towns alone are indicated, but probable towns also...

Look at our island of Manhattan! Sixty-seven years ago there were but one or two small Catholic churches upon it. It was not until 1808 that there was such a personage as a Roman Catholic bishop of New York. Run over the diocese now, and what do we find? Churches, 88; chapels attached to institutions, 29; colleges and theological seminaries, 4; academies and select schools, 23; parochial schools, one to nearly every church; charitable asylums and hospitals, 11; religious communities of men, 6; of women, 10. But this enumeration, as every New-Yorker knows, conveys no idea of the facts. Everything which our Roman Catholic brethren buy or build is bought or built with two objects in view, — duration and growth. Hence massive structures, and plenty of land! Wherever on this island, or on the lovely waters near it, you observe a spot upon which nature and circumstances have assembled every charm and every advantage, there the foresight and enterprise of this wonderful organization have placed, or are placing something enormous and solid with a cross over it. The marble cathedral [of St. Patrick's] which is to contain ten thousand persons is going up on the precise spot on the Fifth Avenue which will be the very best for the purpose as long as the city stands. Yet, when that site was selected, several years ago, in the rocky wilds beyond the cattle-market, no one would have felt its value except a John Jacob Astor or a Roman Catholic Archbishop...

When Archbishop [John] Hughes made up his mind, about ten years ago, that the time had come for beginning a cathedral that would be worthy of the chief city of the Union, the debt upon the old [St. Patrick's] cathedral had not been extinguished, the cemetery fund was almost consumed in enlarging and improving the cemeteries themselves, and the archbishop was dependent for his mere maintenance upon the product of the tax upon the parishes. No matter; the time had come for beginning; and every New-Yorker now sees how perfectly the commencement of the enterprise was timed. But there was no money. If it had been a Protestant enterprise, this fact would have presented a slight impediment. It is only our Roman Catholic brethren who can undertake two-million-dollar cathedrals without having any money. The archbishop caused a circular letter to be written, announcing his design, and... raised three hundred thousand dollars, — enough to buy the land, lay the foundation, and carry up the walls a few feet. About the time the [Civil] war broke out[,] the money was gone, and it was highly convenient to stop. The orphans and the widows of the war were a heavy charge upon all the city parishes. The ordinary collections at Christmas and Easter (sacred to the orphan in all Catholic churches) were utterly insufficient, and the people were called upon for further aid, which of course they gave most liberally. It was obviously not a time to be building marble cathedrals for posterity, and so the walls were carefully boarded over. The war being ended, the new archbishop [John McCloskey] issued a requisition, calling upon each pastor of a parish for a contribution to the cathedral fund, and allowing him a certain time in which to collect it. Work upon the building has been resumed, and will probably go on until it is completed...

Atlantic Monthly 21 (April 1868): 432–51.

44. The Altar and Throne of St. Patrick's Cathedral, New York, 1877

Whereas mainline Protestant houses of worship tended to be constructed by and for the middle class, Catholic churches were often financed with the meager earnings of immigrants. That poor Catholics invested scarce resources for lavishly decorated churches puzzled, and sometimes outraged, social reformers. But art critics were another story. The inclusion of Catholic churches in architectural reviews reflected growing awareness that immigrants valued refinement and beauty as much, if not more, than their Protestant co-religionists.

IN the *Art Journal* for January of last year, we gave a description of the new St. Patrick's Cathedral in New York..., which is one of the most imposing church edifices in this country; and we now engrave the high altar and

6. Main altar, St. Patrick's Cathedral, New York. Although "the urgent demands of economy" forced architect James Renwick to scale back his original plans for the Gothic cathedral of St. Patrick's in New York, its construction symbolized the arrival of the immigrant church in America. St. Patrick's was begun in 1858 and dedicated on 25 May 1879. Its interior was critically acclaimed for inspiring "a sense of vast dimensions and of solemn magnificence." The steeples of the cathedral were finally completed in 1888. *Art Journal* (December 1877).

throne which are intended for the interior, after the designs of the architect, Mr. James Renwick. This work, like the cathedral, will be of grand proportions and equally magnificent in style. Some parts of the work have been executed in Rome, Italy, and others in St.-Brieuc, France. The high altar will be erected at the eastern end of the building, opposite the grand entrance, which is on Fifth Avenue. The design is very simple in outline, but exceptionally elaborate in detail. It will be elevated above the floor of the cathedral so that it can be seen from any part of the interior . . . The table, or altar proper, will be of pure white marble resting on columns, the shafts of which are of precious marbles, with white-marble bases and foliated capitals.

These columns, which are eight in number, divide the front into three large and four small niches. The centre niche will contain a sculpture in high-relief of "The Last Supper," and those on either hand [will contain sculptures of] . . . "The Passion of Christ" . . . Above and behind the altar, extending its entire width, are two marble steps richly inlaid with precious stones, and on these the candelabra, of gilt bronze, will stand . . . The tabernacle, which is three feet wide and six feet high, is made of Carrara marble inlaid with gems and adorned with exquisite Roman mosaics representing the "Crown of Thorns" and another sacred emblem. The door of the tabernacle is brass-bronze, fire-gilt. The columns which support the arch are of the richest marbles, which the arch itself is of white marble, inlaid with gems cut in facets, and on either side are marble figures of angels kneeling . . . The reredos, which is the *chef-d'oeuvre* of the design, is divided into five sections, having a central tower and spire, and two flanking towers and spires . . . A marble canopy covers the tabernacle, and has a rich tracery and a groined ceiling. Under this canopy will stand a magnificent crucifix, with the base resting upon the roof of the tabernacle. The second division or story of the central tower, directly over the canopy, . . . is supported by sixteen polished columns of coloured marbles, with bases and capitals of white marble . . . The finial supports the central cross which crowns the whole design. The cross will be a magnificent one of bronze gilt, with a centre consisting of a single large crystal cut in facets . . . The niches will contain pedestals supporting statues: on the gospel side, St. Peter; and on the epistle side, St. Paul. These two statues will be nearly six feet in height . . . The spires of the two corner towers are twelve feet six inches high. They are of rich pierced tracery, with crockets and finials of foliage, and correspond in elegance of design and harmony with the ornamental carved work of the central towers . . .

Between the central and side towers are six niches . . . [which] will contain six angels bearing shields, on which are sculptured in relief the emblems of the Passion of Our Saviour. These statues are all of white marble, and life-size . . .

The throne, for the cardinal archbishop, is carved of French walnut, and the work was executed by M. Paul Guibé, of St.-Brieuc. The design, which is by Mr. Renwick, consists of the seat, over which there is a square canopy supported on columns with carved capitals. The back of the seat is ornamented above the cushion with a traceried gablet in which are carved the arms of the diocese of New York... The whole is richly decorated with gilding and polychrome-work... M. Paul Guibé, of St.-Brieuc, is also the sculptor of the statuary of the reredos and rich traceried work of the niches and spires. The art-work for the altar proper, or table on which the reredos stands, was done by the sculptor Carimini, of Rome.

The workmen are now putting the finishing touches to the interior of the structure... The floor of the cathedral is laid with tiles, and the woodwork of the pews is of butternut, oiled. The sidewalls are to be coloured in imitation of various marbles, and the interstices of the richly-groined arches of the roof have been painted to resemble Caen-stone. The grand clustered columns which spring from the floor and support the roof are of white marble, and richly sculptured at their bases and capitals.

> "The Altar and Throne of St. Patrick's Cathedral, New York," *Art Journal*
> (December 1877).

45. Dedication of St. Patrick's Cathedral, New York, 1879

Nowhere was the changing image of the immigrant Catholic Church more apparent than in news coverage of the construction of St. Patrick's Cathedral on Fifth Avenue in New York City. The cathedral was designed by James Renwick, the foremost Gothic architect in America. In its account of the cornerstone laying in 1858, the New York Times *predicted that St. Patrick's "will have no parallel on this continent." Archbishop John Hughes took the opportunity to praise the cathedral as a visible reminder of the Irish diaspora which had brought learning and piety "through all the civilized countries of the world," and he reminded New Yorkers that St. Patrick's would be "a great work for the poor," providing honest employment for immigrant laborers. As a result of the outbreak of the Civil War, nearly two decades passed before St. Patrick's was officially dedicated. Its steeples were completed in 1888, and the edifice was consecrated in 1910, after its debt was paid off.*

Special Telegram

NEW YORK, May 25. — St. Patrick's cathedral, the magnificent temple which Catholic faith has erected in this city, was dedicated to-day with such religious pomp and circumstances as has never before been witnessed in this country. In this grand edifice the solemn and gorgeous ceremonies of the ancient church will hereafter be celebrated with a pomp to which we are unaccustomed in America. The corner-stone of St. Patrick's was laid in 1858, over twenty years ago, by Archbishop [John] Hughes. The eminent prelate believed that great advantages would accrue to his church by the building of a cathedral in New York which would have undisputed preeminence among the Roman Catholic churches of the country... It is said that Archbishop Hughes first insisted that the cathedral should EXCEED ALL OTHER CHURCHES in one dimension at least — in its length, its breadth, its height, or in the height of the spires. His wish, however, was not gratified in this, and, though a very large church for the United States, it is not large in comparison with the great European cathedrals. Yet the main wish of that ambitious ecclesiastic has been accomplished. The new cathedral[,]...most eligibly situated on Fifth avenue, imposing in its proportions, grand and noble in its interior, harmonious, symmetrical and magnificent in its adornings, will be a main object of interest in the city, and will attract to its ceremonies vast numbers of people not accustomed to them. When its lofty towers are built, it will be the grandest ornament of Fifth avenue, and the proudest ecclesiastical edifice in the country.

The building of St. Patrick's has gone on slowly and with intermissions, according as the contributions of the faithful came into its treasury. The structure has been built out of the FREE-WILL OFFERINGS of pious Catholics, rivaling in their zeal the religious devotion of the middle ages...The money used to complete the building was obtained at the great fair which was in progress for a month at the cathedral last winter. This enterprise was conceived on a scale only exceeded by the marvelous sanitary fair during the [Civil] war. It was visited by about three hundred thousand people and the proceeds over and above all expenses were nearly $200,000. Thus, through all the long course of its upbuilding, the grandest church structure in this country has risen inch by inch as the humble offerings of the millions have given it strength to grow...

THE HIGH ALTAR, with its white marble canopies and very generally subdued tones of very rich marbles[,] is not over conspicuous when seen from the nave owing to the great body of deeply-tinted glass above the reredos line...A curious feature in connection with the great foliated capitals was the large number of sparrows which have found building room there. These free ramblers of the air have discovered in the cathedral a convenient breeding spot, and for years past have made their nests there. During the whole service to-day they withdrew incessantly and shot from and to their perches through the open windows...

THE SERMON, by Bishop [John J.] Ryan, who spoke vigorously and extemporaneously for nearly two hours[,]...was a plea for the building of magnificent palaces in which to worship God, and for the conservation of all the venerable forms and symbols that are a part of the Roman Catholic worship...

"A Hallowed House: Dedication of St. Patrick's Cathedral, New York, on Yesterday, with Imposing Ceremonies," *Chicago Times*, 26 May 1879.

46. Confirmation Day Parade, Holy Family Parish, Chicago, 1895

In addition to providing widespread coverage of church dedications, national newspapers reflected a deep fascination with the sacramental dimension of immigrant Catholicism. Beyond describing the crowds that gathered for Sunday Mass and weekday novenas and devotions in urban neighborhoods, the press regularly ran features on the participation of children in processions connected with First Communion and Confirmation. Significantly, while editorials routinely excoriated immigrants as a threat to American democracy, news coverage praised Catholic processions as models of order, decorum, and stability.

Yesterday was the annual confirmation day in the great Holy Family parish on the West Side. The day was marked as it has been annually for many years by a parade of all the societies connected with the parish. The procession, in which over thirty organizations marched, was reviewed by Archbishop P. A. Feehan, who presided in the service of confirmation in the Holy Family Church at west Twelfth [Roosevelt Road] and May streets.

The procession started from the Sodality Hall at Eleventh and May streets, and was under the direction of John F. O'Brien, who was chief marshal. He had for aids Thomas Conley, Daniel F. Ryan, James Cleary, P. J. Kennedy, Major Ford, M. Heeney, John J. Lawler, Anthony Bendel, Robert Dugan, John Byrne, John McGraw, W. J. Maloney, John Ryan, P. McGarry, William Sullivan, and Robert Guthrie. All along the line of march thousands of spectators lined the streets to view the parade. One of the chief features of the procession was the band of 800 girls and boys who were to be confirmed and made members of the church. The 500 girls of the confirmation class walked in fours; all clad in white, and beside them, two abreast, walked the boys who were to take upon them their first vows in the church.

Escorted Archbishop Feehan

A platoon of police led the line, and the first organization in the column was the Married Men's Sodality of the parish. This organization numbers about 1,800, and the majority of the members were in line. The society presented a fine appearance. The next organization was the Young Men's Sodality, and after them came the juvenile societies of the parish, including in their membership boys and girls who are almost men and women, as well as little tots who marched proudly in gay uniforms. First of the juvenile band were the Emerald Cadets, preceded by their drum corps. These boys acted as an escort to the first communion boys and girls, who followed in the line directly after them. The crew of the Pinta, a corps of boy cadets in sailor uniforms of blue, attracted a good deal of attention from the spectators, and so did the Columbian Guards, a society of small boys, who were armed with spears. The route of the procession was along May street to Twelfth Street, Twelfth to Morgan, Morgan to Fourteenth Place, Fourteenth Place to Ashland Boulevard, Ashland Boulevard to Taylor, Taylor to May, May to Twelfth, and Twelfth to

7. Confirmation Day parade, Chicago. The annual Confirmation Day parades in Holy Family parish drew thousands of Chicagoans in the 1880s and 1890s. Regarded as public acts of faith — as well as models of order, decorum, and stability — these events strengthened the image of Irish Catholic immigrants as devout urban dwellers. Taken from *Holy Family Parish: Priests and People* (Chicago: Universal Press, 1923). Reproduced with permission of the Holy Family Preservation Society.

Blue Island avenue, where the line was broken up. At Ashland avenue and Taylor the procession was met by a carriage containing Archbishop Feehan and Father [James F. X.] Hoeffer, rector of St. Ignatius College. An escort was formed for the carriage of the Archbishop, and it preceded the procession for the remainder of the march. At the convent of the Sacred Heart on Taylor street, near Loomis, there was a halt while the sisters of the convent school paid their respects to the Archbishop. The latter was presented with a bouquet of beautiful flowers by the pupils of the convent. When the parade again reached May and Twelfth streets it was reviewed by Archbishop Feehan from the steps of St. Ignatius College.

Order of the Parade

The following was the order of the parade;

FIRST DIVISION

Platoon of police.
Patriotic Sons of Father Mathew.
Married Men's Sodality and band.
Young Men's Sodality and band.
Emerald Cadets. First communion boys and girls.

Young Crusaders. St. Joseph's Society.
Holy Family Society. Crew of the Pinta.
St. Joseph's Cadets. Columbian guards.
Temperance cadets. Sacred Heart Convent School.
St. Aloysius' School. St. Joseph's School.
St. Agnes' School. Guardian Angels' Cadets.
Ephpheta Deaf and Dumb School of St. Joseph's Home.

SECOND DIVISION

Father Mathew [Total Abstinence & Benevolent] Band. Father Mathew
    Cadets.
Father Mathew T. A. & B. Society. Annunciation Temperance Cadet
    Band.
Holy Family Cadets. Holy Family T. A. & B. Society.
Divisions 28, 1 and 7 of the [Ancient Order of Hibernians].

THIRD DIVISION

Catholic Order of Foresters. Division marshal, John J. Collins; aids,
    James J. Gillen and James Silk.
First Regiment [Catholic Order of Foresters] and band.
Holy Family Court No. 1.
St. Joseph Court No. 8.
St. Ignatius Court No. 18.
St. Aloysius Court No. 27.
St. Rose of Lima Court No. 70.
Oakley Court No. 128.
Sherman Court No. 224

The confirmation service took place at 4:30 in the afternoon, immediately
after the parade.

> "Their First Vows: Confirmation and Parade of Catholic Children, at Holy Family
> Church," *Chicago Daily Inter-Ocean*, 10 June 1895.

47. Italian Church Dedication, 1899

*Throughout the nineteenth century and well into the twentieth, ethnic compe-
tition continued to manifest itself in church-building. Italian Catholic immigrants
who had been relegated to the basements of Irish and German churches were
eager to establish parishes of their own, and they looked forward to the day
they could worship in structures that reflected and respected their ethnic origins. While newer Italian churches benefited from advances in architecture and
engineering, there was still room for conflict: the Irish firm that designed Holy
Guardian Angel, for example, added a Celtic cross! When it was struck by
lightning in 1904, Italian parishioners regarded it as providential because "they*

8. Holy Guardian Angel Church. Holy Guardian Angel Church, just east of Jane Addams's Hull-House settlement, grew out of a mission established by graduates of Sacred Heart Convent Academy. In addition to donating funds for a permanent church in 1899, the alumnae taught catechism to Italian immigrant children. By 1910, Holy Guardian Angel's Sunday school was one of the largest in the world. Located in the path of the Dan Ryan Expressway in 1959, the parish built a new combination church and school structure at 860 West Cabrini Street, but it was demolished in 1963 to make way for the University of Illinois at Chicago. Marquette University Archives. Reproduced with permission.

strenuously objected to its Celtic form as being more appropriate to adorn a Protestant rather than a Catholic temple."

THE Holy Guardian Angel Church, located on Forquer street, in the center of [Chicago's] West Side Italian colony, was dedicated last Sunday [26 November 1899] by His Grace, Archbishop [Patrick A.] Feehan.

The chancel was appropriately festooned with palms and flowers. The walls of the sacred edifice were adorned with the banners of the following Italian societies: St. Michael the Archangel, Italian Court of Foresters of St. Frances of Paul, Madonna of Monte Viggiano, Lady of Mt. Carmel, Assumption and Sorrowful Mother of Mutual Help.

At the conclusion of the dedication ceremonies, the pastor, Dr. E. M. Dunne, sang High Mass, at which Rev. Frs. Ponziglioni and Bergeron assisted

9. First Communion, St. Philip Benizi, Chicago. Although the Italian neighborhood around St. Philip Benizi Church was widely regarded as a slum by housing reformers, sacramental events such as First Communion provided visible proof that immigrants valued beauty and refinement, from the white dresses and suits worn by the children to the elaborately decorated banners of the parish societies. The statue of the Blessed Virgin Mary was carried in procession around the neighborhood, underscoring the deep connection between sacred and profane space. Servite Provincial Archives, Chicago, Papers of Fr. Luigi Giambastiani, O.S.M., folder 313. Reproduced with permission.

in the sanctuary. The venerable Jesuit missionary Father [Paul] Ponziglioni, delivered the sermon with his usual eloquence.

After the Communion His Grace made a brief address to the congregation. In the course of his remarks the Archbishop highly complimented the zeal of the pastor and said that in architectural beauty the Guardian Angel Church compared favorably with many of the fine churches throughout the city. He strenuously exhorted the people to obey their pastor and to show appreciation of his work among them by giving him their generous support and co-operation.

Mass is said every week day morning at 8 o'clock. On Sundays and holidays the first Mass is at 8 o'clock and the last at 9:15, after which the Sunday school classes are held. Vespers and Benediction Sunday afternoon at 3 o'clock. A

10. First Communion certificate, 1911. By the turn of the twentieth century, ornate churches had become a distinctive element of Catholic identity as well as material culture. Margaret Pelosi's 1911 Holy Communion certificate features the magnificent barrel-vaulted coffered ceiling of Our Lady of Sorrows Church (patterned after the Sistine Chapel in the Vatican) and the carrara marble altar donated by the women of this Chicago "boulevard" parish. Servite Provincial Archives, Chicago. Reproduced with permission.

sewing circle for the Italian girls is held every Saturday afternoon at 2 o'clock in the Guardian Angel schoolhouse...

The new Church of the Guardian Angels is designed in a very simple but highly effective Romanesque style, and though evidently with a strict view to economy, its total cost being only about $15,000. It is so effective, especially in its interior treatment, as to call for the emphatic approval of the Most Reverend Archbishop and the vestry clergy and laity, who freely expressed their pleasure and surprise that such beauty and grace of interior and exterior could be accomplished with such modest outlay.

The dimensions are: Extreme outside length, 105 feet; extreme width, 42 feet. The front elevation is of extreme dignity and simplicity. Conspicuous almost by the absence of the customary tower, but with a gable rising to a height of sixty feet, flanked by graceful buttresses and pinnacles, and adorned by a group of three gable windows and a niche, which is to receive a figure of the Guardian Angel, one does not desire the presence of a tower, but rather rejoices in the ease and beauty of the simple design.

The interior, however, is a revelation to the visitor in its impressiveness. Here the architects [James J. Egan and Charles H. Prindeville] have also, by a departure from customary ideas — at least in the American Catholic churches — produced, in a bold but simple semi-circular vaulted ceiling, an effect which takes the foreign-born citizens back to the remembrance of many more historic continental churches. The total height to the apex of the vault is about thirty-six feet, and the sanctuary is set apart and emphasized by a corresponding arch of fine proportion.

The material is brick and Bedford stone trimmings, a fine quality of red variegated bricks being used in the front.

"Italian Church Dedicated," *New World*, 2 December 1899.

48. Dedication of St. Josaphat's (Polish), Milwaukee, 1901

While many immigrant Polish parishes throughout the United States selected Renaissance styles of architecture for their permanent houses of worship, St. Josaphat in Milwaukee went even further, becoming a pioneer in the field of adaptive reuse. Not only was the Polish church constructed of material from the ruins of Chicago's federal customhouse and post office, but immigrant parishioners contributed their labor, hauling "five hundred carloads of marble, copper, wrought iron, carved stone, and paneled mahogany" sent by railroad to Milwaukee. The ornate dome of St. Josaphat's quickly became a distinguishing feature in a cityscape dominated by German Catholic edifices. Indeed, poet Charles H. Winke celebrated its location "on dull streets, mid huddled houses, where / The groping children of a martyred land / Make their new home..."

In the history of the world, there have never been any ceremonies in any society that excel in solemnity and grandeur those of the dedication yesterday

11. St. Josaphat's Basilica, Milwaukee. Milwaukee architect Erhard Brielmaier created the Polish church of St. Josaphat's in 1901 from the ruins of Chicago's federal custom-house and post office, and the edifice was officially declared a basilica in 1929. Owned and administered by the Conventual Franciscan Friars since 1910, St. Josaphat's is currently being restored to its former glory by a "broad-based coalition of business and civic leaders in the greater Milwaukee community." State Historical Society of Wisconsin WHi(X3)2628. Reproduced with permission.

of St. Josaphat's church on the South side. The robes of the clergymen, from the pope's representative, Cardinal [Sebastian] Martinelli, with his garments of white satin, embroidered with gold and colored silk, to the humblest priest in black and white and the acolytes of all sizes, in robes of different colors, each did his part with dignity and without hurry and impressed upon the 4,000 people in the church the fact that the dedication of a sacred house to the service of the Supreme Being is an affair of the utmost grandeur easily surpassing all occasions merely human and temporal.

Upon reflection comes the thought of sadness attendant upon everything earthly. The master mind, the priest to whose splendid intelligence this magnificent structure stands as a monument, is doomed to an early death. The keenness of his business ability and the foresight with which he grasped the opportunity, enabled him to purchase the material and erect this church at a cost of $175,000, while it is stated by authorities that it could not be erected in the ordinary way for $700,000. Father William Grutza secured the stone of the old federal building in Chicago for an amount which could have been duplicated five times over had he wished to sell the stone before making use of it.

The pastor is sick from overwork in looking after the details of so large an undertaking and has been at death's door for months and physicians say that he will never recover his health.

Procession around the Church

The procession made its way around the church and the central figure was Cardinal Martinelli. Following him were archbishops, bishops and priests and acolytes of all sizes. Another group was the Young Ladies' Sodality all dressed in white, and lastly came the banners of all the church societies, the whole procession forming one vast color scheme, pleasing to the eye and vastly impressive.

The street parade before the dedication was a large one. A company of Polish lancers escorted the cardinal from Archbishop [Frederick X.] Katzer's residence, and it was 10 o'clock when they arrived at Grove and Mitchell streets, where the civic and military societies were waiting. In the procession were the Kosciusko guards, four companies of Polish knights, twelve societies from St. Stanislaus parish, each with 100 men, a larger number of societies from St. Hyacinth's parish with 100 men in each company and about twelve societies from the parishes of St. Vincent and St. Cyril.

The services opened with a sermon by the Rev. Thomas Grembowski in Polish and he in conclusion paid a glowing tribute to the Rev. William Grutza, saying that the pastor had devoted the best years of his life and sacrificed his health in the cause. Archbishop Katzer then celebrated pontifical high mass, assisted by the Right Rev. Fox of Green Bay, the Rev. Henry Willmes, the Rev. Flazcek of Buffalo and Father Schinners, Archbishop Katzer's secretary.

It was nearly 2 o'clock when the mass was finished and Bishop Messmer, who was to speak in English, made only a few appropriate remarks on account of the length of the services. The papal blessing was then bestowed on the congregation by Archbishop Katzer and the church was dedicated by Cardinal Martinelli, assisted by the Very Rev. H. Gulski and the Very Rev. Abbelen. The ceremony consisted of a responsive service and the giving of the papal blessing in Latin by the Cardinal. The service was over and the people slowly filed out...

A sacred concert will be given at the Pabst theater tonight for the benefit of the Italian mission. There will be vocal and instrumental music by the best talent in the city. Cardinal Martinelli will attend and will be welcomed to this city by Mayor Rose and Judge Carpenter...

"St. Josaphat's Dedicated," *Milwaukee Journal*, 22 July 1901.

49. The Celtic Revival at St. Patrick's Church, Chicago, 1912

For many Irish immigrants to America, church-building was a relatively new activity. Although construction of masonry churches in Ireland began in earnest following Catholic emancipation in 1829, the boom was cut short by the Great Famine of the 1840s. For immigrants who had escaped hunger and eviction in Ireland, the construction of a permanent church represented faith and hope in the future. Despite the cholera epidemic of 1854, St. Patrick's, the "mother parish" of the Chicago Irish, forged ahead with plans for a brick Romanesque church, the first in the city when it was dedicated on Christmas Day 1856. By the time the steeples were raised in 1885, however, St. Patrick's had become the old neighborhood parish left behind by upwardly mobile Irish Catholics. But thanks to the genius of Thomas A. O'Shaughnessy (1870–1956), St. Patrick's took on new life and identity, becoming the best-known example of the Celtic Revival in art.

ST. PATRICK'S CHURCH, perhaps the oldest public edifice in Chicago, has become the corner stone of the renaissance of Irish art. When it is reopened on St. Patrick's day it will be the first church in ten centuries upon which the Irish method of church decoration has been attempted, and it will be the first time in the history of the United States that the ancient Catholic art of the Emerald Isle has been conferred upon a public place of worship.

St. Patrick's, built in the honor of Ireland's patron saint [in 1856], at the corner of Adams and Desplaines streets, was for many years a parish all but forgotten. Long ago it was the central Catholic church of the city, but the growth of Chicago gradually deprived it of that distinction. Now, with the modern development of the city, its location again has become central, and its position at the center of Catholic activities here induced the pastor, Rev. W. J. McNamee, to have the building remodeled and redecorated.

From the interlaced designs of the great bronze cross on the southern tower of the church to the last detail in the intricate iridescent mosaic in the win-

12. Celtic stencils, Old St. Patrick's, Chicago. Between 1912 and 1922, artist Thomas A. O'Shaughnessy transformed the interior of St. Patrick's — the oldest public build-ing in Chicago — into the finest example of Celtic Revival art in America, and perhaps Ireland. A cartoonist for the *Chicago Daily News*, O'Shaughnessy drew in-spiration from sketches he made of the *Book of Kells* in Trinity College, Dublin, as well as Louis Sullivan's ornament and Alphonse Mucha's Art Nouveau style of painting. O'Shaughnessy's Celtic stencils in the "mother parish" of the Chicago Irish have recently been uncovered and re-created. Photo by Joan Radtke. Reproduced with permission.

dows of the church, the new decorations are purely Irish. These windows are, perhaps, the most interesting feature...Under the direction of Thomas A. O'Shaughnessy, the artist, an art glass company has prepared the glasses from formulas prepared by him...in the manner of the enamels still to be seen on the most ancient jewels in the museums of Ireland.

The process by which the glass for these windows was made was originated by the artist. The direct light of the sun, even at midday, fails to weaken the decorative quality of the windows, while in the half light of the early morning and the late afternoon they are unusually luminous. The theme of these win-dows is drawn from the oldest school of art, while the windows themselves belong to the newest and most advanced school of window-making.

On St. Patrick's day the remodeled church will be reopened with one of the most impressive series of religious ceremonies in the history of Chicago. Many of the eminent clergymen of the city will participate. At the 11 o'clock mass Rev. H. P. Smyth of St. Mary's, Evanston, one of the most profound

13. St. Brigid window, Old St. Patrick's, Chicago. Throughout the nineteenth century, "Bridget the domestic" was a familiar figure of fun — and derision — in American journalism and drama. So persistent was the stereotype that Irish-American families refused to christen their daughters Bridget or call immigrant female relatives by their baptismal name. Artist Thomas A. O'Shaughnessy (1870–1956) restored Brigid to her rightful role as an educator and patron of the arts in this luminescent stained glass window in Old St. Patrick's, Chicago. Photo by Ellen Skerrett. Reproduced with permission.

Irish scholars of modern times, will preach a sermon rich with the research of a lifetime's study of the ecclesiastical history of Ireland.

"A Renaissance of Irish Art," *Chicago Record-Herald*, 3 March 1912.

50. Memorial to Irish Patriot Terence MacSwiney, 1920

One of the most powerful symbols of Irish Catholic identity and nationalism is the Great Faith window designed by artist Thomas A. O'Shaughnessy in 1920. It constitutes the first American memorial to Terence MacSwiney, the Lord Mayor of Cork who died in London's Brixton prison on 30 October 1920, following a seventy-four-day hunger strike. Here, in his own words, is O'Shaughnessy's artistic credo for the MacSwiney memorial window dedicated on 24 November 1920: "To the GLORY OF GOD and to the honor of Terence MacSwiney and of those men and women living and dead, who have served and who have suffered for the freedom of Ireland."

...Gaelic art is the mother of Christian art.

Irish culture, when released from bondage with the recognition of the Republic of Ireland, will cause Gaelic art to be again recognized in its preeminent fitness to express Christian idealism.

The story built into the window is a brief synopsis of the story of Ireland, from the glorious, happy past to the tragic, glorious present. In the center of the Rose design at the top of the window which typifies Heaven, is the all-seeing eye of God surrounded by symbols of the Trinity, and of Eternity, with insert panels representing the material universe.

To represent the holiness of Liberty, this panel is rendered in the colors of the Irish Republic. The green, white and orange of the Republic are complemented by the deep blue, crimson and purple of ancient Ireland.

The colors play from full chroma through tones and tints to neutral and to purity of almost invisible delicacy.

At the base of the window a half circle represents the Present. Arranged above this in the form of a Celtic Cross, are eight panels bearing historic scenes. The center panel of the Cross is devoted to the Immaculate Conception, as the inspiration of the Irish people. In the left cross arm St. Patrick is shown at the court of the King of Ireland. In the panel at the top of the cross is shown St. Bride, Patroness of Learning, Music and Art. In the right cross arm, St. Columcille teaching the English.

Below the Immaculate Conception panel, St. Brendan, missionary in the sixth century to what is now America.

Below this panel St. Columban, who in 613 A.D. established the first school of Modern Europe.

St. Firgil, seventh century, is shown expounding to the Pope the rotundity of the earth as taught in the Irish schools.

14. MacSwiney window, Old St. Patrick's, Chicago. In a radical departure from traditional stained glass art in Catholic churches, Thomas A. O'Shaughnessy's Great Faith window (1920) at Old St. Patrick's, Chicago, memorializes Terence MacSwiney as a modern-day martyr in the campaign for Irish freedom. The figure at the base of the window depicts the Lord Mayor of Cork who starved himself to death during a seventy-four-day hunger strike in London's Brixton prison. Mass gatherings throughout the United States denounced "English atrocities in Ireland" and urged President Woodrow Wilson to "fully recognize the new Irish republic without delay." Photo by Joan Radtke. Reproduced with permission.

Below this, Duns Scotus the Blessed, expounding the doctrine of the Immaculate Conception.

At the bottom of the Cross St. Malachy, who in the eleventh century predicted that in the twentieth century Ireland would again be free of the English invaders.

Beneath the Rose panel on either side at the top of the Cross in attitude of adoration is the form of an Angel of Faith, rendered in white and delicate tints of color.

Below the Cross arms on either side of an Angel of Hope, in green.

At the base of the Cross are angels of Charity rendered in orange. In each of these panels the angels are surrounded by symbols of the cardinal virtues.

In the center panel at the base of [the] window is shown the soul of Terence MacSwiney being borne to Heaven. Beneath him the palms of martyrdom; on either side the fires of trial and persecution. Above him the Cross of St. Bride, which typifies the ideal of the Irish people in their devotion to law, order and chivalry.

To the extreme right and left at [the] base of [the] window are shown the chaos brought upon the world by England's wars of conquest . . .

Joseph J. O'Shaughnessy. Printed with permission.

51. Eulogy for Terence MacSwiney, 1920

MacSwiney's death by starvation focused international attention on Ireland's campaign for independence from Britain. Irish Americans honored his memory with "monster" demonstrations in New York, Boston, Philadelphia, Washington, D.C., Chicago, and San Francisco. Archbishop George W. Mundelein (1872–1939), a fifth-generation German American who had grown up in St. Nicholas parish on the lower East Side of Manhattan, was well known for his views on the Americanization of immigrants and his vigorous support of the Liberty Loan campaign during World War I. But as his eulogy for MacSwiney makes clear, Mundelein also understood and sympathized with Irish Americans who felt betrayed by the League of Nations.

This is not the time nor the place to discuss a political problem, nor is the archbishop the one to cast the seed of dissension in the hearts of his people in times as troubled as are our own. But it seems only just that some one should free the memory of the man we are here to honor to-day from cruel accusations that have been cast upon it, and to [lift] from the minds of our people any lingering doubts as to the manner of his death. My earliest recollections as a boy center about the description of an incident in the war of the Revolution when a young American soldier seeing his country's flag falling into the enemy's hands, determined to rescue it, and though it meant certain death, he climbed the hillside, while the enemy's fire fell all about and had just grasped the staff, when he fell, his heart pierced by a British bullet. And to-day after the lapse of years, with a man's fancy but with the same undimmed enthusiasm as then, I can see, side by side with this another picture, the youthful soldier of the Irish republic, lying dead on a bed in an English prison, his heart and body broken, but his stiffened fingers clasping the tricolor of the little nation, in whose birth struggle he had participated, and for whose cause he had not hesitated to give all he had.

When the great war was over and the Irish people found that they were betrayed, and that the promised freedom for little nations was to apply only to those that had been in subjection to the vanquished and not to those forcibly held by the victors, there seemed to remain for them only a hopeless, a desperate choice. Either they must drive the invader from their soil by force of arms or continue in the bondage in which they had been held for seven centuries. To have chosen the former would have been suicidal, for the now victorious enemy could have flooded the land with soldiery and literally blotted them out of existence. To have accepted the latter meant sinking out of sight forever, as a people, sacrificing the last chance that might ever come to them. In this difficult position, their leaders, a new type, young men, not politicians, idealists if you will, but with the high purpose of martyrs, with an absolute contempt for their own lives and safety where their unhappy country was concerned, they found another way. An entirely new method of warfare. They called it passive resistance, it meant leaving the enemy entirely unnoticed, his authority disregarded, refusing to submit to his courts of justice, accepting only the decrees of their own. Making their own laws, enforcing their own regulations, inflicting their own penalties. They knew the clash had to come. But this time it was to be a clash not of arms but of wills, with the world as an audience. Their army was to be one of sufferers, martyrs, not of murderers. It might cost their own lives, they were prepared to pay that price, if need be, for their country. The young Mayor of Cork was one of the first to be taken. His course lay plain before him; he completely ignored his captors, he would offer no defense, he refused to accept their sentence, he declined to consider himself their prisoner, he was a soldier of his country; he had done no wrong; he would force them to release him or to be accountable for his death. Was he right? We know from the lives of the Saints that many of them have done things prompted by love of God and under His inspiration that might not be acceptable under other circumstances. The General in battle will ruthlessly sacrifice the lives of men to gain prestige and honor for his country, which at other times would make him guilty of wholesale murder. At least this new type of warfare does not contemplate the forced drafting of unwilling combatants; it does not mean the slaughter of their adversaries, the death and mutilation of innocent men in the very prime of life; it does not mean the slow and painful starvation of countless babies, in order that their fathers' spirit may be broken; it means only the offering of their own lives, not because their lives are not dear to them, but because their country is dearer still. Who are we to sit in judgement! And surely such judgement comes with bad grace from people who have been guilty of these other things. But we are not here either to praise or to blame Terence MacSwiney. He has gone, — and he has gone without fear — before that Judge from Whom nothing is hidden, who reads the thoughts and the hearts of men. And we who have followed the seventy-five days of his purgatory here, who have witnessed his splendid courage, his deep piety, his unshaken confidence in God and his heroic love of country, we feel that his judgement will be a favorable one and his reward in eternity great. And while we honor to-day that starved and shrunken body, that clothed in its coarse brown Franciscan habit awaits the coming of the resurrection day, we ask the great Judge of the universe that He receive into His fatherly arms this noble soul, because he has shown the greatest love that man can show for that unhappy land, which has been the glory of the Church and the home of its teachers and its Saints. But even more, our thoughts go out and our hearts are raised for those at home, whose souls are caught in the grip of terror and haunted by the constant fear of persecution, of danger and death, and we ask the Merciful Christ that He may strengthen them in the struggle and guide their efforts in all things for God and for Ireland. And you of their race and of their blood, God forbid that in this hour of the motherland's greatest need you should fail her, that any spirit of dissension, any selfish interests, any lack of sympathy should part you. Rather may the unselfish, the persevering, the heroic example of this noble soldier of the republic inspire and quicken you that you too may be a source of encouragement and support to your brethren over there and a tower of strength to the cause. They tell us that it is always darkest just before dawn. Perhaps the time is near at hand when the darkness of the long night that now hangs over Ireland will be swept away, and a new day of liberty will dawn. It is our fond hope and our fervent prayer that then in peace and prosperity and freedom the Irish race may continue to be what in sorrow and suffering and bondage they have ever been, — the "natio fidelissima" — the most faithful nation of the Church.

> Transcript of Archbishop George W. Mundelein's eulogy for Terence MacSwiney, in Madaj Collection, 1920, M 46, Archdiocese of Chicago's Joseph Cardinal Bernardin Archives and Records Center. Printed with permission.

52. French Canadians Celebrate Church Reopening, Worcester, Massachusetts, 1996

Changing attitudes toward ethnic parishes were clearly revealed in the 1980s and 1990s when bishops announced the closing of churches and schools built during the heyday of the immigrant church. In light of declining congregations and a continued shortage of priests, diocesan planners regarded these closings or consolidations as evidence of good stewardship. The "view from the pew," however, was often one of bitterness and anger. In scenes reminiscent of the nineteenth-century trustee controversy, St. Joseph's parishioners in Worces-ter kept faith by challenging the authority of their bishop and occupying their shuttered church until they were evicted.

WORCESTER — They say faith can move mountains. In Worcester, it moved an entire city and its new bishop.

At 2 p.m. tomorrow, Bishop Daniel P. Reilly will celebrate a Mass in St. Joseph's Church — the first Mass offered in the church in more than four years. It will be a celebration of the faith of the people who refused to let the parish of their parents and grandparents die.

"The church is the people," Bishop Reilly said Thursday as volunteers buffed St. Joseph's marble floors and vacuumed its red carpets. "This is a great symbol of the faith of the people."

That faith was sorely tested after then Bishop Timothy J. Harrington or-dered the church — its congregation declining, its building needing repairs — closed in May 1992.

But the working-class parishioners refused to quit the 700–seat church. For 13 months, they occupied St. Joseph's.

On June 23, 1993, on order from Bishop Harrington, police evicted 50 of them from St. Joseph's. Several hundred others gathered on Hamilton Street that day, crying and praying and singing "Amazing Grace" as carpenters nailed plywood sheets over the 68–year old church's stained glass windows.

Worcester police, many with tears in their own eyes, led the parishioners out one by one, then locked the heavy oak doors and erected a metal fence across the front steps.

"I turned around and said, We'll be back," Jeanne Ducasse, 49, said as she stood once again in the church's foyer with a huge smile on her face. "This is a miracle, plain and simple. It's a joyous miracle."

The miracle seemed all but impossible after the order to close the church. As in many Roman Catholic parishes around the country, St. Joseph's membership was both aging and dwindling.

At the same time, the church, built by French-Canadian immigrants in 1928 and decorated with dozens of statues and intricate mosaics, needed more than $500,000 in repairs to its roof and brick exterior. Parishioners vowed to raise the money, but Bishop Harrington ordered St. Joseph's merged with Notre Dame des Canadiens, a downtown parish.

Some of the parishioners obeyed. Hundreds of others, however, refused, choosing to occupy the church instead. The dissidents, many of them in their 60s and 70s, took turns sleeping on St. Joseph's oak pews and on confessional benches. Without priests to say Mass, parishioners devised their own services. Finally, they were evicted.

Still the St. Joseph's faithful, as they had come to be known locally, refused

15. St. Joseph's Church, Worcester, Massachusetts. The battle to save St. Joseph's Church in Worcester, Massachusetts, from the wrecking ball pitted parishioners against their bishop in 1992. In addition to filing a civil suit in the state superior court, protesters occupied the Gothic church for more than a year until they were finally evicted. Designed for the French-Canadian parish by architect O. E. Nault and dedicated on 6 May 1928, St. Joseph's was reopened with great fanfare on 4 August 1996. Kenneth R. Desautels, *History of St. Joseph Parish, 1820–1992.* Reproduced with permission.

to quit. They wrote letters to the editor and letters to Rome. Every evening for more than two years, they held rosary services on the steep sidewalk.

"Rain, snow — nothing stopped us," said Terry Turgeon, a 52-year-old mother of four and a leader of the dissidents.

Bishop Harrington retired in December 1994 and was replaced by Bishop Reilly, formerly the bishop of Norwich, Conn. Immediately Bishop Reilly formed a reconciliation committee.

"The fact that this church means so much to these people meant so much to me," Bishop Reilly said. "I grew up in a parish, St. Michael's in Providence, that really gave me a great sense of solidity, an identity to my life and a sense of belonging."

So on Jan. 7, during a Mass said in the St. Joseph's gymnasium and attended by more than 500 people, Bishop Reilly announced that he would leave the reopening of St. Joseph's up to the pastor, Rev. Richard Roger, and the merged parishes, and that he would support parishioners if they could raise $600,000.

Turgeon said the Save St. Joseph's Committee now has $300,000 in the bank and more than $400,000 in pledges.

"I have $600 on my kitchen table right now," said Ron Fortin, 60, the former church custodian and another dissident leader. "People are elated at the decision the bishop made."

Then Bishop Reilly walked through the doors of the church on Thursday and exclaimed, "This is looking nice! This is going to be something special." Turgeon, Fortin and the other parishioners flocked around him.

Paul Della Valle, "Parish Faithful Set to Go Home," *Boston Globe,* 3 August 1996. Printed with permission.

53. Vietnamese Catholic Center, Santa Ana, California, 1996

For immigrant newcomers, the desire to construct a church of their own was as powerful in the 1990s as it had been two centuries earlier for French, Irish, and German Catholics. In much the same way that church-building created community for Catholic immigrants who settled in a largely Protestant-dominated nation, the construction of the Vietnamese Catholic Center announced that Vietnamese immigrants and their children had reached a critical mass and were also putting their imprint on the urban landscape.

When laying out the plan to build this center we had the Vietnamese culture in mind so that it might become an architectural landmark for visitors to see in the area. Messrs. Don Quang Tran and Lam Cuu Nguyen were the architects who responded to our wishes with their outstanding overall design. They have brought to the fore front both our Catholic and national traditions in a splendid way.

Christian Perspective

All the long and square lines of the structure speak of the correctness of conscience. The soaring bell tower with a cross on top reveals a life of sacrifice and the eventual resurrection. Two huge lateral buildings are like open hands to welcome everyone to the place. The square courtyard in the middle calls for a just and equitable way of living. The roofs curving up at extremities extol serenity and peace.

The three magnificent gates under the bell tower may entail multiple meanings. They represent three stages of our religious journey: past, present and future; or three cardinal Christian virtues: faith, hope and charity; or three phases of spiritual life: purgative, contemplative and unitive. They can also portray our philosophical concept of harmony between heaven, earth and man. The cross-shaped shrine tells of the love for the Holy Cross that our ancestors refused to step over on the way to their glorious martyrdom. The roofs over it represent the two-way love for God and neighbors. The entire

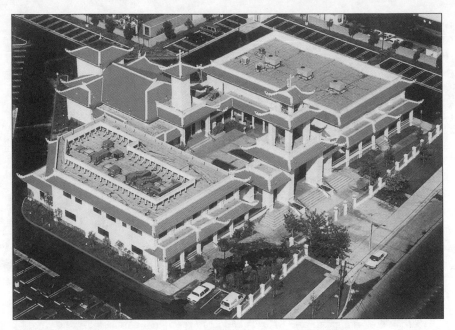

16. Vietnamese Catholic Center, Santa Ana, California. The architecture of the center shows graphically how Asian Catholics are determined to retain their identity while finding a home in a new land. It is at once Christian in its inspiration and national in its form. Reproduced with permission.

structure highlights the intertwined harmony between religion and life, and between heaven and earth.

National Identity

At first sight, visitors may only see it as an Asian architecture, but with deeper analysis they can discover finer Vietnamese lines in it. The slightly curved roofs are different from the Chinese, Japanese or Korean counterparts which are far more ornate and complex. The Vietnamese do not like complicated things and these slightly curved roofs suit their peaceful and simple way of living. The curved lines combined with the long and square ones reveal our philosophical concept of living with dignity and integrity in the world, and in complete harmony with the surrounding environments.

The portico with three gateways (Cong Tam Quan) instigates a triple look at the past, present and future phases of our lives. We look at the past so as to learn the courageous deeds of our ancestors. We build up the present to continue their benevolent works. We look forward to the future to make progress and leave something behind to posterity. In every religion we find the theory of wonderful trilogy. Christianity adores the Holy Spirit. Buddhism venerates Sacred Books of Thien Thai, Hoa Nghiem and Huyen Tu.

We also have favorite numbers for every aspect of our lives. The Vietnamese prefer odd numbers such as three, five, seven and nine. These are positive and powerful numbers which are believed to have caused national greatness in the past. It is not a coincidence that architects build three-story towers, five-room houses, [with] each room of the house having three decorative objects on the outside. We usually find five round shapes on the facade of a building, and five steps in front of the portico. The courtyard is divided into five different lots, and the columns of adjacent buildings form nine continuous spaces...

We hope the City of Santa Ana is pleased with the construction of the Vietnamese Catholic Center as it offers a different form of design which is aesthetically beautiful and pleasant to look at. The Diocese of Orange is also proud of this structure which carries a Vietnamese style and will remain a worthy contribution to the multiethnic legacy of the Catholic Church in America.

"Architectural Features of the Vietnamese Catholic Center, City of Santa Ana, California," in *Vietnamese Catholic Center* (Santa Ana, Calif., 1996). Printed with permission.

Part 3

DIVERSIFYING
THE IMMIGRANT CHURCH

Introduction

Beginning in the 1880s, massive migration from new sources in Europe and America began to diversify the American Catholic community's ethnic composition. At this time, adverse religious, economic, or political conditions in several countries influenced millions of Catholics to leave their homelands to migrate to the United States. These newcomers reshaped the ethnic mixture of the American Catholic community, just as the Irish and Germans had shaped the ethnic profile of the Catholic population since the middle nineteenth century. The impact of new groups did not diminish Irish and German influence since immigration from Ireland and German-speaking Europe continued through the early twentieth century.

The massive immigration from the 1880s to the 1920s, with some twenty-four million newcomers, especially from eastern and southern Europe, brought people to the United States with a range of religious backgrounds such as Jews and Orthodox and Protestant Christians. They along with Catholics diversified the languages, religious cultures, and social structures in communities across the country. The host population often had mixed feelings about the waves of newcomers, leading to a reprise of anti-Catholic and nativist movements. For the Catholic Church, new immigrant groups brought challenges to its leaders and the existing ecclesiastical arrangements.

The largest of the "new" Catholic groups, the Italians, came mostly from poverty-stricken southern Italy and Sicily, where, as tenant farmers, they had struggled to grow enough to eat. Heavy taxation and military service to support Italy's efforts to build up a large standing army were added burdens. In the 1880s, Italians began arriving in growing numbers, and, through the years 1900–1914, some three million came to the United States. Most immigrants were men who came for economic reasons, and many returned home after improving their economic status. Since few Italians, at least initially, intended to stay in the United States, they were not eager to build Italian parishes and communities. As the documents reveal, their encounters with the Catholic Church in the United States were fraught with misunderstandings.

Another large group of Catholics, the Poles, accounted for some two million immigrants arriving between 1870 and 1920. Poland had lost its independence in the 1790s to the territorial ambitions of its neighbors. Three large empires — Germany, Austria-Hungary, and Russia — occupied Polish-speaking areas. In the Kingdom of Prussia, the largest of the German Empire's twenty-six states, the chancellor, Prince Otto von Bismarck, imposed legal restrictions during the 1870s that subjected routine Catholic life to state control and expelled religious orders. This persecution, known as the *Kulturkampf,* brought Catholics in Prussia, including its substantial Polish minority, into protracted conflict with the state. Bismarck also promoted efforts to enforce official use of the German language in Polish-speaking areas. Decades of political oppression in Russian Poland alienated Catholic Poles, who desired the use of the Polish language in education and official business. Poles were better treated in Austria-Hungary with its largely Catholic political leadership. However, for Poles, in addition to political and religious reasons, economic factors entered into decisions to migrate as populations grew and economic growth did not improve their quality of life.

Other eastern Europeans immigrated to the United States in substantial but lesser numbers than the Poles for religious, economic, or political reasons. Closely connected to Poles were their neighbors, the Lithuanians, subjects of Russia, who accounted for some 300,000 immigrants prior to World War I. Also from Russia some 500,000 Ukrainian Catholics arrived. From the Austro-Hungarian Empire about 650,000 Slovaks immigrated, the largest Slavic group after the Poles. From the same empire, hundreds of thousands of Czechs, or Bohemians, as well as Hungarians, Croats, Ruthenians, and Slovenes came to America. Quite apart from eastern and southern Europe, Portuguese came to the United States, settling largely in New England.

Immigrants from other parts of North America chose the United States. Untold numbers of Mexican immigrants came north for economic betterment and, later, to avoid religious persecution. (Their religious experience is treated in another volume in this series.) French Canadians, mostly from Quebec, settled in northern New England to obtain employment in its industries. They added nearly one million to the U.S. Catholic population by 1920.

As revealed in the following documents, the roles of religion, the church, and community life differed among the "new" immigrant groups joining the U.S. Catholic community. These differences challenged the church's mostly Irish episcopal leaders, some of whom may well have thought that one type of Catholicism fits all. However, among such a large group as southern Italians, the formal worship and sacraments of organized Catholicism were to be kept at a distance, while a more popular style of Catholic practice was favored. A similar pattern could be found among Portuguese. On the other hand, Polish Catholics strongly adhered to the formal practices of their faith. Like the Germans, they also saw in their parishes a means of preserving language and culture. Though fervent supporters of Catholicism, Poles also had strong views concerning lay initiative in parish life that embroiled them in conflicts with American bishops. French Canadians avidly supported their national parishes for both religious and cultural reasons in a manner similar to Poles and Germans.

These ethnic groups expanded the American Catholic community with a rich diversity unlike the Catholic populations of many other countries. The size and diversity of these groups led to the undoing of virtually open immigration to the United States. By the 1920s, the American public resisted high levels of immigration and supported federal legislation enacted to restrict the flow of immigrants.

The Polish

54. Panna Maria, Texas, 1866–70

Polish immigrants settled predominantly in urban areas, but the first Polish settlement in the United States began in 1854 at rural Panna Maria (Village of Our Lady), Texas. In 1866, Polish-born Father Adolf Bakanowski of the Polish religious order the Congregation of the Resurrection was assigned to the pastoral care of the Poles in Texas, remaining there until 1870, when he went to the larger Polish community in Chicago. The following excerpt suggests the Texas experience was not a happy one for the Poles.

Adolf Bakanowski, C.R., "My Memoirs—Texas Sojourn (1866–1870)," translated by Marion Moore Coleman

... The beginnings of Polish colonization in Texas were, in truth, lamentable. What had prompted the people to leave the homeland and emigrate to America was the urging ... of a Franciscan, Father Leopold Moczygemba. His superior in the Order had sent him to Texas on a German mission and there he conceived the idea of colonizing this wild country with Poles. So about two hundred families from Upper Silesia, at his prompting, left their native farms and hastened across the Atlantic to a land which they had been promised was flowing with milk and honey.

How great was their disillusion when, after a hard and dangerous journey, they discovered they had been betrayed. To turn around and go back was out of the question ... They had to remain where they were, and endure every kind of misery that bore down on them ... [Bakanowski describes their hard life.]

That is the unpleasant side of their life. But along with this, there was, in the realm of morals, a good side. For one thing, since they did not know the language, they were forced, by the strange and barbarous customs of the southern Americans, to get along together in harmony and to achieve within their own community Christian solidarity. This made it easier later on to establish a model parish organization. The want they suffered, the poverty, the persecution to which they were exposed by the Americans, all these contributed to making them cling to their own Polish manners and customs, and especially to the faith they had brought with them in their hearts from the old country...

When they [southerners] saw a Pole without knowledge of the language, a peasant with no education, these southerners looked upon him as they did upon the blacks, and felt they had the same right to deny him his human rights as they did the blacks...

During those wretched years the settlers had no resident priest. Barely once every year some Catholic chaplain would put in an appearance, but he would be a foreigner, and unable to communicate with the people...

Quickly upon our [the Resurrectionists'] arrival [in 1866] we set to work organizing the parish and getting it in operation. I called all the farmers together for a meeting and we settled many matters: the tax to be levied for our maintenance, the fee to be charged for each service, burial fees, etc. We also arranged for putting the church in order as well as for building a rectory and school. Everything was agreed upon harmoniously, and at once we all set to work. The people were willing to follow my advice and were full of piety. They loved us. It was agreed that without my consent no one, for example, would conduct any festivities in his own home, and that every social gathering with music must not only have my permission beforehand, but must end at a certain time, generally midnight, a rule that was conscientiously enforced...

We organized in the parish the Brotherhood of the Holy Rosary, a separate group for men and one for women. Through the instrumentality of the Living Rosary we organized the parish in accordance with instructions received from Father [Piotr] Semenenko [one of the founders of the Congregation of the Resurrection]... Around the church we built a wooden fence so that we could hold processions inside it... In the churchyard, in front of the church, there was a Crucifix. Certain of our people, being very devout, as they prepared to leave the homeland, brought with them a figure of the Christ, and this we placed on a cross in the churchyard. Everyone who entered the church would generally pause to say a prayer before it, in memory of the homeland. For each and everyone it was a reminder of home, and more than one parishioner here poured out his yearning for the old country in a flood of tears. Or would fortify himself here to endure the strangeness of the new country, so different in spirit from the old. Here everyone felt himself a brother or sister of all, bound together by a common tie of suffering in a foreign country. One woman, her mind confused by longing for the homeland, knelt one day to weep before the Crucifix. She noticed that, like herself, the figure of Christ also had his head bowed in the direction of the faraway land from which she had come, and she cried aloud, "Oh, Lord Jesus! I see that you too long for the old country. You too have your poor head turned toward Europe!" ...

Polish American Studies 25, no. 2 (July–December 1968): 112–14, 121–22. Reprinted from *PAS* with the permission of the Polish American Historical Association.

55. Thomas and Znaniecki on the Polish Parish, ca. 1918

The following selection is taken from the monumental five-volume study The Polish Peasant in Europe and America, *the work of University of Chicago sociologist William I. Thomas and Polish philosopher and activist Florian Znaniecki, published from 1918 to 1920. The two examined the Polish community on both sides of the Atlantic. The following selection portrays the importance of the Catholic parish to the Polish immigrant community.*

[T]he Polish-American parish is much more than a religious association for common worship under the leadership of a priest. The unique power of the parish in Polish-American life, [is] much greater than in even the most conservative peasant communities in Poland... The parish is, indeed, simply the old primary community, reorganized and concentrated. In its concrete totality it is a substitute for both the narrower but more coherent village-group and the wider but more diffuse and vaguely defined *okolica*. In its institutional organization it performs the functions which in Poland are fulfilled by both the parish and the commune...

Its religious character is, of course, important in itself since there is a certain minimum of religious ceremonies — christenings, weddings, funerals — which are considered absolutely indispensable even by the least religious among the immigrants... The majority consider the Sunday service — at least the mass — and even more the Easter confession as also essential. But all these purely religious needs could be satisfied almost as well and at less expense by joining the local Irish-American church with an occasional visit from a Polish priest for confession and a sermon... If the Poles with few exceptions refuse to join Irish-American parishes it is because what the Polish colony really wishes in establishing a parish is not merely religious services but a community center of its own...

[I]t is clear that the Irish-American church, though on the religious side its organization is similar, can never become for the Polish community anything more than a religious institution; its framework cannot be successfully utilized by the Poles for other social purposes, since they do not feel "at home" in a parish whose prevalent language and mores are different... The parish is not "their own" product, they have less control over its management than over that of a Polish parish which they have founded by free cooperation...

William I. Thomas and Florian Znaniecki, *The Polish Peasant in Europe and America* (New York: Dover Publications, 1918–20), 2:1523–26.

56. St. Stanislaus Kostka, Chicago, 1917

As with other immigrant groups, Poles asserted the right to have their own national parishes to preserve their language and faith. When large-scale immigration from Poland increased after 1870, Chicago emerged as the largest center of Polish settlement in the United States, and the Polish national parish there, St. Stanislaus Kostka, became the country's largest Polish parish, possibly the largest Catholic parish in the world, claiming more than fifty thousand parishioners. Though Polish Catholics held the pastor in high regard, Polish laymen could become very aggressive when their wishes were ignored. The following excerpt from St. Stanislaus's fiftieth-anniversary history reflects the importance of the parish to the community, but also reflects the violent side of Polish Catholic life.

...The time about which we are speaking was the year 1867. The settlement counted about 150 families (mostly from Silesia) when they finally began to think about buying land for a church of their own...Four lots were bought at the corner of Noble and Bradley Streets...for $1,700. The place was then quite isolated...but since some decision had to be taken in order to establish at last the much desired parish,...the construction of the church was started in September, 1869...The first floor was designed for school rooms and had a hall for meetings. On the second floor was the church. The entire cost of the building was $6,885...

Priest Jozef Juszkiewicz was appointed the first rector of the parish...In 1870 Priest Adolf Bakanowski...came to Chicago...The growth of the parish promised to be quite good. Unhappily, for various reasons dissatisfaction and misunderstandings arose until finally the parish stood in open opposition to its rector...The parishioners reproached the priest with insufficient care for the parish, which was undeveloped and poor, and finally went to Priest Bakanowski eagerly petitioning him to become their rector...Priest Bakanowski refused...

Meanwhile among the Polonia disorders continued and finally the excitement reached a point where it nearly ended fatally. One night 6 masked men rang the doorbell of Priest Juszkiewicz and when he opened the door [they] beat him severely, threatening him with death if he did not leave the parish...Finally Priest Juszkiewicz left the parish...

St. Stanislaus Kostka Parish, Chicago, *Album Pamiatkowe z Okazyi Jubileuszu Parafii Sw. Stanislawa K.* (Memorial album of the golden jubilee of the parish of St. Stanislaus Kostka) (Chicago, 1917); reprinted in William I. Thomas and Florian Znaniecki, *The Polish Peasant in Europe and America* (New York: Dover Publications, 1918–20), 2:1550–51.

57. Riot in Bay City, Michigan, 1897

Violence was not unusual in hotly contested parish disputes. The following news report of 1897 tells of the troubles of the Polish parish of Bay City, Michigan, in the Diocese of Grand Rapids. The dispute was "over the ownership of parish property."

BIG RIOT: Bay City Poles Stormed the Rectory: Father Bogacki Had to Fly for His Life: One Man Shot and Cannot Recover: Detective Jailed for the Shooting

Bay City, Mich., Jan. 5 — The anti-Bogacki faction of St. Stanislaus church attacked the parsonage at 10:30 this morning and stormed it for over an hour. All the windows were broken and the doors were battered down. The entire police force were called, but were powerless to quiet the mob.

At 3:30 Father Bogacki and his special guard, James Fitzgerald[,] surrendered. The priest was driven to Fr. Rafter's house and the police took possession of the house and placed it in charge of a squad of police. The safe was opened and the disputed books taken to headquarters.

The riot was the result of last night's meeting. The Poles say Fr. Bogacki must go. The rioting mob was fully 1,000 strong. Over 100 shots were fired and many were injured.

James Yachomovich was shot in the body, and will not recover.

Detective Fitzgerald has been arrested, and is in jail for firing the shot.

The police were powerless to protect the priest or property. The mayor refused to call out the militia and says the church must settle the trouble. The dissension has existed since May 1895 and was submitted to [Archbishop Sebastiano] Martinell[i, the apostolic delegate to the United States,] a few weeks ago.

The funeral episode yesterday started it anew. Now the angry Poles say Fr. Bogacki will not be tolerated under any conditions.

Detroit Evening News, 5 January 1897.

58. Zuaves of St. Stanislaus Kostka, 1916

The Polish national parish existed in part to preserve the Polish heritage of the people. The following excerpt, from the fiftieth anniversary booklet of St. Stanislaus Kostka, depicts an honor guard expressly developed to preserve the traditions for the second generation, that is, the children.

Zuaves of St. Stanislaw Kostka. The Zuaves [founded 1915]... wear uniforms, helmets, and swords on the model of the Papal Guard...[The Zuaves are present at all major parish events.] The Zuaves are composed of 30 members chosen from the Society of Altar-boys... They are sons of parents who have belonged to the parish for many years and have been educated in the parochial school. They are obliged to shine as models of devotion, to partake regularly of the Holy Sacraments and thereby to be good sons of their dear parents, to know the history of their ancestors, the great men of Poland, to talk Polish among themselves and at home. In a word, the Zuaves are expected to be the guardians of everything that is divine and Polish in order to grow to be real Polish patriots and defenders of the Christian faith...

William I. Thomas and Florian Znaniecki, *The Polish Peasant in Europe and America* (New York: Dover Publications, 1918–20), 2:1557–58.

59. Instructions to Polish Catholics, Maspeth, New York, 1913

In 1913, a group of Polish Catholics in Maspeth, Queens, New York, broke off from St. Adalbert's Parish (also a Polish parish) in neighboring Elmhurst to establish their own local Polish parish. The following is the memorial booklet published at the dedication of the new church in 1913. The booklet is not merely celebratory — special advice and words of caution are directed at the Polish parishioners. Several of the instructions indicate a working-class congregation, perhaps with a peasant background. Again, the importance of the Polish language is stressed.

TAKE NOTE

Don't think you are a member of the parish if you don't pay your dues, which are $8 per year. You have to have a parish registration book in order to be able to use the priests' services such as blessings for the sick, marriage, or christening...

What Every Christian-Catholic Should Remember

 1. Attend Mass on Sundays and holydays.

 2. Don't be late for Mass...

 5. Don't imagine the homily...[is] only for women...

 8. Don't talk in church.

 9. Don't leave the church during the homily.

10. Don't spit on the church floor.

11. Don't think the holy water font is a sink (some people actually wash their hands in it)!...

17. Don't pass by the church without visiting the Blessed Sacrament.

20. Don't close your eyes or turn your head during collection time.

22. Don't forget to pay your yearly dues to the church.

25. Don't think that frequent confession and communion are harmful.

27. Don't think that public schools are better than Catholic schools.

31. Don't send your children to non-Catholic schools.

32. Don't forget about the big debt our church has.

33. Don't forget that we should try to organize our own school.

38. Don't marry a person of a different religion.

39. Don't forget that marriage in front of a [Protestant] pastor means excommunication.

44. Don't use other [i.e., non-Polish] languages in your church or around the church building.

Our Organizations

The organizations of Holy Cross Church have certain goals, ... duty to one's neighbor, God's glory, and mutual support derived from the love and the preservation of our native language ... It is not our business to check if associations carry on their duties, ... but we have to report an unpleasant fact: in regards to the preservation of our fathers' language, there is still need of more work. [We need] less mixing of this country's language.

A Few Notes about Our Native Language

We don't think we are out of line if we speak out about preservation of our language ... Ignoring our native language and denying our nationality must bring on our ethnic group indifferentism ... Don't expect respect towards your beliefs from members of this society if you don't respect your own beliefs and traditions of your fathers. Since Poland lost its political existence, our only heritage is our faith, language, memory of past battles and martyrdom. The nation is still fighting against its oppressors by protecting these virtues, which are impossible to destroy ... Sons of fathers who escaped from persecution and brought the faith, language, and their treasures here too quickly forget their ancestors and very rarely use the Polish language. A false shame drives some people to deny their native language and traditions and to imitate strange customs ... It is easy to put together a need and a duty: a need of learning the English language and the duty of preserving our own language. Polish schools and churches can carry on this mission.

> *Pamiatka Poswiecenia Kosciola SW. KRZYZA* (Memorial on the blessing of Holy Cross Church), trans. Monika Pochanke-Smith (Maspeth, N.Y., 1913).

60. Waclaw Kruszka on the Polish School, 1905–8

The Polish school was the crucial institution in preserving the Polish faith and traditions. The following two texts stress its importance in maintaining Polish identity. The first is from Father Waclaw Kruszka's monumental Historya Polska w Ameryce *(A History of the Poles in America), consisting of thirteen volumes, with the first published in 1905 (though parts appeared earlier in serial form in newspapers) and the last published in 1908. The following text is taken from a recent translation by Krystyna Jankowski published by Catholic University of America Press and is part of an ambitious project to translate all thirteen volumes.*

From Chapter 6: "History of the Polish Education System in America"

The Polish school stands right next to the church in importance in America. In the full sense of the word, it is the foundation of the Polish church abroad. Without a Polish school, the Polish church, if it is to remain Catholic, will certainly become Irish, English, and "American." The Polish churches, where the Poles so often hear the word of God in their native language, are citadels of patriotism; arks and vessels that protect the Polish people in exile from the flood of the deluge of denationalization and foreigness. But the foundations of these citadels, the hulls of these arks and vessels, are the Polish schools! Without them, the Polish church would sink like a bottomless vessel in a sea of Anglo-Americanism. Polish schools are the best sources and propagators of Polish nationality and patriotism on the foreign American soil. Here, in these Polish parochial schools, not only do our children learn that which is offered in "public" ... schools — that is to read, write, and count — but they also learn faith in God and love for our homeland — Poland. In the other schools our Polish children would hear about Poland only as much as, or even less than, they might hear about the wild tribes of Australia or distant islands.

Our people in America grasped and understood the importance of a Polish school quite early. Organizing themselves into a parish, they would establish a school simultaneously with, and often even before, building a church...

Waclaw Kruszka, *A History of the Poles in America to 1908,* trans. Krystyna Jankowski, ed. James S. Pula (Washington, D.C.: Catholic University of America Press, 1993), pt. 1, 110–11. Printed with permission.

61. Polish Clergy on the Polish School, 1920

In 1920, the General Union of Polish Clergy in the United States submitted a long memorial to the Holy See complaining about the treatment of Polish-American Catholics by the American hierarchy (see also document 67). The memorial also extolled Polish achievements. The following excerpt appeared in the section of the memorial entitled "The Present Situation" and told of the many sacrifices made by the Polish immigrant to support the Catholic school. It also paid tribute to the efforts of the Polish teaching Sisters, without which the schools could not have existed, or at least as inexpensively. By 1920, about two-thirds of all Polish-American children were enrolled in Catholic schools.

After the Church, the *parochial school* was the object of the most zealous care of the clergy and Polish emigrants. Because the American school not only corrupted the native language of the Polish children, but it also separated them from their families and traditional customs, the clergy quickly arrived at the profound conviction that there was no other way to preserve Catholic Polonia for the younger generation than the Polish Catholic school, and such schools were established everywhere with great sacrifice on the part of the emigrants, because the founding of these schools did not free them from taxes imposed by the American government for the public schools. It would not be inappropriate to add here that the annual expense of the parochial schools is 2 million dollars, that is, a half-dollar a head for each immigrant. This cost is one-third the amount which is spent on American public schools, because there are 2,500 Polish Sisters, belonging to different congregations, that literally offer their life for teaching...The number of students who attend the Polish parochial schools is close to 400,000 — of which 47,000 are in Chicago alone — and here we find the opportunity to add that the scope of this instruction is not only to preserve for the youth the faith, their own language, the spirit of the family, and the traditions of Poland, but also to instruct them well...as to the conditions of American life, to introduce them to the American spirit,...and to prepare them for adequate and opportune fields of work. And naturally, since they teach English in these schools, there will emerge from them good and intelligent American citizens, always imbued, however, with a spirit purely Catholic and Polish.

Experience has taught us that the most important goal stated here was reached in general,...[but] people who were separated from this beneficent parochial organization were lost to the nation and also often to the church...

> *I Polacchi Negli Stati Uniti Dell' America Del Nord* (The Poles in the United States of North America). Translated from Italian by Dominic Fasso. Archdiocese of Chicago's Joseph Cardinal Bernardin Archives and Records Center. Printed with permission.

62. Sisters of the Holy Family of Nazareth, 1885

Polish Catholic women religious provided the backbone of the Polish Catholic school system. Religious communities such as the Sisters of the Holy Family of Nazareth, Sisters of the Congregation of St. Felix of Cantalice (Felician Sisters), Sisters of the Resurrection (Resurrectionist Sisters), and Franciscan Sisters came from Poland to staff schools. The Sisters of the Holy Family of Nazareth were founded in the early 1870s by Mother Frances Siedliska and came to the United States in 1885. The following excerpts come from Mother Siedliska's diaries and letters and from early "convent chronicles" and describe the call, the harrowing ocean crossing, and the early ministry. Mentioned in the documents are Father Vincent Barzynski, pastor of St. Stanislaus Kostka in Chicago, and Father Anthony Lechert, Mother Siedliska's chief adviser.

From a Memorial

In 1885 Father Lechert told us that Father Vincent Barzynski, a Resurrectionist, Superior of the Polish mission in Chicago, had requested our Sisters to care for an orphanage and for parish schools for poor Polish children.

From the "Convent Chronicles" — The Trip to America

Having left our luggage at a hotel, we went to Mass at the little church called *Stella Maris*. After a bit to eat, we went on to the port and took our places on the ship which was named *Gottardo*. The Sisters were somewhat worried about the long voyage which we were about to embark upon, but were courageous and happy. Our Mother showed herself full of confidence and of abandonment to the will of God. She watched us with love as her lips whispered prayers to the Lord.

At seven o'clock that evening the ship left Naples; slowly we lost sight of the shores of Italy. In our poor hearts there were sentiments of melancholy, of content and joy to have been chosen by the Lord for His work and to sacrifice and immolate ourselves for His glory...

The night of June 30th there was a violent storm and we were in grave danger. The *Gottardo* seemed like a light shell on the sea. The waves of the sea were all-violence and sometimes we thought we would be submerged into the depths. No one thought of sleep. We all remained awake and called on the aid of the Immaculate Virgin Mary. Father Lechert remained standing, ready to impart absolution in case of imminent danger; many of us prepared for death. Only Mother Siedliska was calm and serene; with short and truly holy words, she encouraged us to have trust in God. She had a completely firm faith, calling upon us to offer ourselves to work for the Lord and His glory across the ocean. It would be He, after all, who would bring us there whither He was calling us.

Finally, on July 4th, we arrived in New York...

[From New York they traveled to Chicago, where they entered their chapel.]

The church was a large room with three wooden altars...[and] a few benches. Poverty superb! The tabernacle was made from wood. A tiny lamp indicated that our Divine King was present. Our hearts were saddened at the sight of such misery and neglect of Jesus. It was a revealing lesson for us about how we should renounce everything and live with complete dedication to the Master...

The Polish women came to become acquainted with us... Seeing us they cried from joy, calling us the good sisters from their native land. We found ten orphans there. Three children from the parish, mostly poor, came to see us also... Our Mother in her goodness and lovableness drew all of them to herself...

From a Letter to Europe Describing the Sisters' Ministry

...Here our life is quite different, different problems, different personalities. The work is unglamorous and simple: the elementary teaching of a few hundred children. Materially the situation is very delicate, because we do not wish to incur expenses for anyone; we accept whatever these good people give us out of their kindness and poverty. All this is precious and welcome, coming as it does from the Lord's holy dispensation for us.

> Archives of the Sisters of the Holy Family of Nazareth, Des Plaines, Ill. Printed with permission.

63. Call for a National Polish Catholic Congress, 1896

By the middle of the 1890s a series of strains began to appear within the Polish community in the United States. The community found itself divided between "clericalists" and "nationalists" as embodied in the Polish Roman Catholic Union (PRCU) founded in 1873 and the Polish National Alliance (PNA) founded in 1880, respectively. The PRCU saw the Polish identity as inextricably connected with Catholicism, while the PNA, still largely Catholic, was more inclusive, allowing socialists, Jews, and schismatics to join – their main concern was the political independence of Poland. In addition to this split was a growing concern over separatism – several priests, discouraged by the way Polish Catholics were being treated by the American hierarchy, broke away from the Catholic Church. By 1896, Father Anthony Kozlowski in Chicago and Father Stefan Kaminski in Buffalo had already become schismatics. To address these problems, Father Jan [John] Pitass of Buffalo, supported by Father Vincent Barzynski, called for a national Polish Catholic congress to meet in Buffalo. The following document announced the congress and listed the concerns to be addressed. The PNA and those who had separated from the Catholic Church were of prime concern.

A Call to the Reverend Clergymen and the Polish-Catholic Societies in the United States of America from the Executive Committee of the Polish Catholic Congress, Rev. John Pitass, Chairman

Reverend Clergymen and Dear Countrymen!

For some time past there [we]re noticeable among the American Poles certain unwholesome and foreign currents, and there appear[ed] various negative symptoms which wholly disagree[d] with our spirit, both that of Catholics and of Poles. In time the evil became more evident ... It came to pass, that the Poles in America, thanks to the instigations of bad and unscrupulous people, divided themselves into two camps, and these camps glowed with a hatred toward each other ... [A] battle is now raging in all the Polish colonies and parishes.

After some time a party was formed among the American Poles, whose followers began an open war against the priests, against all the faithful Poles, and against the entire Catholic Church. Almost in every colony, and in every parish, men were found who took upon themselves the task of bringing about discord and strife among the brethren, and by the use of most unworthy means, they attained their object, for almost a civil war was declared. The liberal party began to teach that religion for the Poles is an unnecessary ad-

dition, that the priests are the tyrants of the people, and that every religion
not excluding even the pagan was better than the Catholic religion...[The]
result...faith began to weaken and morality to lower,...[and] ill manners
and impiety grew at most terrific pace.

In the beginning the evil appeared under various forms and hence it was
impossible to see at the first glance, where was its chief cause. With the organization of the independent churches, however, with the formation of socialistic
and anarchistic societies, then it was noticed whence comes the enemy...

At last the people of good will, who truly love their brethren and are attached both to the Catholic Church and to their country, shook off their
lethargy, and beheld that in the presence of the assaults of the enemy, it is
wrong to be unactive, and hence resolved to take a decided stand against the
attacking host. The question was now of a weapon, and finally all agreed on
the calling of a Polish Catholic Congress...

**In view therefore of the desires of the Polish Catholic party, in the name
of all Polish parishes, with the authority of the immense majority of the
Polish-American clergy and the representatives of organizations and societies, we call the Polish Catholic Congress to meet on the 22nd day of
September, 1896, in the city of Buffalo, N.Y....**

And what shall we discuss in this congress?...

The so-called "Independent Churches," or the Polish American schism is
the greatest evil that afflicts us, and hence the congress must consider how
to put an end to this propagation by the fallen priests and other seducers...
Another plague that afflicts us, is the Polish National Alliance, an organization which spreads pernicious principles, infidelity, and thrusts the people to
impiety and denial of the faith of their fathers...

[The document proclaims that the congress should support the Polish
Immigration House and the Polish Seminary and then moves to other
matters.]

In the presence of the agitation which is brought about among the working classes by the socialists, anarchists and other apostles of perversion...,
[the Congress] should resolve to organize labor societies, which would be in
union with the spirit of Christianity and the Catholic Church...[and] put a
stop to the spread of socialism and anarchism among the laborers of Polish
nationality...

The Poles inhabiting the United States number at least one and a half million souls, they form therefore one-sixth of the Catholics of all nationalities
living in the United States, and therefore it would be proper and just, that
the Polish clergymen should be on equal footing with the clergymen of other
nationalities in the matter of occupation of the highest offices and Episcopal
Sees in this country. [The congress proposes to petition the Congregation of
the Propagation of the Faith and the pope about this issue.]

Let us remember that from the success of this congress...depends the future of the Poles in the United States. Let us remember that upon us are looking not only our countrymen in Europe but also the citizens of the many nationalities in this country! Let us prove that Poland and a Catholic Poland at that, does exist, and that even here in a foreign land, as we have been, so we also shall remain faithful children of the Catholic Church and of our Country. Let us defend our ideals, let us defend our brethren from infidelity, and the loss of their nationality, and then God shall help us to victory!...

Given in Buffalo, this 23rd day of June, 1896,

Rev. John Pitass, chairman of the executive committee

[Twenty-seven representatives from fifteen cities also signed.]

Archives of the Archdiocese of New York. Printed with permission.

64. Waclaw Kruszka, "Polyglot Bishops for Polyglot Dioceses," 1901

Besides being a historian, Father Wenceslaus [Waclaw] Kruszka was one of the great agitators for equal rights for Polish clergy in the United States and for the appointment of a Polish bishop. Ordained in 1895, the following year he became pastor of a Polish parish, St. Wenceslaus in Ripon, Wisconsin, an appointment he came to consider as exile. In 1901, he published the following document, which made the controversial claim that anyone who accepted an episcopal appointment to a "polyglot diocese" but who was not "polyglot" himself "committed a mortal sin." The piece was so controversial it was turned down for publication by the influential Ecclesiastical Review. *However, the setback was only temporary, and the essay was ultimately published in the* New York Freeman's Journal *as a letter to the editor. Today, it is heralded by many scholars as an early articulation of cultural pluralism.*

To the Editor Freeman's Journal:

Unity in variety — this is the law of the whole universe. Even in the Creator of all things we have unity of Essence in variety of Persons. And the same law reigns also in His Church on earth.

The Catholic unity is not an absolute uniformity, but unity in variety, unity of faith in variety of customs, manners and languages. *And only in such a unity there is strength,* because only in such a unity, there is vitality. The rigid uniformity bursts easily, breaks to pieces. Hence, that there are different nationalities in the Catholic Church, is not to be deplored, but on the contrary, it should be for us Catholics always and everywhere rather a reason for joy and congratulation: for the differences of nationalities are not weakening, but they are rather *strengthening the unity* of the Church. Take away the variety, and you take away the strength, the vitality from the unity, and retain in its place a weak, rigid and dread uniformity.

The Catholic Church in the United States is "en miniature," indeed an image of the whole Catholic Church spread over the rest of the world in as far as it embraces here all the different nationalities of Europe, Asia and even Africa. Those different nationalities in the United States may, by and by, become by themselves one nation *of one language,* if not observing the same customs and manners. But is it good policy of the Catholic Church *to make* them "perforce" one nation of one (English) language? Some think it is, for they think that by introducing national *uniformity* they are strengthening the *unity* of the Church.

But this is a great illusion of some of our English speaking Catholics. Nationalities and languages are not of human origin, and the Church has no authority from God to change or destroy them; therefore "durum est tibi contra hunc stimulum calcitrave." Different languages, as we know from Revelation, are a penalty imposed by God upon the human race, for its pride. To try to introduce one language is, as it were, to try to rebuild the tower of Babylon again. It's vain labor. If it is God's will that at least here in the United States the different languages must vanish, they will vanish by themselves, in the course of time. But *hic et nunc,* in our time they do exist, and they will exist for a long time to come, on account of the constant immigration which is pouring in every year. Does this fact endanger the Catholic Church in America? Does such a variety of nationalities weaken the unity of our Church in this country? Not at all, if properly provided; on the contrary, it strengthens the unity of faith.

It is true it is not convenient for our *one-tongued* American prelates to rule and manage and control such a mixed population. For the bishop cannot understand the non-English people of his diocese, and the people cannot understand their bishop; hence, naturally there arise misunderstandings among non-English parishes. This is very true. But can we blame the people that do not speak English? Must the people, as regards the language, accommodate themselves to the bishop, or vice versa, must the bishop accommodate himself to the people? That is the important question: is the diocese for the bishop, or the bishop for the diocese? The answer is evident, the bishop is created for the diocese and not vice verse, and, therefore, if the diocese is polyglot, the bishop must be polyglot, too.

But, is it just to demand from our American bishops that they speak, besides English, also French, German, and perhaps Polish and Bohemian? Why, if there is in his diocese a large percentage of each of these nationalities (say one-fifth) it is just, he ought to speak those languages, otherwise he cannot fulfill his duties as a bishop. Are not our American bishops successors of the Apostles? But what is said of the Apostles? Did they not "speak with *divers* tongues" (Acts ii.,4)? Yes, you say, but this was a miracle, and nowadays miracles are not necessary. Answer *distingueneo;* miracles are not necessary — *concedo;* but that the "gift of divers tongues" is nowadays in America not necessary — *nego simpliciter!* Surely nowadays to expect from God the "gift of tongues" *by a miracle,* and not *by study,* would be really to tempt God! Because every candidate to the priesthood or episcopacy has time and occasion enough to acquire those "divers tongues" by his own study. I know German priests, as for instance the Very Rev. Jos. Rainer, Rector of St. Francis Seminary, Wis., who, besides English and German, speaks fluently also in Polish, Italian, French and other *living* languages. Potuit hic, cur non alii? Polish priests as a rule, are polyglot, too, more than the Germans. Over one-half of the Polish priests in the United States are born or educated here in America, and they speak English just as well as any other native American, but besides English and Polish, they usually speak also German, Bohemian, French, and so on, remembering the Latin proverb: "Toties sum homo, quoties linguis calleo."

I am far from asserting that the gift of divers tongues *alone* makes one fit for a successor of the Apostles; I say only that for a bishop in a polyglot diocese the gift of divers languages is *ceteris paribus* — a quite necessary and indispensable attribute; for, consider it impartially: If God did a miracle to enable the Apostles to "speak with divers tongues," from this fact alone you can draw the conclusion of what great importance in the economy of salvation must be the knowledge of different languages! There was certainly in those days the Latin or Greek language not less common than the English in our days — and nevertheless God did a miracle in order that *all* the people present might hear the Gospel preached *in their own language:* "We have heard them speak *in our own tongues* the wonderful works of God" (Acts ii., 11). Why this? Because it is not a strange language (though known to us, but it is the native tongue), the mother tongue, *"our own* tongue," which gives us a full *understanding* of the truth, especially of a religious truth. People of other languages, for instance, learn English and *can do business* in that language nearly as well as in their own; but they will not *pray nor make confession* in English; they can even hear and understand a common discourse in English, but they fail to understand the word of God preached in English for this simple reason: because the English language has a special and very difficult *terminology* for expressing the religious truths and thoughts.

Oh! If nowadays in this country whenever our bishops come to administer Confirmation in a parish, our people also could say and exclaim with joy: "We have heard them speak *in our own tongues* the wonderful works of God!" What great consolation would it be for them, and what real *confirmation* in their faith, which is surrounded here by thousands of dangers! For, it is in our times also, that "faith cometh *by hearing*" (Rom. x., 17). And "how shall they hear *without a preacher*" (ib. 14) in their own language? I know our right reverend bishops have different priests for different nationalities in their dioceses. But — abstracting from the fact that, for instance, the Polish Catholics are not provided with a sufficient number of Polish priests (for one and a half million of Polish Catholics there are not quite 400 Polish priests in the United States) — I ask has the *priest* the teaching power and authority of a *bishop*? Is a common priest the Teacher and Preacher *proper,* the *Pastor* proper of the Church? No, he is not; for "the Holy Ghost hath placed *you bishops,* to rule the Church of God" (Acts xx., 28). *To rule,* that means not only to translocate priests from one parish to another, but it means in the first place *to teach* and to preach! "Preach the word" (II. Tim. iv., 2). The priest is only a helper of the bishop, and it is quite a different thing for the common people to hear the priest and to hear and understand the bishop. The bishop is the *pastor proper* of the faithful flock, "and the sheep follow him." Why? "Because *they know his voice.* But a stranger they follow not, but fly from him, *because they know not the voice of strangers*" (John x., 4, 5). And how many in the United States fell away from the true faith merely because they never heard, never knew nor understood the voice of their pastor proper — the bishop? Yes, they understood the voice of their priest and they followed therefore their priest, but did they not go astray just by following only the priest? — And how many will fall away in the future on this account, because they have not the pastor proper (bishop), whose "voice they know" and understand? "Faith cometh by hearing — but how shall they hear without a preacher?"

Therefore — salva reverentia of all existing right reverend bishops who entered their office when things looked differently — I do affirm *with certainty,* gained both a priori and a posteriori from experience among non-English speaking Catholics, that *nowadays* in the United States, whosoever (a candidate) dares to assume the duties of a bishop in a *polyglot diocese,* without being a polyglot himself, takes duties upon himself which he knows he is unable to perform, and therefore *he commits a mortal sin.* He should either *learn* "to speak with divers tongues" (for he cannot expect a miracle from God), or he should *refuse* to assume the responsible duties of a bishop in such a diocese. He cannot excuse himself by saying that he is forced by the Holy See to accept the bishopric of such a diocese, for I am certain that the Holy See, if duly informed, will never force him.

In the last years things look differently. The constituent parts of the Catholic Church in the United States during the last quarter of the XIX century changed immensely. The Church here is not now composed exclusively of English and German speaking elements, as it was previous to the year 1870. Since that time the Slavonian immigration, i.e., Poles, Lithuanians, Bohemians, Slovacs, etc., among whom the Poles are the predominant element, grew immensely, so that they constitute now about one-third of the entire Catholic population in the United States. According to the census, made by the author of "Historya Polska w Ameryce" ("The Polish History of America," 1900), there are, for example, 69,300 Polish Catholics in the Buffalo Diocese, or nearly one-half of the entire Catholic population of that diocese; there are 57,200 in the diocese of Pittsburg[h], or one-fifth; 48,500 in the diocese of Scranton, or one-third; 48,200 in Cleveland, or nearly one-fifth; 32,200 in the diocese of Fort Wayne, or one-third; 14,750 in the diocese of Marquette, or one-fifth; 44,100 in the diocese of Grand Rapids, or over one-third; 47,900 in the diocese of Detroit, or one-fourth; 172,600 in the archdiocese of Chicago, or one-fifth; 16,600 in the diocese of Omaha, or one-fourth; 16,400 in the diocese of Duluth, or over one-half; 23,800 in the diocese of St. Cloud, or over one-half; 31,200 in the diocese of Green Bay, or one-fourth; 46,080 in the archdiocese of Milwaukee, or one-fifth; besides, in the dioceses of [33 named] — in each of these dioceses the Polish Catholics constitute a considerable part about or less than one-fifth. We did not, however, take into account the Lithuanians, Bohemians, Slovacs and other Slavanian [*sic*] nations.

Hence the Rt. Rev. Bishop Spalding of Peoria, as long ago as Aug. 14, 1892, in an address delivered on the occasion of a church dedication at LaSalle, Ill., very truly described the present and future numerical strength of the Poles in the Church in this country in the following words: "I am not a prophet, but this I can foretell you, that the Poles will play a conspicuous part in the Catholic Church in America. The immigration of other nations is decreasing, but that of Poles, Lithuanians, Bohemians and Slovacs is increasing every day. And as the Poles constitute a majority, they will play a conspicuous part in the Catholic Church here — and I tell you, that here in America there will begin another Polish History."

Nevertheless, we heard another American prelate saying that there will never be a bishop of Polish nationality in the United States. Why not? Why should the Poles be ignored and overlooked in the ecclesiastical hierarchy of America? Why should only the English and German speaking nations have the exclusive privilege to have bishops of their own language? Why? Because the majority of the English and German nations separated from the Church, whereas the Polish nation, as a whole, remained *always faithful to the Church?* "Polonia semper fidelis," as remarked Pope Pius IX.? Or, because England brought forth a Henry VIII., and Germany brought forth a Luther, who ruined Christianity in their respective countries — whereas Poland brought forth a John III., Sobieski, the king, who, at Vienna in 1683, saved the whole Occidental Christianity from the invasion of the Turks and the deluge of Mohammedanism? — But overlooking the merits of old Poland, we Poles in America do not ask any special privilege, we only ask just and EQUAL treatment in the ecclesiastical hierarchy.

[Rev.] Wenceslaus Kruszka,
Rector of St. Wenceslaus Church at Ripon, Wis.

Wenceslaus (Waclaw) Kruszka, "Polyglot Bishops for Polyglot Dioceses," *New York Freeman's Journal*, 3 August 1901.

65. Francis Hodur, Polish National Catholic Church, 1907, 1901

While Waclaw Kruszka agitated within the Catholic Church, others simply left. Like Anthony Kozlowski and Stefan Kaminski, Father Francis Hodur of Scranton, Pennsylvania, left in 1897. In 1904, the various independent churches came together to form the Polish National Catholic Church of America (PNCC). At issue was what was perceived to be the Poles' second-class citizenship in the American church, as reflected in their lack of lay control of parish property and the appointment of pastors according to models of church governance they had known in their homeland. The following documents written by PNCC bishop Francis Hodur articulate the movement's main concerns. Ultimately, about 5 percent of the Polish Catholics in the United States would join the PNCC.

Francis Hodur, Bishop of the Polish National Catholic Church

"Purpose and Principles" of the Polish National Catholic Church
in America: The Preamble to the First Constitution, 1907

Goal and Purposes of the Polish National Church of America

1. The first and foremost desire of the Polish National [Catholic] Church in America is the sanctification and salvation of the Polish emigrant in America...To create a hearth for the Polish people in the emigration around which they can warm themselves when they have been made cold...

   The Polish nation is undertaking a terrible life-or-death struggle there in Europe, where its land, language and the achievements of a thousand-year cultural labor, and here in America, where under the cloak of the community of the Roman religion Irish bishops try to exploit it, denationalize it, and harness it to their own political chariots. Therefore, it must be on watch...

2. The second principle of our organization is this, that church property should be the direct possession of those people who build and support the church, joined in parishes and dioceses. Management and control over church property belongs to committees chosen by the parish and answerable to them...

Mass in Polish, 1901

To the Polish people in the United States

On the Feast of the Nativity I shall celebrate Holy Mass in St. Stanislaus Church in Scranton, Pa., at 10:30 in the Polish language. I will do this for two reasons: First, for reasons of a religious nature, and secondly, from national considerations...

...[J]ust as a child who wants to talk sincerely with its parents does not do so in a foreign language unknown to itself but in a language in which it can easily express all the love and honor it has for its father and mother, so should we children of God speak at the altar to our Best and Most Merciful Father. The more so, since by this will be removed the barrier which today exists between the priest, offering the sacrifice in a foreign, dead language, and the people in whose name this holy act is being performed. The priest will not be just a translator of the sentiments of the Polish nation before some kind of judge who does not, it is pretended, understand our language, but he will be a true sacrificer and mediator between the people and God, who created us and endowed us with the most beautiful Polish language. And we will thus also prove that we are an independent nation having the same rights to existence, to glory and to happiness as do all those other peoples who have already attained national rites...

That which our forefathers could not succeed in doing in the times of the first Jagielons, when the Polish religious services brought into Krakow after the year 1390 ceased less than a century later scorned by the magnates and by the Roman clergy, will succeed today when the enlightened Polish people will undertake this task. Therefore, I call upon you, working people, exiled people, people scattered across the American land, and ask for your help and protection in this pious work!

Since we are truly today the poorest among the nations and only language distinguishes us before the world and unites all the sons of Poland in one vital nation, then let the people raise up this dear treasure and permit that we will lift it up to the royal throne and the prayer of the holy sacrifice will thunder with its tones.

Our enemies wish to tear out our mother tongue, let us, therefore, loving it all the more because it is scorned and persecuted, make it the mediator between the nation and God...

> Theodore L. Zawistowski, ed. and trans., *Hodur: A Compilation of Selected Translations,* 2d ed. (Scranton, Pa.: Polish National Catholic Church of America, 1990). Printed with permission of Theodore L. Zawistowski.

66. Condemnation of the *Kuryer Polski,* 1912

In 1901, the second Polish Catholic Congress met in Buffalo and sent a memorial to the bishops of the United States calling for the appointment of Polish bishops. "We are convinced that Auxiliary Bishops located throughout the country wherever there are large colonies of Poles, would work wonders towards forestalling the movement of 'Away from Rome.'" When the bishops failed to respond favorably, the congress sent letters to individuals and delegated Father Kruszka to take their plea to Rome. In 1903, Kruszka traveled to the Eternal City, where he believed Pope Pius X made a commitment to appoint a Polish bishop. It would be five more years before a Polish priest in the United States, Paul Rhode, was named auxiliary bishop of Chicago. In the meantime, Kruszka and his brother Michael, editor of the Polish newspaper Kuryer Polski, *stepped up the agitation for Polish bishops. Even after Rhode's appointment, they did not relent, attacking the German archbishop of Milwaukee, Sebastian Messmer. So rancorous did the dispute become that the archbishop and bishops of the province of Milwaukee felt compelled to issue the following condemnations in February 1912.*

Pastoral Letter of February 1912

TO OUR BELOVED BRETHREN of the Clergy and the Laity Greeting and Blessing.

[The letter begins by warning of "the danger of false doctrines" and then continues:] To our great sorrow duty compels Us to warn our faithful flock against a similar movement in our own country which threatens to mislead the people into false doctrines regarding the ecclesiastical authority and to direct its passions into the path of schism and separation. The agitation for Polish bishops in the United States has assumed such a character, especially in our province, that it becomes positively subversive and destructive of Catholic faith, loyalty, discipline and order. No sensible person will blame the Polish Catholics of America for being desirous of having bishops who can preach to them the word of God in their own mother-tongue. Rome...will know the time and way to solve this important problem...Whenever and wherever the Holy See shall see fit to appoint Polish bishops in the United States...the other bishops of the American Catholic Hierarchy will receive them with sentiments of a true and loyal Catholic love and reverence. In the meantime Polish Catholics must rest assured that the bishops...will be just as solicitous and zealous for the spiritual and ecclesiastical interests of the Polish faithful as they must be for all the other children of the Church whatever their nationality or race. But Polish Catholics must also be persuaded that love of one's nation or race or tongue can not be allowed to degenerate into blind passion and narrow-minded sentiment, and that blind nationalism has been the cause of all the great and disastrous schisms in the history of the Church. Nationalism of this kind has no place whatever in God's Holy Church of which St. Paul says, "There is neither Jew nor Greek;...you are all one in Christ Jesus." Gal. III, 28. Of whatever race or nationality we may be, in the Church we are all members of the same mystic body of Christ, children of the same spouse of Christ, being animated and sanctified by the same Holy Spirit of Christ...Where nationalism and nationalistic passions strive to become leading and ruling principles in the affairs of the Church, general or local, they breathe and beget the spirit of disobedience and rebellion and very soon heresy itself. When men of this spirit systematically attack the public acts of ecclesiastical superiors in the exercise of their lawful authority, they undermine that ecclesiastical authority itself and shatter the very foundation of rule and order in the Church. When in the same spirit they claim for the lay people the power of government in ecclesiastical affairs, and the right of management of the church properties, independent of the lawfully appointed bishops, they attack the very constitution and fundamental law upon which the visible organization of the Church is built. When this same spirit becomes a common scandal-monger and blackmailer by spreading broadcast before the masses all kinds of reports of so-called clerical scandals, it destroys effectively the reverence and love of the people for the priesthood and for the religious institutions of the Church. Again, when this uncatholic and unchristian nationalistic spirit denounces as traitors to the holy cause and as apostates from their nation whosoever refuse to submit to its dictates and to follow its call, then it sows the seed of strife and hatred among the children of that same race... to the great scandal of Catholics and non-catholics and to the great detriment of religion and nationality. Finally, when that same spirit, not satisfied with merely preaching its false doctrines, begins to organize the misled masses into combined bodies of agitation, even at the risk of incurring the censures and excommunications of the Church, then it will soon attain its last object, namely, independence from the authority of the Church, separation and complete schism. Unfortunately this spirit of revolt and disorder is at present being fostered to a dangerous degree among our Polish Catholic brethren... The fight against what they maliciously call the "German" bishops of this province of Milwaukee, is but a sham battle to cover the real fight for ecclesiastical independence from non-Polish bishops...

The true spirit of this whole agitation has been most clearly set forth in the call and program for "The American Federation of Polish Catholic Laymen," issued by the *Kuryer Polski* of Milwaukee and the *Dziennik Narodowy* of Chicago. This program calls upon the Polish lay people to organize a national federation embracing parish, county and state federations all over the United States. The purpose of this federation is, first, to demand of the Holy See Polish bishops for the Polish Catholics, a phrase well-calculated to convey to thousands of Polish Catholics the idea of separate Polish bishops independent of the other American bishops, so that Polish Catholics of the United States would form a separate religious body under its own episcopal jurisdiction distinct from other American hierarchy, a Polish church within the Catholic Church of America. Secondly, to obtain civil laws by which control and management of church property and money affairs of the parishes shall be placed in the hands of the laity... The program calls upon Polish Catholics to keep up this agitation even if they had to suffer persecution and excommunication from the Church...

...We hereby solemnly condemn the said *Kuryer Polski*... and the *Dziennik Narodowy*... as publications greatly injurious to Catholic faith and discipline... Therefore, should any Catholics still dare in the face of this solemn warning to read... the said *Kuryer Polski* and *Dziennik Narodowy*, as long as these papers continue their present course and attitude..., let them know that they commit a grievous sin before God and the Church...

Moreover, We strictly forbid any Catholic of our province to join the above mentioned "American Federation of Polish Catholic Laymen"...

> Sebastian G. Messmer, Abp. of Milwaukee
> James Schwebach, Bp. of LaCrosse
> Frederick Eis, Bp. of Marquette
> Joseph J. Fox, Bp. of Green Bay
> Augustine F. Schinner, Bp. of Superior

P.S. This pastoral letter is to be read in all churches where Polish Catholics worship, on Sunday Sexagesima, Febr'y 11th, A.D. 1912.

Archives of the Archdiocese of Milwaukee. Printed with permission.

67. Polish Clergy in the United States, "I Polacchi" Memorial, 1920

By 1920 only two Poles had become bishops in the United States, Paul Rhode and Edward Kozlowski. In that year, the Polish Clergy of the United States, in conjunction with the Polish legation at the Vatican, submitted a memorial to Pope Benedict XV that was quite similar to that of the German Abbelen and Cahensly memorials. In it the Polish clergy warned of the "Americanizing" tendencies of the American bishops and renewed their call for the appointment of more Polish bishops for the United States. The document gave a quick overview of the condition of Polish Catholics in the United States, listed "serious misunderstandings between Catholic Poles and the American clergy," and finally listed four demands. Only the last two pages of the memorial containing the four demands of the Polish clergy are presented below.

Postulates of the General Union of the Polish Clergy in America

The assembled priests have arrived at the common convictions (a) that the theory, now fairly well supported in America — that after the resurrection of Poland the Polish immigrants must be *"Americanized"* — ought to be categorically denied as unjust, and (b) that in no case should the Catholic Church, by means of its Bishops, serve as an instrument of the "Americanization" of the Polish immigrants. It would therefore be (c) a strict obligation of the Polish government to intervene in this question, bringing to the attention of the Supreme Authority of the Catholic Church the current policy of the American episcopacy with respect to the Polish clergy and Polish immigrants, demonstrating that this policy will lead to the decline of the faith of the Polish people, and consequently it will cause the most serious damage to the Holy Church...

The postulates of the Polish Clergy of the United States have been formulated as follows:

1) Most Rev. Bishop Paul Rhode, the first Polish bishop in the United States, was able to eliminate the discord among many Polish associations, and greatly improve many Catholic organizations, he has founded an enormous orphanage in Niles, Ill., has contributed greatly to improving the parochial schools, has strengthened the Catholic spirit among the immigrants by continual and tireless visits to the Polish parishes, and thus earned the gratitude, love, and admiration of all the Polish clergy. For these reasons the latter humbly entreat the Holy See that the Most Rev. Bishop Paul Rhode be assured the succession in one of the Archdioceses where large numbers of Poles reside.

2) This clergy likewise kindly requests the naming of Polish auxiliary bishops in the ecclesiastical provinces of Chicago, Boston, Detroit, Philadelphia, Scranton, Pittsburgh, Buffalo and Milwaukee.

3) In the seminaries of the Archdioceses in which there are many Poles, a substantial and serious study of the Polish language, history and literature, should be ensured, and as for the Polish education of the Sisters who teach in the parochial schools, it must absolutely be provided in a more satisfactory manner.

4) The American episcopate should apply the regulations of the new Code of Canon Law as regards the division of parishes, etc., most cautiously — scrupulously taking into consideration the rights of immigrants...Rome, June 28, 1920

> *I Polacchi Negli Stati Uniti Dell'America Del Nord.* Translated by Michael J. Dalton. Archdiocese of Chicago's Joseph Cardinal Bernardin Archives and Records Center. Printed with permission.

68. Response of the American Hierarchy, 1920

The American hierarchy reacted quickly and forcefully to the "I Polacchi" memorial. In the following document, Cardinal James Gibbons, writing on behalf of the American bishops, reiterated themes that had been formulated throughout the nineteenth century, echoing in part the argument made by Bishop John Dubois in 1827 (see document 2).

[After protesting the interference of a foreign government in internal Church matters the response continues:] For generations the Catholics of the United States have repelled the unjust accusation of disloyalty to the American Government and of subserviency to foreign potentates. Should it become known that the Polish priests of the U.S. appealed to the Polish Government to bring pressure on the Holy See in favor of their pretensions, and that the Polish Government acceded to their wishes, without doubt, the Poles of this country would be accused of unfaithfulness to our Government; and the American Church would be charged with subjection to foreign powers...The consequences would be serious for the Catholic Religion.

Whilst deploring and condemning the interference of the Polish Government in American church affairs, the U.S. Hierarchy blame still more severely those Polish priests in this country, who for selfish ends besought a foreign Government of laymen to bring pressure on the Holy See in matters of a purely spiritual order. Priests should make themselves worthy of episcopal honors, rather than seek them.

What would become of the unity of the Church in the U.S. if Bishops were appointed according to race distinctions, nationality and language? If Polish bishops should be named for Poles here, why should not Indian Bishops be appointed for the Indians, and Negro Bishops for the Negroes? Catholics come to this country from nearly every nation in the world. We have Irish, Germans, Italians, Lithuanians, Austrians, Slovenians, Croatians, French-Canadians, Spaniards, French, Belgians, Portuguese, Dutch, English, Scotch, Swiss, Maltese, Bohemians, Tyrolese, Syrians, Maronites, and other nationalities, in addition to the Poles. Will it be said then that, for each of these races, nationalities, tribes and tongues, there should be a bishop, or rather many bishops, according to their numbers and location? If so, the resultant confusion would surpass any discord recorded in history...

[After refuting a number of the memorial's claims, the bishops conclude:] It is of the utmost importance to our American nation that nationalities gathered in the United States should gradually amalgamate and fuse into one homogenous people and, without losing the best traits of their race, become imbued with the one harmonious national thought, sentiment, and spirit, which is to be the very soul of the nation. This is the idea of Americanization. This idea has been so strongly developed during the last war that anything opposed to it would be considered bordering on treason. The American people and government are today fully determined that nothing shall stand in the way of promoting, in every section of the country and in every portion of the people, this work of Americanization. It will be a real disaster for the Catholic Church in the United States if it were ever to become known that the Polish Catholics are determined to preserve their Polish nationality and that there is among their clergy and leaders a pronounced movement of Polonization. Still more will it provoke mistrust and suspicion among our Protestant fellow citizens and our American government, should they hear that the Catholic Poles of the United States have appealed to a foreign government in support of their un-American endeavors at the Vatican. In the face of the continual hatred and hostility against the Church manifested by thousands of American citizens, this Polish movement is, to say the least, fraught with great danger to the present peaceful and happy relation between the Church and the American people and Government...

The Italians

69. American Bishops and Pastoral Care of Italians, 1884

The arrival of large-scale Italian immigration during the 1880s began a new pastoral challenge to the Catholic Church in the United States. Italians came mostly from southern Italy, where the popular religious culture tended to be more meaningful than regular attendance at Sunday Mass and formal devotional life centered in the parish church under clerical direction. Instead, Italians' religious life focused on private and public practices not always related to the local church and its clergy. The American bishops first had to address the pastoral care of Italians at their Third Plenary Council of Baltimore in 1884. The following is a report of the council's committee on the Italian immigrants submitted to the prefect of the Congregation of the Propagation of the Faith.

Most Eminent Prince,
Prefect of the Congregation of the Propagation of the Faith,

Following the directives given at the meetings held in Rome in 1883, the Fathers of the Third Plenary Council of Baltimore were presented in Title III of the Schemata with those observations that deal with all immigrants, in particular with the Italians that came here. It emerged in a clear and concise way that 1) Italians who have migrated to America rarely thereafter put foot in a church or receive the Sacraments; 2) they live scattered in all parts of the cities; 3) viewing their stay in America as an exile, they come here with the intention of returning to their native country. As a result, they generally do not contribute anything for the building of churches or the support of priests. These were the exact conclusions reached by the Bishops who were commissioned by the Council to look into this matter. Moreover it was evident that Rome was unaware of the fact that the Italians suffered a spiritual destitution greater than that of all other immigrant groups. In fact, if we look at the other groups that have come with the intention of staying in America, it is evident that they are extremely generous in the building of churches and schools. As is evident from the growth and expansion of the Catholic faith, the Irish, the Germans and the French hold tenaciously to their faith and they carefully look after themselves and their children so that nothing detrimental may fall on the Catholic name. On the contrary, the Italians — especially those that come here from the regions of Naples, Calabria, Sicily, etc. — fall into apostasy with the greatest ease, because they have not been instructed in the most elementary principles of the faith. Hence, it is not unusual that they sell their Catholic faith for any price and that they allow their children to be educated by non-Catholics and receive confirmation from heretics.

In order to provide some remedy for these deplorable conditions, their origins and causes must be found. It is not our intention to anticipate the decisions of the Sacred Congregation. However, with all due veneration and humility, we think the following suggestions should be submitted.

The Bishops of the southern provinces of Italy should be pushed over and over again to show pastoral concern in giving religious instruction to those poor and ignorant peasants. It cannot be denied that nowhere among other Catholic groups in our midst is there such crass and supine ignorance of the faith as among the Italian immigrants. This appears very strange, since there are so many priests and religious over there; yet to a man those who come here are religious[ly] deficient. Among the adults, few have received First Communion; if they were confirmed, that was done without instruction. Almost none of them go to confession here, unless compelled or in danger of death. In the hope of material gain, they desert to the side of the enemy and, having rejected the true faith, they embrace the false one.

Therefore it is of the greatest importance that those who are about to migrate be well instructed at least in the fundamentals of the faith. Otherwise when they return to their native land after having grown richer, they will propagate irreligion as though it were the true light. It seemed important to inform the Sacred Congregation of the immense spiritual destitution of the Italian immigrants and at the same time to earnestly beg the Holy Father — may God grant him long life — that he turn his eyes to our humble petitions so that those, whose pastoral concern this is, might at least offer some Christian doctrine to the migrants from Southern Italy who come to America. Such a task cannot be accomplished by us here, both because of the lack of Italian-speaking priests and because the number is inadequate to the size of the task. There is no doubt that what St. Alphonsus once did in his time for the ignorant masses can be done again. Likewise, St. John de Rossi accomplished the same thing among the harvesters and farmworkers. If the Supreme Authority (if I may use the words in the Schemata of the Third Plenary Council of Baltimore) were to send here and to those regions of Italy from which the peasants migrate priests prominent for their good behavior and doctrine and fired by the zeal for souls, priests who, having rejected the sordid desire of temporal gain, might devote themselves *fully* and *permanently* to the spiritual care of the Italians, a work most certainly necessary for the salvation of souls, then, blessed by such auspices, in due time such a work will achieve full results.

We felt that it would be useless to insist with too many words — although there are accounts from priests and very many reports in Rome sent by the Cardinal Archbishop of New York. Perhaps we might offer one example to illustrate the condition of the Italians. It has often been demonstrated in civil courts that the padroni treat the Italians like slaves. They bring Italians here by promising them all sorts of things. However, they make them work for their own gain. They keep them in fear by telling them about the craftiness of our own people and in this manner they rob them in many ways. These and other things can be read almost daily in the newspapers and are really true.

In the meantime, according to the census held in New York, 25,435 Italians disembarked there in 1883. Just as many came for sure in 1884, even though the census has yet to be published. It is well known that there are many societies, especially in New York, under the leadership of even apostate priests and that so far 800 adults have received confirmation from a pseudo Anglican Bishop. We felt that the above observations on this issue had to be made and brought to the attention of Your Eminence. In the meantime, as usual, with all our hearts we are obedient in the Lord and at your service.

By mandate of His Eminence, Apostolic Delegate of the Third Plenary Council of Baltimore [Cardinal James Gibbons].

Thomas A. Becker
Bishop of Wilmington
Sub-Delegate

Archives of the Archdiocese of Baltimore, 79–B-S. Translated from Italian by Silvano Tomasi and Edmund Stibili. Printed with permission of the Center for Migration Studies.

70. Mother Frances Xavier Cabrini and Italian Immigrants, 1889

To minister to the growing Italian diaspora, communities of Italian priests and women religious came to the United States. For instance, in 1887, Bishop Giovanni Battista Scalabrini of Piacenza in northern Italy formed the Missionary Society of St. Charles (the Scalabrinians) to train and assign Italian missionary priests to minister to Italians in the United States and elsewhere. Another group was the Missionary Society of the Sacred Heart, whose superior, Mother Frances Xavier Cabrini, with sisters of her community came to the United States in 1889. The following story, which appeared in the New York Sun, *includes an interview with Mother Cabrini, a future canonized saint, and describes the aims of her missionaries.*

MISSIONARIES TO OUR ITALIANS
Nuns Sent from Rome to New York
at Archbishop Corrigan's Request

During the past few weeks dark-featured women, in the garb of Sisters of Charity, have been going through the Italian quarters in the bend and in Little Italy, climbing up dark, steep, and narrow stairways, diving down into foul basements, and into dens which even a New York policeman does not care to enter without assistance. These women are all slight and delicate. They wear a peculiar veil, unlike that of the usual religious devotees, and few can speak English. They are members of an order entirely new to this country, the Silesian [i.e., Salesian] missionaries of the Sacred Heart of Jesus. It is an Italian organization of nuns who look after the welfare of orphans, and all that are engaged in this work are of Italian birth. The half dozen located in this city are pioneers in the United States, and they came upon the solicitation of Archbishop Corrigan and Mrs. Luigi P. di Cesnola, wife of Gen. di Cesnola, the director of the Metropolitan Museum of Art. The Archbishop and Mrs. di Cesnola wrote to Lombardy, the headquarters of these missionaries, last November, requesting that a branch be started in this country. They were induced to this because of the terrible condition in which many poor Italian children were in in this city. Of the many thousands of Italians in New York a very large majority were sunk in extreme poverty and squalor.

This was particularly so in the case of those newly arrived in this country. Unable to provide with a degree of decency for themselves, they, of course, could do little for their children, and these were allowed to grow up in abject ignorance. Many were abandoned or driven forth into the streets of the big city to beg or steal the means for subsistence. One can not walk the streets without encountering hundreds of little Italian boys whose only knowledge of English lies in the phrase: "Shinaboota, fiva centa, mista." The pennies they collect are not their own but go to some padrone who supplies their outfits, and gives them a mere pittance of the small amount they earn. Of the Italian girls who are homeless and forsaken, their misery may not be so apparent, but it is even greater. The Silesians [Salesians] came here in March, but were not able to begin operations until sometime later. They now occupy a large yellow stone house on East Fifty-ninth street, near Park avenue. It is rather cold and forbidding looking on the outside, but the interior is bright and cheerful. The floors are stained and rugs are scattered around plentifully. The head of the American contingent is Sister Frances Xavier Cabrini, Superior General. She is a dark-hued but sympathetic woman, with large coal-black eyes and a winning smile. She cannot talk English. She is very much in earnest and anxious that her mission should be successful. As soon as the branch is firmly established, she will return to Europe, leaving another missionary in charge here. She is the founder of the order and has done wonderful work in providing refuges for the orphans in Italy.

"Our object," she said, "is to rescue the Italian orphans of the city from the misery and dangers that threaten them, and to make men and women of them. At present we are especially anxious about the Italian girls who have no decent homes, but later we shall look out for the boys. We include under the title of orphans not only the fatherless and motherless, but also the children that are abandoned, or whose parents do not properly care for them. We have found that many children are abandoned shortly after they reach this city. Their parents, who have come here expecting to be rich immediately, now learn their mistake, and being unprovided with money, they set the children to care for themselves. Then, too, there are many poor Italians who are barely able to supply food for the numerous mouths dependent upon them, and they are glad to let us to take some of their children and bring them up properly. Of late things have been somewhat better because of the work of the Italian priests who come to New York at the request of the Pope, but there is still a great deal to be done.

"We take children between the ages of four and fifteen years, house, feed, and clothe them, and train them mentally and physically so that they may be good citizens and good members of the Church. Our mode of work is to go right down into the Italian quarters and go from house to house, from apartment to apartment. We are recognized by all Italians, and many of them are glad to see us. We try to learn about all the Italian children we meet, whether they have proper homes or proper schooling. I have said that we are especially anxious about the girls just now, and the reason must be apparent. The temptations that a big city like this offers to poor, ignorant girls of any nationality are very great, and to abandoned Italian girls who have no means of livelihood and are ignorant even of the language around them, they are terrible. At present our means are limited, as we depend entirely upon private subscriptions, but all the Italians of wealth approve of our course, as well as the Catholic clergy, and we hope soon to be able to do more. As soon as our means will afford, we intend to have a larger house, where we can accommodate all the children who come to us."

The work of these women is very trying and has many hardships. Anyone who has ever been in the Italian quarters where these missionaries go can realize something of the unpleasantness of their task. Sky-scraping tenements in which hundreds of families are huddled together, ill-smelling rooms, drunken men and surly women, all these must be encountered on every trip. Many of these Italians, too, have abandoned all religion and are atheists. They have no sympathy with the meek, kindly faced women who devote their lives to deeds of charity, and frequently are very gruff in their behavior toward them. Still, the missionaries persist in their work, and try to save the children of even these men, unmindful of the jeers and even threats with which they are met. The missionaries all wear a peculiar gold ring as a badge of their order, of which the sign is a heart surrounded by luminous rays.

New York *Sun,* 30 June 1889, 5.

71. Jacob Riis on Italian Religious Festivals, 1899

The religious expressions that Italian immigrants favored had a personal and public dimension that separated them from the churchgoing practices of their coreligionists of other ethnic groups. In the following account, Jacob Riis, one of the leading journalists of the time, turns his reporter's eye to the public religious festivals in New York City, first in lower Manhattan with a profile of festivals for specific Italian saints, then on the upper East Side at the Church of Our Lady of Mount Carmel on 115th Street in Italian Harlem. Riis also brings into his story New York City's police commissioner, Theodore Roosevelt, who within a few years became president of the United States. The article illustrates the interest and fervor of Italians for their religious heritage.

The rumble of trucks and the slamming of boxes up on the corner ceased for the moment, and in the hush that fell upon Mulberry street snatches of a familiar tune, punctuated by a determined drum, struggled into the block. Around the corner came a band of musicians with green cock-feathers in hats set rakishly over fierce, sunburnt faces. A raft of boys walked in front, abreast of two bored policemen, stepping in time to the music. Four men carried a silk-fringed banner with evident pride. Behind them a strange procession toiled along: women with babies at the breast and dragging little children; fat and prosperous padrones carrying their canes like staves of office and authority; young men out for a holiday; old men with lives of hardship and toil written in their halting gait and worn and crooked frames; lastly, a cripple on crutches, who strove manfully to keep up. The officials in Police Headquarters looked out of the windows and viewed the show indifferently. It was an every-day spectacle. This one had wandered around the block thrice that day. President Roosevelt (of the Police Board), who had come out to go to lunch, was much interested. To him it was new.

"Where do you suppose they are going?" he said, surveying the procession from the steps. He was told that some Italian village saint was having his day celebrated around in Elizabeth street, and he expressed a desire to see how it was done. So we fell in, he and I, and followed the band too, at a little distance. It led us to a ramshackle old house in Elizabeth street, and halted there in front of a saloon with the appealing announcement on a swinging sign: "*Vino, Vino, di California, di Italia.* Any kind of Whisky for Sale." The band and the fat men went into the saloon. We followed the women, the children, and the scraggy ones through a gap in the brick wall that passed for an alley to the back yard, and there came upon the village of Auletta feasting its patron saint.

It was a yard no longer, but a temple. All the sheets of the tenement had been stretched so as to cover the ugly sheds and outhouses. Against the dark rear tenement the shrine of the saint had been erected, shutting it altogether out of sight with a wealth of scarlet and gold. Great candles and little ones, painted and beribboned, burned in a luminous grove before the altar. The sun shone down upon a mass of holiday-clad men and women, to whom it was all as a memory of home, of the beloved home across the seas; upon mothers kneeling devoutly with their little ones at the shrine, and upon children bringing offerings to the saint's glory. His face smiled down benignly upon them from the frame of gaudy colors with the coat of arms of the village, — or was it a hint at the legendary history of the saint? — a fox dragging a reluctant rooster by the tail. In his own country the saint is held to be mighty against fever and the ague, of which there is much there. The faith which prompted a stricken mother to hang the poor garments of her epileptic boy close to his hand, in the hope that so he might be healed, provoked no smile in the latter-day spectators. The sorrow and trust were too genuine for that. The fire-escapes of the tenement had, with the aid of some cheap muslin draperies, a little tinsel, and the strange artistic genius of this people, been transformed into beautiful balconies, upon which the tenants of the front house had reserved seats. In a corner of the yard over by the hydrant, a sheep, which was to be raffled off as the climax of the celebration, munched its wisp of hay patiently, while bare-legged children climbed its back and pulled its wool. From the second story of the adjoining house, which was a stable, a big white horse stuck his head at intervals out of the window, and surveyed the shrine and the people with an interested look.

The musicians, issuing forth victorious from a protracted struggle with a fleet of schooners in the saloon, came out wiping their mustachios, and blew "Santa Lucia" on their horns. The sweetly seductive melody woke the echoes of the block and its slumbering memories. The old women rocked in their seats, their faces buried in their hands. The crowd from the street increased, and the chief celebrant, who turned out to be no less a person than the saloon-keeper himself[,] reaped a liberal harvest of silver half dollars. The villagers bowed and crossed themselves before the saint, and put into the plate their share toward the expense of the celebration. Its guardian made a strong effort to explain about the saint to Mr. Roosevelt.

"He is just-a lik'-a your Saint Patrick here," he said, and the president of the Police Board nodded. He understood.

Between birthdays, the other added, the saint was left in the loft of the saloon, lest the priest get hold of him and get a corner on him, as it were. Once he got him into his possession, he would not let the people have him except upon payment of a fee that would grow with the years. But the saint belonged to the people, not to the church. He was their home patron, and they were not going to give him up. In the saloon they had him safe. Mr. Roosevelt delighted the honest villagers by taking five shares in the sheep, albeit the suggestion that it might be won by and conducted in triumph by the band to Police Headquarters gave him pause. He trusted to luck, however, and took chances.

And luck favored him. He did not win the sheep. The names of all who had taken chances were put into a bag with that of the saint, and in the evening drawn out one by one. When the saint's name appeared there arose a great shout. The next would be the winner. Every neck was craned to read the lucky name as it came out.

"Philomeno Motso," read the man with the bag, and there was an answering shriek from the third-floor fire-escape behind the shrine. The widow up there had won the prize. Such luck was undreamed of. She came down forthwith and hugged the sheep rapturously, while the children kissed it and wept for joy. The last of the candles went out, and the shrine was locked in the loft over the saloon for another year.

San Donato's feast-day is one of very many such days that are celebrated in New York in the summer months. By what magic the calendar of Italian saints was arranged so as to bring so many birthdays within the season of American sunshine I do not know. But it is well. The religious fervor of our Italians is not to be pent up within brick walls, and sunshine and flowers belong naturally to it. "Religious" perhaps hardly describes it, yet in its outward garb it is nearly always that. They have their purely secular feasts, — their Garibaldi day and their Constitution day, both in June, their Columbus day, and the day in September commemorating the invasion of Rome and the end of the temporal power of the pope, — and they celebrate them with the enthusiasm of which their hundred and fifty-odd societies in New York have always an abundant store. The rigors of our Northern winter and an unfavorable experience with the police have driven the carnival indoors and turned it into a big masquerade ball. Once, on a temptingly sunny February day some eight or ten years ago, Mulberry street started in to keep carnival in the traditional way; but it had forgotten the police regulations. The merrymakers were locked up for masquerading without a permit, and were fined ten dollars each in the police court. Ball tickets are cheaper, and Mulberry street has confined itself to dancing since. But if one wishes to catch a glimpse of the real man, it is not on these occasions that it is to be had. It is when he is "at home" with the saint in the back yard, the church, or wherever it may be.

To the Italian who came over the sea the saint remains the rallying-point in his civic and domestic life to the end of his days. His son may cast him off, but not the father. Occasionally their relations are strained, perhaps. Such things happen in all families. Inattention to duty on the part of the saint may seem to require correction, or even more drastic measures. You may catch your man, after a losing game of cards, shying a boot at the shrine in the corner, with an angry "Why did you let me lose? I gave you a new candle last week"; but that only goes to prove the closeness of the compact between them. To the homesick peasant who hangs about the Mott-street café for hours, hungrily devouring with his eyes the candy counterfeit of Mount Vesuvius in the window, with lurid lava-streams descending and saffron smoke ascending, predicting untold stomach-quakes in the block, the saint means home and kindred, neighborly friendship in a strange land, and the old communal ties, which, if anything, are tightened by distance and homesickness. In fact, those ties are as real as they were at home. Just as the Aulettans flock in Elizabeth street, so in Mulberry, Mott, and Thompson streets downtown, and in the numbered streets of Little Italy uptown, almost every block has its own village of mountain or lowland, and with the village its patron saint, in whose worship or celebration — call it what you will — the particular camp makes reply to the question, "Who is my neighbor?" For the feuds came over with the fealty, and are of record in the police office. When a fresh record is made, the detectives do not go out haphazard in the Bend and look for the man with the knife. They find out to what village he belonged, and, if it is not a question of cards, which other village is its pet-enemy.

Then there are the saints of wider dominion, whose patronage is claimed by many towns, and whose prestige is correspondingly great. The day before the

Auletta celebration in Elizabeth street, it had been St. Roch's day, — "Rocco" he is called by the barbarians of Mulberry street, — and his partizans had wandered around the block behind the band with the green cock-feathers, resting at intervals in the back yard where the shrine was erected. Indeed, there were half a dozen independent celebrations going on all day in as many yards, always the darkest and shabbiest, which this saint seems to pick out by a kind of instinct, reminiscent, perhaps, of his earthly appearance...

When the July sun shines fiercest, and melts the asphalt pavements of Little Italy, there comes a day when all the bands and all the processions march toward One Hundred and Fifteenth street. There, quite near the East River, stands the Church of Our Lady of Mount Carmel, who, in the language of one of her devout adherents, is "the Madonna they worship most" in these parts. Not only from New York and Brooklyn, but from the far towns of New Jersey and the railroad camps of Connecticut, come hosts to kneel at her shrine. All through the night preceding the feast, wagons loaded with confectionery, fruit, and waxed candles drive up and take position at the curb, as near the church as possible. Before the dawn is announced by the booming of guns, a double row of wagons extends into the avenue at each end of the block. The drivers sleep in their seats. With daybreak there is a sudden awakening. The whole of Little Italy appears to pour itself into the street at once, and such marvelous combinations of color break out from the tenements as are never seen anywhere else. The rainbow is only a feeble suggestion of them. Fireworks go off, the hucksters' cries rend the air. The people cheer and forthwith attack the candle wagons. They are out for a good time, and it is quite evident that they are having it. Women with children in arms elbow the throngs to get near the wagons. Never one goes away without her candle. The venders reap a rich harvest. They have candles from a few cents up to forty dollars — monster ones twice as long and as heavy as the average purchaser, gorgeously decked with gilt, with pictures of the Madonna, and with crucifixes. The big ones go first.

The great basement doors of the church are opened, and the throng takes shape and direction. It moves toward the shrine above which stands the image of the Virgin in spotless, flowing robes. All about are crutches and canes cast away by those whom she has healed. The women throw themselves before her and hold out their babies to be blessed. Men kneel and mumble prayers. The resistless march of the multitude sweeps them on. They clutch blindly at near-by seats and sink into them, repeating incessantly their prayer and telling their beads. Soon the church is filled to overflowing but there is no break in the march. There is none till the last ray of the day's sun has long died in the west and midnight draws near. The crowd presses on and on, stumbles before the shrine in a vain effort to kneel, and catches at the robe of the Virgin for but a single touch, even at the hem of her garment, as it is borne past. Back at the shrine, the priests are receiving the offerings of the people and piling them at the feet of the image. The murmur of a thousand subdued voices in fervent supplication rises above the tread of countless feet marching ever on and on.

By breakfast-time comes the first procession, with a band. Six men bear a banner aloft with a picture of the Virgin made of — greenbacks. Handfuls of bank-notes are pinned to the banner wherever there is a vacant spot. It is an Italian society grateful for past favors, and takes this practical way of bearing witness to the fact. Other banners come during the day, and are borne into the church, to be tendered to the guardian priests. The enthusiasm of the audience is fired at the sight. A woman kneeling in her seat takes off her necklace and flings it at the priest who catches it deftly and pins it to the robe of the Madonna. The eyes of the happy giver shine with joy. A kind of frenzy seizes the audience; watches, rings, ear-rings, and pins are passed up. The image stands forth in a robe of shimmering gold above the moving multitude.

Outside, band follows band, procession upon procession. From every corner of the compass they march into the street, men, women, and children, shouldering candles, little and big, that wilt in the July sun and crook like question-marks long before the church door is reached. A woman carries a mighty candle on her bare shoulder, walking barefoot on the hot asphalt. It is a self-imposed penance, requiring no little fortitude and endurance. Some march barefoot the six miles and over from Mulberry street, choosing the roughest pavement and kneeling on the sharpest stones on the way to tell their beads. Lest there should be none sharp enough, the most devout carry flints in their pockets to put under their knees. Girls walk in white with veils and lighted candles. An elderly woman steps proudly, bearing upon her head a temple of wax candles steadied with pink ribbons held by four matrons. The cry of the chestnut vendor rises above the din. He carries his ware threaded upon a fish-line at the end of a long pole. Dimes in plenty are his catch. Pink lemonade is hawked along the curb, and huge slices of watermelon, red and juicy, make the mouths of the thirsty paraders water. But they cannot stop. At a stand on the corner a boy sits perched on a stool, his whole face buried in an enormous rind, munching for dear life, while with his disengaged hand he waves mechanically a newspaper fastened to a stick to chase the flies from his table. The sun pours down upon his bare head, the bands bray, the show and the banners go by; he eats right on. He has his share of the feast, and on the point of miracles is satisfied.

The processions lose themselves in the struggling crowds only to be evolved again farther on by some undiscoverable process of extrication that works automatically without the assistance of the police, who strive manfully but unsuccessfully to clear the way. A company of fifty or sixty girls crowned with wreathes and each carrying a burning taper are greeted with cheers. In their wake a little fellow labors along bent nearly double under the weight of a monstrous candle. Every garment drips perspiration. He is wet through, but radiantly happy and proud. His gaze is riveted upon the goad that comes steadily nearer, the white-stone steps of the church. Every face is set in the same direction. Children emerge with the hand that touched the Virgin's robe swathed in handkerchiefs to keep the blessing safe and to make it last. At the shrine the pile of golden offerings grows. Twenty or even thirty thousand dollars is not an unusual valuation of it when the feast is over. The money goes to the work of the church among the poor rather than to deck the image with gold and gems that might tempt sacrilegious thieves.

At noon there is a brief lull to enable the paraders to snatch a hasty bite from the wagons. The early afternoon brings more bands, more processions, ever-increasing in invasions from east and west. They come by families, and each member, from father to the baby, must bring a candle to the altar if nothing more. The block is jammed, and every street in the vicinity. The paraders, with canes and martial step, march and countermarch on the outskirts of the crowd. At any time one may hear half a dozen bands playing different tunes within earshot. The throng keeps time to them all. Night comes, with fervor unabated. Colored lanterns are strung across the street. In the church a thousand candles are lighted. The last tired stragglers have their reward. All the hardships of the long, hot day are forgotten as they prostrate themselves before the Madonna and kiss the hem of her robe. The heavy doors are swung to behind them, and locked. The feast of Our Lady of Mount Carmel is past and gone like a beautiful dream. The crowds disperse slowly in the midnight hour. The prosaic Frenchman across the street shrugs his shoulder expressively as he puts up his shutters. "Phantasme Italien," he says, and goes in. Yet he has let his storefront and made money. He too has cause to be satisfied.

Jacob Riis, "Feast Days in Little Italy," *Century Magazine* 58, no. 4 (August 1899): 491–99.

72. Italian Women and the Return of San Rocco, ca. 1890

With the overwhelming number of Italians indifferent to regular churchgoing and many Italian men hostile to formal religious practices, the women had a crucial role in passing on the traditions of Italian religiosity as imported from the homeland. The following newspaper account, though undated, was probably published in the 1890s. It relates the story of women rescuing a statue that held powerful religious meaning for them.

THE RETURN OF SAN ROCCO
Joy of the Potentini When a Legal Tangle Was Solved

There is no longer any danger that sudden fatal disease may strike down the Potentini, the faithful people of the Italian province of Potenza, who dwell by the thousand on James and Oliver and Roosevelt Streets. After being kept for two nights and a day in an undertaker's shop, as a prisoner, and after being touched, sacrilegiously, by hands deemed unclean, San Rocco, the patron saint of the Potentini, who protects them from all evils, but in particular from the death-bringing plague, is now back in his proper place in the little Church of San Gioacchin[o] on Roosevelt Street . . .

Let the truth be told right here; the men took him away — not with their own hands, but by their squabbles in law courts, and their talk of legal right and wrong. And it was the women who early this morning, and with their own hands, carried back the blessed statue of the saint sprinkling with their tears the way over which he had to pass. The women do not care about law, of the right of possession, or such things — who can own a saint, anyhow? All they care for is that the saint be in his wonted place in the dim church, that they may come to him for protection for themselves and their little ones.

Never before was such a scene witnessed, even in these parts of the city, where all sorts of strange and wonderful things are happening every day. After a night spent in . . . weeping and wailing, the frightened women of the Potentian colony learned about ten o'clock this morning that the kind Father Poggio, rector of the Church of San Gioacchino, from which the statue of San Rocco was taken on Tuesday, had succeeded in arranging things. He whose word is law to the Potentini, had had to furnish security, a bond to guarantee that if the suit that is now pending in the Second Municipal Court should be decided adversely, the disputed statue would be delivered up to whosoever was declared by the court to be its owner. They spoke with bate[d] breath of enormous sums, of many hundreds of dollars. As a fact, the two Potentini who furnished the bond had had to give security to the extent of $1,000 or just as much as the other side had had to give before they obtained a writ of replevin, enabling them to get possession of the statue.

Scores of women had spent the night in or near the church, crying and praying lest misfortune of direst kind befall them and theirs on account of the absence of their principal protector. Their numbers swelled as the morning advanced, until more than a hundred were on hand, when at last the glad tidings arrived. It was learned that the bond had been filed and that City Marshall Freeman, who had seized the statue under the writ, had declared his willingness to surrender it at once.

The Release Acclaimed

At first deep silence reigned on the narrow street in front of the gray-gabled church. Then such a shout rose as could have come in equal strength only from an army. Young women and middle-aged matrons, toothless granddams [*sic*] and little barefoot maids, embraced and cried and shouted and danced with joy. Down to the New Bowery the shout spread, hands popping out of every window to find the cause; it ran like electric flashes along a wire to James, to Oliver, to Madison Street, down to the East River. Out of towering tenements tumbled women in noisy eagerness. "To the church," was the cry. In a few minutes the small space in front of the church was blocked — there must have been a thousand women, and hardly a man among them, except old Bacigalupo, the sexton, who was so excited that he stuttered.

Somebody — maybe it was the sexton, or maybe it was young Coluccio, the president of the Societa Fratellanza San Rocco — led the way to the undertaking shop of Vecchio & Maresco on James Street, in front of which the little boys and little girls of the colony spent exciting hours all day yesterday, fighting among themselves to get near the window, and pressing their little noses flat against the pane in order to catch a glimpse of the saint in his cabinet inside. Logito, the old caretaker, stood in the door, with sullen mien as the crowd came by.

"How many of those — those things there are true Potentini? They came from everywhere, even from Napoli. And now they claim our saint — he who belongs only to the p[e]ople of Potenza, and for whose coming all the way from Italy we, the real Potentini, paid our cents and dollars," he cried.

But old Logito has learned that American law cannot be resisted. All he could do was to demand a receipt for the statue from the marshal. Then he stepped sullenly inside and let the on-sweeping flood of hysterical women break against the narrow doorway, where they struggled so frantically to be first that none could get in for a while. But at last a score managed to force themselves into the narrow room where old Logito stood, pressed closer to the wall, fearful in spite of his courage. For the women of Potenza are dangerous if their ire be thoroughly aroused. Not another man was there, the marshal having discreetly vanished.

With a common impulse the women inside fell on their knees and began to pray with passionate fervor, raising now and then their hands up to the saint whose waxen face smiled down upon them with stereotyped benignity. Those outside saw what the little group inside was doing, and followed example. As rings spread on the mirroring surface of a lake when a pebble is thrown into it, so one row of women after another would sink down into kneeling position on the rough pavement, until, look where one may, there was nothing to be seen but heads bent in prayer. This lasted a couple of minutes, perhaps, while from the worshipping crowd rose a murmur as of the swarming of a million bees. Above that sound, that seemed like a silence, rose suddenly a shrill yell, and through the crowd a shock passed visibly. Some beat their breasts in a panic of new fear. Was the saint not there, after all? Or had he shown a sign of his anger that was not to be appeased?

Again the shout was heard, and this time the note of anger was perceived. At once, a thousand tongues were moving in rapid questioning. By degrees the news spread. Oh, those dogs, those — ! The statue was in pieces — a curse on them! No, no — not in pieces, but partly broken. The nose? No, an arm — not, just a fold of the mantle — no, no, it wasn't the statue at all. Glory, glory, it was safe, but the base on which it stood — no, not the base either — and so on. The truth was that a small splinter of wood had been knocked out of the cabinet in which the statue is housed when not on exhibition at special occasions. They found it on the floor and picke[d] it up tenderly.

Then, lest worse befall, they proceeded to move the saint back to his niche in the church. Eight very old women took the statue slowly and carefully out of the cabinet and lifted it on to their shoulders. When they appeared on the street, a cry was sent toward the sky that could be heard many blocks. Women laughed until the tears began to flow afresh. They embraced, not in pairs, three and four together. Others knelt again, with quickly moving lips, and fingers eagerly plucking at the beads of their rosaries.

San Rocco's Return

Slowly the eight old women moved down the narrow street to the corner of Madison Street, some fifty feet away. Behind them followed six women carrying the cabinet. And in their wake again came two younger women who in their joined hands carried the splinter torn from the cabinet. Every now and then one of them bent her head reverently over the bit of wood and kissed it. From all sides the other women surged forward that their fingers might touch the sacred statue or if that were impossible, the cabinet at least. Under the pressure the brightly colored figure swayed as if in danger of falling, but the old women clung to their burden, and continued to push steadily forward along Madison Street toward the corner of Roosevelt Street, only a block away.

A Flower-Strewn Way

In the meantime, a number of women had collected flowers and began to strew them in front of the improvised procession. Others had procured lighted candles and formed in lines on both sides of the bearers of the statue. As the statue progressed, not only the women, but all men who happened along, fell on their knees with hands folded in prayer around their caps. It took the procession nearly thirty minutes to reach the little church. There they were met by the sexton and several of the priests. The crush in front of the building was fearful, but nobody seemed to mind it, or even to notice it. At last the church was entered, and the statue was tenderly deposited on a platform temporarily arranged for it to the right of the altar and by the side of the image of the Blessed Virgin. Immediately a hundred candles were lighted and placed before the Saint on sconces provided for the occasion. Every seat in the church was filled. Down at the door hundreds stood up, while other hundreds tarried outside, awaiting their turn. The numbers decreased gradually during the day, but worshipping groups [were] always in evidence. And along all the streets inhabited by the tribe of the Potentini eager groups were seen discussing the triumphant return of the saint and the trouble that caused his brief exit.

"Clipping concerning the Dispute over Statue of S. Rocco," Church of St. Joachim, in Center for Migration Studies, no. 079, box 5, folder 124. Printed with permission.

73. A Priest's View of Italian Religious Festivals, ca. 1900

The religious festivals held slight appeal to priests ministering among Italians, who seldom attended Sunday Mass or sought church services except infant baptisms, weddings, and funerals. Father Giacomo Gambera, a member of Bishop Scalabrini's Missionary Society of St. Charles, served in several Italian immigrant communities in the United States through the late nineteenth and early twentieth centuries. He left an extensive memoir that reveals his views on ministry to Italians. His objection to festivals, which he calls processions, demonstrates the division among Italians concerning these religious practices.

Processions

It was in Chicago that I saw for the first time the use of processions in our community: carrying statues of crucifixes, Madonnas, and saints through the public streets, but with methods that for me were condemnable in every aspect.

First of all in a city in which you have a mixture of nonbelievers and those of other faiths, this parading of statues exposed our religion to irreverence and derision.

In the second place, the promoters of these external feasts were generally not trustworthy individuals; they were not exemplary, they were not practicing Catholics, and they were suspected of pure speculation. In fact, without any authorization, they used to solicit offerings from their fellow townsmen in the name of the feast and of the parish. Then, when the parade was over, they would strip the saints of the offerings made and not render an account to anyone; at the most, they would give an account to their society as they wished.

They offered nothing to the parish, but only the usual offering for the mass and sermon. It was a speculative administration of a committee which neither the society members nor the pastor could control.

It is clear that such abusive customs could not be favored by the pastor, and in no way did I want them introduced in my parish, even more so because by giving in to one group that would have aroused the yearning among others to do the same. The honor of our religion and the interests of the Church would have been even more compromised, and the veneration would simply have served to bring considerable profits to the shrewd and self-styled devotees.

One day, a committee approached me saying they wanted to carry in procession the crucifix that was in the church which some devotees had donated. I tried with every possible reason to dissuade them, but it was impossible. I promised I would conduct a solemn service in the church at no cost to them, but it was not acceptable. I asked if they were disposed to give the pastor an account of the money collected and to give the parish the net profits, and they refused. Then I opposed the idea with all firmness, but to intimidate me, or to cause more annoyance, they had recourse to the usual threats of death and destruction.

For these people there are neither pastors nor bishops to regulate the way of worship, but they have to do whatever they want to do. If they are contradicted, then beware! Sentences of capital punishment.

It was the first time I found myself in such a dispute.

To avert worse disturbances, I allowed them to take the crucifix from the church, but on condition that it would never be allowed back in again.

When that profane procession was over and after pocketing the money, they placed the crucifix in the nearby Church of St. Stephen, deceiving the frail pastor and scaring the assistant so much that he went insane and was admitted to Columbus Hospital where one night, out of his fixation of persecution, he jumped out of the window, but was saved.

It is not necessary to add that in that procession there were neither any prayers, nor religious hymns, but only shouting and unbecoming exclamation. Some simple women, in their ignorant simplicity, carried candles and walked barefooted. The zealous collectors went from door to door, and many made generous offerings, while they refused even the smallest offering to the church. The statues were carried around only as promotional devices and to increase their business. They expected a priest should also be among them.

It is futile to note that these were methods of the few southern traditions, which are disliked and disapproved by all.

Other societies or individual devotees also celebrated the feast of their towns' patron saints, but in church. If any money was left over from the collections they had taken up, this was turned over to the pastor for the needs of the parish.

To eliminate such serious, shameful, and unbecoming things, the Italian pastors decided as a group to ask the archbishop for a formal prohibition to be read in our churches. But so as not to have disturbances from these dangerous fanatics, at least so it is believed, nothing was done about it, abandoning us all to ourselves in these painful conflicts.

That which I suffered in those moments of rash reaction in the parish while I was only carrying out my sacred duty of putting an end to frauds, profanations, and the waste of money out of pure vanity; and that which I suffered when four swindlers threatened my life, and after having so patiently tried the best I could to revive that congregation, which with difficulty was making progress, I entrust all that to God alone.

The devotion of certain of my fellow-countrymen seemed to me to be a pagan remnant with substitution of idols.

In this connection, the church authorities, together with the civil authorities, should take drastic steps for the honor and good order of the common

Catholic worship, and to protect the clergy and the interests of the Church from dishonest and dangerous elements.

Too many serious cases have been verified.

> Giacomo Gambera, *A Migrant Missionary Story: The Autobiography of Giacomo Gambera,* edited and with an introduction by Mary Elizabeth Brown (New York: Center for Migration Studies, 1994), 157–60. Printed with permission.

74. Italians' Attitudes toward Catholicism, ca. 1900

Father Giacomo Gambera, author of the previous document, also recorded his views on the differences within the Italian immigrant community between those who frequented Italian Catholic churches and those who did not. As an experienced missionary he knew at first hand the layers of responses to pastoral ministry among Italians.

Church Influence among Italians

The most sacred institution, the most revered monument for our emigrants abroad, is the Church. It is the first and authoritative school of religious and social duties. It is the focal point of Christian and civic virtues. It is the meeting place of the most intimate and brotherly union. It is the House of God and of the people, where domestic and national customs are consolidated and sanctified.

Moreover, the Church keeps the Italians' prestige and their esteem in Americans' and foreigners' eyes high, whether they are Catholics or not. A colony of emigrants is all the more valued by the ecclesiastic and civic authorities, the more it shows itself to be faithful to the practices of its religion, which is rightly recognized as the most efficient creator of the highest human education.

But unfortunately in our colonies, especially among the most fortunate and educated class, the so-called *prominenti,* comprising the representatives of our government, gave a general example of irreligion, with rare exceptions.

It was and is a rare exception to see a banker, a rich businessman, an industrialist, a doctor or a judge of our race in church on a Sunday. Very few of them were practicing, or were interested in their national religious institutions.

Furthermore, the newspapers of our language, put out nothing except skeptical professions and propaganda and mocked the divine mysteries of our faith; the lurid *Asino* [meaning "Donkey," an anticlerical periodical] led the bunch. It was favorite reading matter among workers of ours who knew how to read.

So this disgraceful indifference of the upper class certainly did nothing to deserve credit and respect from Americans and foreigners, much less to unite and help to improve our immigrants.

But what is worse is that the example of the upper class was followed by the lower class. I heard it said so many times: neither my *compare* [close family friend] the banker, my fellow townsman such-and-such, a doctor or lawyer, the president of the Don Pasquale Society — that crook who made himself rich, my "boss," nor many others more fortunate than myself, not even our consul, go to church, and I have to go, I who am a worker, a poor father of a family, have to give money to the parish priest. I who am the most poor?

And one takes note that there isn't a people who waste a lot of money on festive vanities, bands, fireworks, flowers, parades, processions, funerals, etc. like ours does. They squander in a few hours treasures which would have been more than sufficient to support churches, schools and orphanages.

Americans who see them spending considerable sums on showy appearances and neglecting their public institutions, religious and humanitarian, and end up saying, as I have also heard many times: "The Italian people is crazy!"

In these big cities our colonies have the example of Catholics — Irish, German, Polish, Slav, Belgian, etc., — right in front of their very eyes, who almost all attend and maintain splendid religious and national works.

They are seen to be well organized, with their most distinguished citizens as leaders, all in agreement and united in the apostolate of their priests. But all this edifying example has served for little or nothing; even today 80 out of 100 of ours are non-practicing, with the *prominenti* leading the way.

From this state of affairs, it arose that the Catholics and Protestants criticized us, condemned us, were scornful of us and said, "the Italian people who came from the center of Catholicism and Christianity, and who should be the first to give an example of a Christian spirit and way of life, is instead the one who in its ignorance and irreligion scandalizes believers."

These accusations might be rather unjust and exaggerated, but our people have regrettably given reason for them to be made.

One doesn't forget that our immigration resembled a dispersed flock, disorganized, divided, without language, without power, and on the whole coarse and illiterate, and was therefore more exposed to all the moral and physical dangers than any other nationality. It thus had an absolute need for wise leaders and superior examples. If the superior and more influential class had been united with the missionary fathers by consensus or leadership, the colonies would have become more united and disciplined. They would have provided educational and charitable institutions, and their descendants would have inherited the language of their fathers and would have grown up with a greater attachment to their religion and to their fatherland of origin. Instead those who are supposed to have the power and obligation, refuse to support our work, and they have left us alone in our churches with the minority of our faithful and with the poorest element. Thus we stayed at the tail end of it all. Even today in almost all the colonies, we are forced in the most wretched of cases to run to the foreign institutions, who either do or don't accept and help us. Many of the young people have lost their love of, even the memory of their faith, or their language and of the blessed and glorious land of their forefathers, when they are not feeding on hatred and aversion.

For lack of example and guidance and to better protect themselves on their own, our exiles founded societies of mutual assistance. They became split by *campanilismo* [loyalty to native village] with a disastrous dispersal of strength. What is worse, the societies were presided over by people completely lacking the most basic qualities necessary to morally elevate their associates — when they weren't astute swindlers, capable of any dishonest exploitation.

Many societies carried the name of the patron saint of their village and celebrated their annual ceremony with splendrous and noisy parades, and with a mass and even a panegyric.

But the societies were rarely present in church. Everything began and ended on the outside.

In conclusion, the sorrowful example of irreligion given by the upper class and disseminated by unbelieving journalism has brought the following disasters to the colonies: divisions, impotence, contempt, weakness, and finally exclusion. The example of Cincinnati, and later on of other colonies, were proof that when a few respectable Italians are the first to promote and finance religious institutions, they are fervently followed by the others, [and] success is ensured and the foreigners admire and praise.

> Giacomo Gambera, *A Migrant Missionary Story: The Autobiography of Giacomo Gambera,* edited and with an introduction by Mary Elizabeth Brown (New York: Center for Migration Studies, 1994), 89–91. Printed with permission.

75. Social Worker's Report, San Francisco, 1917

St. Peter's and St. Paul's Church is a landmark in San Francisco's Italian community. The parish social worker, Irida (?) Martini, made home visits on behalf of the parish's Sunday school program. Her reports excerpted here address a concern for the Italians' faith life as she records baptism (B), confession (C), confirmation (Cf), and Sunday School (SS). Apart from remarks on these benchmarks for formal church affiliation, her reports reveal aspects of Italian-American life as of 1917.

Report Month of April 1917
SS. Peter's & Paul's Sunday School

Made a number of visits to old friends that needed looking up. Among them:

Chiatello — This family consists of the father who is really a bad type, alcoholic and all that, a mother who is always in poor health and goes to the clinic-hospital nearly every year for something or other, [and their children:]

Katie 15,	B.	C.	Cf.	–	In Juvenile Home.
Joe, 13,	B.	C.		–	Sickly
Angelina 8,	B.			–	Badly nourished
Louisa 5,	B.			–	" "
Baby 1,	not B.			–	" "

These children seldom go to Church. The mother claims that it is because they often lack clothes. I saw to it that the children received some clothes not very long ago, but still they do not come. Joe is at present a dip[h]theria carrier and the mother has just returned from the isolation hospital with it. Katie is in the Juvenile Home under treatment for one of the social diseases. A few years back a man was sent to the State prison for contributing to her delinquency — with the father's consent — and in 1914 Katie was committed to the Associated Charities for legal control. Since then Katie has been under good observation, but very lately she got in with a loose company of "friends" and is now in trouble. Miss Ashe of the Telegraph Hill Assn. has been hovering around this family and is now trying to send off to Hill Farm Joe and the rest for their health.

The father is a cook by profession, but if he works one day a month he believes firmly that he has done his noble duty toward his family and spends the rest of the month drinking and loafing.

Something ought to be done in regards to this family otherwise they are lost absolutely. They live now at 839 Greenwich St.

Marrone — Carolina — 3012 A Steiner St. 11 years old.

This child's mother died a few months ago with Tuberculosis in the City and County Hospital. Since then she has been living with her father. He is the janitor in the Hawaiin [sic] Bldg. at the Exposition. The child has been neglected spiritually.

A few weeks ago Miss Storti called at the Haawaii [sic] Bldg. with an officer and removed the child to the Detention Home where her case is pending now. It seems as though the child slept in the same room with her father — in the basement of the Hawwaiin [sic] Bldg. and the place was an awful sight — dirty, unhealthy and not calculated to have a beneficent influence on the child.

There is an older sister who lives with an aunt and works.

The father is willing to pay $5.00 for the child's support in a foster home. He receives $45.00 a month salary.

Federico — Alice, 9 years old. Gave her note to take to Sister for H. Communion. The mother is an alcoholic also. The father died a few months ago and the family is in need now, but the child has been rather wild all along and never — or seldom — came to S. School. She promised to come, but will need looking after to make her keep her promise as there is no co-operation from the mother. They live at 656 Greenwich St. Sicilian.

Bitelli — 1241 Kearny St. Miss Ashe has been, and is interested in this family. She is now wanting to send them to Hill Farm to recuperate from malnutrition she says (the children — Rosie 11, Frank 6, Tessie 10, Antoinette 7).

The girls were there last year and unless they could get something from the Italian Church seldom come near it. The girls especially promised me time after time to come regularly to S. school [*sic*], but so far they have kept their promises very poorly. Sicilians.

Defelippo — 19 Salmon Alley. Joe 13, Bennie 8. The mother died in this family 5 years ago and they have had no one to look after them (there are 8 in the family) except the father. They have been sadly neglected as far as their spiritual training goes. And the boys are rather a wild bunch. Lately they have been contaminating other boys and the case had been referred to me by the Juvenile Protective Assn. Mr. Mario Forno has been going after them too, with me, but they do need someone to keep after them constantly. The father is a property owner and independent. Sicilian.

Cassetta — 459 Chestnut St. (9 children in the family) but Vincenza, 13, B, C [and] Jim, 10, B, [s]eldom go to S. School and [need] looking after. Also Paul, 9, who started S.S. but has not continued going.

Cassasa — Charles, 7, B, goes to SS once in while. Mother goes to Mass pretty regularly but father sleeps on Sundays. Genoese. 557A Filbert St.

Ditto, 163 Jasper Place,

Lizzie, 13,	B	C	Cf	Does not go SS.
Millie 11,	B	C	Cf	Does not go SS. reg.
Emilia 10,	B	C		" " "
Josephine 6,	B			
Angelina 4,	B			

Children are negligent about Sunday School. Mother has been sick lately and the girls have had to keep house. Father is a bootblack and works on Sundays. Sicilian. Need constant looking after to make them come to S.S.

Paccella, 553 Filbert St. Father is a bootblack. Calabrese.

Biaggio 16,	B	C	Cf.
Pasquale, 14,	B	C	Cf.
Salvatore, 11,	B	[C]	Does not come to SS.
Joe, 6,	B		
Jimmie, 5,	B		
Rosie, 15,	B	C	Cf.
Flora, 9,	B		Is now preparing for SS.
Marie 2,	B		
Ida, 8 mos,	B		

Some Hard Cases

Pennisi, F. Father is a cooper. Sicilians. 2035 Taylor St.

Bastiano 15,	B	no C or Cf.
Ida 13,	B	" " " "
Mike 12,	B	" " " "
Grace 8,	B	" " " "
Lucy 6,	B	" " " "
Frank 4,	B	" " " "

Father will not let children go to Church. Says they can pray at home as well. Mother is of same sentiment. Spent half an hour trying to make them think differently but no results.

Balestreri, V. Laborer. Sicilian. 2037 Taylor St.

Josie 9,	B	Goes to SS very irregularly.
Salvatore 7,	B	
Mario 5,	B	
Frank 6,	B	
Peter 14 mos.,	No B.	

Mother says children would rather play than go to SS. Parents negligent.

Scribante, I. Cement Contractor. Piedmontese. 2039 Taylor.

Pompilio 14,	B	no C or Cf.	Have gone to SS very irreg.
Marie 13,	B	" " " "	" " " " " " "
Laurina 10,	B	" " " "	" " " " " " "

Parents seldom go to Church. Father works and mother is ill. Five years from Italy. Want them now to receive all together — the Holy Sacraments. Have been very negligent. Talked to the mother at length regarding her duty towards her children. Hope that it may produce results.

Messina, A. Fisherman. Sicilian. 1041 Taylor St.

Joe 16,	B	C but no Cf.
Salvatore 15,	B	No C or Cf.
Peter 13,	B	" " " "
Mary 11,	B	" " " "
Vincent 8,	B	" "
Luciano 3,	B	
Frank 9 mos.,	B	

Mother says she can't do anything with the boys. Beyond her control to make them go to Church. Gave her a talking to, also. Doubt if it will produce desired results, though.

Romeo, A. Fisherman. Calabrese. 2036 Taylor St.

Marie 4 mos.,   not B.   Will soon.

D'Acquisto, V. Husband invalid. Sicilian. Fisherman. 2021 Taylor St.

Jim 14,	B	C	no Cf.	Doesn't go to S.S.	
John 10,	B	No C		Goes very irreg to SS.	
Peter 9,	B	" "	" "	" " " "
Antonio 4,	B				
Mary 18,	B,	Miss Ashe is keeping her at the Tek			

Found some 412   Italian children   under 14 yrs of age
248   "   "   over 14 yrs of age
41 Mexican, Spanish, etc. under 14 yrs of age
15   "   "   "   over   "   "   "

I find that the minister of the Evangelist [*sic*] Church on Filbert St. near Mason has been canvassing the neighborhood for Sunday School children with apparently indifferent results, but he is keeping it up with the assistance of some of his followers. This man was a priest in Italy formerly.

The Green St. Church has a new minister also, a young man who speaks the Italian language very fluently. This man is working and worrying himself sick over the distressing poverty which he fancies exists among our Italians, I am told. He is feverishly seeking to give material aid right and left — with the assistance of the Associated Charities and other organizations on the Beach — ingratiating himself in the good graces of these people and often leading them to his Church.

As a matter of fact, there is *comparatively* little poverty among our people this year. Here and there one finds a case that needs tiding over for a few weeks on account of illness in the family, or need more clothing for their many children, often they need medical attention and medicines, but they are not destitute in the real sense of the word. The trouble with this promiscuous distribution of charity is, that instead of being constructive it tends to pauperize the recipient and leaves them more helpless than before. They often become slaves to begging — an art which often deceives the less learned in the idiosyncrasies.

I have established the habit of meeting the cases I come across that need material assistance at the Associated Charities Bldg. on Tuesday between 2 — 4 and with the assistance of Miss Kane go over the merits of the case.

I have renewed my efforts to get the Curfew Law enforced. The Vittoria Colonna Club, the Juvenile Protective Assn. and the San Francisco Federation of Women's Clubs are going to take it up further with the Police Commissioners of this city.

The Mexicans, Spaniards, Porto Ricans, et al, which I have met this last month, especially those on Salmon Alley and Himmelmann Place (across the street from the Spanish Church) live very poorly. I have found as many as ten — men, women, and children [—] crowded into four, dark, dirty rooms (19 Salmon Alley). These people seem to choose the most unlivable places — the darker the place the dirtier they'll keep it, and sometimes the smell in their home is more than any other mortal being could possibly stand for. Naturally, this sort of existence is not conducive to spiritual or moral perfection and complications often arise.

Archives of the Archdiocese of San Francisco. Printed with permission.

76. Sicilians Lay Merlo Away Like a Monarch, 1924

In the nineteenth century, Catholic clergy routinely criticized ostentatious floral displays at funerals, first for Irish immigrants and later for Italian newcomers. But the tradition persisted in rural and urban parishes and became even more elaborate in the 1920s as automobiles replaced horse-drawn carriages for the procession to the cemetery. Although Italian labor leader Mike Merlo was waked at home in a traditional manner, the funeral cortege bearing his remains to St. Clement Church in Chicago included a life-sized wax effigy dressed in a "suit" of blue flowers.

Michael Merlo, president of the powerful Union of Sicilian Societies, was buried to-day like the monarch he was. Thousands of Italians — wealthy merchants, shabby laborers, women riding in limousines and shawled women trudging through the rain — followed the body in a procession that stretched a mile through the streets and was an hour in passing.

The slow procession from the Merlo home at 443 Diversey parkway to St. Clement's church, at Deming place and Orchard street, and then to Mount Carmel cemetery was a richly colorful spectacle, accompanied by pomp befitting the man who, all unknown to half the city, exercised regal powers during his life.

Two hundred and sixty automobiles were in line behind the hearse, many of them heaped high with the countless flowers that had been laid in and around the Merlo home.

Wax Image in Limousine

At the head of the cortege, giving it a strange and foreign air, was a glittering limousine, in which, quite alone, sat a life-size image of Merlo, dressed in a suit made of woven blue flowers. Following that lead car were twenty-one automobiles almost hidden under burdens of flowers. Then came eighty-eight automobiles bearing representatives of the Sicilian societies. The hearse followed. Behind it rolled the many automobiles of the family, relatives and friends.

For hours traffic was utterly disorganized through the vicinity of the home and church. Long before the body of the Italian leader was taken from the home, where a ceremonious wake had been going on incessantly for days, a crowd of 3,000 Italians assembled in Diversey parkway. Outside the church another great crowd was waiting. The streets for blocks in every direction were impassable.

In spite of the fact that Merlo's passing has exerted mysterious influences in the underworld, there was no disorder at the funeral. Fewer than twenty policeman had been assigned to the funeral, and they had nothing to do.

Merlo's Name Used by Slayers

The death of Merlo is connected in a vague, mysterious way, with the subsequent murder of Dion O'Banion. The gunmen who shot O'Banion down in his flower shop on Monday spoke Merlo's name. Somehow Merlo is supposed to have held in check forces that have now become disorganized and uncontrollable, the police do not know how.

Solemn requiem mass in Merlo's honor was celebrated at St. Clements by Mgr. Francis Rempe. Burial was made at Mount Carmel. Honorary pallbearers were Mayor Dever, Francis X. Busch, State's Attorney Crowe, Joseph Esposito, Judge Francis Borrelli, J. E. Burke and Edgar A. Jonas, Martin J. O'Brien, Arthur O'Brien, Michael Kenna, Chief of Police Collins and Anton Cermak.

"Sicilians Lay Merlo Away Like a Monarch," *Chicago Daily News,*
13 November 1924.

The Slovaks

77. Matthew Jankola, Sketches from a Slovak Catholic Parish in Pittston, Pennsylvania, 1900

Slovak immigration to the United States increased during the 1870s. By 1920, more than six hundred thousand Slovaks had immigrated to the United States. Close to 80 percent of these immigrants were Catholic. In the following document, Father Matthew Jankola provides his perspective on the Slovak Catholic community. Jankola emigrated to the United States at the age of twenty, and he then completed his studies for the priesthood. He was ordained in 1895 and assigned to St. John the Baptist in Pittston, Pa. He ministered to the Slovaks of Pittston and of seven neighboring towns. He later assisted in the creation of a community of Slovak Sisters in 1909, the Congregation of Saints Cyril and Methodius.

My Parish

Twenty years ago there wasn't a single Slovak soul here. No Slovaks, except me, live in the city of Pittston itself. The nearest Slovaks have to walk about twenty minutes to get to church. For this reason, I have one of the worst parishes in America. Whenever it is cold, or it rains, I always fear that few people will show up in church. My parishioners live in seven "places" around Pittston. These are: West Pittston, with 7 families; Sturmerville, with about 40 families; Wyoming, with 10 families; Port Griffith, with about 40 families; Smithville, with 24 families; Duryea, with about 16 families; and Pittston Junction, with 14 families. About 30 of them own their homes. Three or four parishioners own 3–4 houses.

The majority of my parishioners hail from Spis County in Slovakia. For instance, Port Griffith houses Slovaks predominantly from the northern Spis region of "Pod Magura" (from the villages of Nedeca, Trips, Vysny and Nizny Laps, Kacvin, Cierna Hora, and so on). Others come from Abauj, Zemplín, Saris, and Uzhorod Counties. Only a few originate in Orava or Trencín Counties. These statistics cover only parishioners, that is, those who regularly support the church. About 200 boarders, plus 60 families, support my parish. Another 200–300 boarders never set foot in the church, and are not parishioners.

In America there are three kinds of Catholics. The majority are good, they fulfil their Christian duty, live as Christians, support their parish and priest, the organist and so on. Then you have the lukewarm Catholics, who hem and haw; and finally, the boarders, who don't give a hoot, live a carefree life, pay no attention to their souls, and plan to live a Christian life only in the Old Country! To this group also belong the "enlightened ones" and various other individuals.

You might be surprised that I can give you only an estimate of the number of my parishioners. That's because our people are always looking for better work, and always on the move, like the Jews. In my Annual Spiritual Report for the Bishop I estimated 800 "souls." The Slovaks care about their religion in spite of the fact that they are abroad and have to fend for themselves in a land which proclaims "liberty of conscience" and has many temptations. We have no patrons, no foundations, no church property, and the state does not support us. The people have to take the initiative, build their churches, and support their priests and bishops by themselves. Priests are paid between $600 and $1,000 yearly and the parishes have to pay a church tax to the bishop of between $25 and $200 per month (my poor parish pays only $50 per month). In America we have a sixth Commandment: support your parishes.

How do Slovaks support their churches and parishes in America? In various ways. Where there is no debt or where there are a lot of parishioners, they contribute in small amounts. In some places parishioners pay up to $1.00 monthly, in other places 75 or 50 cents or only 25 cents (as for instance, in Freeland). With me families generally pay 75 cents and individuals 50 cents, for a total of about $6.00 per year. In addition, because this year we will be building a church (our present church was purchased from the Germans and is too small and ugly), families are supposed to contribute an additional $10.00 and individuals $5.00 more per year. In some parishes these monthly contributions are gathered by "collectors," in others, such as in Irish churches, the people bring the money directly to the parish. We have two "collectors" at each location and, as soon as payday arrives, they visit every Slovak home and collect their dues. I went out collecting for the new church myself on two occasions. That's how it is in America! All gifts go into the parish treasury and all expenses are paid out of it: the building, the priest, the organist, the churchwarden, and the church and rectory decorations. The American priest, who is really a missionary, owns only his vestments and his books. He simply cannot afford to own any furniture or other material that he would have to transport from parish to parish.

Ownership — The Role of the Priest

All churches, schools, cemeteries, and so on are church property and are registered in the name of the bishop in trust. In our parish the property is registered in the land registry office as follows: St. John the Baptist Roman Catholic Congregation in Pittston, PA, in trust of the Rt. Rev. M. J. Hoban, Bishop of Scranton, PA. In other places the property is registered directly in the name of the bishop, or in the name of the bishop and the parish council; that depends on diocesan laws and state laws. The bishop does not concern himself with parish finances unless a problem appears in the annual report. In my case I control everything. The parish finances are in my name and I write the checks. Once a year I call a meeting of the parish collectors, who are also the trustees, and I show them the books. After that I announce these figures in church: what was our income, expenses, and how much of our debt we have retired. Other priests post these figures on the church doors; still others publish them and hand them out to their parishioners.

Those church finances! They have caused many uprisings in American parishes. In some places the priest has no control over the finances, he receives his pay, and that is it. But these are exceptions (among Slovaks they rarely arise), and very bad ones, and such priests are to be pitied. If the people see that their pastor is devoted, active, a good administrator, pays his debts (especially this, or he will be warned), is not arrogant (with some people you have to be very tactful), rude, cheap, demanding, snobbish, and lazy, and does not shirk his duties on Sunday after Mass, then the people will support him. The Slovaks are very good in this regard. However, if one's predecessor ruined everything, then it is very difficult to regain the people's trust. From this you musn't conclude that the priest here is a servant of the people and has no authority. We all know that in Hungary, if the priest sides with the nobles, he will triumph, but what do the people think of him? I know that people value good priests more in America than they do in Hungary. We live in a land of 40 million Protestants and atheists but it is unheard of that someone would insult a Roman Catholic priest, as often happened in Hungary. We don't normally wear vestments in public, but we do wear Roman collars, and even without it people recognize us and address us as "Father." Here, as in the old country, people do complain to the bishops about us, and especially here where there are so many trains and streetcars, and most often about that miserable treasury, and mostly it is by the smartalecks and loudmouths who wish to control the parish. We do not have great formalities here, we address the bishop simply as "Bishop" (and usually he also serves as his own secretary) and, if he so wishes, he simply tells you that he is removing you from the parish. You are now on vacation and can travel wherever you want (provided you have the finances). However, since America is a "free country," you can appeal to the Apostolic Delegate in Washington, or even to Rome itself! Here you can do it.

The Spiritual Life

If we did not have those dissolute "boarders" among us, I could safely say that our people would be the best, the most moral and religious of all. Those who were raised in a religious way in the old country are good Catholics here as well. The work of priests in Slovakia is evident here. My Spis Slovaks are the best of all those in Pittston — they attend services the most, they support the parish the most, and they obey and respect their pastor. Forty children attend the parochial school and if they lived closer, over 100 would attend. The people go to confession 2–3 times a year. We have a Rosary Society of the Sacred Heart and a Living Rosary Society; both have many members. Thirty of them subscribe to the religious magazine *Posol*. In the last year my parishioners raised almost $4,000 for the support of their church. This is how we live in distant America, torn from our motherland, but very few of us wish to return. It must really be better here for the poor working person. Indeed, it is!

Tovarysstvo (Ruzomberok, Slovakia, 1900), 3:303–5. Trans. M. Mark Stolarik.

The Lithuanians

78. Lithuanian Dispute in Shenandoah, Pennsylvania, 1877

Lithuanians began immigrating to the United States in the late 1860s, numbering over three hundred thousand by 1924. After arrival, they generally attached themselves to Polish parishes and societies. Though distinct in language and customs, the Lithuanians felt a kinship with the Poles as a result of their proximity in Europe, but more importantly, because they were both oppressed by tsarist Russia. In time, according to William Wolkovich-Valkavicius, "national sentiments" arose which created ethnic conflict between the Poles and the Lithuanians. One area settled by the Lithuanians was the Shenandoah Valley in Pennsylvania. In 1877, the Lithuanians petitioned the archbishop of Philadelphia for a Lithuanian priest. As indicated in the second document, the relationship between the Polish pastor and the Lithuanians deteriorated significantly.

Shenandoah, Nov. 3rd, 1877

Most Right Rev. J. F. Wood, Archbishop of Philadelphia

We have been down to see your Lordship on the 17th of Sept., and then humbly requested you to send us a priest that could speak the Lithan language. We would not be so troublesome and anxious only we cannot go to confession to our present Priest as he speaks only the Polish language, which we do not understand, nor does the three fourths of the population of this place. We would humbly and respectfully represent to you that many of us are working in the mines and in danger of a sudden death almost daily. In such cases a priest speaking our language is absolutely necessary to us, to administer the last sacraments of our holy church.

We have had a letter on the 31st of October from the Rev. Father Koncz of Milwaukee who speaks both the Polish and Lithan languages. He says he will come here with a recommendation from the Bishop of Milwaukee, if you will be kind enough to give your approbation, for which we will be ever grateful.

We would also humbly remind you that our children are deprived of Sunday school instructions. They not having any knowledge of the Polish language.

Your lordship would confer an everlasting benefit on us your children, by giving us a favorable reply to our request for which we will be ever thankful.

We are your obedient servants in Our Lord and Saviour Jesus Christ

John O. Leth
Peter Kozakawich

Letter in the Shenandoah Newspaper, 1877
An Explanation of the Polish Catholic Church Difficulty:
Six Hundred Lithuanians Unite in Representing Their Case to the Public

To the Editor of the Herald.

We, the Lithuanian portion of the Polish Catholic Church, have been misrepresented by all the newspapers throughout the country. They called us devils in human form, which every one knows is untrue. The Lithuanians are an honest people, and the charge that we are compelled to submit to the dictates of our leaders is an unfounded statement. We do no harm to anybody and have never molested the citizens of any place in which we have resided, and in presenting this letter we aim only to speak the truth.

Last Sunday we went to church and waited for the priest to come to show him the true number of Lithuanians — men, women and children — who were in the parish, and to ask him when we were going to get a Lithuanian priest to whom our poor people can confess their sins. Having previously informed him of the fact by a gentle letter that we would be present on the morning in question, there was no necessity of calling out the police force for what the pastor terms an aggravation[,] as in the eyes of any impartial man it was no transgression of the law. When the pastor arrived at the church we asked him the same question we did in our letter, but he gave us no answer, and instead of showing any disposition to comply with our demand he, in assistance with a police force, began to maltreat and arrest the poor women who were present, and a large number of credible witnesses have testified that the pastor struck a number of the parishioners with a large bunch of keys, which he had in his hand. The people of the town know how we were confined in the lock-up for a whole day, and we need say nothing of it, as the act was so cruel that it cries out for itself. Rev. Alex Lenarkiewicz did not tell the truth when he stated we used knives, pistols and stones on Sunday, as we had no intention of raising a fuss, and our priest, as a father, should have asked us what we wanted, but he acted in the manner we have described above. He knew what we desired, and in not granting it what is to become of us and our poor children? Every religion wants to follow its church, but Rev. Alex Lenarkiewicz and his few Poles want to separate us from our church and religion. We Lithuanians built the church in very hard times, during a sixth month's suspension.

The Poles, with the exception of two, who together contributed $8, did not lend a helping hand to erect the church, and there were as many of them in this neighborhood at that time as there are now. When we asked for help to build the church the Poles said that they wanted no priest or church, and they do not now contribute to the support of the one they have. The Poles want to prosecute the Lithuanians because they are such, and Father Lenarkiewicz stated in church that we should go up the hill further and build a church for ourselves if we were not satisfied. We would do this but for the hard times... Now every person who sees the case right will only say that what we have done is commendable, and we intend to keep our religion which Jesus Christ left us. Every Christian should stick up for his religion, and we should live as brothers, not clubbing and kicking at each other like dogs. Poor Mrs. Mary Ann Mencenweicz, she may die soon through the violence she received on Sunday, and our Father Lenarkiewicz don't care for us, and if we saw even a dog kicked undeservedly we would feel sorry for the poor brute. We, as the whole world, carry the picture of Jesus Christ in our souls and deserve to be treated as such, and now, citizens of Shenandoah, we intend asking you for some assistance in our coming letters to the officials of the church.

Yours respectfully.   About 600 Lithuanians

The Czechs

79. Bohemians in Chicago, 1908

The first urban Czech parishes in America were St. John, founded in 1854 in St. Louis, and St. Wenceslaus, organized in 1863 in Chicago. A minority among immigrant Catholics, Bohemians also had to compete with freethinkers who supported a wide range of organizations, including benevolent societies, newspapers, cemeteries, and homes for orphans. St. Procopius at Eighteenth and Allport Streets in Chicago's Pilsen neighborhood, founded in 1875, became the center of Czech Catholic life and culture in the Midwest. Under the direction of the Bohemian Benedictines from St. Vincent Abbey in Latrobe, Pennsylvania, the parish established a high school for boys (the nucleus of Illinois Benedictine University in Lisle, Illinois); Narod, a Bohemian daily Catholic newspaper; children's magazines; and an orphanage. St. Procopius Church, dedicated in 1883, was consecrated in 1908 after the mortgage had been liquidated.

The demonstration of the Bohemian Catholics of Chicago, which began Saturday with the opening of a quadruple religious celebration and the first consecration of a Bohemian Roman Catholic church and a chapel in the Chicago archdiocese, was brought to a successful conclusion last evening.

The second day of the celebration — which is the silver jubilee of the blessing of the church, the one thousandth anniversary of the birth of St. Wenceslaus, the patron saint of Bohemia, the golden jubilee of the ordination of Pope Pius X, and the golden jubilee of the apparition of the Virgin Mary of Lourdes — was opened with the solemn celebration of pontifical high mass in [St. Procopius Church] by Archbishop [James E.] Quigley. Thirty priests were in attendance.

Many Parishes Represented

In the afternoon there was a parade of fifty benevolent, literary, social, dramatic, singing, and other organizations of the Bohemian Catholics from parishes throughout the state. After the procession, which began at 1:30 and lasted until 4 o'clock, a musical festival and mass meeting was held in the evening in the Bohemian Slavonian Catholic hall, 508 [1310] West Eighteenth street. A banquet in the same hall was held immediately after the concert.

Seven thousand members of the Bohemian laity participated in the parade. There were 1,600 young women, dressed in white, who carried streaming banners, and scores of small girls, who held aloft symbolic crosses, anchors and hearts representing Faith, Hope, and Charity. After the girls 1,100 uniformed cadets, knights and veterans followed in the pageant. The representatives of the women's organizations, who rode in thirty carriages, the civic foresters and kindred associations made up the rest of the procession.

Bishop Blesses Statue

This procession started at the church and ended at the new [Lourdes] chapel. Father Svrdlik then delivered a sermon entitled, "The Devotion of the Blessed Virgin Mary." Prior to the sermon Bishop Peter Muldoon blessed the statue of the Virgin which is set in the grotto of the chapel.

"Bohemians Hold Sacred Festival," *Chicago Tribune,* 5 October 1908.

The Hungarians

80. Hungarians in Chicago and Cleveland, 1905

Monsignor Count Péter Vay de Vaya and Luskod, an aristocratic Hungarian priest, took a personal interest in the welfare of Hungarian immigrants by serving as a chaplain on ships bringing them to the United States. His extended visit to the United States in 1905 included stays at Hungarian Catholic communities in New York, Chicago, and Cleveland — industrial areas that attracted Hungarians. His visits to the first Magyar (Hungarian) Catholic parish in the United States, St. Elizabeth Church, established in 1893 at Cleveland under the leadership of Father Charles Boehm, and to Our Lady of Hungary Church in Chicago, whose dedication in 1905 was the occasion for his trip, are described in the following excerpt from his memoir.

The reason of my visit to Chicago was...to inaugurate the little Catholic church, erected by the immigrants recently arrived from the shores of the Danube and the Tisza...On arriving in Chicago I found that the place of my destination was rather difficult to get at, and a good way off, being situated in the southernmost suburb of the town...

At a little distance among the marshy pasture land I detected the small wooden structure. From its roof waved the American and Hungarian flags, stars and stripes and the tricolor (red, white, and green) harmoniously blending together. "That is the church, and the school is underneath," some one proudly volunteered. A humble edifice truly, but speaking of much sacrifice and labour. These simple folk have built it with their hard-earned savings, for the glory of God and the religious education of their children.

More than half the population of Chicago are foreigners...There are over 200,000 Italians, and the Hungarians proper, not included in other categories, must be estimated at nearly 15,000 new arrivals within the last few years. These latter are chiefly employed as butchers in the slaughter-houses, and as blacksmiths and carpenters in the Pullman establishment. It was at the expense of these people that the little church was built which now met my view. It stands like a beacon amid the surrounding marshes; it is the nucleus of a new suburb, which will spring up around it, and will certainly be no less important a part of the metropolis than the others which have arisen at 16 miles from the centre of the town. It is a first step towards progress, another foundation stone of civilisation and culture.

The workmen and their families awaited me at the entrance of the building. For the greater part they were still dressed in their simple costume "from over the sea," and their whole demeanour showed that they had not long since arrived in these parts. Set adrift in that great city, without knowing the language, without friends or any one to advise them, these poor folks are at the mercy of chance. And, in addition to all the other difficulties and problems which the municipal authorities have to face, we can well understand that this question of dealing with the foreign population of inferior civilisation is one of the greatest and hardest to solve. They have not only to be fed, they have also to be protected and educated. The church and the school are their only safeguards. As long as the people will go to church and are willing to have their children brought up on religious principles there is nothing to fear. As long as they recognize their duty towards God they will also recognise and fulfill their duty towards their neighbour.

The inauguration of that humble little church and its simple worshippers left an indelible impression upon me. It was one of those never-to-be-forgotten scenes which, in spite of their apparent unimportance, form a page in the annals of history. This small beginning, representing the accumulated savings of those hardy workmen, is the centre of new efforts and new struggles. Let us hope these may lead here to as successful an issue as they have done in other parts of the town. Let us hope that the little church may grow into a cathedral, and its elementary school into a great scientific establishment. And although in the past the place has so often been shaken by strikes and tumults, let us hope that henceforth faith and culture may ensure peace and prosperity to this marvellous city...

Our church, a modest wooden building of two stories, used also as a school and as a habitation of the priest, rises like a landmark in the midst of a desert of factories, for here are the ironworks of the Illinois Steel Trust, and the famous workshops of the Pullman Car Company. In both of these great enterprises the number of hands employed greatly exceeds 10,000, drawn for the most part from Austria-Hungary. That is why this parish was formed. The population, called into existence by these works, required the consolations of religion, and their numerous progeny needed education and care, in an atmosphere impregnated with smoke and alcohol.

When at last I arrived, after a long journey, I found the church crammed with workmen and their families, all persons who earned their daily bread by the sweat of their brow. This sympathetic crowd, and the warmth of their reception, almost made me forget that the congregation had gathered in an erection made of planks, more like a barn than a place of worship.

What was my surprise at the end of my sermon when the priest appealed to the generosity of the worshippers, and, a sheet of paper in his hand held a meeting of the congregation, asking them to furnish the empty building. The altar-cloth, ornaments — everything was subscribed with a truly Christian generosity, and if ever Providence should again take me back, I am certain that I should find that humbler parish a most flourishing centre.

At Chicago I witnessed the initiation of an American cure of souls, with its preliminary work; at Cleveland, on the contrary, I was able to admire the full development of one of these immigrant parishes. This was the first and incontestably the most important of the Hungarian communities. The number of Magyars alone exceeds 30,000. They have numerous churches, several newspapers published in their language, and many societies and clubs. I knew all this beforehand, and yet on my arrival was surprised at the importance and size of the church of the first Hungarian parish in the United States.

I had promised to pass the feast of Whitsuntide there, and, thanks to my stay of several days, I was able to understand the phenomenal growth and immense influence attained in so short a period. The Church of Cleveland, like that of Chicago, had been founded only a few years before, in a suburb far from the town. The priest arrived there alone, without either help or acquaintance, finding nothing, knowing nobody. It would have been difficult to believe that such had been the state of affairs if I had not already known something of the work and the marvels accomplished by the faithful in these new States. My reception, in which all the different associations took part, their banner unfurled, was a most touching exhibition of hospitality and affection. The church and all the galleries were crowded with worshippers, thousands of voices sang the hymns, and the ground was strewn with flowers which perfumed the air, laden with incense which mounted in silvery clouds toward the blue heavens — the priests prostrate before the altars of God, make a beautiful picture, and was quite the most edifying scene in the whole of my mission, rich though it was in heart-warming recollections. Good Father B[oehm] may well be proud of his work, and of the results of his apostolate.

Such results, attained in the short duration of a single life, are only possible in new countries. They afford the greatest encouragement to the humblest parsons in their work. The bishops on their side give full liberty of action, so that it may vary with the necessities of the different localities, and in order that the activity of each place in their diocese may be developed to the very utmost. Thus both agent and work increase in force, and existing parishes make new ones. Gradually independent dioceses are formed, for as soon as a parish priest has more members in his congregation than it is possible for him to know and care for, a further division is made. In Europe there are parishes of forty or fifty thousand souls. In America, on the contrary, the number rarely exceeds twelve or fourteen thousand. The dwellers in each parish form, so to speak, a large family, in which the members know one another, at least by sight, and each is known to the priest. Thus they constitúte, as I have said, large families, each member contributing according to his power to the welfare of the community. This is how the success to-day recognized by the world is made possible, and why the Catholic Church in the United States has risen to her place of general respect and honour.

> Monsignor Count Péter Vay de Vaya and Luskod, *The Inner Life of the United States* (New York: E. P. Dutton, 1908), 181–85, 336–40; in John Tracy Ellis, ed., *Documents of American Catholic History* (Milwaukee: Bruce, 1956), 2:555–60. Printed with permission of the estate of John Tracy Ellis.

Eastern Rite Catholics

81. Archbishop John Ireland and Eastern Rite Catholics, 1889

Immigrants belonging to several Eastern Rites of the Catholic Church began arriving in the United States in the late nineteenth century with Ruthenians initially the largest group. American bishops were ill prepared by education or direct experience to understand the rights of these Catholics — who are in communion with the Holy See and are thus sometimes called Uniates — to preserve their ancient liturgies in vernacular languages as well as the tradition of a married diocesan clergy. These Catholics of Eastern Rites were just as fully Catholics as Catholics of the Latin Rite. Unfortunately, American bishops such as Archbishop John Ireland feared the arrival of these groups with what was thought to be their exotic worship and customs that reinforced the impression that Catholicism was foreign. Perhaps, above all, American bishops feared the Eastern Rite Catholics' noncelibate diocesan clergy would inspire thoughts of marriage among Roman Rite priests. In response to American bishops' request, the Congregation of the Propagation of the Faith instructed Eastern Rite bishops in eastern Europe to send only celibate or widowed priests to minister to their immigrant flocks in the United States. The exclusion of married Eastern Rite clergy from the United States was affirmed in decrees in 1907 and 1929. The following account of Father Alexis Toth's interview with Archbishop John Ireland reveals the tragic ignorance and hostility of Archbishop Ireland in dealing with Catholics, including priests of other rites. Subsequently, Father Toth led thousands of Ruthenian Rite Catholics into the Russian Orthodox Church.

I was a Uniate when I came to America...I knew that here in America as a Uniate priest I was to obey the Roman Catholic Bishop of the particular diocese in which I happened to work. The Union demanded this as well as the various Papal Bulls, Briefs and Decretals as there was no Uniate Bishop in this country.

When I came to Minneapolis, I was there a while, when a Polish priest came up to me and said, "You better come up with me, I introduce you to the Bishop of Minneapolis, of St. Paul, Bishop Ireland." This Polish priest was called away to some sick and I went up myself to see him. I had my priest's clothes on and I introduced myself and showed him my papers...

Moreover, in my credentials the following instruction was clearly given: *Dilectio tua debet, in cuius territorio habetur locus destinationis suae.* The place of my appointment was Minneapolis, Minnesota, in the province of Archbishop Ireland. As an obedient Uniate I complied with the orders of my Bishop, who at that time was John Valyi[,] and appeared before [Arch]Bishop Ireland December 19, 1889, kissed his hand according to custom and presented my credentials, failing, however, to kneel before him, which, as I learned later, was my chief mistake. I remember that no sooner did he read that I was a "Greek Catholic," his hands began to shake. It took him fifteen minutes to read to the end after which he asked abruptly — we conversed in Latin:

"Have you a wife?"

"No."

"But you had one?"

"Yes, I am a widower."

At this he threw the paper on the table and loudly exclaimed: "I have already written to Rome protesting against this kind of priest being sent to me!"

"What kind of priests do you mean?"

"Your kind."

"I am a Catholic priest of the Greek Rite. I am a Uniate and was ordained by a regular Catholic Bishop."

"I do not consider that either you or this bishop of yours are Catholic; besides, I do not need any Greek Catholic priests here; a Polish priest in Minneapolis is quite sufficient; the Greeks can also have him for their priest."

"But he belongs to the Latin Rite; besides our people do not understand him and so they will hardly go to him; that was the reason they instituted a church of their own."

"They had no permission from me and I shall grant you no jurisdiction to work here."

Deeply hurt by the fanaticism of this representative of Papal Rome, I replied sharply: "In that case, I know the rights of my church, I know the basis on which the Union was established and shall act accordingly."

The Archbishop lost his temper. I lost mine just as much. One word brought another, the thing had gone so far that our conversation is not worth putting on record.

...[T]wo days after meeting with Bishop Ireland, the Polish priest Jacob Pocholsky called on me. He spoke as if terror-stricken. "For God's sake, your Reverence, what have you done? The Archbishop writes me I must have no intercourse with you. He does not accept you as a regularly ordained priest and I am under strict orders from him to announce this at the altar, forbidding your people to be ministered to by you or to take sacraments from you..."

This was my reply: "This is your concern. Do what you think is best. I shall not surrender one step and shall not be influenced by anything you and your bishop can do."

The Archbishop's demands were made public. He sent complaints to Rome and my flock began to hear rumors which frightened them. The Archbishop, it was said, was going to send away their priest in ignomiy, etc. In the meantime, I received letters from several of my fellow priests of the Uniate Rite, who wrote that there were a good many of us who had been treated by Latin Bishops and priests just as I had been. I informed the Uniate Bishop of Eperjes of all this, asking his instructions, but be never answered me. Naturally so! As if a Uniate Bishop dared to contradict a Latin Archbishop. I wrote a second and third time, still without obtaining any reply. At last, I received from Canon Dzubay the following instruction: "For God's sake, be patient and, if the Archbishop doubts that you are a faithful Catholic, let him know that you are willing to take your oath on it!"

After a while I received another letter from him, proposing that I should write a detailed account of the way the Archbishop received me and advising me to write very carefully, as the letter was to be sent to Rome. This I did, but later on the same Reverend Dzubay informed me that the truth was too harshly stated in my letter for it to be sent to Rome. However, some measures had been taken and Rome was told that Latin Bishops must respect the Holy Union.

Keith S. Russin, "Father Alexis G. Toth and the Wilkes-Barre Litigations," *St. Vladimir's Theology Quarterly* 16, no. 3 (1972): 132–34; original in *Testimony: Greek Catholic Church et al. v. Orthodox Greek Church et al.* (Court of Common Pleas, Luzerne County, Wilkes-Barre, Pennsylvania, 1894), 1:235ff. Printed with permission.

The French Canadians

82. Bishop Antoine Racine on French-Canadian Catholics in the United States, 1892

In the late nineteenth century, the rapidly growing French-Canadian population in Quebec faced bleak economic prospects with a shortage of arable land. Because of their close proximity to New England and the prospect of steady employment in textile mills there, French Canadians entered the United States in large numbers. With nearly a million French Canadians in the country by 1910, large French-speaking Catholic communities arose in such cities as Woonsocket, Rhode Island, Lewiston, Maine, Worcester, Massachusetts, and Manchester, New Hampshire. In considering the pastoral challenges of this situation as of 1892, Bishop Antoine Racine of Sherbrooke, Quebec, whose diocese was adjacent to the borders with New York, Vermont, New Hampshire, and Maine, described the issues of French-Canadian Catholic life in the United States in the following letter submitted to the Congregation for the Propagation of the Faith.

Memorandum on the Situation of French Canadians in the United States of America, by Monsignor A. Racine, Bishop of Sherbrooke — Paris, Librairie de l'Oeuvre de Saint-Paul, 6 rue Cassette, 1892.

Rome, February 29, 1892

To His Eminence Cardinal Ledochowski, Prefect of the Sacred Congregation for the Propagation of the Faith

I. At the present time, knowing how to treat Canadians in the United States of North America for the sake of their faith and for the sake of religion in general is a subject of concern for many people.

Here is our opinion on the subject. We know that it is sincere and we believe that it is moderate. As we keep all the voices of sympathy quiet and as we leave aside all the reasons of detail, we will only consider the greatest amount of good to be obtained.

II. We will not speak here of the fact that it would be advisable, convenient or necessary to appoint bishops of Canadian origin for the United States to the dioceses where Canadians make up the greatest majority of the Catholic population. This is a delicate point, fraught with difficulties and it presents various aspects that we leave to the study of the concerned parties, especially to the apostolic zeal of those who, in this vast country, have received the mission to rule the Church of God, and, above all, to the wisdom, the perspicacity and to the prudence of the Holy See.

We cannot ask for anything more than for bishops to be liked by their Canadian flock and not to clash in any way with their legitimate customs. If need be, bishops may not even have to speak their language. However, in this last case, we think that it would be more appropriate if they had a vicar or an important priest who is capable of understanding them in order to give them confidence and to facilitate their rapport with the episcopal authority.

However, over and beyond everything else, what is really essential is that pastors or missionaries to Canadians should be priests who know how to speak their language well, understand their mores, be aware of their aspirations, willingly enter into the current of ideas that characterizes them and, at the same time, foster the development of their particular institutions, as long as they are not conflicting with the laws of the land. It seems to us that the good of these people and the good of the Catholic faith do require this.

III. The mere fact of emigration, transplanting people from the country where they were born and lived for a long time on a foreign land, is something that is too deeply disturbing for their moral structure. Therefore, it would be imprudent to increase the intensity of these shocks by useless attacks on their ancient and strong traditions. This is the case for all peoples although we believe we can state that this situation does exist, *a.fortiori,* for French Canadian people because of the particular circumstances in which they were born and developed.

In some way, as they barely emerged from childhood, they were uprooted from their homeland, they saw their country handed over to a powerful nation which did not share their faith and which had little to do with the outside world. Because they had to concentrate their energy to preserve their national and religious existence, the Canadian people had to live their own lives apart, withdrawn in the midst of rural areas and with their patriarchal customs. In order to resist the seductions and attacks of heresy, to take possession of the land and to expand their colonies, they did cling to their admirable parish system and despite the greatest obstacles, they established French schools where Catholicism ruled masterfully. They tightly rallied, en masse, under the leadership of their priests on whom they lavished the respect which is due to kind friends, protectors or fathers in such a way that French Canadians became used to seeing their customs, language, traditions and their discipline as the remnant of a sacred heritage and even the external continuation of their beliefs. Whoever attacks all these things which are dear to them is indirectly attacking their faith. They show great strength in resisting Protestantism, atheism and indifference but if you take away this protective setting of their old customs, we might say that they become like Samson: they are already in the power of the enemy.

Unfortunately, examples of this sad experience are all too frequent. When French Canadians do not have in their neighborhood priests to administer the sacraments and to instruct them in their own language, all too often, they stop going to church on a regular basis and, little by little, they slip into the most complete indifference. If you assign to them priests who are opposed to their traditions, they become unhappy, insubordinate and difficult to control. Hence, their hearts are open to the worst influences of heresy. For all these reasons, before there was a bishop in Burlington, in Vermont, numerous families whose ancestors were French and Catholic were speaking English and they were Protestant. Once such an evil had occurred, it was irreparable.

On the contrary, give French Canadians zealous priests who speak their own language and know their customs and, as it can be seen today in many industrial centers of New England, you will have fervent and generous *Congregations* that are building splendid churches, separate Catholic schools, convents and charitable institutions as they bring about the blossoming of the faith in the midst of circumstances that are, at times, very difficult. A way of being which produces such good effects deserves to be preserved.

IV. Human beings do not easily escape the influences of the milieu in which they are living. Almost in spite of themselves, they give in to the doctrines and customs of that milieu.

What are the doctrines which are generally prevalent in the intellectual and moral world of the United States for the majority of the people? They are the doctrines of Protestantism, religious indifference or atheism. A thirst for gold dominates everything and a passion for riches invades almost every soul. This materialistic trend is encouraged by what people see and hear, by the public school system which is a cause of the ruin or the weakening of faith of Catholic youth. Although there are noble exceptions, we might fittingly say that the exception confirms the general rule.

What are *generaliter loquendo,* the customs of the country? Are they customs of comfortable and easy living, material pleasure or customs of feverish work in the pursuit of wealth? *Virtus post nummos.*

Having to move in the midst of such an atmosphere, Catholics find it very difficult not to come under its pernicious influences, at least to some degree, and although they may preserve the integrity of their faith and even a strong zeal in terms of religion, it is hard for them not to give in unconsciously to the practical mores and the intellectual tendencies of their compatriots. At times, it may happen that, far from seeking to defend themselves against these tendencies, they encourage them by the excessive attraction they profess for the ways of being of American society which is permeated by Protestant morality and by exasperating tolerance. In the United States, this form of indifference with regard to religious belief has taken away thousands of souls from the true faith. And even though religion has greatly increased recently, this is not due to conversions from Protestant groups but rather, to Catholic immigration which was rapidly coming in waves from Ireland, Germany, Canada and in the past few years, also from Italy. The quick organization of these scattered forces by a shrewd episcopate and the resounding realization of its importance in terms of numbers, something unknown until then, may have led some to believe in the intrusive propaganda of the church in the midst of American people but, unfortunately, we cannot deny that the number of perversions far surpasses the number of conversions.

Therefore, against the invasion of these pernicious influences, for French Canadians, their customs and language, which kept them apart, also constituted a rampart and a powerful barrier. A rampart and a barrier which it would be wise to preserve and to fortify instead of striving to bring them down. We see the same results happening among French Canadians and for the same reasons as the results that can be seen with the Maronites in Lebanon or among the Polish faithful in Prussia or Russia.

V. "But they say, if all Catholics in the United States spoke English, it would be much easier to serve them."

This may be true but they do not speak it. Are we going to jeopardize their faith in order to make it easier to serve them? The Holy Spirit granted the gift of tongues to the apostles, not to nations. It is up to the priests to learn the language of the people that their zeal leads them to evangelize, rather than being up to the people to learn the priests' language. Every day, we see missionaries beginning to learn the languages of the tribes to which they have undertaken to bring the good news. They would have to wait for a long time for their conversion if they required those tribes to learn their own language, French or English, in order to hear the truths of salvation. The main purpose of the church is to form citizens for heaven rather than to undertake to amalgamate all the different nationalities that may exist within a country into one for motives of temporal interest.

"But they add, English must inevitably become the language of North America. Therefore, it is better to start to speak it right away."

Well then, if that is the case, let us leave it to time. Do not go faster than the natural evolution of ideas. In the meantime, by not clashing imprudently with the feelings of the present generation and by complying with their tastes, let us preserve their faith so that this second or third generation who, according to some, must necessarily speak English, may continue to profess Catholicism. In any case, as long as emigration from Canada to the Unites States continues on a large scale, as it is now, it is impossible to make the bulk of the Canadian population speak English. Even if you succeeded in anglicizing the young generation, you would still have to face older people and new arrivals and the problem to be resolved would have to be started all over again with the same difficulties and the same dangers to the faith. Therefore, let us take things as they are, leaving enigmas to the future and for the time being, let us use the most efficacious means to save souls.

When around 1820, because of disease and famine, the Irish were forced to abandon their homeland to emigrate to Canada, the bishops of Quebec and Montreal lost no time in providing them with priests from their own country or, at the very least, priests who were well versed in their own language since in those days, there were few Irish priests in our country. And since that time, the few English-speaking parishes existing in French Canada have continued to be served by English-speaking priests. In their schools, catechism is taught in English and in their churches, homilies are given in English. Wedged in a French majority, these heterogeneous groups happily and satisfactorily develop according to their own customs. Why should not the Canadians in the United States be treated the same way as the Irish in Canada? To our knowledge, they are treated that way in some dioceses: therefore, religion is making great strides there.

VI. Before concluding, let us briefly indicate a few motives of general interest in favor of this policy of fatherly benevolence:

1. If we know how to preserve this profoundly Catholic spirit of Canadian people with its present guarantees, it may serve to offset the spirit of indifference which is permeating the people of the United States of America from everywhere and with time, it may become a good leaven for the nation.

2. The energy and the generosity, with which Canadians build and support their French and Catholic schools and their deeply rooted principles on

the question of separate schools, may be a great contribution and a powerful help to American bishops in their efforts, depending on the times and circumstances, to put into practice the decrees of the third Council of Baltimore dealing with the subject.

3. The zeal and the spirit of the apostolate, characteristic aspects of the French people in America, the large number of priests, sisters and missionaries who came from it, demonstrate that it is a good policy to preserve, in its characteristic form, this breeding ground for priestly and religious vocations that has done so much in the course of the past two centuries and that is still doing a great deal now for the spreading of Christianity in the new world.

4. The rapid growth of Canadians, when they are allowed to develop freely in the shadow of their parish institutions, will bring Catholicism to predominate in several states of the great nation before long. On this topic of the high birthrate of the French in America and for your Excellency's information, along with this memorandum, we are including two short and precise works which are filled with facts and figures: *On the Movement of Catholic Population in English America* and *Canadian Colonies*. Their author, M. E. Rameau de Saint-Père, Paris, France, is a thinker, an untiring investigator whose philosophical mind knows how to go back from the effects to the cause. He is also a staunch Christian.

5. Finally, these French Canadians have deep Roman Catholic feelings and by the good fortune of providential circumstances, they have escaped from Gallican errors, as well as from Jansenism, Protestantism and modern atheism. At a given moment, in some difficult conjunctures which the future in America could bring about, these people could certainly be very helpful in leading to the triumph of the visions, policies and guidelines of the Roman Curia.

VII. For all these reasons, we conclude that for the good of religion in general and for the good of Canadians in particular, the following is important:

1. Canadians of the United States should be allowed to develop with their own language, customs and their traditions.

2. It would even be desirable to foster this traditional development since for them, it is a safeguard and protection for their faith.

3. In order to attain this goal, they should be provided with priests and missionaries who know their language well, who are familiar with their mores and who support their ways of being.

4. Finally, insofar as it is possible, these priests or missionaries should belong to their own nationality. We do not consider this last point to be absolutely essential, even though it is extremely important. In fact, if Canadians did not have priests of their own background at the head of their parishes, they would end up being mistrustful: hence this could be a source of endless tribulations for ecclesiastical superiors and for their subjects.

In the hope that your Excellency will find that this presentation of our opinion concerning this complex and delicate question is a reserved and moderate view, we remain with the highest consideration and the most profound respect for your most distinguished Excellency,

> Your very humble and devoted servants.
> Antoine, Bishop of Sherbrooke
> J. B. Proulx

Antoine Racine, "Mémoire sur la situation des Canadiens-Français aux États-Unis de l'Amérique du Nord," *Revue franco-américaine* 1, no. 6 (September-October 1908): 482–86.

83. French-Canadian Mutual Aid Societies, 1910

French Canadians in the United States, where both Protestants and their Irish-American coreligionists regarded them with some suspicion, developed strong attachments to their parishes and ethnic institutions. In these settings their aim of survivance *encompassed the cultural imperative of preserving the Catholic faith, family traditions, and the French language. In addition to the religious and educational dimensions of parish life, French Canadians supported mutual aid societies similar to those of other immigrant groups. The following selection describes the function of the union of such mutual aid societies in French-Canadian Catholic life.*

The Mutual Aid Society of St. John the Baptist of America

If, ten years ago, someone had predicted that the French American element would have the best organized mutual aid society in the United States today, in all likelihood, such a person would have been considered a dreamer. Besides, if our memory serves us well, it is precisely what was said in 1900 to the promoters of the sound federation of the French American national societies. The same critics whom we have been able to observe on more than one occasion as they were siding with those who were hosting dinner parties, are now again found attacking the same institution on behalf of politicians. All the latter ever knew about this national movement is what they were able to get out of it. However, all of this will quickly pass and the national work is sufficiently well established to resist even more serious attacks.

We have been able to see that in the enthusiasm that was displayed on March 28 in Woonsocket, on the occasion of the tenth anniversary of the first Congress of the Mutual Aid Society of St. John the Baptist of America.

We have already mentioned this society to our readers. More than once, we have even expressed the desire to have this society come to the Province of Quebec to develop an influence that would be the expected antidote against neutral societies and against the intensive "Columbus mania" which slowly destroys the roots of our sense of national organization. While we are waiting for the day when "we could hold one another's hands over and beyond borders," we want to express to this society all our admiration for the work of convocation and of salvation which it is accomplishing for the most important group of our people after the group of our Province of Quebec. We especially want to say this to the leaders of this society. Through countless ups and downs and even after ten years of difficult work, these leaders have never given up their enthusiastic fearlessness of the early days.

They have never lost sight of the goal of the society which is "to gather, in the same feeling of fellowship, all the people of French origin who are living in America." This was, indeed, the most formidable difficulty of their task. However, they have been able to take advantage of the history of their own national organizations. As founders of parishes, builders of schools, untiring supporters of the traditions of their ancestors, even in their new homeland, with the same spirit, they have founded works of Catholic faith and militant works: in addition to their wonderful Peter's Pence Society, they continue to publish a powerful little newspaper, the "Union," that is to say, the voice of their society. This paper best represents the French American ideal in its truest sense.

After that, why should they be surprised by the relentless attacks against them or by the fact that, if need be, the Irish American hierarchy joins forces with politicians to attack their most zealous companions? They are going to experience worse things yet. May they hold on. All the true friends of this cause are with them. Ad multos annos!

Leon Kemner, "L'Union St-Jean Baptiste d'Amérique," *Revue franco-américaine* 5, no. 1 (1 May 1910): 53–54.

The Portuguese

84. Portuguese Mission in Boston, 1896

Portuguese immigrants, mostly from the Azores, began arriving in the United States during the 1860s, and the immigration peaked during the era 1890–1924 when more than two hundred thousand arrived. Most settled in the New England area, though a sizable portion made their way to California. Portuguese religiosity was similar to that of Italians, with emphasis on festas and processions, such as the Holy Ghost Festival. In the following document, a Jesuit mission preacher gives his impression of the Portuguese community in Boston.

THE MISSION OF PORTUGUESE [JESUIT] FATHERS TO THEIR
COUNTRYMEN IN THE UNITED STATES, 1896
A Letter from Father [J.B.] Justino, [S.J.] to the Editor
The Mission at Boston

The Portuguese population of Boston and its suburbs amounts to several thousands souls. They are scattered over all parts of the city, and occupy no special quarter of their own. For some years there has been a growing tendency among them to move out of town, owing to the increasing difficulty of finding cheap homes. It would be an easy matter for these people to attend to their religious duties were they so minded. They are living in the vicinity of Catholic churches where they could hear Mass and approach the sacraments, and they are surrounded by Catholic schools where their children would receive a solid religious and liberal education. Unfortunately they are not church-goers, their own Portuguese church having seemingly as little attraction for them as the Italian and other churches. The children go chiefly to the public schools, and if they know any catechism at all they know it in English. As many of the older persons speak only Portuguese, there are families where from their early years the children converse among themselves in a language not understood by the parents. The inconveniences of such a state of things are more easily imagined than described. A few mothers are still to be found who do not hesitate to box their sons' ears at the first word of English they hear them pronounce. Others submit to the inevitable. Happily, the evil results are neither so many nor so widespread as at first sight might be expected...

It may be truly said that of all the foreigners that come to make America their home, with perhaps the exception of the Italians, the Portuguese hold the very lowest rank in all that concerns religion. They are pointed out everywhere as ignorant and irreligious. I have no doubt that the fault lies in the fact that they arrive in the country utterly lacking those solid religious principles, which would be their safeguard against the dangers to which they are exposed.

[Father Justino describes efforts at providing a mission in Portuguese, then notes:] Meanwhile the feast of the Immaculate Conception was fast approaching. Besides being celebrated with much solemnity in the Archdiocese of Boston, it is also the patron feast of the Portuguese societies of this city. They were to come to the church in a body in full uniform, with their badges, banners, and music. The carpenters were actively at work putting the new windows in place, for the donors were anxious to have the names of their respective islands conspicuous on the great day...

On the morning of the eighth of December, the services began at half past eight o'clock. The children were all present in their first Communion dress. The ordinary ceremonies of the renewal of baptismal vows, consecration to the Sacred Heart of Jesus and to the Blessed Virgin, etc., were gone through with such admirable spirit and fervor, that many were moved to tears. At 10 o'clock there was a solemn high Mass, the subdeacon being Mr. Duarte, a countryman of ours born in the island of Pico, now a member of the Society and a professor of Boston College. The different colonies of Boston, East Boston, Cambridge, etc., had marched to the church in order of parade, the American and Portuguese flags floating at the head of the procession. After the gospel, there was a patriotic sermon appropriate to the occasion, for which the consul, overflowing with enthusiasm, came to thank the preacher in the name of all the colonies. At three o'clock in the afternoon the church was again crowded to its utmost capacity. A short farewell sermon was preached, the mission-cross was erected, and the way of the cross was made. Then there was the blessing of the children, and to conclude, a procession wherein the statue of the Immaculate Conception was borne, preceded and followed by the children and the members of various confraternities. The delight and enthusiasm of the people were visible on every countenance...

Woodstock Letters (1896), 25:447, 452, 450.

Part 4

AFTER 1924: THE PERSISTENCE AND TRANSCENDENCE OF ETHNICITY

Introduction

For more than a century, the Catholic Church in the United States had defined itself in terms of caring for wave after wave of Catholic immigrants. The Immigration Act of 1924 dramatically redirected that dimension of Catholic life. The new law greatly reduced the number of people entering the country, and its national quota system discriminated against immigrants arriving from Catholic areas of southern and eastern Europe. For some church leaders, the restriction of immigrants provided an opportunity for the church to complete its task of Americanizing the immigrants who had already arrived. Many believed that as immigrant generations matured, they would lose their foreign characteristics and languages and adopt the English language and American ways. To a certain extent this assimilation did occur. Third- and fourth-generation German Americans may not have differed much from their Irish-American coreligionists of the same generations.

In the post–World War II era, the American Catholic community was even further removed from its roots in the massive immigrations of previous generations. Catholics increasingly began to advance up the economic ladder. Along with other veterans who had served in the armed forces during World War II, young Catholic veterans took advantage of the educational benefits offered under the G.I. Bill of Rights. More Catholics than ever before began pursuing higher education, transforming Catholic and other institutions of higher learning. The boom in Catholic college graduates resulted in increased social and geographic mobility for Catholics. Young adult Catholics left their old ethnic neighborhoods and parishes in the central cities for the open spaces and larger houses of the growing suburbs. They left behind the imposing churches and extraordinary parish structures that reflected their immigrant ancestors' hard work and devotion. The membership of many historic ethnic parishes declined significantly, as fewer and fewer parishioners made the journey from the suburbs to their old ethnic church. The trend of diminished membership accelerated with the decline of general church attendance by the 1960s.

The decline of the Catholic presence in old urban neighborhoods reached a critical point by the 1980s. Parishes with diminishing memberships and burdened with rising maintenance costs for aging parish buildings found survival difficult. Dioceses were often called upon to provide subsidies to keep declining parishes afloat. Many dioceses began the process of consolidating old urban parishes. This trend made sense from an economic point of view. The dramatic decrease of priests available to serve in parishes reinforced the trend to consolidate. From every rational perspective the closing and/or consolidation of ethnic parishes made sense, but in nearly every case the closing of parishes generated enormous protests and spurred a resurgence of ethnic pride. Despite all the social and economic advances of American Catholics and their apparent abandonment of ethnic roots, ethnicity continued to persist. In the following selections we highlight the problems confronted by the Archdiocese of Boston in attempting to close Polish parishes, but its experience has been repeated in many dioceses across the country with other ethnic parishes.

Beyond the persistence of ethnicity the era also witnessed concerns that transcended ethnicity; the response to these concerns was deeply rooted in the experience of the immigrant church. Throughout the nineteenth century, "race suicide" was not an issue regularly discussed by parish priests in Sunday sermons. In the wake of increased immigration from southern and eastern Europe, however, civic leaders — including President Theodore Roosevelt — began to voice concern that native-born Americans of Protestant stock were not reproducing to the same extent as Catholics and Jews, and that Negroes in the South might soon outnumber whites. *The Ladies' Home Journal* of February 1906, for example, claimed that President Roosevelt regarded race suicide as "more important to him than railroad rate legislation, or the tariff, or even the substitution of the merit system in public life for the regime of patronage and spoils." Although mainline Protestant denominations also opposed the widespread use of contraception, birth control increasingly emerged as a "Catholic" issue thanks in large measure to Margaret Higgins Sanger, the most prominent American figure in the birth-control movement from 1912 until her death in 1966.[1] The daughter of a socialist father and religiously devout Irish-Catholic mother who bore eleven children, Sanger believed that large families imperiled the lives of mothers and perpetuated poverty among immigrants. Her strategy in portraying the Catholic Church as the major opponent to birth control gained momentum following the U.S. bishops' pastoral on

---

1. See Kathleen Tobin-Schlesinger, "Population and Power: The Religious Debate over Contraception, 1916–1936" (Ph.D. diss., University of Chicago, 1994); and idem, "The Changing American City: Chicago Catholics as Outsiders in the Birth Control Movement, 1915–1935," *U.S. Catholic Historian* 15, no. 2 (spring 1997): 67–86.

contraception (26 September 1919) and the papal encyclical *Casti Connubii* (31 December 1930). Not only did opposition to birth control become a distinctive marker of American Catholic identity from the 1920s on, but it transcended ethnicity.

The Persistence of Ethnicity

85. John V. Tolino, "Solving the Italian Problem," 1938

Despite the restrictions on new immigration to the United States enacted in the Immigration Act of 1921 and the Johnson-Reed Act of 1924, the so-called Italian problem lingered well into the 1930s. The following document chronicles the Archdiocese of Philadelphia's attempts to resolve the issue finally. The way to solve the Italian problem was, apparently, to Americanize Italian Catholics and ease them away from the national parish. Father John Tolino was born in Italy in 1904 and immigrated to the United States in 1911. He was ordained in 1930 and spent most of his priestly life as pastor of Annunciation Parish in South Philadelphia (1933–69).

... To meet the needs of Italian-Americans of the Archdiocese of Philadelphia, the greatest portion of whom live in South Philadelphia, an intelligent and far-seeing plan of reorganization of parishes was put into effect by the Archbishop [Dennis Dougherty] a few years ago. Up to that time all the Italians of South Philadelphia, a densely populated section, were assigned to a few national parishes, which in time became inadequate for the increasing numbers. Meanwhile, many canonical parishes were left almost deserted by the migration of their members, although these empty churches were surrounded on all sides by lax Italians, who were fast drifting away from all religious influence. There was a church on the corner, it is true, but the Italians did not enter, because they received no special invitation. There were no priests assigned there who could hear confessions in Italian, or who, they felt, were specially interested in them. It was still the "Irish" church, and they passed by it. For several parishes such as these, new boundaries were set, and all the Catholics of whatever nationality living within the boundaries, became members of those parishes. As a matter of fact only about one percent of the population was of non-Italian blood. The pastors who were appointed to these parishes were either Italians or Americans of Italian parentage. The assistants were Americans, who not only spoke Italian, but what is more important, were deeply interested in the Italian people. The other canonical parishes of South Philadelphia which still had a large proportion of "Irish" in their memberships, but with a considerable number of Italians and Italian-American families also within their boundaries, retained their American pastors, but were given at least one assistant able to speak and preach in Italian. In this way almost all

Italians of South Philadelphia became identified with canonical parishes rather than national parishes, without sacrificing any of the advantages of a national parish for these people.

It seemed like a daring move to some when these changes were brought about, but the wisdom of the provisions cannot be denied in the light of later experience and actual results. On all sides in this section of the city there has been a genuine revival of the religious life of the Italian and Italian-American people.

Speaking for my own parish, which was formerly a great old "Irish" parish, but which, still a canonical parish with new boundaries, is almost solidly Italian or Italian-American now, I give the results of a few years' work under the new system. From the very first days of the reorganization we saw the dire need which the people had of being instructed in Christian doctrine... With the help of three young American assistants, we established classes in Christian doctrine for both young and old. In addition, catechetical instructions are given not only at all Sunday Masses (and at no Sunday Mass is instruction ever omitted), but at the many week-day services and novenas as well. The only religious confraternities and societies officially recognized are the Holy Name Society, the Sodality of the Blessed Virgin Mary, and the Christian Mothers. The various religious societies which small groups of people have formed among themselves have no official standing as legitimate units of parish life. Every effort is concentrated on building up our recognized societies, both by religious and social functions.

The people have been trained to a sense of punctuality by having all Masses and religious services begin precisely at the hours designated...[The author then notes that abundant time for confessions and accessibility for sick calls were provided.]

Having won the loyalty and affection of so many of our people, we gradually eradicated the quasi-superstitions connected with outdoor religious processions. These had so degenerated through the years as to become disgraceful to the beautiful traditions both of the Church and of the Italian people themselves. There is no denying the spiritual value incidental to well-conducted processions, when due regard is had to time, place and other conditions. It was my experience, however, that such processions had come very close to "rackets" in this section. There was little of the truly religious in any of them. They were conducted on the following basis. First, a largely lay-committee, which as a rule owned the statue of a saint (either loaned to the church or kept in a private home), would canvass the people of the parish for money to celebrate a feast. After the money had been obtained, the next step was to visit the pastor in order to haggle over the "price" of a Solemn Mass, street-procession and panegyric in honor of the saint. After a satisfactory agreement, the committee would arrange the time of the Mass, often with utter disregard of the regular Sunday schedule of Masses. Sometimes they would actually appoint the preacher for the occasion. After the Mass, which would begin when the committee found itself ready to grant permission, the procession would follow. Many taking part in the procession had not attended Sunday Mass, either that day or for years previously. These would follow the statue, with stops being made at strategic places where devotees of the saint might pin money on the ribbons strung from the statue. Along the sidewalks would stand groups of people, some devout, some sneering, the majority indifferent, and the youth humiliated and ashamed. Frequently a band playing profane airs accompanied the marchers. After the procession was over, the greater part of the participants, who usually had not been to confession or Holy Communion for a long time, would desert church and processions for another year.

Outdoor processions in my parish have been discontinued. No exceptions are ever made. The people have been instructed about the reasons for the prohibition. Within a short time they showed themselves completely in accord with this policy. In place of holding processions, the people have been taught to honor their patron saints by a good confession and by receiving Holy Communion...

...The solution [to the Italian problem] is simply this: "Conduct the Italian parish along the lines of a first-class American parish." Give to the Italian parish zealous, energetic, intelligent priests...Let the people be treated with sympathy and kindness, but always with the firmness of righteous authority. Conduct the church services along strictly liturgical lines. Teach the people above all things the sacredness of the authority of the bishop, and they become thereby more impressed with the sacredness of the authority of their pastor.

American Ecclesiastical Review 99 (1938): 252–56.

86. Italian Procession, Bunker Hill, Michigan, 1939

Despite efforts by Father Tolino to Americanize Italians, ethnic traditions persisted. From the 1890s on, processions and festas *had become commonplace in American cities with large Italian populations and national parishes. While the need to assert ethnic identity and claim sacred space was equally compelling in outlying areas, the process often took much longer to develop. As the following document attests, the feast day celebration of Saint Ippolito drew crowds from three states, including Italians who had participated in similar celebrations in their native Sicily. Significantly, women as well as men vied for the privilege of carrying the statue.*

Bunker Hill, Aug. 14. — Men and women shouted with joy and fought for the privilege of carrying the statue of St. Ippolito at the first solemn celebration of the saint's feast in this country, held here yesterday.

More than 5000 visitors from Southern Michigan, Indiana and Ohio poured into this little village for the ceremony. The religious observance was held at the Church of SS. Cornelius and Cyprian.

The ceremonies opened on Saturday evening, when the new statue of the saint was installed in the sanctuary in a place of honor. A guard of honor kept an all-night vigil, praying before the Blessed Sacrament, in honor of the saint, asking blessings upon all those who were to take part in the celebration.

Two Masses Celebrated

On Sunday morning at 9 o'clock a low Mass was celebrated for the benefit of the visitors and many received Holy Communion. At 11:30 the crowd, which had formed into a procession, marched into the church, followed by Bishop Joseph H. Albers, of Lansing, the attending clergy and the officers of the solemn Mass, which was celebrated by the Rev. Ignatius Brady, O.F.M., assisted by the Rev. John F. Duffy, pastor of the Church as deacon, the Rev. Mr. Francis Timmons, sub-deacon[,] and Mr. Paul DeRose, master of ceremonies...

Bishop Speaks in Italian

During the course of the Mass, Bishop Albers addressed the Italians in their own language. He encouraged them to be worthy Catholics even though they were 7000 miles away from their native Italy and stressed the importance of being faithful to Sunday Mass, the Sacraments, devotion to Christ in the Blessed Sacrament, the Mother of God whom the Italians love so tenderly, and to the saints to whom they are so attached.

Immediately after the Mass, Bishop Albers solemnly blessed the strikingly beautiful statue of St. Ippolito, representing a young Roman officer gripping in his right hand a large sword, symbol of his office in Valerian's army[,] and in his left hand holding the martyr's palm.

Accompanied by the Bishop and the clergy, the statue was carried outdoors where it was placed upon a carrier and then borne in procession.

Older Italians Weep

Many of the older Italians who have come directly from Italy wept for joy at the sight of their Santo. To whom it recalled fond memories of the many feasts they attended in their little city of Saint Ippolito in the Province of Cosenza, Calabria, Italy. Jubilant — they shouted with joy and strove with each other for the privilege of carrying the statue on their shoulders. Both men and women vied for the privilege. It was eventually accorded to all. To satisfy the crowd the committee ordered the carrier to be put down every 20 feet so that everyone could have the opportunity.

As the statue was being carried, the Italians chanted their beautiful ancient hymns in honor of the Saint and pinned votive offerings on a silk ribbon suspended from the neck of the statue. The men and women bore burning candles in their hands while the little children carried flowers.

After the procession, spaghetti with meat balls or chicken was served to the visitors. Games were played throughout the afternoon. At 7:30 p.m. the large Church bell rang for the solemn Benediction service that closed the religious festival.

> "Italians Vie in Effort to Carry Saint's Statue," *Michigan Catholic,* 17 August 1939. Printed with permission.

87. Closing Polish Parishes, Boston, 1990s

By the 1990s significant demographic changes within urban centers left many dioceses with too many national churches with too few parishioners. Along with this was the fact that many ethnic groups had third-, fourth-, and fifth-generation members, who preferred attending a regular parish, not the national parish. Several dioceses across the country, including Detroit, Philadelphia, Chicago, Boston, and others, attempted to close many of these national parishes or to consolidate them. The effort has often been met with staunch resistance by the ethnic groups involved. The strong attachment to ethnic parishes has repeatedly surprised chancery offices. The following three articles from the Boston Globe *chart the attempt of the Archdiocese of Boston to consolidate or close some of its Polish national parishes.*

James L. Franklin, "Archdiocese to Reduce Polish Parishes," 1995

The Archdiocese of Boston yesterday announced a plan to reduce the number of ethnic Polish parishes from 14 to four, a change that could lead to mergers involving 10 parishes in old urban neighborhoods.

The plan, which follows 16 months of discussion involving most of the affected parishes, orders the closing of one Cambridge parish outright, and directs the remaining nine to take part in a process that could lead to consolidation with neighboring parishes.

It was a decision driven by the changing needs of Polish Catholics, a shortage of priests and the needs of newer immigrant groups.

Cardinal Bernard F. Law said he had accepted the recommendations of a parish based planning process, "conscious of the sacrifices many persons will be asked to make."

But the cardinal added he expects that by maintaining four Polish parishes the archdiocese "will be responding responsibly to the true pastoral needs for a Polish apostolate while at the same time continuing to provide for all the people of the archdiocese"...

The changes announced yesterday call for closing St. Hedwig Parish, Cambridge. The four remaining Polish parishes will be Holy Trinity in Lowell, St. Michael in Lynn, St. John the Baptist in Salem, and Our Lady of Czestochowa in South Boston.

Parishes directed to talk to their neighbors about merger or consolidation include Our Lady of Ostrobrama in Brockton, Sacred Heart in Ipswich, St. Casimir in Maynard, St. Peter in Norwood, St. Adalbert in Hyde Park, St. Michael in Haverhill, St. Stanislaus in Chelsea and Holy Trinity in Lawrence.

One of the Polish parishes, St. Joseph in Peabody, may become a national parish for Korean Catholics, according to an archdiocesan source. Members of St. Joseph who want to continue to affiliate with a Polish parish are being encouraged to turn to St. John the Baptist in Salem, but some parishioners already have expressed willingness to share the property with another ethnic group, according to the archdiocesan source.

Boston Globe, 20 January 1995, 21 (Metro). Printed with permission.

Diego Ribadeneira, "Parishioners Plead for Polish Church," 1997

A group of Ipswich parishioners made a personal plea yesterday to Cardinal Bernard Law not to merge their Polish church with two other Ipswich churches.

The parishioners said their church, Sacred Heart, is more than just a building — it is a vital part of their Polish heritage and an important way of passing on ethnic traditions.

"We don't think of Polish as being just our spoken language," said Shirley Ogiba, one of the leaders in the fight to stop Sacred Heart from being merged with St. Stanislaus and St. Joseph's, the other Roman Catholic parishes in Ipswich. "We think of Polish as being our culture, and our culture is intertwined with our religion."

After a meeting that both parishioners and church officials described as cordial and respectful, Law told the six representatives he would take their concerns into consideration before making a final decision.

"I don't think that Cardinal Law knew how strongly we felt that we hadn't been heard," Ogiba told reporters after the meeting at Law's Brighton home...

Boston Globe, 21 February 1997, B4 (Metro). Printed with permission.

Zachary R. Dowdy, "Archdiocese Warns Peabody Parish against 'Illicit' Mass — Excommunicated Priest Offers Service to Members of Closed Church," 1997

Just days after closing the doors of a Polish church in Peabody, the Archdiocese of Boston is praying that parishioners there resist attending a Mass that will be said tomorrow by an excommunicated priest who belongs to a breakaway church.

In a letter from the Rev. William Murphy, the archdiocese urged Roman

Catholics not to attend services conducted by the Rev. Gerry Clements, a priest with the Catholic Apostolic Church of North America.

"It is illicit for Roman Catholics to seek or receive communion from him because he and the church he represents are not in communion with Roman Catholics," Murphy says in the letter...

But Clements, 40,...said he will hold the service at St. Michael's Hall in Peabody anyway, despite meeting yesterday with Murphy.

Clements, who has been married for 18 years, said he became a Catholic Apostolic priest because he refused to take the vow of celibacy required of Roman Catholic priests.

He said he is conducting the Mass at the behest of parishioners at St. Joseph's Church, one of many parishes that were closed July 1 as part of the archdiocese's mergers. The request came about a week after he attended a meeting of the Save St. Joseph's committee.

"I'm trying to heal a wound, not create a bigger one," Clements said. "If I had canceled Mass, that would have hurt them"...

Murphy's letter steers Roman Catholics to the five other Roman Catholic churches in Peabody, and the Polish churches in Lynn and Salem. The merger plan, which comes after three years in the making, was geared to reduce the number of Polish parishes from 14 to four...

Boston Globe, 5 July 1997, B2 (Metro). Printed with permission.

88. John Radzilowski, "Why Are They Wrecking Our Churches? Once Center of Polonian Life, Churches Are under Attack," 1998

Polish-American John Radzilowski, a frequent contributor to the Polish American Journal, *expresses outrage at the destruction of parishes and churches built by his immigrant forebears. Again, the persistence of ethnicity can be observed.*

Parish churches have long been the center of Polish American life. Once, nearly all Polish Americans lived in compact communities centered around a parish church. That church was a Polish church. Today, although many Polish Americans have left the old neighborhood and live in the suburbs, I suspect that the church is still an important part of life for many, even if they no longer "feel Polish."

The Problems

Polonia faces two church problems. First, is the wholesale wrecking of our lovely old Polish churches, sometimes for no good reason at all. Second, is the "depolonization" occurring to Polish American Catholics. It is no secret that Polonia has long had its problems with the Catholic Church, not with doctrine but with efforts by non-Polish pastors to stop Polish customs, language and ethnicity...Today, such problems should be behind us, but they are not.

Vatican II wrought great changes in the Church, many of them for the better. Some American pastors, however, took things too far. Many used it as an excuse to root out ethnicity (which they considered "old-fashioned"). This happened at the same time many Polish Americans were moving out of the old neighborhoods. Although we retained our faith, we lost our ethnicity. Old customs and rituals that were the backbone of everyday Polonia life were suddenly gone. In some cases, pastors refused to allow older people to follow customs and rites they had known all their lives.

Immigrant Sacrifice

Most unconscionable was the desecration of beautiful old Polonia churches. Many were built by our poor but hard working immigrant ancestors who lovingly paid for each decoration, statue, and window with backbreaking toil, with children who never went to college, and by doing without any luxuries. In some parishes, the work of a lifetime was swept away in a matter of weeks. Parishioners found statues smashed and broken in garbage dumps, or left on a street corner for the trashman. Stained glass windows were bricked over, frescoes whitewashed...The pain and rage that this caused in so many parishes remains just under the surface like a festering wound. I will always remember the time I found stained glass windows dedicated to the perpetual memory of someone's Polish grandparents lying in the dirt in a church basement.

Unfortunately, the war on churches has not ended. In Minnesota, for example, one old Polish parish was combined with two others (a German and a French church). The other two churches were demolished. The Polish church is slated for the wrecking ball, too, only to be replaced by a brand new church.

Another old Polish church in the same city is also under threat, but this time for a different reason. The current pastor is making a major effort to de-emphasize the parish's traditional Polish character. Unfortunately, this, too, is not an isolated case...In my own parish, the local church hierarchy tried to end the Polish-language ministry without providing for the needs of the many Polish-speaking people in the area...Only vigorous protest stopped this plan. Similar stories of church closings and efforts to stop Polish ministry can be heard in other places as well — New England, New York, Pennsylvania, and so on.

What Can We Do?

What is happening and what can we do about it? First, although there are pastors and bishops who dislike Poles (for whatever reason), and they constitute a major threat, the much bigger problem is that the American Catholic Church doesn't understand that we are still Polish Americans even though we no longer live in Polish neighborhoods. Many pastors and bishops, like Americans in general, don't understand ethnicity, period... They understand racial problems, but not ethnicity. Our continued existence bewilders them. On top of this, pastors and parishioners are afraid... to speak up in favor of Polish customs, songs, and rites...

Many of us go to parishes with people of different ethnic backgrounds. That's okay. We can live with and learn from each other. If we celebrate Cinco de Mayo, why not combine it with May 3d festivities? If we sing black spirituals at Christmas, why not some Polish carols, too? Can't Italians enjoy Swieconka as much as Poles? Our parish and our Church should be big enough to accommodate everyone. The Church is and has always been about diversity and we need to remind everyone of that and see to it we are not left out. The burden is on us. There is nothing anti-Church about this. The Catechism enjoins Catholics to respect and celebrate cultural diversity within the unity of the Church...

Polish American Journal (July 1998): 4. Printed with permission.

89. Lithuanian Cemetery, Chicago, 1999

For many Catholic immigrants, burial in consecrated ground with "your own kind" was a final, visible badge of ethnic identity. These cities of the dead, generally located at the edge of town, symbolized the growth and evolution of an immigrant group. Paradoxically, as families moved from city to suburb, leaving behind their "mother churches," their cemeteries came to symbolize fading ethnic identity in the post–Vatican II church. As the following document illustrates, the issue of ethnic exclusivity has reemerged among plot holders in the nation's largest Lithuanian Catholic burial ground.

Nearly 100 years ago, in 1903, the memberships of 13 immigrant Lithuanian parishes jointly bought the ground and established Chicago's St. Casimir Lithuanian Cemetery at 4401 W. 111th St.

Over the years, more than 60,000 people, mostly of Lithuanian descent, have been buried at St. Casimir. The saint for whom the cemetery was named was born in 1458, the third son of Poland's King Casimir IV, and became patron saint of both Poland and Lithuania.

It is one of 42 cemeteries operated by the Catholic Archdiocese.

In the beginning, as with their churches and schools, most Catholic cemeteries were created by, and identified with, ethnic groups — Irish, Italian, Poles, Germans, Bohemians and others.

Also, over the years, as neighborhoods changed and people emigrated to the suburbs and the archdiocese began closing churches and schools, the ethnic identity of Catholic institutions faded and became more diverse.

Gradually, pastors and their parishes relinquished their cemetery proprietorship to the archdiocese, and in the mid-1960s the archdiocese moved to eliminate ethnic designations and refer to all its cemeteries as Catholic.

The idea was, and is, as one official put it, to "welcome all people of all ethnic origins...Churches are for all people, and the cemeteries are for all people."

More than 30 years later, however, that still doesn't go down agreeably with some in the Lithuanian community, three of whom recently wrote to Chicago's archbishop, Cardinal Francis George, objecting to removal of the word "Lithuanian" from the name of St. Casimir Cemetery.

In May, in a letter to George that was published in a Lithuanian language newspaper, Birute Matutis, president of St. Casimir's Lithuanian Cemetery Plot Holders' Association, and Salomeja Dauliene, secretary, expressed deep disappointment in the way the long-running disagreement over the name issue has been handled.

They cited the enduring faithfulness of Lithuanian Catholics even through 50 years of Soviet communist rule and of Lithuanian Americans who want to be buried in a cemetery identified with Lithuanian national and spiritual pride.

In a June 28 response to Matutis and Dauliene, the cardinal wrote that he is "very appreciative of all that the Lithuanian Catholic community has done to build the Catholic Church in Chicago."

He said theirs was the only complaint he has received about changing the name of the cemetery, which was done years before he became archbishop here.

George also noted that the directors of Catholic Cemeteries and the Rev. Patrick Pollard, who is in charge of them, are planning garden crypts for Saint Casimir in a new project that will "enhance the beauty of the cemetery and affirm our commitment" to it and to the Lithuanian community.

Then last week, Joe Kulys, who is a plot holder at St. Casimir and president of the Marquette Park Neighbors organization, wrote to George expressing concern over recent reports that the cardinal has declined to address longstanding concerns of the Lithuanian community "regarding this most important and hallowed burial ground."

The "harsh actions" taken in removing Lithuanian from the cemetery's name "struck at the very heart of who we are as people," wrote Kulys, who told me his "grandparents, parents, uncle, aunt, a cousin are all there" in St. Casimir, where he expects to join them.

Kulys proposed that the current name be kept, but that "a permanent line of subtext[,]" such as "an inspiring Lithuanian Catholic heritage," be added to the name and signage for the cemetery.

Pollard told me he is sorry that some individuals might feel otherwise, but that cemetery directors see what is being done at St. Casimir — building new crypts; planting new trees and gardens; importing new artwork from Vilnus, Lithuania; investing in the property — as representing a "very clear affirmation" of regard and respect for the cemetery, its heritage and its future.

"We don't want to make anyone feel unwelcome," Pollard said.

Raymond R. Coffey, "Name Change Still Bothers Some," *Chicago Sun-Times*, 24 August 1999. Printed with permission.

The Transcendence of Ethnicity

90. Birth-Control Clinics

On 1 May 1916, five months before she opened the nation's first birth-control clinic in Brooklyn, Margaret Higgins Sanger exhorted women at a Chicago rally "not to bear children if they expected them to 'grow up to be wage slaves.' " Sanger's experience as a nurse had convinced her that poor Catholic and Jewish women deserved ready access to contraceptive information, and she began to write and lecture on the subject. Although middle-class Protestant club women initially shunned Sanger for her socialist views, they embraced the idea that birth control would improve American society by limiting the number of morally and physically deficient children born to immigrant mothers. One of the earliest Catholic opponents to birth-control clinics was Mary Onahan Gallery (1866–1940), a graduate of Sacred Heart Academy on Taylor Street in Chicago and the mother of eight children, five of whom survived to adulthood.

The women of Chicago are watching with grave concern the effort to foist a birth-control clinic on their city. I attended the first lecture of Margaret Sanger in this city in the West Side auditorium [1916], having been warned that it was unfair to condemn without a hearing. One third of that audience consisted of boys and girls of high school age. They came into the hall giggling and snickering, furtively eying each other. My heart ached for those children.

The proponents of control say: "There are poverty, bad housing, slums in the world, therefore let us prevent the birth of more children." The conclusion is a non sequitur. Do away with the poverty, the bad housing, the slums. Don't do away with the children. They say: "A woman has had six idiot children. It is a crime to permit her to have any more." Certainly, it is. It was a crime to permit her to marry in the first place, but the remedy is to segregate her permanently.

There was no birth-control clinic here in Illinois when Abraham Lincoln was born in poverty. Had there been, doubtless it would have severely reprehended bringing a child into the world in such surroundings. Yet Illinois [and] the world are the richer for that boy.

Spare us the birth-control clinic now!

Mary Onahan Gallery

"Birth Control Clinics," undated *Chicago Daily News* article attached to Mary Onahan Gallery letter, in Madaj Collection, 1924 M75, Archdiocese of Chicago's Joseph Cardinal Bernardin Archives and Records Center. Printed with permission.

91. "Are Irish Catholics Dying Out in This Country?" 1922

Concern over declining birthrates was not limited to American Protestants. In addition to worrying about birth-control clinics in poor immigrant neighborhoods, Catholic leaders expressed alarm at the smaller size of middle-class Catholic families living in cities. Particularly ominous was the pattern of delayed marriage among the Irish, who were finally enjoying the benefits of upward social and economic mobility. Although the custom of late marriage — and fewer resulting births — made sense for survivors of the Great Famine in Ireland in the 1840s, parish priests regarded its persistence in America as sinful.

THE question as to whether there are enough children in the Irish Catholic families of this country to replace their fathers and mothers and keep up the representation of the race among our population would seem to be gratuitous. Everybody seems to presume that the Irish are a prolific race and are beyond all doubt not only reproducing themselves but besides that distinctly adding to the population of the country...

In the light of such impressions it is extremely interesting to take a series of families belonging to what is usually considered the successful group among the Irish in practically any part of the country and see what has happened to them in the course of three or four generations. The first generation out from Ireland, usually beginning its career in poverty, had an average of a little more than six children in the family who lived to adult life. The child death-rate was very high seventy-five years ago, and the infectious diseases, cholera, typhus, typhoid, as well as the children's diseases carried off a great many in their younger years. Of these six who reached adult life not more than half, as a rule, married. This may be astonishing considering the usual Irish attitude toward marriage, but it will be found to be true. In some of the cases there was a priest or two in the family and not infrequently one or more of the girls entered the convent. In others the apparently inevitable old maids and old bachelors, so commonly to be found in Irish families of the better-to-do classes here in America[,] accounted for the rest...

Apparently from what I have found, if the Church is to depend on the reproductive increase of the Irish Catholics of this country for its membership[,] the future looks blank indeed. This is not at all a new view, I know, but has been expressed by at least half a dozen who have looked into the question somewhat before this. The one reason for calling attention to it once more is to try to tempt people to look into these conditions in their own neighborhood and let us know the facts. After looking over the data that I have in hand already I am forced to the conclusion that while the fewness of children in the families represents a very prominent factor in the unfortunate situation that is evidently developing, it is by no means the only factor, and I doubt whether it is even the most serious factor.

[The most serious factor] is to my mind the very large number of old maids and old bachelors who are to be found in Irish families in this country...[I]t is not unusual to have half the children of the family remain unmarried. Sometimes it is actually more than that. That question is too large to treat properly at the end of this article, so I am asking the Editor of *AMERICA* to let me tell a little of the story of old maids and old bachelors in a succeeding contribution, and to touch upon the question of our college graduates not having nearly sons enough to represent them in the next generation in college, as another phase of this very interesting and, it seems to me, extremely important question.

James J. Walsh, M.D., Ph.D., "Are Irish Catholics Dying Out in This Country?" *America*, 5 August 1922. Printed with permission of America Press, Inc. ©2000. All rights reserved. For subscription information call 1-800-627-9533 or visit www.americapress.org.

92. Mary Onahan Gallery, Letter to Archbishop Mundelein, 1924

On 22 January 1924, Judge Harry M. Fisher of the circuit court of Cook County denied a petition by Archbishop George W. Mundelein to set aside his earlier decision permitting the establishment of a birth-control clinic in Chicago. According to the Chicago Daily News, *"Following testimony given by expert witnesses, introduced by counsel for the archbishop, Judge Fisher declared that he was convinced that a free clinic for the poor is as legal as are other clinics which are not required to have licenses." Birth-control advocates rejoiced, and the Family Limitation Committee of the prestigious Chicago Woman's Club mailed each of its members a copy of Judge Fisher's decision, calling it "the sanest contribution on scientific birth control." In the following letter, Mary Onahan Gallery, the mother of eight children, discusses the dramatic shift in attitudes about contraception that had occurred since 1912.*

1612 Chase Avenue
Chicago
Jan. 25, 1924

Most Reverend and dear Archbishop:

Would it be advisable for the Catholic Women's Clubs of the city to come out in a protest against the establishment of this noxious birth control clinic? They have a membership practically of 50,000 not including great organizations like the Foresters.

It seems too bad that a little bunch of radicals should swing things as they are doing. The trouble is the conservative people, the people who are against it are silent. They do not like to come out publicly on an unpleasant subject.

This Mrs. [Helen] Carpenter who heads the project is quite active in the Chicago Woman's Club. We drove it out of the club twelve years ago after I made public protest against it but it has crept back again under the title of "Family Limitation Committee."

Of the twenty who went before the Board at that time to protest only three were Catholic. The rest were Presbyterian, Episcopalian, Methodist, Jewish. In fact I had more backing from the non-Catholics than I did from the Catholics

I am sorry to say. But the Catholic Women's Clubs can be swung into line if you think it advisable & I have no doubt many of the Men's clubs as well. And if the women came out overwhelmingly against it the thing will be killed. What would you advise us to do? . . .

Cordially yours,
Mary Onahan Gallery

[P.S.:] It was a great joy to have John home at Christmas! His brother Dan is still gallivanting out on the Riviera. He has been over a year & a half on the flagship & is now a lieutenant. *[John Ireland Gallery, named after the archbishop of St. Paul, Minnesota, was ordained in 1926 and served as a priest of the Chicago diocese until his death in 1995. During World War II, Rear Admiral Daniel V. Gallery made military history when his crew on the Guadalcanal attacked and seized the U-505 on 4 June 1944. According to the Chicago Museum of Science and Industry, where the submarine is now on display, this constituted "the first time in American history since 1815 that a foreign enemy man-of-war had been boarded and captured on the high seas."]*

Archdiocese of Chicago's Joseph Cardinal Bernardin Archives and Records Center. Printed with permission.

93. James M. Gillis, C.S.P., "Will Ye Fight or Will Ye Run?" 1932

The promulgation of the encyclical Casti Connubii *(On Christian Marriage) on 31 December 1930 was widely interpreted as a reaction to the decision of the Lambeth Conference of Anglican Bishops allowing married couples to use contraceptives. The issue of family limitation took on new layers of meaning as the Great Depression deepened in America. Increasingly, "keeping faith" meant opposition to birth control for Catholic men and women of very diverse ethnic and economic backgrounds. The following article, full of martial metaphors, illustrates the degree to which the birth-control issue had already become a marker of American Catholic identity by the 1930s.*

I have consistently refused to debate the question of birth control. There are certain matters of morals that do not admit of debate. Onanism is one of them.

But there are supplementary questions that cling to the fringe of the essential matter. For example, loyalty to the Church in her fight against the neo-pagan movement in general, and race-suicide in particular.

We all remember the questions put by the captain of a company of soldiers to his men as the battle was about to begin, and the enthusiastic though enigmatic answers: "Are ye with me or are ye agin' me?" "We are!!" "Will ye fight or will ye run?" "We will!!!"

May I be pardoned if I confess the suspicion that the reply of some Catholics to the questions of their Church is equally enigmatic? The gage is down, the battle is crucial. In preparation for that conflict the Church should know how many are under her banner, and how many follow the flag of the enemy. There are only friends and foes. No one can be neutral. "He that is not with Me is against Me," said the Master, and the Church echoes His words. He also said, "I know Mine and Mine know me." Just at this moment, as the birth control fight commences, the Church cannot say those same words. She doesn't know where some "Catholics" stand...

And now, for example, Mrs. Margaret Sanger, leader of the birth control movement, recently received a gold medal known as the American Woman's Association Award, at a testimonial dinner in her honor at the club house in West 57th street, New York.

It happens that some Catholic women belong to that Association, and that some other Catholic women lived in that club house. They are in general women who have had superior educational advantages, and also are therefore presumably persons of unusual intelligence... They must be aware that the A.W.A. has slapped their Church in the face... Also they must see that the A.W.A. in insulting their Church has insulted them. The association has said to them in effect, "You don't count. You pay your dues, or your rent, or both, but we don't have to reckon with you. We know that your Church is against birth control. You also know it. But we go ahead regardless, and award honor to the champion of a cause that your Church holds in abhorrence. And what are you going to do about it?..."

There is the challenge. And now we shall know those that have spunk and those that are yellow. Those that take it without protest are "Catholics." Those that stand up and protest and who being voted down as an insignificant minority, resign, are Catholics...

Well, the issue is not to be fought out in a club house. This battle is due to rage all over the world. But whether it be on one small spot of the earth's surface, or on the entire globe, the Church must know her friends and her foes. Incidentally, the call to arms will demonstrate those that lack the courage either to be friend or foe. Kind reader, under what banner do you fight? Or are you — God forbid — of those that are afraid to fight, and so either lie down or run away?

> Rev. James. M. Gillis, C.S.P., "Will Ye Fight or Will Ye Run?" in "Sursum Corda; Or, What Is Right with the World," syndicated column distributed by the National Catholic Welfare Conference News Service, published in *The New World*, 13 May 1932. Printed with permission.

94. Catholic Sacramental Practice and Birth Control in Chicago, 1932

In May 1932, the congressional Ways and Means Committee of the House of Representatives and a subcommittee of the Senate Judiciary Committee held hearings on the Hancock and Hatfield bills, aimed at opening the U.S. mails

to the dissemination of birth-control information. The following letter, written
by George Cardinal Mundelein to Mrs. Rita C. McGoldrick, president of the
International Federation of Catholic Alumnae, outlines pastoral policies adopted
in the Chicago diocese against birth control.

Chicago, Illinois
July 18, 1932

Mrs. Rita C. McGoldrick,
191 Handsome Avenue,
Sayville, Long Island,
New York.

My dear Mrs. McGoldrick:

...I read your testimony in both hearings with a great deal of interest. I agree with you that we are looking at this matter with entirely too much complacency and that before we are aware of it, we will wake up to find all barriers removed. Under the circumstances I have decided to protect and instruct my own people. At least it will not be said later that we were asleep and did nothing to protect those under our care. In a word we are endeavoring to instruct and protect our Catholic people against this evil. To instruct them in the pulpit is not so easy because of the mixed audiences before us. So we found other avenues. In enumerating these, there is of course no intention of criticizing other dioceses or sections...

In the first place, you will notice that marriage with us is not the haphazard affair it has been in the past or still is somewhere else in the country. There is a long interrogatory to be answered, filled out and sworn to by both parties, with express mention of avoidance of birth control practices. This is kept on file for future references, and is obligatory before every marriage. Second, our promises for a mixed marriage are signed by both the Catholic and the Protestant party, and both expressly obligate themselves to abstain from the practices of birth control. Third, all confessors are required to satisfy themselves by interrogation in the confessional of both men and women, when a family is small or apparently spaced, that there is no practice of birth control. Should there be any such practice, absolution is withheld until the promise to abstain in the future is given. This has been productive of much good in the past year with women, and now the same inquiry takes place with men. There can be no such excuse as ignorance or good faith. Finally, recognizing the fact that an economic difficulty often enters, we established our own [Lewis Memorial] maternity hospital for the service of small wage-earners, the white-collar class... Twenty-eight hundred children born in seventeen months and 247 babies born in this hospital in the past month of June. Everything included all for fifty dollars and our record is better than any other maternity hospital in Chicago, even the most expensive. So you see, we have the premises well policed as far as our people are concerned. As for the rest, I told one prominent man, that unless the non-Catholics safeguard themselves in this manner as we had done, in the lifetime of one generation we would own and control this city of Chicago, because we would have the votes. This letter became a little longer than I had intended, than I usually write, but the subject is interesting, and it makes up for past neglect ...

Chancery Correspondence, 209, 1932, Archdiocese of Chicago's Joseph Cardinal Bernardin Archives and Records Center. Printed with permission.

95. Margaret Sanger on Catholics and Birth Control, 1934

From the 1920s on, Margaret Higgins Sanger (1883–1966) emerged as the nation's most influential birth-control advocate. Born in Corning, New York, Sanger was a keen observer of Irish-American community life and mores. Her immigrant Irish father, Michael Hennessy Higgins — a fiery socialist and a disciple of Henry George — carved headstones for a living. Sanger's mother, Anne Purcell, had been raised Catholic but did not go to church after her marriage, yet she bore eleven children. Sanger remembered that there was always "another baby coming" in her family and that she preferred the Virgin Mary to the Crucified Christ because "she was beautiful, smiling — the way I should like to look when I had a baby." As the following letter reveals, Margaret Sanger succeeded in casting the debate over birth control as a fight against the power and authority of the Catholic Church.

SIR: The Catholic opponents of birth control are evidently unaware of the dissatisfaction among the intelligent men and women of their own faith regarding the attitude their Church has taken on birth control. To satisfy this element there was recently published a book called "Rhythm," loudly praised by Catholic prelates and press, which explains in detail, and to the hour, when conception *cannot* take place. Most of us have long ago discarded the safe-period theory as a method available for general application. This book, however, was written by a physician [Dr. Leo Latz] and is published with "Ecclesiastical Approbation," which means that it has the approval of the Roman Catholic Church.

Our opponents are evidently unaware of the contents of this book, for every argument they have ever used against contraception is supported in the book on behalf of the safe-period method. All the ballyhoo of "race suicide," "the race dying out," "immorality," is answered by the author with fearless intelligence and in a spirit that one respects.

On the general principles of limiting or controlling the size of the family — on the needs, rights, and morality of the practice, we seem to be in perfect agreement. *On methods we entirely disagree.* The Catholic opponents advocate a safe period. The non-Catholic proponents desire to place all responsibility concerning methods in the hands of the medical profession.

The federal laws, however, state clearly that *"any"* information to prevent conception sent through the United States Mails is illegal. The Post Office has informed us that "Rhythm" by Dr. Latz, is mailable, but that "Contraceptive Practices," by Dr. Hannah M. Stone, is unmailable.

The twenty million members of the Catholic faith now have a method of birth control legally sanctioned by the Post Office authorities and morally sanctioned by the hierarchy. But what about the one hundred and four millions of non-Catholics who prefer *other* methods of birth control or who do not think the safe period is safe?

Margaret Sanger, "Catholics and Birth Control," *New Republic,* 13 June 1934. Reprinted with permission.

Part 5

ASIAN IMMIGRANTS

Introduction

Asian immigrants have posed interesting challenges to the Catholic Church in the United States. First, the earliest Asian immigrants, the Chinese and Japanese, were overwhelmingly non-Catholic; thus much of the church's ministry was missionary in character. Second, the scarcity of Catholics among these groups meant that there were few priests, religious, or lay catechists to minister to them in their own languages. And, third, Asian immigrants faced intense racial hostility from Americans on the West Coast and elsewhere in the country. Until 1952, they were designated "aliens ineligible for citizenship," regardless of how long they had lived in the United States. Unfortunately, U.S. Catholics were not immune to the prevailing societal prejudices.

Asian immigration to the United States was quite limited until the California Gold Rush of 1849 inspired a large migration from China. By the end of the 1850s more than thirty thousand Chinese had immigrated to California. During the 1860s the Chinese provided the bulk of the workforce in the construction of the western portion of the transcontinental railroad. Despite their contributions, the Chinese were the most despised of people, derided as "cheap coolie labor." By 1882 anti-Chinese hysteria culminated in the Chinese Exclusion Act, which severely restricted Chinese immigration, reducing it to a trickle. By the early twentieth century many Chinese had migrated to the eastern urban centers of New York and Boston, ostensibly to escape West Coast hostility.

Since few Asian immigrants had contacts with the Catholic Church in their homelands, they did not look to the local Catholic community for spiritual care when they arrived. As the "immigrant church" preserving the faith of its own ethnic members in a hostile environment, the Catholic Church was not a presence to early Chinese immigrants arriving on the West Coast.

Japanese encountered a similar pattern of hostility and neglect. Beginning in the 1890s a significant number of Japanese immigrants began arriving in the United States, numbering seventy thousand residents by 1920. They worked as migrant workers in California agriculture with a significant number enjoying success as truck farmers. In 1906 San Francisco's Asiatic Exclusion League was formed to extend the provisions of the Chinese Exclusion Act to the Japanese. When San Francisco's Public School Board planned to segregate Japanese in "oriental schools," anti-U.S. demonstrations erupted in Japan. In 1907 President Theodore Roosevelt responded by negotiating a "Gentlemen's Agreement" with Japan, in which the government of Japan voluntarily limited immigration to the United States. Even this did not inhibit anti-Japanese feeling. In 1913 the state of California passed legislation forbidding Japanese to own land in California.

Catholic ministry to Chinese and Japanese began in fits and starts in the nineteenth century. After several unsuccessful attempts to establish missions for the Chinese in San Francisco, the Paulist Fathers established the first successful Chinese mission at Old St. Mary's Church in the city's Chinatown in 1903. In 1921 it was formally named Holy Family Chinese Mission while continuing to be known as St. Mary's. Local archdioceses began a Chinese mission in New York in 1910 and sponsored ministry to Chinese in Boston around the same time. The first Japanese mission was established in Los Angeles in 1912 by Father Albert Breton of the Paris Foreign Missionary Society. The following year he established another Japanese mission in San Francisco.

Since few Chinese and Japanese immigrants were Catholics, the missions' main purpose was conversions to Catholicism. Interestingly, Japanese and Chinese mission parishes operated much as other Catholic ethnic parishes had — the missions sought not only to preserve the immigrants' faith (or to provide immigrants with a new faith) but also to preserve their language and culture. In most cases, the language and culture were not intimately connected with the Catholic faith, as was the case with other groups, such as the Polish or Irish. Nevertheless, in Los Angeles, San Francisco, and New York, the Catholic missions operated Japanese and Chinese language schools. The vast majority of students were not Catholics, but were sent to the schools by their parents to ensure that they did not lose their language and culture. The Catholic Church thereby played an important role in preserving the culture and language of many second- and third-generation Japanese and Chinese, despite the fact that so few were Catholic.

In contrast to the Chinese and Japanese, Filipino immigrants were mostly Catholics. Though the United States acquired the Philippine Islands in the Spanish-American War of 1898, few Filipinos came to the United States before 1920. During the 1920s, a wave of Filipino immigrants — over 90 percent male — arrived to find work mainly in agriculture and canneries on the West Coast. Like the Chinese and Japanese before them, they encountered discrimination. In 1934 federal legislation all but ended Filipino immigration, which did not resume until after World War II.

The Catholic Church's response to Filipino immigrants, according to Filipino historian Fred Cordova, was uninspiring: "Filipino American Catholics kept the faith even though many had not become regular church goers... [T]he institutional Catholic Church's commitment to Filipino Americans was one of indifference if not benign condescension."[1] Since the Filipino population was predominantly male, church leaders responded with the creation of Catholic Filipino Clubs for them in Seattle and San Francisco in the 1920s. Since they arrived in the 1920s, at a time when many bishops were discouraging the formation of ethnic parishes, national parishes for them were slow to be established. Nevertheless, in 1925 the Seattle diocese experimented with the founding of a mixed Japanese and Filipino national parish, Our Lady Queen of Martyrs.[2] In Los Angeles, the diocese founded St. Columban's parish in 1947 for Filipinos. It served as the only Filipino national parish in the United States. For the most part, Filipinos have been encouraged to become part of their local parishes.

The crucial event in enlarging the Catholic Church's relationship with Asian immigrants was passage of the Immigration Act of 1965. The U.S. Congress framed this legislation during a period of strong support for eliminating discrimination against African Americans. The 1965 act eliminated the blatant discrimination against Asians and southern and eastern Europeans embedded in the 1924 immigration law. As a result of this reform, immigration from Asia, Mexico, and South America soared. By 1990 Asians and Latinos accounted for over 80 percent of all immigrants to the United States.

While increased immigration added to existing American communities of Chinese, Japanese, and Filipinos, a major political event — the fall of Saigon in 1975 and the collapse of South Vietnam's government — gave rise for the first time to large-scale immigration of Vietnamese. A second wave of Vietnamese refugees, the "boat people," who fled their country by sea, crested around 1980. A third wave of Vietnamese arrived in 1986 as part of the Orderly Departure Program. Though Vietnam was only about 10 percent Catholic, the number of Catholics among the refugees was much higher — in the initial wave close to 40 percent. Vietnamese Catholics brought a pre–Vatican II understanding of the Catholic faith and adhered to many devotional practices of the preconciliar era. In relating to the Vietnamese, church leaders have had to nurture the traditional expressions of the faith, while easing them into contemporary Catholicism.

Other Asian groups have arrived in large numbers since the 1970s, most notably immigrants from Korea, Hong Kong, Laos, Cambodia, Taiwan, and India.

---

1. Fred Cordova, *Filipinos, Forgotten Asian Americans* (Dubuque, Iowa: Kendall/Hart, 1983), 172.

2. Madeline Duntley, "Japanese and Filipino Together: The Transethnic Vision of Our Lady Queen of Martyrs Parish," *U.S. Catholic Historian* 18 (winter 2000).

The documents in this chapter address the varied experiences of Asian Catholics and the Catholic Church's reactions to their presence. In doing so they reveal some of the enduring challenges of welcoming new immigrants to the U.S. Catholic community.

Chinese Immigrants

96. Father James Bouchard, S.J., "White Man or Chinaman — Which?" 1873

Father James Bouchard, S.J., was a popular mission preacher who ministered along the West Coast during the latter half of the nineteenth century. The following speech was given in 1873 at St. Francis of Assisi Church in San Francisco as a fundraiser for the Presentation Sisters — a sum of three thousand dollars was raised. The speech reflects commonly held attitudes of San Franciscans, Catholic and otherwise, toward the Chinese. The flood of Chinese workers who returned to the city following the completion of the transcontinental railroad in 1869 created intense competition for jobs, a tension that was exacerbated by the onset of the panic of 1873. In 1877, violence erupted with three days of rioting against the Chinese followed by the creation of the anti-Chinese Workingmen's Party of California, whose slogan was "The Chinese Must Go!" The Workingmen's Party was led by Irishman Dennis Kearney, who repeated themes similar to those articulated by Bouchard. One final note — Bouchard was a Native American of the Delaware tribe (though his mother was of European descent), but he studiously avoided reference to that part of his heritage. Indeed, Bouchard endorses the white racist theory that was later used against Catholic immigrants from southern, central, and eastern Europe.

The importation of the Chinese is a question of serious import to the people of this country. Whether it will redound to our benefit, or add to our injury, are points which are worthy of discussion at the present time; and I am glad to find that many of our fellow-citizens are waking up to the question. The influx of thousands of ignorant idolators can, it seems to me, be productive of no good to our country. Yet it appears that a portion of the press, in dealing with this subject, most generally dilate on the amount of wealth which may be gained by employing the cheap labor or servitude of the Chinese...[But what] are the results of cheap labor[?] We find in countries where the prices of labor have been reduced to their lowest rates, that their forms of government are more or less despotic. Their people, by a lifetime of labor barely obtain the necessaries of life, and the aristocracy of a favored few fatten and grow rich in luxuries and all the refinements of life at the expense of the toiling and downtrodden many. In such countries we shall find magnificent public buildings, fine roads, and the results of cheap labor in a thousand ways. But we also find that in proportion as the wages of all labor have been reduced to their lowest possible rates, the moral and intellectual status of the people has fallen.

[After haranguing that cheap Chinese labor would have no benefits, Bouchard continued:] I know there is a class among us, which is ready to meet us with this argument. The Chinese are greatly benefited...: that our philanthropic citizens and our religious zealots (their works are very commendable; I am not going to condemn them for the efforts they are making to benefit them) lead them by the dozens and hundreds, on the Sabbath, into the various churches, and there teach them to spell and read; and then, having taught them to read, place in their hands the Bible; and, of course, when this is done, they must necessarily become Christians. Well, this has been going on for a considerable time, even in San Francisco... Now, tell me how many of these people have ever converted to Christianity?... Have the papers of our city yet heralded the baptism of a single Chinaman as the fruit of their labor?... It is, so far as the effort is concerned, commendable, I say, but the result, certainly, is not equal to the effort. In fact the whole labor seems to be abortive, so far as the conversion of the Chinese is concerned; and I have very little confidence that any considerable number, if any one at all, of all the Chinese population will ever be converted to Christianity here. It is almost impossible even to convert them in their own country...

But suppose that these Chinese that come into our country are all free; could come and sojourn in our country and become citizens if they wished — and Christians too, if they like — still I maintain that they are an inferior race of people and consequently can not be a safe class (that is, if introduced in any considerable number) of people in our country. Their immigration should therefore be opposed — legitimately, of course — I do not countenance violence, or violent and illegal measures; but certainly the immigration of an inferior race must result in great injury to our people and country...

I have said sufficient to show you the inferiority of that race, and the disadvantages to us, as a people, of bringing them among us;...[t]hey are not a people we want; they are far from being the laboring class that our country needs, and must have, to develop all its resources — to enrich and ennoble it — to perpetuate its grand and noble institutions. 'Tis the white race we want. The white man — the head of all his kind in bone and muscle, and pluck and endurance; in intellect a head and shoulder above all other races; a man, even in the natural order, more or less governed by sentiments of honor and the obligations of honesty; and, in addition, more or less under the influence of a conscience trained in accordance with the teachings of Christianity, and controlled by Christian morality in his everyday life; the only race that has ever proved itself capable of self-government, or of really progressive civilization. According to our public journals, hundreds and thousands of the white race — for example, the Celt, the Saxon, the Gaul, the Teuton — arrive annually in our country, to seek new homes and remunerative labor, invited hither by our free government and fruitful soil. They come from the islands and from the continent of Europe; are bone of our bone — our own kind...Will you place an obstacle to the coming of these people into our country? Will you invite, and bring in by the thousands and hundreds of thousands this inferior race; these pagan, these vicious, these immoral creatures, that are incapable of rising to the virtue that is inculcated by the religion of Jesus Christ — the world's Redeemer[?] Be assured...that if you bring in this people numerously...you will not only prevent the immigration of the European races to our country, but you will drive out those that have already taken up their residence among us...Is there a man or woman in the breadth and length of this Republic that has so little American Spirit,...so little love of country, as to be willing to give any aid...to the introduction of a mass of inferior people, that must drive away, or prevent from coming, a class of immigrants that would be a credit to the country — a benefit to the country, and that would help to make this the greatest and grandest nation on the face of the earth?

San Francisco Catholic Guardian, 1 March 1873, 302–3.

97. Archbishop Joseph S. Alemany Requests Assistance with the Chinese Apostolate in San Francisco, 1871, 1874

Spanish-born Joseph Sadoc Alemany, O.P., first archbishop of San Francisco (1853–84), demonstrated remarkable solicitude toward the Chinese in the San Francisco Bay Area. In the following documents Alemany writes the superiors of the Jesuit mission in California to obtain Jesuits to serve as missionaries to the Chinese. He relates his hard luck in his previous endeavors. As early as 1854, he had obtained a Chinese priest, Father Thomas Cian of the Congregation of the Holy Family in Naples, Italy; unfortunately, Cian spoke the wrong dialect, so he was almost completely useless. Successful ministry to the Chinese in San Francisco did not occur until 1903, when the Paulist Fathers began their mission at Old St. Mary's Cathedral in the heart of Chinatown. One of the recurring difficulties in ministry to the Chinese was acquiring qualified Chinese-speaking priests, Sisters, and catechists.

San Francisco, April 27, 1871

Very Rev. J. B. Ponte, S.J., Supr.

Very Reverend Dear Sir:

We have so many Chinese in this diocese, that we should make some provision for their souls...I therefore beg you to accept the care of this poor people, whose souls have a great claim on our ministry and charity...

Your most humble and devoted servant,
Joseph S. Alemany, A.S.F.

San Francisco, Aug. 5, 1874

Very Rev. Aloysius Masnata, S.J., Supr.

Very Reverend Dear Sir:

I am obliged to write you on a very peculiar subject, in which I think you can help me. It is on the Chinese question.

I have made many efforts to have our Chinese attended to in their spiritual affairs. I wrote to Cardinal Fransoni. I got a Franciscan missionary, who after building a little chapel for them, left in bad health. Then I obtained Father Thomas Cian, who could not do much for them, and he finally had to go. Then I visited the Chinese College at Naples, but saw that I could scarcely entertain any hope of succeeding there. Then Father Valentini came, but he needed a catechist, whom I obtained from Hong Kong, and he also needed a school and chapel, which, when established, were not over successful. I also wrote to our missionaries in China, who could not help. I spoke to our old friend, Father Ponte, who was very anxious to undertake it, but he desired first to communicate with the General, but the General did not encourage immediate action. Then I wrote to the General, and he recommended me to write to Bishop Languillat of China, but, naturally enough, this good Bishop thinks he needs what missionaries he has. Therefore, what is to be done? Must I abandon all hope? Must I leave the large number of Chinese here and through the diocese without any efficient provision for them, and without any missionaries to work for them? The question is a serious one and should be faced...

Yours truly in Christ,

+J. S. Alemany, A.S.F.

Joseph Riordan, S.J., *The First Half Century of St. Ignatius Church and College* (San Francisco, 1905), 166, 195–96.

98. Francis Leo Lem and Chew Yee to Archbishop Patrick W. Riordan Requesting Chinese Pastor, 1910

As with all immigrant groups, the Chinese desired a priest who could speak their language. Despite the beginning of the ministry of the priests of the Missionary Society of St. Paul the Apostle (Paulists) to the Chinese in San Francisco, the Chinese still desired a Chinese pastor. In 1904, the Sisters of the Helpers of the Holy Souls, who had been working in Shanghai, arrived in San Francisco to work with the Chinese. Included in the group was Mother St. Ida, a native Chinese, a Eurasian to be exact.

San Francisco, Cal.
Jan. the 13th, 1910

Most Reverend Archbishop,

We would like very much to have you assign a pastor [to] come to this city permanently preaching in Chinese because there are [a] good many of our Chinese has [*sic*] joined the Church and they do not understand [E]nglish languages [*sic*]. We are already so proud of the kind interest you take in us by sending us the Sisters and hope soon [we] will have a missionary from China to hear confessions in Chin[ese].

Thanking you cordially, yours truly

Francis Leo Lem
Chew Yee

Archives of the Archdiocese of San Francisco. Printed with permission.

99. Chinese Ministry in San Francisco, 1945, 1942

The following three letters reflect the difficulty of obtaining Chinese-speaking ministers. In the first letter, San Francisco resident A. Wong writes the editor of the archdiocesan newspaper, The Monitor, *expressing his desire to hear the Catholic faith preached in Chinese. In response, Father Charles Donovan, C.S.P., pastor of the San Francisco Chinese mission, St. Mary's, relates the work being done for the Chinese at the mission. Integral to the Chinese mission was the work of lay catechist John Yehall Chin (see document 100). In the final letter, Donovan requests that Chin be exempted from military service during World War II because of the centrality of his work at the mission.*

Letter to the *San Francisco Monitor* [Newspaper of the Archdiocese of San Francisco], 1945

May, 1945

Question:

Where could Chinese have faith explained to them in [their] native tongue?

Reverend Father: Explanation for above question — the war has made great difference to Chinese people — hundreds of Chinese are turning from paganism to Christianity — but mostly through Protestant religion in San Francisco. In Catholic mission no religion explained or confessions in Chinese. The Chinese people think in Chinese — each year some adults follow children into Catholic Faith but do not understand. Grace Cathedral, YMCA, Baptists all have catechism taught in Chinese. Protestant missionar[ies] waiting to return to China are working among tenements in Chinatown — speaking language — Catholic Sisters do not speak language — one sees in *Monitor* Chinese language class announced at Chinese mission — like class at Jesuit Fathers, but no religion class. Mr. Chin drafted in army after Pearl Harbor could teach religion but he was not replaced at mission. Above question not so important to appear in *Monitor* but, Reverend Father may use influence to have Chinese speaking priest hear confessions and explain meaning some time to people. Chinese speaking Sisters might call on people — like Protestant Sisters. Thousands are looking for the truth, but do not know where to go and many baptized do not understand... Please give petition your consideration. Thank you kindly,

A Wong —

Reply of the Director of the Catholic Chinese Social Center

May 24, 1945

Most Reverend John J. Mitty, Archbishop of San Francisco...

Your Excellency:

This is in reply to the question sent to the *Monitor*'s office which asked where a Chinese could have the Catholic faith explained in his native tongue.

Since I have been working with the Chinese for the past five years, I think it is my duty to clarify the situation which prevails here at the Chinese Mission and to let you know that this problem has always been sufficiently met by us. If at any time anyone is desirous of having the truths of our Church explained in his native tongue, this opportunity is always present and can be adequately fulfilled by the Mission. Since I have been here, there has never been one person who has come to me with this desire who has gone away discouraged. If such persons have, then I am not aware of it.

The questioner likewise refers to Mr. John Chin, our former catechist, now in the armed forces. As regards this problem, I have made repeated attempts to have him returned, and only recently with your kind help also, I have again requested his dismissal from the services for the sake of the Mission. During his absence, however, there have been at the Mission young Chinese women, as well as Chinese mothers, who are fully equipped to pursue the task of catechizing in their native tongue.

At our Chinese Mission, there are Confessions heard in Chinese. I happen to hear them myself every Saturday and Sunday, and once in a while I try to give a sermon in Chinese. For the past year and a half, I have been studying to master this language...

Our religious faith is likewise explained in Chinese to those who so desire it and to those who cannot speak English when under instruction... As for the children, and younger people, they all speak English, and we have Friday night classes for those children who attend public schools...

May I say also that our Chinese Mission averages fifty to sixty converts a year, that our Mission is far more influential in Chinatown than the questioner states, and that our Sunday Mass attendance far exceeds the attendance of any of the seven Protestant Missions in Chinatown. Some of the leaders of these other missions have openly lauded the equipment and facilities which our Mission offers to the Chinese.

Two groups of Sisters visit our Chinese people continually: the Chinese Sisters from the Helpers of the Holy Souls and our own Sisters of St. Joseph of Orange who teach daily at the Mission. Day and night the Sisters, as well as myself, are on the watch for more souls, and I can never overstress the excellent accomplishments of these hardworking Sisters. All their time is Chinese time. I, myself, likewise visit our Chinese people and, moreover, teach in the homes all those who, because of multiple duties, cannot visit me at the Mission or at the rectory of Old St. Mary's...

I hope the facts I have set forth may give you a clearer idea of the scope of our work in this regard at the Mission.

Praying God's blessings upon you and your work.

> Respectfully yours
>
> Rev. Charles A. Donovan, C.S.P.

Request to Have Gim Ham [John Yehall] Chin Exempted from Military Duty, 1942

To: The Chancery Office
San Francisco, Ca

> January 24th, 1942

Your Excellency,

[Father Donovan explains he is trying to have Gim Ham Chin exempted from military service as a "minister of religion." He continues:]

The duties of Gim H. Chin are as follows.

Instruction in prayers and Christian Doctrine of the first four Primary grades as well as the kindergarten of our Parochial School. A companion-interpreter and helper with me on sick-calls, census work, hospital and house to house visitations, at Baptisms, Marriages, Funerals. Instructor and Catechist of all our elderly Chinese converts. On every Sunday and Holyday as well as on other special occasions he preaches our messages, announcements and Gospel sermons to the assembly and to the congregation. He serves as a link, a medium of exchange for me in my dealings with the Chinese in their manifold problems as well as being interpreter to the various Chinese agencies and Chinese leaders in Chinatown. [He is] [t]he Directing Supervisor of our entire Chinese Evening School which numbers over 550 students. Therein also he carries on Religious Instruction.

I may add that Mr. G. H. Chin has undertaken these duties exclusively since the year 1931...I may say too, that there seems to be some difficulty not so much concerning the duties of Mr. Chin, but about the title "Minister" which he lacks. On his Questionnaire he ascribed his duties as Catechist[,] which apparently holds no weight with the Local Board.

I hope with all my heart Mr. G. H. Chin can be deferred. I wish to thank you so much Your Excellency for your deep kindness and understanding solicitude in the problem.

> Sincerely,
>
> [Rev.] Charles A. Donovan, C.S.P.

100. Chinese Language School, 1936

In addition to conducting a regular parochial grammar school, one of St. Mary's Chinese Mission's most significant contributions to Chinatown was the Chinese language school. Many parents feared their children would lose their native language, so both Catholic and non-Catholic Chinese sent their children to the school in large numbers. Despite the school's nonreligious emphasis, a Paulist priest in 1956 noted that it had been "the instrument of Christ used to bring so many people of our neighborhood into the Faith." The school was established by Dr. Chu Chew Shong, described at his death as "the beloved patriarch of St. Mary's Chinese Mission." He was assisted by the equally beloved John Yehall Chin. The following excerpts give an account of some of the mission's activities in 1935–36. Absent from the report is what became one of St. Mary's most popular groups — the St. Mary's Drum Corps and Girls Drill Team, founded in 1940.

... The Chinese are a wonderful race and they have an age-old culture. The key to it is the language. Therefore, the Center maintains a Chinese Language School which had an enrollment of four-hundred and fifteen in 1936. One out of every five children in Chinatown attending the various language schools goes to St. Mary's.

In connection with this a music school is carried on to educate the children in their national music. Various instruments are taught, but emphasis is put on the yang k'am or butterfly harp. Dr. Chu Chew Shong, the leading Catholic layman, is the Principal of the Language School, John Yehall Chin, the Supervisor. There are nine native teachers. Mr. Chin also edits the *Aurora*, the quarterly published by St. Mary's Chinese Catholic mission...

The Center also maintains a Social Service Department. During 1935, six hundred children's garments were distributed... Full-time work was secured for one hundred and twenty. Over three thousand visits were made to the sick and needy...

Since the Paulist Fathers inaugurated this work, they have made over a thousand Chinese converts. During 1935, seventy-four Chinese were received into the Church... There were eight thousand Communions during 1935. Sixty-two people were confirmed...

> William A. Lynahan, "A Home Foreign Mission," *Extension Magazine* (October 1936). Printed with permission.

101. Chinese Mission, New York, 1959

Though San Francisco was the major Chinese center, by 1910 significant numbers of Chinese had established themselves in New York City and Boston. Chinese missions were established in both cities. In New York, Transfiguration Parish, which had previously worked with Irish and Italian immigrants, served as the Chinese center. In 1945, the Maryknoll Sisters arrived, followed shortly thereafter, in 1949, by Maryknoll missioner James F. Smith. The following is a

*report of activities from Transfiguration Parish in New York. Note the similarities
to the efforts in San Francisco. One major difference: during the 1950s Catholic
centers had to assist refugees fleeing from Communist China.*

Report on Some Phases of Chinese Work in Transfiguration Parish, Chinatown, New York City, 1959

The year 1959 brought increases in almost every phase of our work here
in Chinatown, New York. There was increased enrollment in our parochial
school, as well as in the Chinese Language classes after school; more Chinese non-Catholic children joined the released time classes and in the First
Communion Group it was noticeable how many more Chinese children
were included compared to other years. A good half of these receiving the
sacrament of Confirmation were Chinese...

New refugee families, most of them already baptized, came from Hong
Kong or Formosa, to find a new home here. It is usual for us to include in our
welcome to them help in finding an apartment, or places in school for the children, sometimes even employment, or medical aid in hospitals, or help with
immigration problems. We try to encourage the mothers and fathers to attend
our adult English Classes, and, of course, there is always interest in Citizenship study for those who meet the requirement. Working Mothers present a
problem now, but often this extra work is necessary to pay off debts incurred
when they first came to America.

The 11 o'clock Mass is a good yardstick for measuring growth in the parish.
This is the parish Mass during which we follow the priest at Mass with prayers
in Chinese, the gospel and sermon are preached in Chinese and the hymns are
likewise sung in Chinese. The church is really well filled for this Mass by both
the local parishioners and other families who live outside the parish limits.
Attendance is steady at the Mass and as new families come in, they swell the
attendance. It is well to note, however, that all of the 6 Masses on Sunday are
attended by Chinese families — the 9 o'clock Mass by the school children and
their parents[,] and those who speak and understand English like to attend one
of the other four Masses. The altar rail is filled with communicants. The children who attend 11 o'clock Mass are the Released Time Catechism Children,
most of whom are not yet Catholic...

One of the big needs here has been special language help for small children
from homes where only Chinese is spoken. Without this help these children
would find it very hard to cover the work in the first grade. A little school
was set up for them in an old-fashioned grocery store and they have regular
language classes there...Chinese is used for the first few months until the
children are able to understand simple directions. It takes a few months more
before some of these children can say anything in English on their own. It is a
long hard pull, but worth the effort when they take the First Grade in stride
the following term. It is the beginning of religion for the majority of them,

too, and they fairly drink in the lessons. Usually, not more than one-third of the children are Catholic when they start out in language school, but they receive Baptism later on in the upper grades.

[The report reviews work with sodalities, released time programs, Chinese Sunday school, summer school for refugee children, parish visiting, and hospital visiting. It then continues:] Calls come from other parishes or schools where the priests or Sisters come in contact with Chinese families and are asking about instruction for the parents of children interested in receiving Baptism.

An interesting story was that of Mrs. Julia Young[,] instructed in the faith in Kowloon about five years ago. She had to leave to come to America before receiving Baptism, but she never lost her interest. Sister Madeleine Sophie kept in touch with her over the years, sending Chinese books and pamphlets to her. Father Dougherty in St. Paul, dropped in occasionally at the Hankow Restaurant for a Chinese meal and became acquainted with the family. Mrs. Young asked about Baptism. Father Dougherty could speak no Chinese, but tried to contact several mission societies who had Chinese speaking priests. None spoke Mrs. Young's dialect. A partial solution of the difficulty was for Sister to send Father Dougherty a correspondence catechism course in Chinese modeled on "Father Smith instructs Jackson." There are true and false questions at the end of each lesson and Mrs. Young can point to the Chinese character for the true or for false in answer to the question.

Kwong Ming Hang is one of the latest converts to be baptized in the parish. In the ten years he has lived, there has been much suffering, bewilderment, sorrow and now, here in America, joy and many graces. He was born in a little village in the interior of China, just at the time the Communists were beginning to take over in China. His parents were farmers and hard put to feed their children after the Communist State had taken its share of the harvest. Finally, when things got too hard, they held a family council and it was decided that at least one of the children should be smuggled out from the land of bondage to the freedom of Hong Kong. The boy was smuggled aboard a Chinese boat and hidden away during the day. In Hong Kong he was taken care of by relatives. Later, it was arranged that he be sent to his uncle's home in America. More and more of God's graces began to pour into his life — he found a new home in a good Catholic family and a place in a Catholic school. He began to study the Catechism and to prepare for Baptism, every Sunday he was at Mass. Soon, within a few weeks he is to make his First Holy Communion. His little face is always wreathed in smiles now — his eyes are dancing with happiness — life is very wonderful.

102. Resolutions of the Tenth Chinese Catholic Conference, 1961

In 1952, St. Mary's Chinese Mission began holding the Pacific Regional Chinese Catholic Conference in San Francisco. The conference gathered Chinese Catholics from throughout the West Coast and Hawaii to "exchange ideas and discuss our common problems and to promote a better understanding of the Catholic faith among the Chinese people on the West Coast," according to conference chair, Rachel Chun. The initial gathering had representatives from San Francisco, Los Angeles, Vancouver and Victoria, Canada, and Hawaii. The following document provides the resolutions of the tenth annual conference. Chun was still the chair, with the conference acknowledging that "the phenomenal growth and prodigious successes of this conference are due almost solely to her personal sacrifice."

San Francisco, California
June 30, July 1 and 2, 1961

We, the delegates to the Tenth Annual Chinese Catholic Conference on this second day of July of the year 1961 of our Lord[,] do hereby adopt the following resolutions after having carefully reviewed the theme, YOU ARE A CHOSEN GENERATION.

1. WHEREAS, the overwhelming majority of lay men are not formally trained in their vocation, BE IT RESOLVED that each delegate area explore practical means of instilling into its parishioners a sense of the Mystical Body, a sense of doctrine, a sense of vocation and personal sanctification...

2. WHEREAS, the definition of being a good Catholic requires, besides passive obedience to the Faith, an active offensive on her behalf against this age of secularism, BE IT RESOLVED that we join civic organizations for the purpose of expounding our Christian ideals by being outspoken and that special efforts at evangelization be directed toward the Chinese community in each delegate area.

3. WHEREAS, the traditional Chinese values regarding ethics and morality have been overshadowed by this age of secularism, BE IT RESOLVED that an attempt be made in each delegate area to revitalize this traditional outlook and to reconcile the tenets of Chinese philosophy with the doctrines of the Catholic Church...

6. WHEREAS, on the issue of non-admission of Communist China to the United Nations is of great importance and concern to all the Chinese Catholics, as well as the world at large, as loyal, good Catholics, and for the love of God, BE IT RESOLVED that the following resolution of the Fifth Annual Pacific Regional Catholic Chinese Conference be reaffirmed and adopted; namely,

The Tenth Annual Chinese Catholic Conference, now in session in San Francisco, hereby registers vehement denunciation of the philosophy and practice of atheistic Communism. This Conference strongly protests against the cruel persecution and inhuman treatment to which millions of Catholics in China are being subjected, and the hundreds of millions of Catholic as well as non-Catholic men, women and children who are unwilling subjects of the slave state of Communist China.

This Conference urges the United Nations to refuse recognition of the Communist regime in China and admittance of this same regime to the halls of the United Nations organization.

Archives of the Archdiocese of San Francisco. Printed with permission.

103. Veneration of Ancestors, 1990

Recent ministry to Chinese has tried to accommodate ancient Chinese practices and customs, particularly the veneration of ancestors. The following is a short interview with Deacon Felix Soo of San Francisco conducted by Franklin Fong, a Chinese-American Franciscan. Deacon Soo was born in Canton, China, in 1912 and was raised in a Buddhist family. He learned English while working for the Chinese government, being sent to the United States in 1945 to study. In 1949, he fled China to Hong Kong following the Communist takeover. In 1961, he converted to Catholicism following the death of his mother. About 1968, Mr. Soo immigrated to the United States. He began assisting at a Catholic parish in San Francisco and in 1979 was ordained to the permanent diaconate. Following a brief excerpt from the interview, a copy of the program used for the veneration of ancestors as conducted at the Chinese New Year's Mass in San Francisco in 1990 is provided.

Franklin Fong: You have a unique background in having spent a large part of your education and life in China and being trained in the very traditional Chinese education before coming to the United States, and then coming to the Catholic Church as an adult. I'm wondering what parts of Catholicism do you see that are especially important in the Chinese perspective, in the way the Chinese see the world.

Felix Soo: From the beginning I have been thinking that the Chinese civilization and Confucian thought do not contradict with the teaching of our Catholic Church. For example the really strong support for piety towards our parents but in our Church we also teach respect your father and mother, no conflict. From the beginning I cannot see any conflict with the Catholic Church teachings.

FF — Do you think there's something that the Chinese can teach the Church? How does the Church learn from how God has worked in the Chinese people?

FS — From the beginning when I spoke with the Church supervisor and the reverend fathers I didn't hear any opposition or even opinions towards our Chinese civilization. They never say any words against Chinese civilization.

FF — One of the big things that happened in the Chinese Catholic community has been the controversy around ancestral worship. During the years that you were the deacon, actively working, are you happy with what's happened, with the way we now do ancestral worship as part of the liturgy?

FS — For the past ten years many clergy, Chinese clergy, also support ancestral worship. In New York City almost all churches where there are Chinese priests they have ancestral worship on the Chinese New Year. I also presided for many years to be celebrant at the end of the New Year Mass and we had ancestral worship ceremony. I preside over that, even now.

Chinese New Year Eucharistic Celebration and Ceremonial Tribute to Ancestors, 1990, San Francisco
[At the end of the Mass]
Ceremonial Tribute to Our Ancestors

1. At the opening of the ceremony: All rise.

2. The servers arrive: All the parish representatives take their places.

3. The master of ceremonies arrives: All the clergy take their places.

4. The main celebrant arrives: The celebrant takes his place.

5. Music.

6. Scripture reading I (Please sit).

> Sirach 44:
> Now will I praise our ancestors,
> Whose virtues have not been forgotten.
> Their wealth remains in their families;
> Their heritage with their descendants...

8. Prayer of a dutiful son and daughter (Please stand).

> My soul is from God, my body is from my parents. Creator and nourisher of life, all praise to you. Gift as high as the mountains, and as wide as the sea. Being careful [about] the funerals for our parents, [t]racing the merits passed down by our ancestors, [r]epaying our debts and expressing our gratitude. The spring festival [brings] a new year, a bright and happy day. The first day of new beginnings — a new spring. Returning to life's source, true son and daughter shall I always be...

12. Offering of the gifts: flowers, wine, fruits.

13. Ceremony of respect: 3 bows to the ancestor shrine.

14. Group reverence: offering to the Lord.

New Year's congratulations: each one bows to his or her neighbor and wishes him or her New Year happiness.

15. Celebrant's blessing...

16. Recitation of Our Father.

17. The celebrant leaves the shrine.

18. Music. Conclusion.

Archives of the Archdiocese of San Francisco. Printed with permission.

104. Zong Ming, "What It Means to Be a Chinese Catholic in America?" 1990

The following reflection was written for the National Pastoral Center for the Chinese Apostolate Newsletter. *The center is in New York City. Zong Ming is described simply as "an immigrant from Mainland China. Mr. Zong came from an old Catholic family. He is now a businessman."*

Chinese presence today in America is often felt in the Chinese restaurants flourishing in every small town and on the faculty rosters of higher educational institutions. As a minority in the U.S., outnumbered even by immigrants from many smaller countries, Chinese Americans have now nevertheless reached a most respectful and important status in various social sectors. This success should be attributed to the rich cultural and historical background of China and the enduring characters [*sic*] of her people.

However, it should be pointed out that in terms of status within the U.S. Church, we Chinese Catholics, have yet to strive harder in this largely "Christian" land.

Two questions are revealed here. First, have we devoted ourselves entirely to our ethnic Chinese parishes and organizations, as some other minorities here already have, e.g. Polish and Koreans? Secondly, other than the characteristic appearance as ethnic Chinese, are there any other outstanding features which make us known as Chinese Catholics?

As disciples of Jesus Christ and citizens of the United States (or soon will be), as well as ethnic Chinese, we must first examine the order of priority and relationship among these three roles before any answers to the above questions are attempted.

First and above all, we believe in God, the Creator of the Universe. We believe in the Holy Catholic Church, founded by our Savior Jesus Christ... [T]he Catholic Church is characterized by her universality. It is our inalienable right to believe and worship God our Creator. Any man-made laws...which oppose this right will not be acceptable to us, even at a great cost of sacrificing our lives. As we all know, thousands of martyrs in the history of our Church, including those in Mainland China, have borne witness to this first priority.

Secondly, we are also citizens of the United States. At the naturalization sworn-in, we pledge allegiance to our new country. A Catholic must also be a law-abiding and patriotic citizen, as long as laws of the government do not contradict those of the Church... More Chinese Catholics should be engaged in social services, such as the care of un-wed mothers, drug addicts, AIDS patients, etc. to express our belief as well as to ascertain our role in today's Church in America.

Last but not least, our hearts and minds are tied to our ethnic roots. It is our obligation to see that our motherland becomes prosperous and democratic as long as what we do would not contradict our faith and the laws and interests of the U.S.

In the past century, our forefathers in the U.S. struggled and built Chinatowns all across the nation. [The] situation of Chinese Americans today is far better than one hundred years ago. What are we struggling now to provide and leave behind for our children and grandchildren? Worth mentioning is the Chinese language and cultural education that many ethnic Chinese Catholic parishes and lay communities are providing to our next generation. It is quite an outstanding achievement in the efforts of preservation of Chinese culture in America.

In conclusion, as a multicultural country, America is great in her ability to preserve, absorb and unify all cultures. While we Chinese Catholics should not neglect our cultural background, it is also unwise to be blind to the strength and richness of all other cultures around us, as well as the weakness and inadequacies of our own culture. Attempts should be made by Chinese Catholics to enrich American culture, especially the American Catholic Church, with our cultural strength and our faith. This then will give us a recognizable identity as Chinese American Catholics in a multicultural country.

(Special essay written for this Newsletter by Mr. Zong Ming.)

National Pastoral Center for the Chinese Apostolate Newsletter (April 1990): 7–8. Printed with permission.

Japanese Immigrants

105. Request for a Japanese Mission, San Francisco, 1912

As of 1912 the Japanese population in San Francisco remained relatively small and the Japanese Catholic population even smaller. Nevertheless, like the Chinese, the Japanese desired to hear the faith preached in their own language. The following letter addresses a recurrent theme in requesting such assistance — if Catholics neglect this ministry, the Japanese will become Protestant.

San Francisco, April 30, 1912

Most Rev. P. W. Riordan,
Archbishop of San Francisco

Dear Sir:

I wish you would excuse me for the rudeness of writing you so abruptly without having any previous knowledge of you personally. My name is Francis Risaburo Hamai. I am a new convert . . . I am Japanese.

I regret that there is not a single Japanese catechist in this coast who can interpret the Catholic doctrine to the Japanese people [which] they need very badly. There are some eighty thousand Japanese in California and forty thousand in the north (Oregon and Washington). And the population are growing every year.

A good many become Protestants because, as they have Japanese preachers at hand, they are more accessible to protestantism than to Catholicism. But, as protestantism itself is a false doctrine by nature, those protestant preachers can not give a complete satisfaction to the men of common sense. And as they study along the doctrine in what they call "Bible Class," they are lead astray and finally to infidelity.

It was a curious thing to find that the Catholic Church has been neglecting Japanese people alone for so many years on this coast. She should have some attempt. So I wish you would consider the matter, and would consent to the immediate attempt for the missionary work to save Japanese souls.

I should like very much to see you some time about this matter . . .

I am afraid that this letter is not polite enough. If I used any rude expression I beg your pardon, for don't mean it.

Yours truly,
(signed) Francis Risaburo Hamai

Archives of the Archdiocese of San Francisco. Printed with permission.

106. Father Albert Breton on the Beginning of the Japanese Missions on the West Coast, 1912–19

In 1912, a Japanese Catholic in southern California by the name of Leo Kumataro Hatakeyama wrote the bishop of Hakodate, Japan, asking if he could have his confession heard through the mail, as there was no Japanese-speaking priest to whom he could confess. Bishop Berlioz denied his request but wrote the bishop of Los Angeles, who forwarded the request to the newly formed Maryknoll Mission Fathers, who in turn referred the request to the Paris Foreign Missionary Society. The latter responded by sending Father Albert Breton, a seasoned Japanese missionary who was recuperating from an illness, to California before he returned to Japan. It is Father Breton who established the Japanese Catholic Mission on the West Coast, first in Los Angeles, then in San Francisco. The following is an excerpt from Father Breton's memoir. He places particular importance on the arrival of the Japanese Sisters, initially known as the Lovers of the Cross, but who ultimately became known as the Sisters of the Visitation. Breton returned to Japan in 1920, where he was eventually named bishop of Fukuoka, Japan.

Los Angeles

12 October, 1912. I arrive in Los Angeles. Canvass all city parishes. Reside at Cathedral rectory.

25 Dec., 1912. Say first mass for the Japanese Catholics at Brownson House, Mexican settlement...Less than 10 attend, my first two parishioners were Leo Hatakeyama who wrote the letter to Bishop Berlioz of Japan. He was living in El Monte, but soon moved to Los Angeles to be near me — and Tonari from Oshima Island, who was a gardener at Mr. Spalding's estate, Point Loma, San Diego.

He came to see me on an early morning of October 1912. Went right away to the Cathedral to attend mass. Seeing there was no altar boy with the priest, he bravely walked up the aisle and answered mass in a perfect manner to the amazement of the celebrant, Msgr. Hartnett, Vicar General.

1913, Holy Saturday. The first 3 Japanese adults are baptized by Bishop Conaty at the Cathedral.

1913 — I canvass the Southern part of the then Los Angeles diocese i.e. San Diego, San Bernardino, Redlands, Riverside to get in touch with the various Japanese settlements — then to Santa Barbara, Watsonville, Monterey and to Fresno, Bakersfield in the San Joaquin Valley. I find that the majority of the Japanese have stores catering mostly to the Japanese or do gardener's work (settled in country ranches; those living in town are in small number). They seem to live apart from the Americans, and there is a good reason to it. The Japanese life is far below the American standard life, they work more, spend less and aim at going back to their mother country for good, after saving as much money as they can. Hence mistrust, jealousy and hard feeling against them. However personally as I am a French missionary ad gentes nobody puts in doubt my good intentions and I am welcomed by all Catholic circles and known as the missionary to the Japanese...The worst that non-sympathizers would say was: "My dear Father, I am afraid you are losing your time on those people. You had better tell them to go home"...

For the Japanese scattered in the country, all I could do was to visit the

Catholics as often as I could to foster their faith by the reception of the sacraments, to tell the pagans that I was interested in their welfare and they should not be afraid of going to the local Catholic Church, school, or hospital.

In the city of Los Angeles (pop. 300,000 at that time) and vicinity. I tried to establish some kind of concrete work as follows:

1913 — Evening class adults (teaching of English).

1914, Feb. 1. Japanese Catholic Club is opened... From the Cathedral rectory where I have been residing so far, I move in the club with a few young Japanese...

1915. But the work of the Japanese Catholic Mission in Los Angeles got its real start when four Japanese Sisters of the Visitation arrived from Japan in March 1915...

On May 1, 1915, the Japanese Sisters Home for orphans and non-orphans is opened...

In May 1, 1915 the Japanese Sisters Kindergarten is opened... in the center of the Japanese settlement... Thirty-five children answer the call. The staff is composed of Sr. Angela, Japanese nun[,] and Miss Gilroy, an American lady. English and Japanese are taught to these children, not so very many yet, who were soon to be known under the name of Nisei. A special course of Japanese language is held every afternoon for children attending public schools.

In Sept. [1918,]... a regular Grammar school begins with the first grade...

In the Fall of 1916 I went to Japan to recruit some young Sisters. In the spring of 1919 I went again for the same purpose. The Sisters of the Visitation were eleven at their highest point. Mother Margarita Matsumoto died in L.A. 1919.

San Francisco

Nov. 1912. Francis Kusama and Hamai [see previous document], 2 Japanese Catholic young men hearing of my work in Los Angeles, ask me to come to San Francisco.

[Mission Center established in San Francisco.] For one year I paid a regular monthly visit to San Francisco. Then I told the archbishop that it was necessary for the good of the work to have a priest residing at the Mission... [Jesuits take charge.]

Archives of the Archdiocese of San Francisco. Printed with permission of the Paris Foreign Mission Society.

107. Bishop John J. Cantwell on Japanese Sisters, 1921

Bishop John J. Cantwell, ordinary of Los Angeles, 1917–36, and subsequently archbishop of the same see until 1947, expresses a commonly held attitude toward the immigrant Japanese — they should become American. In 1920, the newly formed Maryknoll Sisters arrived in Los Angeles to serve the Japanese mis-

sion. Father Breton's Japanese Sisters were invited to join the Maryknoll Order —
one did, but the others declined, ultimately returning to Japan, though several
assisted in San Francisco until 1925.

Diocese of Monterey and Fresno —
[Office of the Bishop] May 25, 1921

Most Reverend Edward J. Hanna, D.D.,
Archbishop of San Francisco

My dear Archbishop:

Father Moore [pastor of San Francisco Japanese Catholic Mission] suggested to me that I should write you and ask you to accept the so-called Japanese Community which I have in Los Angeles, into the Archdiocese of San Francisco.

I don't wish to go into a long story about the Japanese settlement work here until I see you. I may say, however, that I object to a perpetuation in our midst of a Japanese Colony entirely out of sympathy with the spirit of the Church in this country.

The Japanese Sisters under the direction of Father Breton, wished to perpetuate themselves not by taking into the Community native born Japanese, but rather by bringing me some more from Japan from time to time. I do not think that under present circumstances, it would be good for the future of the Japanese Colony, such as is in this country, to permit it to develop as a foreign colony.

The Maryknoll Sisters are giving great satisfaction, with the help of two catechists. The Japanese Sisters would not affiliate with any religious community, nor would they accept direction from any religious community of women.

Father Moore says that as Father Breton is obliged to go back to his Congregation, that he would look after their spiritual interests if they went to San Francisco. One of the Sisters is leaving today for Maryknoll to begin her novitiate. The others, if not accepted in San Francisco, will from time to time return to Japan...

I want to be as kind as possible to these devoted Sisters, who according to their lines did splendid work here, but are entirely out of sympathy with the American spirit of the Church. The good Frenchman who has been looking after them, did nothing to bring them into harmony with American traditions...

Father Breton was for many years practically the Superior of this house, but it seems to be a man is not born who can govern a community of women...

Ever affectionately yours,
(signed) +John J. Cantwell
Bishop of Monterey and Los Angeles

Archives of the Archdiocese of San Francisco. Printed with permission.

108. Discrimination in Seattle, 1936

Beginning in the 1920s, the Maryknoll Sisters staffed the Japanese-Filipino mission in Seattle. What follows is an all-too-typical example of anti-Japanese discrimination recorded in the Maryknoll Sisters' house diary. Of note, the Sisters lament that this attitude is a problem among Catholics as well.

Maryknoll Japanese Mission Seattle, 1936 — House Diary
Jan. 18 — Church Unity Octave Begins

Interesting case of race discrimination reported. A group of Immaculate Conception High School girls arranged a skating party at a public rink. About 50 or 60 attended among them one of our girls. All were allowed entrance except this girl. She was offered her money back but refused it. Was told she could watch the others from the door. All became angered and were about to leave. Were told other places were the same. All entered except two or three who escorted our young lady home. Much indignation among the girls next day. They arrange a large theatre party for our Japanese young lady — as heart balm. Hope she isn't denied entry to theatre. Japanese ladies wept when they reported the incident. The trouble is like incidents have been recorded against some of our Catholic institutions. God forgive them!

Maryknoll Mission Archives, Maryknoll, N.Y. Printed with permission.

109. Maryknoll Protest of Japanese Relocation, 1942

The lives of the Japanese on the West Coast were dramatically altered on 7 December 1941. On that "day of infamy" naval and air forces of the Japanese Empire attacked Pearl Harbor and thus began U.S. entry into World War II. The long-held anti-Japanese sentiments on the West Coast exploded with war hysteria, and 110,000 Japanese were "relocated" to internment camps away from the coast. The Maryknoll Fathers and Sisters had built a thriving Japanese mission in Los Angeles. At the helm was Father Hugh Lavery, who came to the Los Angeles mission in 1927, three years after his ordination. He was placed in charge of the mission in 1935 and remained until 1956. In the following document one senses the outrage of Father Lavery at the treatment of the Japanese, but also the realization that there was little the Maryknollers could do to quell the hysteria.

Maryknoll Mission Los Angeles, 1942

January 27, 1942

Dear Father General: —

There have been groups of Californians who have for years been doing their utmost in every way to down the Japanese. They dispossessed them of everything possible and are partly the cause of the war between the two countries. These same people are now trying to work up the populace to a condition of hysteria against all Japanese...

[Second Letter – Same Date]

Your last word to me when leaving here the other day was to notify you if any serious effort was to be made by the lunatic fringe to put all the Japanese in concentration camps. Well it has reached the stage where it is not only the lunatics that are urging this but nearly all the leaders of the community...

I write you tonight to ask if something cannot be done toward preventing such an unreasonable crazy scheme...

Let me know as soon as possible what you think I can do here...

What are the people going to do? As American citizens the government has the obligation to protect the rights of American born Japanese...

With best wishes, I am

Sincerely yours in Christ,
(signed) Hugh Lavery

[written in pencil at bottom of the page]
Nothing we can do from here.

Maryknoll Mission Archives, Maryknoll, N.Y. Printed with permission.

110. Sister Paul Miki's Account of Manzanar, 1940s

Antoinette Yae Ono, a member of the Los Angeles Japanese community of the Nisei generation (i.e., she was a second-generation immigrant), converted to Catholicism shortly before being sent to the Manzanar Relocation Camp. While at the camp she decided to become a Maryknoll Sister. The following is Sister Ono's account of life at Manzanar. Maryknoll personnel did what they could to ease a most difficult situation. Two Japanese Maryknoll Sisters from Los Angeles went to the camps – Sisters Susanna Hayashi and Bernadette Yoshimachi.

Newsclipping – September 22, 1944
"Japanese Internee to Be Missionary"

Antoinette Yae Ono, resident at Manzanar, West Coast Japanese Internment Camp, left for the Maryknoll Motherhouse, New York, on Aug. 28, with the intention of becoming a foreign missionary. During her two year period at camp, Miss Ono was directly responsible for several converts.

An article in "Manza-Knoll," Catholic newspaper at the camp, reports there have been six vocations at Manzanar in two years. Three girls and three boys departed for Maryknoll foreign mission schools in the East. All are American born Japanese of pure Japanese parentage. They speak Japanese and English fluently, and it is expected they will eventually be sent to Japan to secure converts in post-war years.

Sr. Paul Miki (Ono), Manzanar Relocation Center (Internment Camp), Rec'd
August 1946

Manzanar Relocation Center was situated in Owens Valley about 200 miles
northwest of Los Angeles. Manzanar amongst all other centers was considered
the ideal camp. It was made up of 36 blocks. In each of these blocks there were
14 barracks, one mess hall, a laundry room, shower and latrine, and a recreational hall. Each barrack was divided into 5 or 6 rooms, each room housing
one family. The approximate number of people residing in each block was
275 — the total population of the entire camp about 10,000.

Manzanar was known to all its inhabitants as the "dust bowl." The wind
blew through the valley at a terrific speed and since the country itself is desert
land, one most always had sand in his shoes, hair, and occasionally on the
dinner table.

From the very beginning of evacuation to the very day that Manzanar was
closed the Maryknoll Fathers and Sisters aided the Japanese in every way possible. Maryknoll will always be remembered by the evacuees for their kind
sympathy, generosity, material aid, and most of all for the great interest Maryknoll took in looking after the temporal and spiritual needs of all Catholics
and anyone who needed it.

When the first group of evacuees (mostly bachelor men) arrived in Manzanar in April of 1942, the Maryknoll Fathers drove up in their car in order
to help the evacuees where help was needed. They heard the first confessions
in their car. The first Holy Sacrifice was offered in a mess hall. The Fathers
were not only loved for their Christ-like charity but for the great consolation
the evacuees felt knowing that "Maryknoll" was there with them in camp. To
many of the non-Catholics, the name "Maryknoll" meant more than a Catholic organization; it was the name they used most frequently when speaking
of a friend.

In May, 2 Japanese Maryknoll Sisters, Srs. Susanna and Bernadette, arrived
in camp with more of the evacuees. The Sisters voluntarily interned themselves[,] seeing the opportunities that would come their way to help their own
people spiritually. The Sisters were given one room like the rest and a number, a number by which each family was recorded. The Sisters found it very
difficult at first for camp life meant using the shower, etc. with the rest. The
showers and latrine did not have partitions which made it extremely hard for
everyone.

From the very first week that the Sisters arrived catechetical work was
started beginning with the children and soon afterwards the adults were under
instructions, also. Each Saturday catechism lessons were held for any children whose parents did not object to their attending catechism. Individual
instructions were given during the week for those who were actually interested in the Faith. Srs. Bernadette and Susanna taught the older Japanese in

their own language. The younger people were taught by older boys and girls who volunteered to help the Sisters in teaching catechism.

In November of 1942, Father [Leo] Steinbach was appointed pastor of the Manzanar Catholic Church. Up till this time the Maryknoll Fathers were not able to receive any building which could be set aside just for the use of the church. However, after much difficulties, the Catholic Church was permanently established in one of the barracks and the Blessed Sacrament reserved. All the equipment in the church were made by its own parishioners such as the altar rail, collection boxes, holy water fonts, book shelves, and the altar itself.

The Sisters not only did catechetical work but they also visited the sick and taught in the hospital and helped many many persons who came to them for their own personal difficulties. Through the great zeal of Father Steinbach, the Sisters, and many of the Catholics, there were 246 baptisms recorded, many of the converts were required to study for more than a year to make sure they had the Faith. The majority of these baptisms were adults.

During the 3 yrs. of the Maryknoll Church in Manzanar many clubs were formed by old and young. There were two Sodalities (boys and girls), a study club for the young people which later was known as the "Aquinas Circle," a "Fugin-Kai" for the mothers, Holy Name Society, Altar Boys society, and a club for the girls of high school age which was called the "Knowleens." There were two choirs, a boys choir which consisted of little boys from 7 years old to 13 years old and the other was the young people's choir. The first morning the little boys' choir sang for Mass was a Saturday morning and Father promised them a picnic if they sang well. That very morning the choir increased in number with new faces but all went well and all went to the picnic.

The various clubs were instrumental in bringing non-Catholics to Mass. The girls and boys made it their business to invite their friends and to make friends with the non-Catholics. Many times the girls around 14 or 15 years old would attend the first Mass on Sundays and then offer to take care of babies in order that the young mothers will have time to attend second Mass, there were two Masses each Sunday. In this way, these young mothers who were under instruction attended the Holy Sacrifice long before they were baptized.

There were 3 Confirmation groups, one each year, held in camp and through the sacrament many became zealous for other souls and performed many apostolic works among their own families and friends.

From this little Manzanar Catholic Church there were 8 vocations, two to the Maryknoll Sisters' Motherhouse, 5 to Maryknoll seminary and one to the Jesuit Seminary.

It was a hard life in camp in the beginning but as time went on everyone was happy and no complaints. Through the eyes of a Christian, more good came out of evacuation and internment camp than evil.

It is worth mentioning the charity and humility of Father Steinbach who will never be forgotten by any of the Catholics and many non-Catholics who lived in Manzanar. Father lived in Lone Pine, a small town about 11 miles from camp and drove each morning into camp for 6:30 Mass and stayed all day teaching and helping everyone and every evening he drove back to Lone Pine. In camp there were 2 stores, one food canteen and the other a dry goods store. Since it was impossible to get some necessaries in camp the people would come to Father to do shopping for them. It is truly surprising but Father would have a regular list twice a week to purchase articles for the evacuees from the stores in Lone Pine. Sometimes the list would read: half-dozen baby bottles and nipples, 2 cakes, 1 loaf of French bread, 4 yards of oil cloth, 1 chicken, baby shoes and a bottle of cough medicine. Through these most charitable acts, Father won many souls for Christ.

The summer of 1943, a summer school was conducted by the Sisters and the purpose of this school was to teach the children manners. This was a great success for the majority of the children were non-Catholics ranging from 5 years old to 16 years old. Sister Susanna taught the children Japanese manners which pleased the parents very much. The older girls and boys taught etiquette in English. By conducting the school, the Sisters were able to make new contacts and more students for the catechism classes on Saturday.

Maryknoll Mission Archives, Maryknoll, N.Y. Printed with permission.

111. Advice to Relocated Catholics, 1945

Returning from the camps was very difficult for the internees, who faced overt hostility from other Americans. In the following letter, Father Leo Steinbach, M.M., who had accompanied the Japanese to Manzanar, chastises the Japanese who had returned to Los Angeles for their lack of courage. The letter is taken from a mimeographed newsletter published by the Japanese Catholic community at Manzanar.

Manza-Knoll, October 19, 1945

"Advice to Relocated Catholics"

After visiting several scores of newly baptized Catholics who now reside in the L.A. area, I was amazed to discover that many people who confessed and received Holy Communion at least every Sunday and some even daily while in camp, are now barely performing their Sunday obligation. They attend Mass crouching in the rear pews but lack the courage to walk up to the communion rail...

I asked [one Caucasian] doctor if there were any Japanese attending his church. He replied in the affirmative but added, "I don't think they are Catholic however. I have never seen them receive the sacraments. Maybe they come to church out of curiosity or perhaps to spy on us." I was saddened to hear this remark for I knew those very people were thoroughly instructed in Manzanar where they had received Holy Communion every Sunday.

If the Japanese people would only recall...that every Catholic Church is as much their church as anyone else's, if they would brace their shoulders and walk up to the communion rail and receive Holy Communion, they would not only become more acceptable in the Eyes of God, but they would also win the confidence and esteem of fellow Catholics.

Leo Steinbach

Maryknoll Mission Archives, Maryknoll, N.Y. Printed with permission.

112. James Y. Sakamoto, "Catholicism at Minidoka Internment Camp," 1941–44

James Y. Sakamoto, publisher of the Japanese American Courier, *a Seattle English-language newspaper for Nisei (second-generation) Japanese, spent the war years in an internment camp at Minidoka, Idaho. Although blinded from amateur boxing injuries, Sakamoto's disability did not impair his involvement in community life: he presided over the local Japanese American Citizens League, ran the St. Vincent de Paul Society, and sponsored athletic associations for Japanese-American youth. Before the war, Sakamoto and his family were baptized and confirmed by Rev. Leopold Tibesar, a Maryknoll missioner. Tibesar served the Japanese mission from 1935 to 1946. He had previously served as a missionary in Japan and Manchuria. The selection opens with a brief description of the Seattle Maryknoll mission parish, Our Lady Queen of Martyrs (founded in 1920, and a combined Japanese and Filipino parish by 1925), and continues with events affecting the Japanese-American members of this parish from 1941 to 1944.*

As the sun slants westward, its warm golden rays invariably encompass the backyards of the Maryknoll Sisters' Convent and the Nursery next door, Our Lady Queen of Martyrs Church, Maryknoll Grade School, the Blessed Virgin's Grotto, a tennis court and combined Maryknoll Father's House, clubhouse and workshop. Sunday, Dec. 7, 1941 dawned bright and sunny. Mass was over and the congregation had gone home. Then the news suddenly broke over the radio...Pearl Harbor was bombed by Japanese planes. Gloom and darkness overtook the Japanese community. Some couldn't believe it. To them it was just another dramatically imposed anti-Japanese propaganda concocted by over-imaginative radio commentators and news correspondents. Soon the telephone wires kept up a busy hum. The receiver was in a continual clamp on Father Leopold H. Tibesar's ear. His voice was telling the callers to keep calm...Lips that had lapsed from prayers began laying importance to them. Maryknoll drew record attendance from all faiths.

Hectic days and weeks chronicled the prologue to evacuation. The sudden impact of war had left the Japanese population stunned and panicky...With the early flush of 1942, talk of evacuating the Japanese, both citizens and aliens alike, from the coastal regions spread particularly throughout the Western States... Bank deposits of Japanese aliens had been frozen immediately... Confiscation of firearms, cameras, maps and all articles that were termed as contraband was ordered. Registration of all Japanese, Germans, and Italians as enemy aliens took place... In April the order for evacuation came from the headquarters of the Western Defense Command...

What to do now about property holdings, bank accounts, children's schooling, employment, clothing, food, shelter, new-born babes, expectant mothers, [those] sick in the hospitals, sanatoriums and asylums, parents separated from children in Japan and vice-versa, where to go, unpayable bills and sundry other problems of significant importance to the lives of every individual about to be evacuated? They became the panorama of problems with all their minor details for Father Tibesar to click his camera for clear, correct, and snapshot solutions... The Maryknoll Sisters, thirteen in all at the time, headed by Sister Superior Consolata and Sister Denise, as assistant, bore their crosses with the people, silently ministering to uncounted families and persons. Hope and courage were not the least of the ministrations by the Brothers and Sisters...

The start of evacuation fell on the final day of April to continue to May 16th, until Seattle's Japanese population had been temporarily settled at the Assembly Center, in the fairgrounds of Puyallup, Washington... Camp Harmony, as the Assembly Center was called, was divided into four areas, A, B, C, and D. It was supervised by the Wartime Civilian Control Authority...

Daily Mass was seldom missed. It was held in one or another area and without fail. On July 25th, Seattle's Bishop Gerald Shaughnessy... c[a]me to administer the Sacrament of Confirmation to new converts. [Other] American friends were constant visitors from the first to the last week of visiting permitted at the gates of Camp Harmony. They were neighbors, friends, sympathetic casual acquaintances and persons related in a direct or indirect manner in business with the evacuees... Maryknoll Sisters were visitors as were missionaries of other churches. They were given special permission to visit the children, parents and friends of their church. Each time the Sisters concluded their visits large numbers of children and parents followed them to the gates, choked words whispering farewell.

The August sun poured hot. Orders came early in the month for the removal of Camp Harmony residents to their new home... [C]ontingents of 500 evacuees were moved at short intervals [by train] throughout the month. A large majority had never gone out of the state of Washington and for many another it was their first train ride. For 26 hours they rode on hard-backed day coaches. Hospital patients, however, were transported in an up-to-date Pullman. The only other deluxe carrier was the air-conditioned diner. It afforded a menu-treat on the Army and relief from the sweltering heat of the coaches.

By early September the 7,200 from Camp Harmony and 2,100 from the Assembly Center at Portland, Oregon, filled the Minidoka War Relocation

Center at Hunt, Idaho. The new home was under the supervision of the War Relocation Authority...Laid out in a crescent shape the barrack-lined, prairie community stretched out over rolling plains spotted luxuriantly by sagebrush and cactus. It was a settlement apart from the general stream of life.

A barrack row houses six families or groups of people. The two end apartments are sixteen by twenty feet accommodating two to three persons. The two inside apartments next to them are twenty by twenty-four feet accommodating five to seven persons. The two middle apartments are twenty by twenty feet for the accommodation of four to five persons. There are three entrances to a barrack building, with each one opening into a vestibule-like hallway and two apartment doors facing each other.

When the people first arrived they trudged through sand ankle deep... [R]oads...were tracks made by trucks and cars of the project. On windy days the visibility was obscured by the flying dust and sand that became the bane of every person and apartment as well. When it rained the mud sucked the rubbers [boots] from one's shoes into the slime.

Today, after a year and a half, the automobile tracks are like crude country roads. Where faint footprint paths once existed, between the blocks and the barracks, dirt walks bordered with rough-edged rocks and an irrigation ditch beside it have now replaced them. Trees were planted not so long ago to break the monotony of the sagebrush and the sand hills. Getting around in this community meant walking. Cars are available only for business...

Father Tibesar now resides in Apt. F...in Block 22.[1] The next apartment serves as the Chapel where Daily Mass is held weekdays at 6:50 a.m. On Sundays [Mass] is held in the Block recreation hall which has been improvised into the semblance of a church auditorium. The chapel will long be remembered by all who knew it...After Mass the curtain would be drawn around the Altar where the Blessed Sacrament was kept, and the Chapel would be turned into a library and clubroom for both adults and children. There was a collection of religious, biographical, historical and fictional books in both English and Japanese proving of interest to both young and old. It was a collection that could bolster the pride of any library. The Chapel transformed served also as a clubroom. Meetings were held there in the afternoons and evenings...On Saturday afternoons, especially the children make it their playroom while awaiting their turn to go to confession in Father's quarters across the vestibule-like hallway.

In this barrack Chapel, clubroom and playground for children, Father Tibesar has witnessed and experienced the emotions of people from sorrow

---

1. During the first two months at Minidoka, Father Tibesar commuted the thirty-six-mile roundtrip from Jerome, Idaho, where he lodged with the secular priest, Father Eric Schermanson. Camp administrators gave Father Tibesar the special privilege of an apartment inside Minidoka, but no other Caucasian clergyman or church worker of any denomination was allowed to live inside the center.

to gaiety, deaths to christenings, baptism, confirmation, weddings and comradeship in club activities to fond farewells. None who relocated has failed to reminisce about Mass in the barrack Chapel and the meetings with friends. One convert, who [with] his family [was] relocated[,] wrote how he missed Mass in the barrack Chapel. The great Cathedrals and Churches in the East could not make him forget it, he professed.

At first, Daily Mass [at the chapel] was well attended. On Sundays, there was no difficulty in counting more than 300...present. Since the active institution of the relocation program, the number has come down to half with further decrease expected. Slightly better than half now attending Sunday Mass are not Catholics. They are in the main people who have come to know Father's devotion to the community and the work of the Church.

[M]eetings were held for the Holy Name and St. Vincent de Paul Societies, Legion of Mary, weekly Genko-Kai [women's association] and Our Lady Queen of Martyrs meetings and evening study clubs for old and young in Japanese and English. The Catechism lessons for the children were taken over by the members of the Legion of Mary after Sunday Mass. There was one important program missed, however. It was the education of the children as it was so diligently, efficiently, and carefully accomplished at the Maryknoll [Catholic parochial] School in Seattle by the Sisters.

Then Christmas [1942] approached with nature's white blanket covering the landscape from the night before. It was celebrated with Midnight Mass. Some two hundred...people, Catholics and others, [waded] their way [through the snow] under a cold, bright moon to the Chapel. They filled the Chapel and Father's adjoining quarters to smothering closeness. Mass was beautiful. Excepting to a few, it was their first Midnight Mass. Early on Christmas Day, Father again said Mass for the old and children who were not able to attend the Midnight Service...

Early in February [1943] the [military] registration of all center residents took place. Then came the call for volunteers of Japanese Ancestry for the Special Combat team of the United States Army...Minidoka's response was the largest of any relocation center. Of the more than 300 volunteers, almost twelve percent were Maryknoll boys, a relatively large percentage since the entire Maryknoll membership in the center amounted to some four percent of the population. The volunteering program about cleaned out the Holy Name Society of its American-born Japanese members. There was something akin to an undertone of objection to the volunteer program by an unknown alien element among whom were some younger generation people. Young Maryknollers and others didn't have to have the flag flown in their faces to follow the line of action...Each morning in Seattle at the Maryknoll School the boys had stood with the rest of the children before the flagpole on the corner of the grounds to pledge allegiance to and salute Old Glory. The significance of the practice had taken root with their souls and hearts.

Joining with their sons in the spirit of their action, Catholic fathers and mothers accepted the volunteer program with good grace...There were parents, however, throughout the center who could not accept the action of their sons as cheerfully or even resignedly...To them the question was, "Why must our sons volunteer for the Army when they were ousted from their homes though they were citizens of the United States?"...Little did the population realize, however, that through the volunteering of the boys the relocation of themselves into the general stream of American life...was to be helped considerably...

Today in the vestibule-like hallway that separates the Chapel from Father's quarters, there hangs Maryknoll's own service flag. It has 35 stars. One of them is gold. The luster of the yellow star shines more brilliantly than if it might have been woven there in threads of gold. It is the star of a favorite son of Seattle's Maryknoll[,] Peter Fujiwara...The Stars and Stripes that draped his coffin and belongings were brought to his parents in this center. Father Tibesar conducted a memorial service for this first Maryknoll boy and the first [Japanese American] from the state of Washington to die for his country. The flag hangs proudly across the wall of Papa Fujiwara's barrack apartment. He wears [the] fatigue cap as if to assure himself that his son is still with him...[Fujiwara] would not part with that cap for all the money or comforts in the world. To him it represented his pride in his boy.

Early in the year [1943] Father Tibesar had taken some...members to a monthly meeting of the Holy Name Society at Jerome [Idaho]. The meeting was held at Father Schermanson's residence. It was probably the first time the visitors had been in a home since they left their own in Seattle. The over-stuffed furniture, straight backed chairs, tables,...bedroom set, bathroom, the kitchen with its sink and faucet and all, brought back nostalgic memories. The cheerful atmosphere of Catholic fellowship recalled meetings of a past and happier day in Seattle.

...[A] gathering of all Holy Name Society members of the entire district [was planned for] Minidoka. The occasion arrived on Feb. 14th. Fully seventy priests,...members and friends from Jerome, Wendell, Twin Falls, Buhl, and nearby [Idaho] vicinity, joined with the Minidoka [Holy Name] Society. The affair will remain long in the memory of those who attended...Here was assembled Americans of Irish, English, Polish, Italian, Scandinavian, German, Japanese, and other stock ancestry with [Issei, or first-generation] Japanese members, technically enemy aliens. There was also a lieutenant of the United States Army and several men of his staff who had come to register volunteers for the special combat team.

This had been followed [a year] later...with preparations at Minidoka for a farewell dinner...before relocation of the relatively few remaining Maryknoll [Holy Name] members. The meeting and banquet was held Sunday, March 12 [1944]. Some thirty-four Jerome [Idaho] members attended the affair...[A] native Japanese dish of Tendon claimed the attention of the diners in the mess hall...[T]he Maryknoll ladies and some of the menfolk pitched in to help prepare the dish. The chopsticks and food provided a novelty to the visitors from Jerome and the half dozen [Minidoka] project officials who had been specially invited. The dinner meeting was probably the only one of its kind to be held in the United States and the world, for that matter, under the conditions.

...In June [1943], Sisters Consolata and Rose Carmel came to Minidoka for a two weeks' visit. Their coming was looked forward to with high expectancy and especially by the children and their mothers...[T]hey visited every possible Catholic home as well as others which they had known in Seattle...Sisters Rosaire and Thomas Marie then came to spend July and August with their people...conducting daily catechism classes, Legion of Mary meetings, choir practices...Those two months will probably stand out as the most normal period, mentally and spiritually, spent by the children and parents of Maryknoll in the Minidoka center.

[In 1944] the Legion of Mary joined hands with the young people of Twin Falls at the latter's Church. The visit outside by the Minidoka girls and boys proved both exhilarating and encouraging to them. It gave them the feeling of still being a part of the general stream of American life...The St. Vincent de Paul kept on...None who were helped [by St. Vincent de Paul charity] ever became known to the public. Yet the records show the wide sphere of Catholic action taken by a small but staunch band of Maryknoll men...Each Sunday some reading material was distributed to patients in the hospital who were constantly visited by members seeking to help them...Tobacco, candy, clothing, electric stoves and other necessities were distributed to persons and families in less fortunate circumstances than the majority...

[Our] Lady Queen of Martyrs meetings at the Chapel on Monday afternoons were...helping both morale as well as keeping up the faith...At these meetings Father Tibesar would take up various problems after the regular prayers and spiritual conference. They would chiefly deal with relocation. Almost every week there would be some report of letters received from members who had been relocated. The cheerful note struck in these letters encouraged many within to relocate. Those who could not [relocate]...were gladdened to learn that all was not against them on the outside. On Friday evenings the young people gathered at the Chapel. Following his discourse, Father would listen to questions and ideas as they would arise in the minds of the young people...[A]dult meetings...where Father Tibesar talked in Japanese were proving highly interesting to those who attended. This is attested too, by the attendance of a Protestant minister...for a period of several months...The Protestant ministers were obviously impressed for Catholic books and other literature on the Church were borrowed for further study.

Yet Father did not lay special emphasis on conversions in the center. Those who sought conversion he baptized...Since evacuation at Camp Harmony and Minidoka there were...41 who were baptized and more than 30 con-firmed...Father had his ideas about conversions in the center where people lived under extraordinary circumstances and conditions. His thoughts ran more toward laying the foundation for future conversion among those whom he thought would develop into true Catholics...Letters from those who had been baptized, some of them one-time Protestant Sunday school teachers, denote more than ordinary humility in their appreciation and gratitude at having been able to join the Church while still at Minidoka.

...So the fortunes of evacuee life, as it were, flowed and ebbed with the times of optimism and pessimism on the shores of an uncertain future. Laugh-ter at times turned to tears. Cheerfulness merely cloaked the poignancy of past history...Maryknoll in Seattle...is enshrined within the hearts and minds of her Minidoka members with a love and devotion for the unending work of the Almighty Father, exemplified by the Church. At this Lenten Season [April 1944], the story of evacuation is not finished. The story of Maryknoll [and] devotion for the people of her Japanese parish...also continues "as it was in the beginning, is now and ever shall be world without end."

> "Report on Seattle's Maryknoll, April 1944," the only English-language chapter found in the book *Chibesa-shi no Kotodomo* (About Father Tibesar), published in Japan in commemoration of the American and Japanese ministry of Father Leopold H. Tibesar. Tibesar Collection, Quincy University Library Archives. Printed with permission. The text as printed here was edited by Madeline Duntley.

113. John Hayatsu, "The Role of the Japanese American in the Church," Seattle, 1992

John Hayatsu is a Japanese American Catholic in Seattle who, born in Septem-ber 1941, spent his early years in the Minidoka internment center. He attended Catholic grade and high schools, as well as spending one year at a Catholic col-lege. He is a truck driver, married with four children. He wrote the following observations on the condition of Japanese-American Catholics as a response to a request from his parish Sister in 1992.

I am not sure that the role of the Japanese-American is any different than any other Catholic of any other race. We all come to worship and serve the Lord. We might have different styles but I think that we are all basically the same.

I am not sure if I have interpreted this question correctly or not, but if I may go off in a little different direction and ask you this question. What do the spotted owl and the Japanese Catholic have in common? Answer is, we are both endangered species. Now I am not an expert on this subject, but have you ever seen more than a half dozen Japanese Catholics in any church on Sunday morning at one time? Sometimes I wonder why. After the war in the 40's and 50's, a whole flock of them used to gather to worship at the old Mary-knoll Church on Jefferson Street. The church was torn down and is now part of Providence Hospital. Could that be part of the problem? They do not have a common church building in which to worship? Could it be parish boundaries? Other denominations of Japanese Christians such as the Presbyterians, Methodists, Baptists, and Episcopalians all have their own full, active and vibrant church communities. But they have no boundaries. They come from all over the city and county. The Korean and Vietnamese Catholics gather on Sundays in their own churches. Why not the Japanese? There are a few that gather once a month at the Maryknoll House, but never more than a couple dozen. Could it be the old Japanese mentality of be seen but not heard? Are Japanese parents encouraging their children in the Faith? I remember all the Japanese families from old Maryknoll sent their children to Catholic schools, elementary and secondary, and even college. Not any more. There are some but not that many. There are a lot of third and fourth generation Catholics leaving the Church. But why?

Other Asian Catholics are thriving in the Church. But why not the Japanese? Are we really a vanishing species? I hope not!

Archives of the Archdiocese of Seattle. Printed with permission of John Hayatsu.

Filipino Immigrants

114. Catholic Filipino Club, Seattle, 1922

The first major wave of Filipinos arrived in the United States during the 1920s. Because these immigrants were over 90 percent male and over 80 percent were between the ages of eighteen and thirty-four, the Catholic Church's main concern was their moral rectitude when as newcomers they were beset by temptations of every sort in the United States. To assist them with their struggles the dioceses of Seattle and San Francisco established Catholic Filipino clubs. The following document is an announcement sent out by the Seattle club detailing its services.

CATHOLIC FILIPINO CLUB,
416 Fifth Ave., Seattle May 23, 1922

DEAR FILIPINO FRIENDS AND FELLOW COUNTRYMEN:

The Catholic Filipino Club extends to you its greetings, and bids you welcome to these United States.

In the course of your sojourn here, many courtesies will be extended you, and many functions arranged for your entertainment and edification.

In coming here, you come not as total strangers, for you know that the Government and the people of the United States have an interest in your progress and welfare; besides, many of you have visited here before; furthermore, there are 2500 or more of your young generation sojourning amongst us, and of this number about 800 are in the vicinity of Seattle. About half this number are now in Alaska, working in canneries.

The lot of the Filipinos in America, particularly those attending school, is rather hard; and on account of their youth and the absence of restraint, frequently fraught with peril. /

In an effort to alleviate these conditions, the Catholic Filipino Club was formed. We have been operating one year. About 600 of your boys are registered with us...

The same sentiments of practical religion and charity that was brought to the Islands by the Friars is the motive that inspires us, and while there may be an accident of color that distinguishes the Filipino from his American friends, at heart and in spirit we are ONE in the bosom of God, and in the fold of our Holy Mother, His Church.

While formally we address you as friends, in reality we greet you as members of one large family, and not with ostentation, but in the spirit of family familiarity, we shall try to acquaint you with a few things our Club has done for your countrymen — our brothers — because we feel that you are interested and would like to know.

Employment. We have obtained positions for the boys in families and elsewhere on an average of one every other day.

Sickness. We have provided medical attention [once a week]...[T]hese cases ...ranged all the way from flu and infected tonsils to phthisis and tubercular peritonitis. In one instance, where the patient had the latter malady, we maintained and kept the boy in one of our Catholic Hospitals for half a year, and this service [was] gratuitously rendered by the sisters and doctor in charge...

Legal. Apart from advising the boys in legal matters, we have ever been a friend to them in securing their legal rights: We have helped those who were discharged from the army and navy in obtaining medical aid and vocational training. In one instance we assisted in recovering wages for seven Filipino boys against a bankrupt ship; and in another case, where a local attorney, purporting to have authority from the Philippines to act as guardian for one of the boys, and collect the wages that he had toiled for in Alaska, we pledged Liberty Bonds to the extent of the wages involved and secured a release...

Support. In one case involving the youthful marriage of a Filipino and a Filipina, we not only arranged for the details of confinement, but we stood sponsor to the child, and for six months past have provided the family with rent, fuel, and provisions...We have also given material relief in many other cases.

Education. We have placed five boys in a boarding college conducted by the Benedictine Fathers at Lacey, Washington, and several day scholars in our local Jesuit College...

Death and Burial. We have attended the death-bed of several Filipinos. We have seen that they were all provided with the last sacraments of Holy Mother

Church, and we have accompanied the remains of eight of them to their last resting place. In every instance Mass was celebrated, and a priest officiated at the grave...

Returning Needy Filipinos. Last summer when Manuel Quezon was here, we took up the question of returning to the Islands Filipinos who were anxious to go back and were without funds...Recently, through the cooperation of the National Catholic War Council, we have succeeded in working out an arrangement with the Admiral Line and the Shipping Board by which we are now enabled to return needy and deserving Filipinos back to their beloved Philippines.

Spiritual. Finally, (and we consider this our best accomplishment) we are impressing the boys with an intelligent conception of their duties to Almighty God, and are leading them back to the practice of their religious duties and the sacraments...In these days of material progress and education without God, it is difficult enough to keep morally straight at home, let alone venturing into foreign countries, hampered by human conceit and the inexperience of youth...

We feel that we have the blessing of God on our work. And we know that if you are interested in yourselves, you cannot help but be interested in us.

> Fraternally yours,
> (signed) Lorenzo Zamora, President
> V. C. Edades, Chairman of the Executive Council
> L. J. Esterman, Secretary

Archives of the Archdiocese of San Francisco. Printed with permission.

115. Letter of Thanks for Catholic Filipino Club, San Francisco, 1927

A Catholic Filipino club provided practical assistance to Filipino immigrants. The following document is a letter thanking Archbishop Edward J. Hanna of San Francisco (1915–34) for sponsoring the club.

Walnut Grove, California, June 10, 1927

Most Reverend E. J. Hanna, D.D.,
Archbishop of San Francisco

Dear Father:

We the undersigned Filipino boys who have just arrived in America, although not personally known to you thought it best to write you this letter because of the great help we have received from the Catholic Filipino Club founded by you.

We were passengers of the S.S. President McKinley that arrived last May 23rd. Our suit cases were stolen by the taxi driver, Matas. He took our suit cases and did not return them anymore. Because we stopped at the Catholic Filipino Club we reported the matter to Mr. McCarty, the present head of the club. He helped us claim our suit cases, and although it was not returned anymore, the taxi driver paid us $92.55 according to the decision of the Court of Small Claims. Had we not come under the roof of the Catholic Filipino Club which you founded, we would have lost entirely our suit cases.

We thank you very much . . . We shall do our best to tell our countrymen here and in the Philippines the great service that this club is rendering to the Filipino people.

> Very respectfully,
> (signed) Geronsio F. Molina
> Mariano Forrifos[?]

Archives of the Archdiocese of San Francisco. Printed with permission.

116. Report on Filipinos in San Francisco, 1941–42

In 1942, Archbishop Amleto Cicognani, apostolic delegate to the United States, inquired of the dioceses on the West Coast about their care of Filipino immigrant Catholics. The inquiry was inspired by a letter of concern by a federal government official, Monroe Sweetland, who lamented the plight of the Filipinos. The first document is Sweetland's letter, followed by the response of Archbishop John J. Mitty of San Francisco (1935–61). Mitty's response, which was addressed to Archbishop Cicognani, provides a window into the condition of Filipinos in 1942.

> Office of Production Management,
> Social Security Building, Washington D.C.
> October 14, 1941

Mr. Bruce M. Mohler,
National Catholic Welfare Conference
Washington, D.C.

Dear Mr. Mohler:

This letter is to call your attention to a situation which I consider one of the most unfortunate faced by any minority group in the nation. It seems to me . . . that it is particularly the province of the Catholic Social Agencies to undertake responsibility in this matter, if you will pardon an outsider and non-Catholic for being so bold . . .

As you know, most American Filipinos live in the states of Oregon, Washington, and California. Nearly all of them were born in the Philippine Islands and are excluded from citizenship under the interpretation of the Oriental Exclusion Act, in spite of the fact that most of them now in this country were born under the American flag and educated in American schools. They were brought to this country by the inducements of sections of industry interested in cheap, unorganized labor . . .

...[N]o national group in the United States finds its constitutional and human rights so frequently and flagrantly violated as our Filipinos. They are ostracized socially from nearly every group...

Economically, the Filipino population is restricted to a very narrow category of employment. On the west coast there are three chief sources of livelihood for them: 1. Agricultural labor; 2. Culinary crafts (busboys — but not waiters and domestic service); and 3. The floating canneries which pack salmon off the Alaska Coast. Of these three categories, the third is by far the most lucrative and employs a great proportion of the west coast Filipinos during the summer season.

The civil rights of Filipinos are generally disregarded...During recent years, the Communist Party has been the only group which has taken any effective action in defense of the Filipinos...I am writing this extensive memorandum to you because I believe this problem should be the particular concern of the progressive social agencies of the Catholic Church...The one faint connection which American Filipinos have with a major element in our nation is the fact that most of them are nominal Catholics. I think that for the most part they do not attend Mass or take part in Church functions excepting that their funerals and weddings are usually conducted in a church. I think the American Filipinos are in desperate need of an effective defense agency...

Sincerely yours,
(signed) Monroe Sweetland

31 January 1942

No. 660/41

His Excellency Most Reverend Amleto G. Cicognani, D.D. [Apostolic Delegate:]

...[In response to Monroe Sweetland's letter,] I have been gathering information from various sources: my social welfare group of priests, the Chief of police of San Francisco, the International Institute, and a Captain Sulit, who is an army officer and a Filipino. As a result of the information gathered, I present the following points:

1. As far as our knowledge goes, the problem of the Filipinos in California is not as black as painted in the letter of Mr. Monroe Sweetland...

2. The Filipinos cannot become citizens unless they have completed a term of three years in the Army or Navy or proved that they have fifty percent white blood in them.

3. There are very few Filipino women here. The ratio is from 15 to 25 men to one Filipino woman, differing according to locality. This creates a serious problem because it makes them consort with simple country girls or cast-off prostitutes.

4. California's State Law forbids marriages between Filipinos and whites. Nevada and Arizona have a similar law. Oregon allows the Filipinos to marry whites.

5. There is social discrimination against Filipinos as against other races. The Filipinos find particular difficulty in securing meeting places... The Filipino people are very much interested in their native songs, dances, and plays. The fact that they cannot find meeting places, therefore, creates a more serious hardship for them. However, as Filipinos form friendships with other Filipinos who come from the same locality in the Philippine Islands (that is either from the North or South and so forth), one center, perhaps, would not really be the answer to this problem. While most of them speak English, there is a great number of dialects in their native language.

6. It is not true that in California human rights of the Filipinos are violated by false arrests, mob violence, individual violence, unjust treatment at the hands of the courts, juries and police. Chief of Police Dullea... agrees with this statement... The International Institute feels that in some cases their rights have been violated; these are few... As far as I can see, there have been only a few flagrant cases of their rights having been violated.

7. To my knowledge, the Filipinos in this part of the State do not belong to any unions... The Sulit Family [766 Fell St.] states that about ninety percent of the Filipinos belong to [u]nions. They agreed that a great number of them belonged to the Ucapawa Union... They also belong to the... Federated Agricultural Labor Association in Salinas... Both of these [u]nions are quite radical, according to statements of the Sulit family. The unions have done a great deal for these people...

   ...[T]here is little doubt but that they have been taken advantage of in the way of low wages and sometimes no wages at all...

8. Several years ago, the United States Government gave free transportation to Filipinos who wished to return to the Philippine [I]slands. Very few (2,082) accepted the offer.

9. Filipinos are very much interested in education and have given very satisfactory service to those who employed them. They are the most satisfactory laborers of the foreign groups... It is true that they want white-collar jobs but have been unable to secure them. In some cases they were equipped for the jobs but were rejected because they were Filipinos.

10. The Filipinos are congregated in this Archdiocese in the following places: in Stockton there are always at least five thousand, and during

the agricultural season this number goes up at times to fifteen thousand. There are from three to five thousand in San Francisco, three thousand in Oakland, and one thousand in San Jose. There is a large group in Salinas. In San Francisco they work as domestics, bus boys, dishwashers, cooks, and in the canneries. In other districts they work principally in the field of agriculture...

11. The Catholic Filipino Club was organized in 1922 as a welfare center for all Filipinos in San Francisco. A plan of constructive and recreational activities was adopted, which consisted principally of advice, housing, employment and habilitation of the newcomer. Individual groups were to be organized and united under the Catholic Filipino Club... There had been only one welfare worker employed at the Club... An abrupt influx of Filipinos into San Francisco from the Islands started in 1923, which required all the attention and service of the one worker and the full facilities of the Building, which was taxed beyond its capacity.

    Concentration on immigration work was of prime importance. The constructive and recreational activities of the Catholic Filipino Club and the organization of resident Filipino groups were, of necessity, curtailed.

    In 1924 the Catholic Filipino Club became a participating agency of the Community Chest of San Francisco, which required, in addition to immigration work, that the Club undertake direct relief, such as free employment, free housing, free meals, etc., for the destitute resident Filipinos.

    Relief work practically became the sole activity of the Catholic Filipino Club, reaching a climax in 1929, and terminating in September, 1933, when the City, State and Federal Government took this responsibility...

    On May 1, 1934, the immigration of Filipinos... was placed at a quota of 54 per annum.

    The Community Chest of San Francisco suspended the Catholic Filipino Club from budget participation March 30, 1934...

12. Most of the Filipinos have come to the United States without any or with very meagre religious education or training. They have really very little knowledge of the faith. The Methodist Church... has a Filipino minister, and the Episcopal Church... has been doing some proselytizing among the Filipinos. Their sense of inferiority keeps the Filipinos from attending Church with white people. It might be possible to go further into this question by gathering more information through social gatherings. We have been striving to find some method of handling this problem, and it may be that now, through Captain Sulit, we may be able to accomplish more.

13. Because of the heroic work of the Filipino troops in the recent attack on the Philippines, I feel there is already a changed attitude toward the Filipinos here in the United States and that the outlook is far more promising.

Faithfully yours,
John J. Mitty
Archbishop of San Francisco

Archives of the Archdiocese of San Francisco. Printed with permission.

117. Report on Filipinos in Stockton, California, 1956

In 1956, Archbishop Egidio Vagnozzi, apostolic delegate to the Philippine Islands, wrote the Sacred Consistorial Congregation in Rome, complaining that Filipino immigrants were being neglected by the church in the United States. He suggested that Filipinos were not comfortable in "Irish churches" and that there was a danger that the Filipinos were slipping into masonry or freemasonry. Vagnozzi suggested that Bishop Alessandro Olalia of Lipa in the Philippines visit the United States to investigate the status of Filipinos. Archbishop John J. Mitty denied the accusation that the Filipinos were being neglected and discouraged the visit of Bishop Olalia. Mitty canvassed those priests working in areas with large numbers of Filipinos. One of the more interesting replies came from Stockton, California, where Franciscan Father Alan McCoy was working. From his reply, it is evident that women religious provided a great deal of ministry to immigrants. McCoy and his Franciscan confreres also became noted for their ministry to Spanish-speaking Catholics and migrant workers. The extraordinary work of St. Mary's among the Filipinos was, unfortunately, more the exception than the rule in Filipino ministry.

St. Mary's Church, Stockton, California

August 30, 1956

The Most Rev. John J. Mitty,
Archbishop of San Francisco

Your Excellency:

...It is estimated that there are about 11,000 Filipino people in this area during the harvest season...[T]he great majority of these workers are either single men or men who have left their wives in the Philippine Islands...

When we first came to Stockton we heard that the vast majority of these people had been lost to the faith. However, we soon found that this was exaggerated. There have been serious inroads made by the Methodist and Presbyterian sects, but they were not so serious as we had been led to believe...

In December, 1955, the Benedictine Sisters of Ilocos Sur, Philippine Islands, arrived and took up work here among the Filipino people. The Filipino community had picked out a house and pledged to pay for the property...The

Sisters have proven a tremendous blessing to the entire area. The following is a list of the activities of the Sisters and the services offered to the Filipino people of the community.

First, January, 1956, the Sisters opened a religious pre-school class, in which they taught the Filipino children daily...

All Filipino families of the parish were visited by the Sisters or the priests. Fourteen marriages were validated and a large number are awaiting validation. The President of the Filipino Community has been won back to an active part in the affairs of the parish, and the former President, who had joined the Methodists, came humbly back to ask for readmission...

Each time a birth is recorded of any of our people, a member of the Legion of Mary calls on the family, bringing a medal from the pastor together with a greeting card. The parents are then reminded of their obligation to have the children baptized soon. I think it is safe to say that all the Filipino children are baptized, although it is hard to get them to come soon. They often want to await the arrival of a relative to act as sponsor.

The Filipino camps within the boundaries of the parish were visited during the asparagus season. The Sisters would go with a Father or Brother, and often with one or more members of the Legion of Mary. They would instruct the men, preparing them for the sacraments, teaching them prayers and hymns. Then, after due preparation, one of the priests from St. Mary's would say Mass in the camp, hear confessions... and distribute Holy Communion. The response was very gratifying. Over 50% of those attending the Mass would ordinarily receive Holy Communion. Although the Sisters would not always know the dialect of the men, they were able to find members of the Legion of Mary who could do this and thus help them in their work...

The Filipino youth are included in our regular youth program... Also, an entirely Filipino youth club meets in our hall... A number of Filipino youngsters take an active part in the helpers section of the CCD.

Of the five praesidia of the Legion of Mary... one was for the Filipino people and has proven quite successful. In the first praesidium, which is for the entire parish, our president is a Filipina woman. Also, there is a Filipina woman at the head of a praesidium established at Edison Villa, a federal housing project.

Our St. Vincent de Paul Society has two Filipino members, and full coverage of all needy cases among their people is assured.

A society named Our Lady of Antipolo Society has been formed to further the work of the Benedictine Sisters. The Filipino patients in San Joaquin General Hospital are visited every week by the Sisters and members of the Legion of Mary...

A special novena was held in the Church during the last part of May in honor of Our Lady of Antipolo, during which a painting of Our Lady of Antipolo by a local Filipino Doctor was unveiled... The novena concluded with a special service with a sermon in the Tagalog dialect by Fr. Francisco Reyes, OFM. The same evening the Filipino Catholics had a parade with floats and a dinner, followed by entertainment.

During the recent high school drive the Filipino men played a very active part. And, they have been very faithful in their pledges.

We were able to take every Filipino child of the parish that applied for entrance to St. Mary's Assumption Elementary School. During the past Summer the Benedictine Sisters assisted us with a Summer Religious School...

Personally, I have found the Filipino people a very likeable people. And, although I know it will take a long time to really understand them, the work with them has been most pleasant and gratifying. They are most generous. And I believe that if we can provide the youngsters with a good education, and somehow bring more Filipina women to the United States for these single men, we will be able to build solidly.

The attendance of the Filipino people at Mass has been encouraging...

Respectfully yours in Christ,
(signed) Fr. Alan McCoy, OFM

Archives of the Archdiocese of San Francisco. Printed with permission of Father Alan McCoy, O.F.M.

118. Inquiry and Response on Filipino Ministry, 1980

Following the Immigration Act of 1965, the number of Filipino immigrants increased dramatically, and ministry to Filipinos became a growing concern. In the following document, Philippine-born Noemi Castillo addresses Archbishop John R. Quinn of San Francisco (1977–95) about the sad state of ministry to the Filipinos in the archdiocese. The document which follows Castillo's letter articulates the view of the Filipino clergy. As with many previous groups what is desired is assimilation rather than isolation. What is interesting is that it is the Filipino clergy that are pushing for assimilation.

Diocese of Oakland—
Vicariate for the Filipinos
September 2, 1980

Most Rev. John Quinn,
Archbishop of San Francisco

Dear Archbishop Quinn,

Let me start this letter by introducing myself and the reason for this letter.

I am Noemi Castillo, a parishioner of St. Elizabeth's [San Francisco]. I write to you because I am concerned about the lack of a genuine Filipino ministry in the Archdiocese not because you are closed to it, but more because no one is willing enough to take on the difficult and challenging task nor has the understanding of what this ministry calls for...

I am... involved in the Filipino ministry in the Diocese of Oakland. I find this very ironic because I belong to the Archdiocese of San Francisco but I have to cross the bay every morning to work for the Diocese of Oakland helping different parishes develop their Filipino communities and draw them into the mainstream of their parish life.

I feel sad about this fact, your Excellency, especially because I see so much need for a similar ministry in our Archdiocese and there is none like it happening here. True, there are these individual ministries on [a] parish level, but there is none on an archdiocesan level which, I feel, is very important in bringing the Filipinos together.

In the past I had hoped and looked for leadership among our Filipino clergy but I was and am greatly disappointed. I would like to see our Filipino clergy lead our Filipino people from the external religion and folk Catholicism that many of us, especially those from the provinces, know of, to something more solidly based on faith as our response to God's call.

Instead I see some of our Filipino priests "playing along," if not encouraging a very sentimental devotion to Sto. Nino, for example. There is nothing wrong with having devotion to Sto. Nino. If that is where the faith of the people is, then start from it but move on to a deeper and a more genuine life with God. What I see as wrong in this "religious" devotion is that it stops at it as if it is the ultimate of our Christian faith, and what is worse, is, it is incorporated into beauty contests and fundraising activities. Why can't they incorporate it into the liturgy and help people find its meaning in light of the Gospel values and in the heart of the liturgy...?

I write this letter to ask you for an opportunity to speak to you about the needs of the Filipino people in so far as spiritual formation and leadership development is concerned...

Sincerely yours,
(signed) Noemi Castillo

Archives of the Archdiocese of San Francisco. Published with permission of Noemi Castillo.

[Suggested Reply Given by a Filipino Pastor, 10 September 1980]

After reading your letter...with the interest and attention it deserved, I remembered that our Filipino priests in the archdiocese had met with the... Archbishop three years ago on how to minister more effectively to the spiritual needs of the fast-growing Filipino community in the archdiocese. Well aware of the deep faith of the Filipinos and their potential for active participation and leadership in their respective parishes, the Filipino priests had decided on an approach quite different from yours, it seems.

They believe in bringing the Filipino Catholics into the mainstream of American Catholic life, not by emphasizing too much what pertains solely to their culture as a people, but by working on what they have in common with their American fellow-Catholics. This is why, unlike most Filipino leaders in this country, they do not see the need for a special ministry to Filipinos or for a formation of a Vicariate for Filipinos — things which they feel would only serve to foment a spirit of isolationism, perpetuate differences, and delay the day when the Filipino Catholic will feel at home in an American Catholic community, either as a leader or as a simple parishioner...

Archives of the Archdiocese of San Francisco. Printed with permission.

119. Filipino Catholic Affairs, Archdiocese of San Francisco, Annual Report, 1983–84

Despite the wishes of the Filipino clergy, by 1983 an archdiocesan office for Filipino Catholic Affairs had been established in San Francisco with Noemi Castillo as the key staff person. (She had previously served the Diocese of Oakland in a similar office.) What follows is an excerpt from a document explaining the goals and approach of the office. The document ends with a listing of the strengths and weaknesses of Filipino Catholics.

The activities of the Filipino Catholic Affairs for the year 1983–84 are classified into:

    I. Leadership Formation and Spiritual Development

    II. Celebrations

    III. Service to Parishes and Schools

    IV. Archdiocesan Activities and Inter-agency Cooperation

    V. Coordination with Filipino Clergy, Sisters, Brothers, and Deacons

I. Leadership Formation and Spiritual Development

    a. Formation of a Council of Filipino Parish Representatives

        This process began with a whole day goal-setting activities participated by 35 Filipino leaders coming from 18 parishes. These leaders were designated by their pastors as the official representatives of their parish to the Archdiocesan Filipino Catholic Affairs. [The group reflected on the "experience of Church in (the) Philippines and in the United States," and a mission statement was formulated.]...

II. Celebrations

The faith experience of the majority of Filipinos revolve around religious celebrations. The Filipino Catholic Affairs recognizes this basic reality and makes use of these events as the starting point of evangelization and a means to bring together the Filipino people in the Archdiocese, in joy and unity. At the same time, these celebrations enable the Filipino people to share their culture and Christian heritage with the larger community of the Archdiocese...

Two main religious celebrations were coordinated by the Council:

1. "Salubong" — celebrated on an inter-parochial level... "Salubong" is a traditional Filipino Easter Celebration of the meeting of Christ and His mother on Easter morning.

   [From appendix: "When the Spanish came to the Philippines, one of the modes of evangelization they used was dramatization. They were impressed by the closeness of the family members of the natives and saw it as a witness of the closeness of Jesus and Mary. They dramatized this special relationship of Jesus and His Mother in the 'Salubong.' The celebration brought the entire family to this special religious activity in Easter dawn"].

2. "Flores de Mayo" — celebrated on an Archdiocesan level at St. Mary's Cathedral... "Flores de Mayo" is a traditional Filipino devotion to Mary during the month of May...

Prepared by Noemi Castillo, Staff Person, Filipino Catholic Affairs, August 30, 1984.

Appendices

1. Weaknesses Filipinos Bring to the American Church [Compiled by Council of Filipino Parish Representatives]

   Lack of unity or "kanya-kanya"

   Clannishness and regionalism

   Inferiority...

   Lack of understanding of American parish system

   Shy and reserved people...

   Obsession to establish themselves economically...

   Overemphasis on religious devotions...

   Not supportive of church financially

   No sense of belonging to parish

   Lack of knowledge of the doctrines of our faith

   Superstitious beliefs

   Lack of religious formation; very limited understanding of liturgy and Vatican II

2. Filipino Experience of Church in America

   Involved only when there is a Filipino priest

   Filipinos group themselves according to their regions and/or devotions

Hesitant to attend church meetings...

Attend Church on Sunday as a family unit

Filipinos do not feel a sense of belonging in parish

- celebrations lack warmth...

- few statues in church

- practice of religion is businesslike...

Free offerings for the sacraments of Baptism, Matrimony and funerals

The clergy do not know or understand the Filipino culture

Archives of the Archdiocese of San Francisco. Printed with permission.

120. Jose Arong, O.M.I., Survey of Filipino Priests and Religious — Ministry Focus, 1995 – 96

The following survey was conducted by Father Jose Arong, O.M.I., a Filipino-American priest, for the Office for the Pastoral Care of Migrants and Refugees of the United States Catholic Conference. The survey polled Filipino priests throughout the United States.

Top Priority

63.4%	Filipino youth who are coping with being second generation Americans, and with Filipino culture and religious devotions.
57.1%	Filipinos come to the U.S. as "cradle Catholics." They need continuing religious education.
51.2%	Evangelize devotional practices and traditions which now sustain the faith of first generation Filipinos: Santo Nino, Fatima, Nazareno, San Lorenzo Ruiz, Simbang Gabi, Grief prayers and support, novenas for the dead, Flores de Mayo, home masses. There are some sectarian and/or devotional groups which need special attention: Banal na Pag-aaral, El Shaddai, etc.
43.9%	Filipinos need to be encouraged to financially support their local parish and to use them for their weekend liturgies, baptisms, weddings and sacramentals.
41.5%	Support Filipino marriages challenged by more liberal social environment and the pressures of financial stability often resulting in the break-up of family life.

Printed with permission of Father Jose Arong, O.M.I.

Santo Niño De Cebu Controversy
(Documents 121–24)

121. Agreement between Cebu Association and St. Joseph's Parish, San Francisco, 4 February 1979

In 1968, a group of Filipinos led by Filipina Sally Famarin formed the Cebu Association of California in San Francisco, which encouraged traditional devotions to the Santo Niño de Cebu. The devotion originated in the sixteenth century. During the explorer Magellan's visit to the island of Cebu in 1521, he left a small statue of the Holy Child Jesus (Santo Niño). The Spanish invaded Cebu in 1565 and burned the native settlements to the ground. Amid the charred ruins the statue was found unscathed — its escape of the flames was considered miraculous. The Spanish built an Augustinian monastery on the spot where the statue was discovered. There, the statue became the object of popular veneration. In the mid–eighteenth century the devotion grew in influence and became a major celebration on the island of Cebu. The Cebu Association of California began celebrating an annual novena and fiesta in San Francisco. By 1977 it had become a major Filipino celebration, complete with a banquet, fiesta, beauty pageant, novena, and a substantial procession through the streets of San Francisco. In 1979, the statue of Santo Niño was enthroned on a marble altar at St. Joseph's Church. The following document is the contract entered into by Irish pastor Father James McGee and the Cebu Association.

...Both parties agree to permanently enthrone the Santo Niño de Cebu at St. Joseph's Church from date hereof. Masses and novenas will be held in His honor by the pastor of St. Joseph's, Rev. Fr. James McGee or any of his designees with no fees to the association...

All fiesta celebrations will be sponsored by the Cebu Association of California, Inc. every year from the date of the enthronement...

Both parties agree that a Marble Altar be constructed exclusively to House the Santo Niño de Cebu where He is presently located. This will be built contiguously so as to become a permanent fixture within the church...

St. Joseph's Church agrees to render full services during the Filipino Fiesta celebration and understands that the cultural heritage of the Filipino people in conjunction with the Holy Roman Catholic Church be followed during the fiesta celebrations...

(signed) James A. McGee
Pastor, St. Joseph's Church

Comm. Sally B. Famarin
Fdr. Pres. Emeritus, World Emissary
Filipino Fiesta, Santo Niño de Cebu

122. Warren Hinckle, "Hinckle's Journal/The Philippine Priest and the Philippine Saint," 1984

By 1982, the appointment of Filipino-born Father Fred Bitanga as pastor of St. Joseph's Church in San Francisco disrupted the fiesta and novena devoted to the Santo Niño de Cebu (see previous document). Father Bitanga opposed the devotion on the basis that it represented one region of the Philippines, not the whole Filipino people; that placement of the statue on the altar violated proper liturgical norms; and that the procession made the Filipino people appear "too foreign" — they needed to adapt to America. He encouraged the Cebu Association to return the devotion to their homes. The Cebu Association protested mightily. In the following document, San Francisco columnist Warren Hinckle provides his assessment of the controversy. Following Hinckle's article is the protest letter of the foundress of the Cebu Association, Sally Famarin. To the dismay of the Santo Niño devotees, the statue was ultimately removed from St. Joseph's Church.

"That priest," said the devout Sally Famarin, furiously drumming her two inch pewter and mauve fingernails, "he gives me one big headache."

"That woman," said the Rev. Fred Bitanga, running a finger down the neck of his Roman collar to allow for the righteous anger swelling in his throat, "she is my baptism of fire."

Father Bitanga, a native of the Philippines, is the new pastor of St. Joseph's Church...in San Francisco. Dominating his altar is a beautiful shrine to Santo Nino de Cebu, the Filipino patron saint. Father Bitanga wishes dearly to get this shrine the hell out of there.

The solid marble shrine holds a jewel-encrusted statue of the Christ child. It cuts through the altar floor and is bolted to the very foundation of the church. It was erected in 1980 during the reign of the previous pastor, the late and much-loved Rev. James McGee, by Ms. Famarin, who is a woman of piety, money and determination. She built it to stay.

Now the new Filipino pastor says he is going to tear down the Filipino shrine that the Irish pastor erected. Father Bitanga does not approve of the annual processions made by Filipinos through the streets of San Francisco to the Santo Nino Shrine. He says such outdoor devotion is "not American." He also says the shrine's location on the altar is incorrect, liturgically speaking...

The beef over the shrine has been going on for two years. Last week it grew into the type of religious war where neither side seems disposed to take prisoners.

Father Bitanga said he sent Ms. Famarin a registered letter in her capacity as head of the Santo Nino de Cebu Association, giving her 30 days to remove the shrine from his church.

"If she doesn't take it down, I'll take it down," Father Bitanga said. "We'll get a forklift and lift it up or use a jackhammer or something."

Ms. Famarin said that, if it appears canon law has forsaken Santo Nino, she will seek redress in civil law.

"That priest," said Ms. Famarin, "if he as much as touches the shrine I am going to sue him and the archbishop, too. I am going to court to ask for an injunction against him destroying Santo Nino"...

The battle royal over the jeweled statue of Santo Nino has embarrassed the archdiocese, which has been unable to effect a compromise between the willful woman and the stubborn priest...

...[T]he archbishop...last month furthered the controversy when he would not allow archdiocesan priests to say an outdoor Mass in front of City Hall before the annual Santo Nino de Cebu procession to the St. Joseph's shrine. However, the ever-resourceful Ms. Famarin found a Jesuit priest from USF to say Mass, and she herself assisted in giving out Holy Communion.

I walked in the procession, which went from City Hall down Ninth Street and then up Howard to St. Joseph's. In the march there were hundreds of Filipino faithful plus a sprinkling of politicians...

When the worshipers reached the church, there was no priest to greet them. They knelt before the marble shrine and touched the protective glass over the Santo Nino with the religiosity seen at Lourdes.

"We are used to seeing no priest at this church," said a young Filipino girl dressed in white.

"I could be there to greet them," Father Bitanga said. "I do not believe in that kind of devotion. It would have been hypocritical for me to be there."

At one point last year Father Bitanga and the shrine worshipers were at such loggerheads that the church doors were locked and the faithful knelt on the sidewalk outside the church to say their prayers.

This was Father Bitanga's explanation for that scene: "They are such a small group, I told them to have their devotions at home. I said I would come to the homes, instead of opening the big church with all the expense of light and the heat and so forth."

Father Bitanga said that things like getting locked out of the church would not happen to Ms. Famarin "if she weren't so stubborn." He said there were two Santo Nino de Cebu groups and that he supported the one that meets a few blocks away from his church at St. Patrick's... "The original group split up,..." he said.

The Filipino priest said that he was not simply removing the Filipino shrine from the altar but that all statues in the front section of the church, including the statue of Santo Nino now in the shrine, were being moved to the area that formerly was the bapistry. "We're going to have a chapel of saints," he said.

Ms. Famarin says the shrine cannot be moved because it, along with the church, have been registered as a national landmark. Father Bitanga is not impressed. He has described the Santo Nino statue in polite ecclesiastical language as a piece of junk.

"This is just one of those statues that they sell on the streets in the Philippines," he said. I wonder how he would explain that to the elderly Filipino gentleman I watched kiss the glass protecting the statue...

San Francisco Chronicle, 27 February 1984. Reprinted with permission.

123. Sally Famarin Protest Letter, 1982

For the background of this letter, see the introductions to documents 121 and 122 above.

October 18, 1982

Re — Fiesta of the Santo Niño de Cebu, St. Joseph's Church

Most Rev. John R. Quinn, Archbishop of San Francisco[:]

We are again appealing to you, hoping this approach will bring results knowing that the time is getting so near for this most important event in question.

Fr. Fred Bitanga had agreed to meet with us... regarding the coming Filipino Fiesta of the Santo Niño de Cebu Week this coming January 14–23 but to our dismay, the meeting ended up to practically nothing. We met him again... but still the ridiculous attitude of eliminating the Traditional Procession and the perpetual novena with mass for nine consecutive days and we cannot use any facilities in the Social Hall at all, and all of these activities are important factors of the festival.

Since the Santo Niño de Cebu was enthroned at St. Joseph's Church, for the past three years the late Father James A. McGee had given us the privilege of using the church and social hall,... the social hall for the coronation of the festival Queen and the Banquet after the Traditional Procession... Father Bitanga will only book us for the mass, that is, if we eliminate the Traditional Procession outside.

As of now, we don't know what's going to happen during the nine days mass and novena nights, he wants us to take the Santo Niño home and do our novena at home. We have met with the concerned community, we cannot take the Santo Niño home with us for the Shrine is at St. Joseph's Church, it's something the people believed in, they said it is there that we will say our prayers even if we have to crowd the doorsteps...

Most reverend Archbishop, we know deep in our hearts that you are the only solution to all these problems,... for more and more damage is happening in this most important event of the Filipino people regarding their religious cultural heritage. We have promoted this heritage of the Filipinos since 1968... [P]eople from all walks of life, including the young who have not seen the country where their parents came from[,]... have directly participated in this ancient tradition. We have reached up to its heights of distinction . . . [W]e reached the zenith of happiness . . . [T]hen out of nowhere, one person, and a Filipino priest at that, came and wants to destroy our religious ideologies? This we cannot allow. Has the church really changed that much that our pleading for all of this will bring no results? . . .

The Traditional Processional Parade is a great part of this religious cultural heritage of the Filipino people, an expression of the highest values of their religious culture. We still could have the procession of the Miraculous Santo Niño de Cebu even if no priest would walk with us . . .

Most sincerely yours,
(signed) Sally B. Famarin

Archives of the Archdiocese of San Francisco. Printed with permission.

124. Final Settlement, 1984

In 1984, the controversy ended unhappily for the Cebu Association; however, by 1991 the devotion had resumed at St. Dominic's Church in San Francisco, though on a more modest scale.

October 11, 1984

Receipt

The undersigned on behalf of the CEBU Association and Sally B. Famarin hereby acknowledges receipt in good and sound condition of the statue of the Santo Niño de Cebu from Father Fred Bitanga, pastor of St. Joseph's Church.

Sally B. Famarin

Archives of the Archdiocese of San Francisco. Printed with permission.

125. Nontraditional View of Santo Niño, ca. 1997

The following interview represents a contemporary view of the Santo Niño. Marina, a filmmaker, is identified as a Filipina in her late fifties. Her father had been a labor organizer in the Philippines, had been persecuted, and had perhaps been murdered. This excerpt comes from a thesis by Rachel Bundang, who appropriately titled a talk to the American Catholic Historical Association in 1998, "This Is Not Your Mother's Catholic Church."

Interview with Marina

Marina: I do believe in God. I just don't want you to think that I do it in blind obedience. Just as the military colonized the body, the Church colonized the mind and the spirit . . .

I thought by decolonizing the mind, I should also decolonize the spirit. So I made a film about Santo Niño. And in my film the Santo Niño spoke . . . to a thief. [The Santo Niño] said, "You have forgotten that I am the son of a carpenter, of a laborer. You have dressed me in this gold lamé, gold crown, scepter, silver boots, diamond rings" — and these are real jewels! I really did research on the Santo Niño, one of the richest icons in the Philippines — with a monthly salary!

Finally, I had a thief, who is a dévoté of the Santo Niño. And to his amazement, when he knelt in prayer, the Santo Niño began speaking to him! He said, "Take off this crown, this coat, these boots. Sell them and give [the money] to the poor." In the film I had previously shown the condition of Tonda [an extremely poor neighborhood], so there's no need to explain that. So what you see is a mother able to buy medicine or food for her children, wooden shoes for the kids...

Rachel Bundang, "Sojourners-Women Warriors-Exiles: Faith, Memory, and Survival among Filipina Immigrants to the United States" (M.Div. thesis, Harvard Divinity School, 1997). Printed with permission of Rachel Bundang.

126. From the Peter Bacho Novel *Cebu*, 1991

The following excerpt comes from Filipino-American novelist Peter Bacho's novel Cebu, *in which a second-generation Filipino-American priest struggles to come to terms with his roots. The following scene captures the tension of two generations of Catholic immigrants.*

"Bless me, Padre," said a voice Ben didn't recognize and could barely hear. It was a young, male, and heavily Filipino.

The boy was anxious, mumbling, mixing English words with what Ben recognized as Tagalog phrases. Finally, the tumbled monologue was entirely in the latter.

"Pardon," Ben interrupted him. "In English, please." Ben was uncomfortable in these situations; it made him feel patronizing. He had been on the receiving end often enough himself in the past...

The voice on the other side of the black screen partition seemed terribly confused. "I, I thought you was Pilipino," he said clearly, his accent substituting a "P" for an "F."

"I am," Ben said, then paused before adding in Cebuano, "Pero natawo 'ko sa Amerika." It meant he was U.S. born and raised. He hoped the boy would understand but doubted it. From Remedios [his mother], he learned that speakers of Tagalog, the national language, rarely bothered with other dialects.

"But, but,..." the boy stammered.

"Please, son," Ben interrupted. "I don't speak Tagalog."

The boy sighed, "Padre, I..." he whispered.

"Yes," Ben said as he moved his ear closer to the mesh screen.

"Never mind," he said quietly. "Never mind."

There was nothing else, just the sound of quiet movement, and a door opening, then slowly closing.

Peter Bacho, *Cebu* (Seattle: University of Washington Press, 1991), 162. Printed by permission of the University of Washington Press.

Vietnamese Immigrants

127. Report on Vietnamese Ministry, San Francisco, 1977

After the fall of Saigon in 1975, thousands of refugees fled Vietnam to escape the Communists. Though Catholics represented only about 7 to 8 percent of the general population in Vietnam, the number of Catholics among the refugees has been estimated as high as 40 percent. Many Catholics were dual refugees — they had fled North Vietnam after the Communist takeover there in 1954. According to the following report, Catholics made up more than 50 percent of the refugees who settled in San Francisco. Included among the refugees were many priests, who upon their arrival sought to provide sustenance to their people. Father Tran Dinh (Anthony) Phuc, a Redemptorist, filed the following report on activities among the Vietnamese in the first two years following their arrival in the United States. As with other immigrant groups, the priest played a key role as intermediary between the immigrant and the new culture.

I. GENERAL SURVEY

A) Statistics

According to the last statistics, there are about 1700 Vietnamese in San Francisco and Marin County, of which 856 (in my file) are Catholic. The exact number is certainly higher...

B) Personnel to Help Them

1). Fr. Anthony Phuc, CSSR,... has been in charge of those in San Francisco and Marin County, and Fr. Jos. Tinh, in San Mateo and Santa Clara counties.

2). Sister Rosaline is a Vietnamese nun of the Order of the Lovers of the Holy Cross, VietNam... Besides being choir director [for the Vietnamese community choir], she teaches catechism to Vietnamese children, works with Liturgy and interprets for Vietnamese people in St. Mary's Hospital and Clinic...

3). To share the responsibilities and to assist in our work, ten Vietnamese people of different ages and from different areas have been chosen to form the "Staff and the Board of Consultors."

II. PASTORAL CARE

1). Mass: As scheduled, solemn Mass in Vietnamese has been celebrated regularly in San Francisco at St. Benedict's Center every other Sunday at 11:00 A.M....

The average attendance has been 150...

The reason for Mass every other Sunday [is, according to Father Phuc], "I would like that while keeping their own religious traditions and praying in their own language, the Vietnamese people participate also in the life of their own parishes."

...3745 Communions were distributed from September 1975 to December 1976, and 2237 from January to September 1977...

2). Confession: Confessions are heard one hour before Sunday Mass. For people having valid reasons, I hear their confessions at their homes, hospitals or convalescent homes. From September 1975 to December 1976: 1557 confessions were heard, and from January to September 1977: 1215...

[Baptisms, confirmations, marriages, catechisms, and adult education are then reported.]

Visits

We have visited almost all Vietnamese Catholic families in San Francisco and some in Marin County, at least once, for the purpose of getting closer to my people, knowing them better and letting them speak freely of their problems. Many times, they themselves asked us to come because they had family difficulties: relationships between husbands and wives, parents and children, elderly and youths; disputes, conflicts, separation, risks of divorce. We managed to bring peace back to a certain number of families, but some others are still in trouble and require our attention and help.

Many other people affected by depression or homesickness invited the priest or nun to their homes hoping to get appeasement or relief of their suffering. In every case, we counseled them to go to "Mental Health for Indochinese Refugees Project Office." But, as they said, they "feel easier and more confident talking with a priest or a nun." So we tried to help them as much as we could...

III. SOCIAL ASSISTANCE

A) In the actual special circumstances, sometimes, the priest has to function as a medium between people looking for jobs and some employers, or as interpreter for some people in Social Service Office.

B) To conserve and develop the Vietnamese culture — a valuable way to enrich the multifaced American society — the Vietnamese Youth Association in San Francisco, under the direction of Sister Rosaline and the supervision of Father Anthony Phuc, organized a Lunar New Year Festival at the War Memorial Building on February 12, 1977, featuring Vietnamese folk dances, songs, instruments and plays.

C) Some political organizations — Communists, Rightists,... — have been trying in different ways to use us for their aims. As a Community, we refused categorically and we are vigilant in order not to be involved in such matters...

Archives of the Archdiocese of San Francisco. Reprinted with permission.

128. Request for a Personal Parish, San Jose, California, 1984

In 1979, Archbishop John R. Quinn of San Francisco established a Vietnamese Mission in San Jose, the largest Vietnamese settlement in northern California. Before this was accomplished, however, the new Diocese of San Jose was formed in 1981, with Pierre DuMaine serving as its first bishop. DuMaine set up a Vietnamese center, but this did not satisfy many Vietnamese. Like other immigrant groups before them they wanted their own parish to preserve their faith and culture and to ensure their children would learn the sacred traditions in the new land. In the following petition the Vietnamese Catholic community presents its case for a "personal parish," the equivalent of the national parish of the nineteenth century. Many of their arguments are similar to those of the Germans, Polish, and other groups who had sought their own national parishes. The document provides a cogent presentation of the Vietnamese Catholic viewpoint. By 1984, the Vietnamese community included a large number of "second-wave" immigrants, known popularly as the "boat people." After several years under Communist rule, these people escaped Vietnam in any way they could, either fleeing by foot to Thailand or Cambodia, where they were placed in refugee camps, or getting aboard practically anything that could float. Their plight is highlighted in the following memorial.

Vietnamese Catholic Community in Santa Clara County
San Jose, California

June 18, 1984

The Most Reverend Pierre DuMaine, D.D., Ph.D.
Bishop of San Jose

Following the petition of almost 2,000 Vietnamese Catholics in Santa Clara County submitted to you a few days ago, we, the VNCC and the Ad Hoc Committee for the Establishment of a Personal Parish for the Vietnamese Catholic Refugees in the Diocese of [S]an Jose, as their official representatives, are writing you this letter to support and elaborate their aspirations. In 1981, we requested a Mission and a church but you gave us a Pastoral Center, dedicated in February 27, 1983. After over a year of operation, we see that this center is just a temporary solution because it is limp and still does not satisfy our special needs as refugees. As you know, our needs are different from those of other groups of immigrants.

Lately, we have been deeply concerned about your plan to press us to join the local parishes and assign Vietnamese priests to serve as associate pastors. We feel that this plan will eventually destroy our Catholic heritage as well as the unity of our community, and is detrimental to our salvation and that of our children... We would like to repeat once again our petition to establish a special parish for the Vietnamese Catholic refugees in the Diocese of San Jose.

[The text then cites canon law on personal parishes and says the proposed parish will be "transitional." It continues:]

1. The Vietnamese Catholic Heritage

Before we came to America, we had gone through an ordeal which, to many people, was even more dangerous, adventurous and challenging than the EX-ODUS in the Bible. By the time we took small boats to sea to escape the communist regime, the chance to survive was one to ten. Hundreds of thousands of our people were perished in the Pacific Ocean due to its adverse conditions, starvation, raping, or killing by sea pirates, or a combination of all of these. That was a traumatic experience.

Now we have reached the Promised Land of America. Things have calmed down a little bit to give way to the painful reality of having to leave behind or on the bottom of the sea our parents, husbands and wives, children, brothers and sisters, relatives, or friends, and of course, our Mother Catholic Church, now under communist control and persecution. God has brought us to America. We are living from the dead: What a relief it is to know that we are now free to worship God and to live our Catholic life. We strongly believe that only with God's help and protection could we go through the ordeal because human effort was impossible.

Like Abraham and Noah, we feel the strong urge to set up a place to glorify God and to thank Him for all His help, and to preserve our Catholic heritage wherever we go. We are very proud to have had 130,000 martyrs in the history of our Catholic Church, 117 of whom have been beatified. We feel we have to build a place to venerate them and to emulate them so that we will not be discouraged in our faith ... We think that if we have a home for ourselves to live in, why can't we have one for God and for our Martyrs[?] ... This is our most cherished aspiration ever since we set foot in this land of freedom ...

2. A Common Destiny — Staying Together for Survival

In many ways, the Vietnamese refugees are in a very special circumstance because they all came to America in large groups with one being after another in a very short time. Only a few (mostly young kids) have been able to mainstream into American society and culture. Other groups of immigrants, such as the Chinese, Japanese or Koreans, on the other hand, came here far apart from one another in time with many people already having become "Americanized" to fully mainstream [and] to help newcomers in their communities. Seen in this way, it is easy to understand that, at least for the time being, the Vietnamese in America still need to stay together to survive, materially and spiritually. This is a matter of survival.

For this reason, it is no wonder that the Vietnamese Catholic Community in Santa Clara County, established in 1975, has grown into a very well organized community from the top to the grassroots. This community is presently divided into 9 areas ... and is represented by a Council composed of 27 elected members. There are 9 committees and 9 associations or movements. It is estimated that about 250 youths, men and women, are actively participating in various social, cultural, and evangelical activities of those associations, groups and movements, including a successful vocational training program. If you decide to establish a personal parish for the Vietnamese,...they will be very encouraged to participate even more actively in their voluntary work. On the other hand, if you assign Vietnamese priests to local parishes, our community will be automatically disbanded and our unity as a group will be in jeopardy...

3. Assimilation into the Mainstream

Being able to integrate into American society is our ultimate goal. However, we are convinced that we still need more time to acculturate and then assimilate into the American Church life and society. We know that late teens or older people, psychologically, have gone through their "Imprinting period," meaning the process of new language acquisition and acculturation leading to cultural assimilation and integration can no longer be 100% complete, and that this process will become slower with...age...

In addition, many of the refugees are loaded with different kinds of emotional problems; some are caused by cultural shock, some by feeling of insecurity in an unfamiliar environment, some by family problems, and many by a guilt feeling for leaving behind their dear ones...

As can be seen above, refugees of this age group have many special needs, temporal and religious. A personal parish...will be the best answer to this situation. Here, we can worship God in a "personal" environment with rites and traditions we are familiar with, the language we can understand both cognitively and affectively. Some of the Church traditions that are still practical in Viet Nam, but no longer in America, can be cited to illustrate this point: evening praying together in the Church, eucharistic visits, devotions to the Virgin Mary in May, the Sacred Heart in June, St. Joseph in March, Holy Roses in October and so on.

The assimilation problems of young children and youths are different. Refugees of this age can mainstream relatively fast into the American society and church life. However, experience with other groups of new immigrants has shown that children can do so often with grave danger to their Catholic faith and morals. To the great concern of many Vietnamese parents, their children are becoming more Americanized than Americans. Here, the personal parish comes into play to help these children preserve their home language, Vietnamese religious and cultural heritage, while they are being mainstreamed...

4. The Question of Salvation

...Who will be responsible for the loss of salvation and grace of thousands of our brothers and sisters?...

How about non Catholic refugees? Most Asians are polytheistic. When they come to America, there is a vacuum in their belief. As a result, they are ready to be affiliated with a new faith. Various Protestant denominations have taken advantage of this situation to increase the number of their adherents among different groups of Asian immigrants such as Koreans, Chinese, Philipinos, and Vietnamese. Can we do the same or better? The answer is Yes, if we are allowed to set up a personal parish. We will be able to offer a variety of cultural and social activities to attract these newcomers. Korean Methodist churches, Chinese Baptist churches, etc. . . . have been doing this and they have been very appealing to these groups of new immigrants.

5. Legal Basis

[After citing the New Code of Canon Law on personal parishes, the text continues:]

b. Precedences . . . The establishment of a personal parish for Vietnamese Catholic refugees . . . is not a new creation. In the history of the Catholic Church in America, and in San Jose, various parishes have been established in response to the special needs of various groups of immigrants (St. Patrick's for the Irish, Our Lady of Guadalupe for the Mexicans, etc.). Up to now, there have been 14 Vietnamese parishes in the United States, including two in California (Sacramento and Fresno).

[The letter describes the history of their appeal for a personal parish. Archbishop Quinn approved in 1979, but in 1981 San Jose became a diocese separate from San Francisco. The letter then describes the search for a site for the parish:] . . . A piece of land was found on McLaughlin Ave., San Jose . . . Unfortunately, because there was not enough room for parking, we had to find another place. When the search for another location was in full swing, the Diocese of San Jose came into being under your leadership. It was a very important *vested interest* of our community. In 1981, the VNCC submitted a petition to have a Mission with a church but you just gave them a Pastoral Center. This was not what the people expected when they gave their money to purchase the existing Center. To many people, you just reversed the decision that had already been made by your predecessor. Common sense dictates that this situation should not happen even in a secular organization . . .

7. Philosophical Considerations

a. Pluralistic Approach to Solving a Religious Issue. What we envision here is to have a church built in an Asian style to reflect the origin of those who helped to establish it. A few decades from now, when this church ceases to be "personal," historians will say that this was really a pluralistic approach . . . Our Vietnamese children will then be proud of the contribution of their parents or ancestors to the Diocese. We think that it is a marvelous idea. Here, the old idea of the melting pot is replaced by the more meaningful concept of cultural pluralism or the American Salad Bowl theory.

b. The Question of Free Choice. We know that freedom is one of the most cherished American values and that most of us are on our way to mainstream. However, many are still not fully ready for it yet, and thus, we should have a free choice. This is a human rights question. As of today, it is estimated that more than one thousand of Vietnamese Catholics have joined the local parishes in the Diocese. We congratulate them. However, it should be pointed out here that they still want to participate in many activities of our Vietnamese Catholic Community.

Your excellency,

We have just presented to you our views for your benevolent consideration ... As a new group in the Diocese, at least for the time being, we need to stay together to help one another, especially in our spiritual and Catholic life, for our salvation and that of our children. We also want to emphasize our mission as Catholics to bring more people to our Mother Catholic Church ... Everything we discussed in this letter tends to support the petition of almost 2,000 of our brothers and sisters in the idea of setting up a "personal parish" for the Vietnamese refugees in the Diocese of San Jose ...

Respectfully yours,

For the VNCC and Ad Hoc Committee

(signed) Tran Cong Thien, VNCC President, concurrently chair of
the Ad Hoc Committee; Former Secretary General of Pax Romana
Viet Nam and Consultant of Archbishop of Saigon
[12 others listed as Ad Hoc Committee]

Vietnamese Conflict in San Jose
(Documents 129–34)

According to Vietnamese theologian Rev. Peter C. Phan, "Vietnamese Catholics are deeply attached to their Vietnamese churches and hold their pastors in high esteem. They spare no resources to have their own churches and their own priests so as to be able to worship in their mother tongue and to preserve their religious and cultural customs." This description fits almost every Catholic immigrant group. This desire to have their own church and priest often resulted in conflict with the local bishops. While disputes between the Vietnamese communities and the local ordinaries did occur, Phan notes that "only extremely rarely has the relationship between the Vietnamese Catholic community and the local ordinary been marked by controversies" (Encyclopedia of American Catholic History, 1435). Two of these disputes, however, caught the attention

*of the media, one in Port Arthur, Texas, and the other in San Jose, California.
While these conflicts may not have been typical of the Vietnamese community,
they were typical of most immigrant communities in their adjustment to the
church in the United States. In the following document, reporter Teresa Baggot
provides the viewpoints of the different sides of the conflict that erupted in
San Jose. For a fuller exploration of Vietnamese-American Catholicism, see Peter
Phan, "Vietnamese Catholics in the United States: Christian Identity between
the Old and the New," and Carl L. Bangston III, "Vietnamese-American Catholicism: Transplanted and Flourishing," U.S. Catholic Historian 18 (winter 2000):
19–35, 36–53.*

129. Teresa Baggot, "Feud Erupts as Vietnamese Split over Pastor: Excommunications and Death Threats in San Jose Parish," 1986

The appointment of a new pastor to a Vietnamese Catholic mission here [San
Jose, Calif.] has opened a Pandora's box of excommunications, death threats,
defiance, fear and reports of communist infiltration...

Since July 21, a group of lay Vietnamese opposing the appointment have
occupied the property of Our Lady Queen of Martyrs Mission and prevented the pastor, Father Luu Dinh [Paul] Duong, from entering. Hundreds of
protesters have heckled participants at mass and during Duong's installation
ceremony. San Jose Bishop Pierre DuMaine excommunicated two dissident
leaders. Yet, while the controversy has been framed as an internal church
struggle, some say it is strictly a political power play.

Lay leaders have lined up on each side of the almost two-year dispute, which
centers on the rebels' demand for immediate establishment of a personal parish
and has revealed deep divisions within the 4,000 member Vietnamese Catholic
community. This, however, is the first time demonstrations have been held.

The dissidents consider Duong's assignment an indication of the bishop's
"scheme" to "destroy the unity of this community," according to Thien Cong
Tran, a local junior college counselor and chairman of the Vietnamese Catholic council. However, another member of the mission community, Van Vo,
a 37–year-old photographer who founded the committee for Defense of the
Catholic Faith to counter the rebels, said 95 percent of Vietnamese Catholics
in the area support DuMaine.

An estimated 70,000 Vietnamese have moved to Santa Clara County, of
which San Jose is the county seat, since 1975. About 10 percent are Roman
Catholic, according to Father Eugene Boyle, diocesan spokesperson...

The excommunicated leaders, Thien, 50, and Bai An Tran, 46, intend to
appeal their Aug. 18 censures for organizing large demonstrations that interrupted an Aug. 9 mass of unity at the diocesan cathedral and disrupted
Duong's Aug. 16 installation ceremony, where police cited two protesters for
disorderly conduct. The bishop has promised to lift the excommunication if
the two leaders publicly accept Duong.

The rebel group, composed of members of the Vietnamese Catholic Council, an unofficial organization unrecognized by the diocese, and the Committee for the Defense of Justice and Peace of the Diocese of San Jose, has taken its case against Duong to Archbishop Pio Laghi, papal pro-nuncio in the United States. After receiving a letter from Thien Cong Tran on behalf of the council, along with 1,454 Vietnamese Catholic signatures protesting the new pastor's appointment, Laghi said he would consult with DuMaine.

"In the meantime, I would ask you to avoid any action that might contribute to dissension or disharmony,..." Laghi wrote Thien.

The diocese has threatened to file a restraining order to force the dissidents to leave the church property, but has delayed action in the hope that recent negotiations with three unidentified intermediaries will forge a reconciliation. Both Thien and Bai claim the mission is rightfully the Vietnamese community's, because they have paid nearly half of the $340,000 price tag, including a $75,000 down payment and a $2,875 monthly mortgage. The diocese made the loan to purchase the property and holds the title. The leaders warned of the "danger" of any efforts to evict them.

"The faithful are ready to confront the police power," said Bai, a real estate broker who was a judge in Vietnam. "Nobody can imagine the situation."

While Bai contended his group of "devoted Christians" will not resort to violence, but, like Jesus, turn the other cheek, Thien was not so sure.

"I have the feeling there might be violence or strong resistance from our faithful" if they are evicted, he said. "We will fight for our rights. If we're attacked, we are ready to defend ourselves."

DuMaine and the new pastor have received death threats,... according to Boyle. Bai scoffed at the notion that his group could have any part in such threats. But, according to Sister of Mercy Marilyn Lacey, diocesan director of refugee resettlement, even some of DuMaine's lay Vietnamese supporters fear for their lives.

"They're playing hardball," Lacey said of the dissidents. "I am convinced this has nothing to do with religion. There's insidious motivation of other sorts, political, and perhaps economic." She said the previous pastor, Father Joseph Nguyen Van Tinh, whom dissidents claim Duong deposed, allowed them to "wield considerable influence and power." Boyle said Tinh, appointed in November 1985 as the mission's first pastor, requested a sabbatical leave he is currently taking in West Germany. Tinh was also the diocesan director of the first Vietnamese apostolate.

Describing herself as "deeply involved" in ministry to Vietnamese people, Lacey said she was appalled at the irreverence of screaming protests she witnessed inside a church. She likened the din to a "rock concert."

"It's simply not the kind of behavior you see from Vietnamese Catholics," she said. "Something else is going on."

Said Bai of the protest, "We have no choice; we had to react."

Because a mission, known in the new code of canon law as a quasi-parish, must provide all the sacramental, educational and pastoral services of a normal parish, Boyle said he also believes something more is at issue than a personal parish.

"My personal feeling is what they truly want is a personal power base and a political power base," he said. Many minority groups throughout history have gained power through church communities, he added.

Bai said his group's actions have a "religious purpose" only, but "may have a political effect." Lacey said she had heard that radio broadcasts and newspapers published in Hanoi last month are "celebrating" the discord in the California Vietnamese community. "The word is all around San Jose that several of the inside circle have known ties with the government of Vietnam," she added, referring to the rebels. Bai emphatically denied any such connection in his group.

The dissidents contend they "deserve" a personal parish and have shown all the signs of stability and unity, as well as the financial resources, required by the bishop before he will approve their request. Boyle said the diocese has seen no evidence of the dissident's means to raise as much money as is needed. Financial means alone, he added, are not sufficient to satisfy the bishop.

The rebels also claim that the bishop wants to assimilate them quickly into the mainstream (which Boyle denied), and that many of the nation's 17 Vietnamese personal parishes have fewer members. They also stress that a "mission" no longer exists in canon law and that they have a majority, at least 2,000 people, on their side.

"After Vatican II, the faithful are very important members in the church," said Bai. "I think the church is a democracy. If not, we have to do something to bring democracy to the church"...

DuMaine's supporters claim the sophisticated dissident leaders mislead people by mistranslating the bishop's statements of his intentions. Lacey agreed. A slick magazine, called *Right Reason* in Vietnamese, published by the rebels for the past few months, is "full of lies," she said. Bai denied it.

Vo said his group will try to "neutralize" the dissidents' efforts by publishing articles in Vietnamese newspapers. They have also started boycotting the dissident leaders' businesses. Though he fears physical retaliation from the rebels and has spent nights with his family away from home as a result, Vo said, "we have to protect the church, the truth, the faith. I feel that God gives me the strength to do so." He guessed the dispute could last up to a year.

Said Bai, "We believe in our right reason. The church is very powerful. We still believe we are going to win."

National Catholic Reporter, 5 September 1986, 4. Printed with permission of the *National Catholic Reporter* and Teresa Baggot.

130. Diocese of San Jose Report, 1988

As the dispute lingered on, the Diocese of San Jose ultimately sold the land to the dissidents but refused to allow them to hold Catholic services on the property. A new center for the Vietnamese Catholics was sought. Despite this arrangement, the dissidents continued to hold services on the property. In the following document, the whole controversy is explained from the Diocese of San Jose's point of view. Following that is Bishop DuMaine's letter to the Vietnamese community explaining his actions.

Diocese of San Jose — Office of Vicar General
MEMO August 1, 1988
TO Priests of the Diocese of San Jose
    ...In 1982, the Diocese of San Jose purchased property on Singleton Road ...to be used as a Pastoral Center for the Vietnamese Catholics. This made it possible for the Vietnamese apostolate to set up an office, to provide catechetical instruction, and to celebrate weekly Masses for the Vietnamese Catholics. In 1985, it was elevated to the status of a Mission and thus Masses of obligation (Sunday and Holy Day) as well as Baptisms, Marriages and Funerals could be celebrated at the facility.

In July, 1986, with the appointment of Fr. Paul Duong as pastor, some members of the Vietnamese Catholic Community took possession of the Mission and prevented Fr. Duong from entering and exercising his ministry. Because of this, all priests were removed from the Mission. The dissident group continued to occupy the Mission to prevent Fr. Duong from coming back at another time.

In September, 1986, those who were occupying the Mission filed a lawsuit against the Diocese for "Quiet Title" — claiming that they should hold title to the Mission, not the Diocese. In March, 1987, as those occupying the Mission still were not allowing Fr. Duong to enter and exercise his ministry, the Diocese filed a cross-complaint...

    ...Before going to trial, the parties involved were mandated by the court to participate in a settlement conference...

    ...[A] settlement was reached through which the Diocese would sell the property to a group of Vietnamese people for a cultural center...

    ...The Diocese refused to sell the property to "The Vietnamese Catholic Community, Inc." as this would indicate recognition of the group as "The Vietnamese Catholic Community, Inc."...

    ...Once the property is purchased from the Diocese, all signs and religious articles that might identify it as a Catholic Church facility will be removed and returned to the Diocese. It was clearly stated during the settlement conference that the Bishop has denied permission to hold religious services [there]...

131. Diocese of San Jose — Office of the Bishop, 1988

December 2, 1988

Dear Friends,

I am writing this letter to all the Vietnamese Catholics of the Diocese of San Jose to apprise you of the status of the Vietnamese Mission of Our Lady, Queen of Martyrs...

1. I am conducting an intensive search...to identify an appropriate permanent location for the Mission of Our Lady, Queen of Martyrs...

2. ...The pastor and parish staff will continue to provide and increase the schedule of weekend Masses in Vietnamese (currently offered at four parish locations with attendance over 2,300)...and other normal parish services.

3. The former mission site...no longer belongs to the parish or to the Diocese of San Jose...

4. I will not authorize, and I have explicitly forbidden any Roman Catholic Masses, sacraments, sacramentals, public devotions, or pastoral services on these private and secular premises...

5. In accord with this prohibition, any priest who officiates at religious services on these premises does so without the approval of the Bishop of San Jose...

I want to take this occasion to express my abiding gratitude to all the Vietnamese Catholics of the Diocese of San Jose, especially those who joined me on Thanksgiving Day for the first solemn celebration of the Feast of the Vietnamese Martyrs.

I repeat to all of you the assurances I gave the more than 1,000 Vietnamese Catholics assembled for that event: I will continue, with the zealous help of the three full time Vietnamese priests I have assigned to the pastoral care of our Vietnamese Catholics, to provide ample and accessible sacramental and parish services in accord with the language and traditions which our Vietnamese faithful properly want to preserve and which greatly enrich the Catholic life of our local church...

Sincerely in Christ,
(signed) Pierre DuMaine
Bishop of San Jose

Printed with permission of Diocese of San Jose.

132. Misuse of Former Mission Site, 1993

By 1993, the "dissidents" continued to hold religious services. In the follow-ing letter a San Jose diocesan official chastises a visiting Vietnamese priest for offering services at the former center.

Vicar for Parish and Pastoral Ministry — Diocese of San Jose

April 2, 1993

Rev. Nguyen Duc Viet Chau, SSS
Gretna, LA

Dear Father Nguyen:

It has come to my attention that the Rev. Joseph Nguyen Quoc Hai is intending to preach a mission during Holy Week here in the Diocese of San Jose at a secular site, used for religious celebrations contrary to the explicit directives of the local bishop...

Clearly, Father Nguyen Hai's preaching will be interpreted as an act of public defiance of the Bishop of San Jose and will be a cause of great scandal to the thousands of Vietnamese Catholics who participate in the religious and sacramental life of Our Lady Queen of Martyrs Vietnamese Mission. This action of Father Nguyen Hai will add to the present scandalous action of a priest who is conducting a ministry at this site against the expressed will of the local bishop and against the direct obedience of his provincial minister.

Since Father Nguyen Hai presents himself as the Vice President of the Federation of Vietnamese Clergy and Religious in the USA, this entire organ-ization will suffer if Father Nguyen Hai proceeds with his intended actions in public defiance of the local ordinary...

Sincerely,
(signed) Alexander C. Larkin
Vicar for Parish and Pastoral Ministry

Printed with permission of the Diocese of San Jose.

133. Letter of Bishop Pierre DuMaine to St. Patrick Proto-Cathedral, 27 November 1993

In 1993, Bishop DuMaine sought to defuse the tension by naming the historic St. Patrick's Church in downtown San Jose as a permanent site for the Viet-namese mission. St. Patrick's had served successive waves of immigrants, most recently Spanish-speaking immigrants from Mexico and Central America.

Dear Friends,

Over the past few years, as you know, there have been major changes in the population of our Diocese of San Jose and in the pastoral needs of our Catholic people...

Foremost among these developments has been the changing character of downtown San Jose and of St. Patrick's Parish, as well as the need for a permanent home for the Vietnamese Mission of Our Lady Queen of Martyrs.

Today I want to announce the first stage of a process designed to meet both of these realities.

I am appointing Father Joseph Van Thu as pastor of St. Patrick Parish and Proto-Cathedral, effective, January 1, 1994. He will continue to serve as Pastor of the Vietnamese Mission of Our Lady Queen of Martyrs. Father Van Thu will be responsible for maintaining all present parish services at St. Patrick as well as the liturgical and pastoral services of the mission in various locations throughout the diocese. To assist him in his ministry, Father Robert Moran, Father Dominic Dinh and Father Peter Chinh will continue in their respective positions at St. Patrick and Our Lady Queen of Martyrs...

I have asked Father Van Thu and Father Moran to work with the Pastoral Councils of St. Patrick's and Our Lady Queen of Martyrs to develop a Pastoral Plan to address the needs of the trilingual and tricultural population that now comprises St. Patrick Parish: English, Spanish and Vietnamese...

Pierre DuMaine,
Bishop of San Jose

Printed with permission of the Diocese of San Jose.

134. Office of the Bishop — Diocese of San Jose, 1999

In 1999, after almost twenty years of struggle, the Vietnamese Catholic community was given its personal parish. St. Patrick's was made a personal parish for Vietnamese Catholics, but it also retained its status as a territorial parish. The only group to complain about this development were the Spanish-speaking parishioners who believed the new designation of the parish would reduce ministry to Latino Catholics.

April 16, 1999

Dear Friends,

We wish to announce to you a revised pastoral plan for ministry to all the Vietnamese Catholics in the Diocese of San Jose...

In response to the long-standing request for a Personal Parish by many in the community of Vietnamese Catholic faithfuls, the Mission of Our Lady Queen of Martyrs will be elevated to the status of a Personal Parish, known as St. Patrick Parish. At the same time, St. Patrick Parish will remain a territorial parish for all the Catholics who choose to affiliate with that parish, regardless of their language or ethnicity. It should be noted that St. Patrick Parish is the third oldest in the Diocese and has a venerable tradition of ministry to every influx of immigrants since 1871.

The new Vietnamese Cultural Center on White Road will be known as "Our Lady, Queen of Martyrs, Vietnamese Cultural Center." It will be the gathering place for all the Vietnamese of this diocese, regardless of their parish affiliation.

In further recognition of the maturing of the community of Vietnamese Catholic faithfuls in the Diocese, we will name a priest to the new position of Vicar for Vietnamese Ministry...

> Sincerely,
> Pierre DuMaine, Bishop of San Jose
> Patrick J. McGrath, Coadjutor Bishop of San Jose

Printed with permission of the Diocese of San Jose.

135. Generational Concerns in Sacramento, California, 1991

As with all immigrant groups, the problem of second-generation Vietnamese was serious. Vietnamese youth were caught between the traditional world of their parents and the new ultramodern United States. They were at home in neither world. Many parents felt helpless in assisting their children's adaptation. In the following document, Vietnamese writer Anthony Lam reflects on a bizarre case. Though the incident is extraordinary, it does highlight the difficulties of first- and second-generation Vietnamese in the United States.

Love, Money, Prison, Sin, Revenge, by Andrew Lam

On the afternoon of April 4, 1991, fifteen years, eleven months and twenty-seven days after the end of the Vietnam War, four Vietnamese youths armed with semiautomatic pistols stormed into a Good Guys electronics store on Stockton Boulevard in Sacramento and held forty-one people hostage. Speaking heavily accented and broken English, they issued what the *Sacramento Bee* described as "a series of bizarre demands." They wanted a helicopter to fly to Thailand so they could fight the Vietcong, four million dollars, four bulletproof vests, and forty pieces of 1,000 year-old ginseng roots.

While a crowd, some enthusiasts equipped with their own camcorders, gathered across the street, TV reporters informed viewers that three of the gunmen were brothers — Loi Khac Nguyen, twenty-one; Pham Khac Nguyen, nineteen; and Long Khac Nguyen, seventeen — and that the last, Coung Tran, sixteen, was Long Nguyen's best friend. The Nguyen brothers had come from a poor Vietnamese Catholic family headed by an ex-sergeant of the South Vietnamese army. All four were altar boys. Three of the youths had dropped out of school or had been expelled. None had been able to find a steady job.

The gunmen could be seen on live television behind the store's glass doors, strolling back and forth with their firearms, bound hostages at their feet. Sacramento County Sheriff Glen Craig, who had implanted listening devices in the store, reported that the gunmen were jubilant at seeing themselves...on TV — "Oh, ah, we're going to be movie stars!" The sheriff had also told reporters that the gunmen belonged to a loosely knit gang called the Oriental

Boys — an error, as it turned out, since the police couldn't prove membership in any gang...

[The stand-off ended with the SWAT team storming the building and killing three of the four young men. The latter, in turn, had killed three hostages and wounded eight others.]

As I watched this tragedy unfold on my TV set that night, I remember being overwhelmed by an irrational fear. It was the fear that the Vietnam War had somehow been renewed by those gunmen and by those helicopters hovering over the store. And though I was on the safe side of the TV screen now and judging their barbaric acts, I was not without this singular sense of foreboding: Six years ago I could have been one of them.

If the story of the Good Guys ended in carnage on the linoleum floor of an electronics store, it began an ocean and an epic journey away, nourished by numerous subterranean streams. It is those streams I am foundering in. I am at once too close and too far from their story. Though an American journalist now, I came to this country as a Vietnamese refugee, the son of a South Vietnamese army officer. The young men and I, through our fathers, are veterans of a civil war we never actually fought. In their demands, I hear the thematic echo of vengeance, which forms and shapes all Vietnamese youths who grow up in America. Perhaps all this binds me to the Good Guys hostage-takers nearly two decades after the last U.S. helicopter hovered over a burning Saigon before heading toward the South China Sea...

[The article then explores the youths' fascination with "high-tech consumerism" — TV, movies, video games.]

...Thanks to CNN, satellite dishes, cable TVs, VCRs, jumbo jets, camcorders, and fax machines, integration turns retro-future-active. Technology renews old myths, shrinks oceans, packages memories, melts borders, rejuvenates old passions, redefines the assimilation process. For Asian children immigrating to America today, their parents' homelands are no longer as far away as they were for children in earlier times...

Two days after the Good Guys Siege, a *Sacramento Bee* photo that ran the length of the page showed the Nguyen brothers' parents standing in their living room as if facing a firing squad. Though stricken with grief, Bim Khac and Sao Thi Nguyen admitted journalists into their tiny two-bedroom unit...

The photo shows a sagging sofa, a VCR and, of course, a large TV set. On top of the TV stands a South Vietnamese flag — three red horizontal stripes against a gold background — representing a country that no longer exists. On the opposite wall, a three-tier shrine displays crucifixes, statues of Mary, Joseph, and Jesus and various martyred saints, all with mournful faces.

The Nguyens and their six children spent four months in a refugee camp in Indonesia before coming to the United States in the early 1980s. In Sacramento they were receiving Aid to Families with Dependent Children. The ex-sergeant from the South Vietnamese army, who is active in church, said through an interpreter that he was no help to his children when it came to explaining American things such as homework or news on TV. Still, wasn't what he wanted for his children the same as what any Vietnamese parent wants — that they do well in school and keep "Vietnamese traditions"?

"Please tell the people of Sacramento I am very sorry for what my sons have done," the patriarch offered. Asked how his quiet obedient boys wound up becoming hostage-takers, Nguyen and his wife provided only a miserable silence.

This is the silence of an older generation of Vietnamese refugees who no longer feel anchored anywhere but in their impoverished homes. The exterior landscape belongs to America, strange and nonsensical, not their true home. Inside, many Vietnamese refugees tend to raise their children with stern rules — the way they themselves were raised back home. Vietnamese is spoken, with familial personal pronouns — youngest son, older sister, aunt, father, great uncle and so on — lacing every sentence to remind the speakers and listeners of their status in the Confucian hierarchical scheme of things. These parents are unprepared for children who lead dual lives, who may in fact commit rash and incomprehensibly violent acts — not at all the docile and obedient Vietnamese children they had hoped to raise.

"They are no longer really Vietnamese, nor are they really Americans," said a former teacher, who recently came from Vietnam and now lives on welfare in Sacramento, of his own children. He called their tangled assimilation "crippled Americanization."

For Loi, Pham and Long Nguyen and Coung Tran, who failed school and grew up between the Good Guys electronics store and the Ngoc Thao [a video store that featured Asian martial arts films], there existed two separate notions — notoriety and revenge, revenge being the stronger impulse. One encourages public displays (i.e. confessing on "Oprah," or holding shoppers hostage and giving incoherent speeches) that may lead mainstream America to acknowledge that they exist. The other fulfills the old man's extraterritorial passion — "helicopters to Thailand to kill Viet Cong" — and rejects America as a wasteland.

To grow up Vietnamese in America, after all, is to grow up with the legacy of belonging to the loser's side and to endure all that entails. To grow up in America is to desire individual fame and glory, a larger sense of self. Driving on Stockton Boulevard, it suddenly occurs to me that, while I myself have learned to walk that strange Vietnamese-American hyphen, it continues to hurl young and hapless Vietnamese down into a dark and bottomless pit...

...But there were deeper currents that fed this second-wave refugee family that the media failed to detect. According to one Vietnamese who has been their social worker and knows the family well, the Nguyen parents had been burned not once but twice by communism. They fled to the South in 1954, when Catholics were persecuted by Ho Chi Minh and his army, and they fled Saigon as boat people a few years after the communists ransacked the south in 1975. Communist crimes, Vietcong crimes, human-rights abuses by the Hanoi regime — all are meticulously documented by Vietnamese Catholic newspapers and magazines in the United States. The Vietcong, whom the eldest Nguyen boy barely remembered, nevertheless figured as the prime villains in the household cosmology — the chief cause of their family's suffering in America, the robbers of their father's dignity, blasphemers of the crucifix in their church, called the Vietnamese Catholic Martyrs...

...[N]o matter how articulate a Vietnamese becomes,... when we set foot on the American shore, history is already against us. Vietnam goes on without us. America goes on without acknowledging us...

The Vietnamese refugee's first self-assessment in America is, inevitably, of his own helplessness... As for the Vietnamese child, at some point he comes to the brutal realization that "his" side has lost, and "his" nation is gone; that his parents are inarticulate fools in a new country called America, and he must face the outside world alone...

I am not a Catholic. There is no three-tiered shrine in my family's living room for martyred saints. My mother is Buddhist but she stopped praying for a time when we lost the war. My father, born a French citizen when Vietnam was a colony, was given a Christian name but never went to church...

"The Northerners are fanatics," my father said at dinner one night after the Good Guys incident... "The Northerners immolate themselves and talk too readily of martyrdom... Those boys must have ingested all the plots for tragedy from their Northern Catholic parents..."

...According to the *Sacramento Bee*, the Nguyen brothers had folded their arms, the Vietnamese filial pious gesture, and asked their parents for permission to leave the house that fateful day. This image haunts me. They tried to bring dignity to their father by fighting his war. They coveted being good Vietnamese sons; to assuage the old man's grief, the young man must defeat his old man's enemy...

De Tran, Andrew Lam, and Hai Dai Nguyen, eds., *Once upon a Dream...The Vietnamese-American Experience* (Kansas City: Andrews and McMeel, 1995), 80–89. Printed with permission of Andrew Lam. Andrew Lam is associate editor of Pacific News Service.

Korean Immigrants

136. Anselm Kyongsuk Min, On Korean Catholicism, 1999

Korean immigration to the United States did not begin in earnest until after 1970. Prior to that, small numbers of immigrants had arrived at the turn of the twentieth century and again after the Korean War (1950-53). After 1970 Korean immigration exploded; the Korean population rose from 70,000 in 1970

*to more than 350,000 by 1980 to more than 700,000 by 1990. Large settle-
ments were established in Los Angeles, New York, and Chicago. While a large
percentage of Koreans are Christians, only about 10 percent of the immigrants
are Catholic. In the following document, Dr. Anselm Kyongsuk Min, professor of religion and theology at Claremont Graduate University, reflects on the
background of his Korean Catholic faith.*

... I was born Kyongsuk Min, or rather Min Kyongsuk in proper Korean, Min
standing for my clan, Kyong for my generation and shared by my brother and
three sisters, and Suk for me as an individual, although the generational and
individual components are usually combined — Kyongsuk — to make up the
equivalent of the personal name in Western languages. When I was born in
Korea in 1940, my family had not yet become Christians; they were Confucian in human relations and shamanist in times of crisis. The country was
under Japanese domination, well noted for its brutality, to the point of forcing
Koreans to adopt Japanese names and drafting teenage girls for sexual service
to front-line troops fighting an imperialist war in the Pacific.

One day in 1944, one of my two uncles was away on a trip through
Kangwondo, the province directly east of Seoul, on his mission, according
to a family legend, of delivering funds collected at home to the Korean
troops fighting the Japanese in Manchuria. He was crossing a bridge, fell, and
drowned to death. Like all mothers, my grandmother was inconsolable with
tears for days and weeks. Finally, my father suggested that she join a church.
When she was baptized and received into the Catholic Church, so were all
in the family under her matriarchal authority, my mother, aunt, myself, and
my brother, but not the adult males, my grandfather, father, and uncle, who
joined the Church many years later. It was and still is a Korean custom to
give the newly baptized a *bonmyong*, a name "proper" for a person born into
a new, true life in Christ. This was different from the *sogmyong* or "secular"
name given at birth. The "proper" name was taken from that of a saint, often
the saint whose feast day coincided with one's own birthday. I was born on
April 21 (according to the lunar calendar), so I was named after St. Anselm...

My earliest and most indelible memory of Church life is that of the Sunday
Latin Mass followed by Benediction of the Blessed Sacrament in the evening. I
still remember the scent of incense, the Kyrie and Gloria to the Credo to the
Agnus Dei, as well as the Tantum Ergo and O Salutaris Hostia. As I joined
the altar boys, I went to Mass not only on Sundays but also on weekdays, especially during the summer and winter holidays. Serving the 6:30 Mass under
the dim light of candles, even on freezing winter mornings, was an experience of divine presence complete with mystery, silence, awe, and grace. Also
deeply etched in my memory is the spectacle of the annual National Eucharistic Congress that would begin at the seminary and proceed, in a public display
of Catholic faith, to the Myongdong Cathedral across town. Again I remem-

ber the seminary choir singing the Eucharistic hymns in Gregorian chant, so uplifting, angelic, and mystical.

Korean Catholicism dates back to 1784, when a government official named Sunghoon Ri, baptized Peter in Beijing, returned and baptized fellow Confucian scholars. The first hundred years were years of persecution, producing over 10,000 martyrs, of whom 103 were canonized by Pope John Paul II in Seoul in 1984. Originally a Church of the scholar-official class, as persecution intensified it became largely a Church of the poor and uneducated. As a mission of the Foreign Mission Society of Paris, Korean Catholicism was a transplant of the French in its theology, liturgy and spirituality. Receiving its freedom of religion in 1886, the Church spread its roots among farmers, concentrating on parochial work rather than, as did Presbyterians and Methodists, on medical work and education, out of which came the predominant majority of Korean leaders of the first half of the twentieth century.

June 25, 1950, is an unforgettable day for every Korean over fifty. On that day began the Korean War (1950–1953) that would shake Korean life to its very foundation for decades to come. Some three million people out of a population of less than thirty million were killed, maimed, wounded, or displaced. Whole cities were razed to the ground through street battles and saturation bombings from the air. It was a period of universal, unrelieved suffering for Koreans. It was also a period of religious awakening and conversion for many. The war was an existential demonstration of the vanity of all things, the fragility of life, and the radical perversity of human nature. I too felt there was no hope for the world, apart from God.

It was my grandmother's simple piety that nourished my faith. She was the one who insisted on our going to church every Sunday, our saying morning and evening prayers, our going to confession regularly, and our fulfilling other obligations of traditional Catholic piety. She was most active in the parish, involved in women's activities, never failing to visit the sick and dying. She was also a most devoted wife, mother, and grandmother at home, even receiving an award given to devoted wives. Without the persistence of my grandmother, I would not have become a Catholic; without the enduring example of her piety, simple and unsophisticated, perhaps I would not have remained a Catholic even to this day...

Like most Korean Catholics of my generation I grew up and spent most of my youth liking and taking for granted Korean Catholicism in all its Western forms, in its theology, liturgy, and spirituality, which still largely remain translations of *Roman* Catholicism even after all the postconciliar changes and adaptations. Like most Koreans of my generation I also grew up liking and taking for granted American culture, its language, its commercial goods, its political ideologies of free enterprise, democracy, and anti-Communism, Presidents Washington and Lincoln, even General MacArthur. Americans saved us first from the Japanese and then from North Korean Communism. We were all so eager to learn English and study in America. I remember, as a high school senior, memorizing Washington's Farewell Address and Lincoln's Gettysburg Address. In the fifties any questioning of Korean Catholicism for its Western form would have been simply unthinkable; to be Catholic was to be *Roman*, period. To question American presence in Korea would be tantamount to defending Communism...

Anselm Kyongsuk Min, "From Autobiography to Fellowship of Others: Reflections on Doing Ethnic Theology Today," in Peter C. Phan and Jung Young Lee, eds., *Journeys at the Margin: Toward an Autobiographical Theology in American-Asian Perspective* (Collegeville, Minn.: Liturgical Press, 1999), 135–37, 144. Published with permission of Anselm Kyongsuk Min.

137. Korean Pastoral Mission, San Francisco, 1980

As with previous immigrant groups, Koreans wanted a parish of their own, in which the Korean language was spoken. In the 1970s, the Korean community in San Francisco began to grow. Catholic ministry to the Koreans was provided by San Francisco's Japanese National Parish, St. Francis Xavier. This arrangement did not satisfy the Koreans, who petitioned for their own parish. The following document decrees the erection of a Korean Catholic pastoral mission in an old San Francisco parish, Holy Cross, that had been closed previously due to declining attendance.

DECREE: Erecting a Korean Catholic Pastoral Mission

1) We hereby establish a Korean Catholic Pastoral Mission under the provisions of the Constitution *Exsul Familia* of Pope Pius XII, August 1, 1952, Caput IV, nn.34–39, and the Motu Propio *Pastoralis Migratorum Cura* of Pope Paul VI, August 15, 1969, Caput IV, B, n.33, Caput A, and Caput VI.

2) This Mission will serve all native Korean and Korean speaking people who live in the Archdiocese, who are not affiliated with a territorial parish and choose to affiliate with this Mission. The choice shall be signified by enrollment in the Mission records.

3) This Mission will have its center of worship at Holy Cross Church in San Francisco.

4) This Mission is to continue for as long as the spiritual needs of the Korean people in the Archdiocese require the use of their mother language.

5) The Missionary of this Mission shall be appointed by the Archbishop of San Francisco.

6) Such Missionary will have personal and cumulative jurisdiction over those affiliated with the Mission. Thus, any of these has the right to choose to receive the sacraments either at the Mission or from the local pastors. He will also enjoy all the faculties and be bound by all the duties which belong to pastors under the laws of the Church and Statutes of the Archdiocese

of San Francisco (including the power of assisting validly at the marriages of couples of whom one or the other is affiliated with the Mission).

7) Koreans and Korean speaking people who are affiliated with territorial parishes may attend religious services in this Mission. The Missionary may marry them or baptize their children without the permission of their respective proper pastors.

John Rafael Quinn,
Archbishop of San Francisco

June 26, 1980

Archives of the Archdiocese of San Francisco. Published with permission.

138. Bishop of Overseas Korean Catholics, 1981

As with previous immigrants, Catholics in the country of origin expressed deep concern over the fate of their countrymen and women in the United States. The Korean Episcopal Conference appointed a Korean bishop to monitor the care Korean Catholics were receiving in the United States. One wonders how Irish-American bishops at the end of the nineteenth century would have responded to this appointment.

Bishop of Cheju to Archbishop of San Francisco, 20 April 1981

Your Excellency,

First of all, I must introduce myself. I am the bishop of Cheju Diocese, a large island located southwest of the Korean Peninsula, and also the administrator of the Korean Episcopal Pastoral Commission for Overseas Korean Catholics. In writing this letter I wish to send you my greetings, and also ask for your special pastoral concern for the Koreans living in your diocese.

At present, there are approximately 500,000 Korean immigrants who live in the United States. Each year the number is increasing by 20,000 to 30,000. Also, presently, there are twenty-two priests devoted to their full time pastoral care and seven working part time.

I ask Your Excellency's special care for Korean Catholics residing within your diocese. May I also dare to request your positive support for Fr. Gregory Cho's pastoral ministry in working among the Korean faithful there?

Sometime when I am in your area for the pastoral visitation of Korean Catholics I hope to be able to meet you personally and discuss these matters more fully.

Wishing Your Excellency every blessing, I remain.

Michael J. Pak, Bishop of Cheju

Administrator of the Pastoral Commission of the Episcopal Conference
of Korea for Overseas Korean Catholics

Archives of the Archdiocese of San Francisco. Published with permission.

Other Asian Immigrants

139. Report on Asian Hearings: The Experience of Church in the United States, 1990

The ever-increasing flow of immigrants from Asia consisted of other groups be-sides the Chinese, Japanese, Filipinos, Vietnamese, and Koreans. Large numbers came from Cambodia, Laos, India, and the Pacific Rim. In response to the "Asian presence," the National Catholic Educational Association, the United States Catholic Conference's Office of Migration and Refugee Services, and the Office of Pastoral Research and Planning of the Archdiocese of New York held national hearings between October 1989 and January 1990 in which Asian parents, clergy, and lay ministers were asked to share their experiences and concerns. Non-Asian ministers who worked with the Asian community also testified. Hearings were held in the dioceses of Baltimore, Boston, Chicago, Honolulu, Los Angeles, New York, Oakland, Philadelphia, Portland, San Francisco, Seattle, and St. Paul–Minneapolis. The following document provides a brief summary of one aspect of the hearings.

Most respondents see the United States as a place of opportunity and freedom. Thus, they believe there is a possibility of "making it" here. They see profound differences in many cultural values between the United States and their homelands; however, the ethic of hard work is seen as common. They want everything for their children and experience deep pain in the value clashes which are arising between themselves and their children[,] who are being educated in U.S. schools...

Especially poignant were the new immigrants' and refugees' stories of their search for an experience of community within the U.S. Church, while at the same time struggling to earn a living, find shelter for their families, educate their children, and forge an identity within this new society.

The respondents reported that they experience the Church in the U.S. as unwelcoming. "Coldness" was a descriptor used on many occasions. There were many reports of attending Mass in an "American" parish and feeling totally isolated. Because Asians were accustomed to spending a great deal of time in Church, both before and after Mass, in personal and communal prayer, they find the rigid Sunday Mass schedule offensive...

They feel they are barely tolerated in the parish and at Mass. Many have been deeply offended at having to pay rent for a Church in order to have Mass in their native language. Also, the time set aside for their Mass was generally at an inconvenient time such as mid-afternoon on Sunday. There were many such reports during the hearings. As hard workers, they indicate they would offer the Church far more financially than what they were being charged for rent if only the Church would welcome them and not put them in a position of being paying clients. They feel like visitors and see this as a reflection of American "big business."

A further example relating to money is the consistent report about the use of collection envelopes. Again, this is seen as offensive and bureaucratic — not a reflection of the Church the respondents knew in their homelands.

There was a strong call for ethnic, pastoral "centers" which, after responding to the enculturation needs of the various Asian ethnic communities, could dissolve. This was not a demand for national or personal parishes; to the contrary, the people voiced specific fears that such parishes might lead to separate Catholic churches within the U.S. and this was not seen as desirable by the Asian respondents...

Related to this, the respondents asked for priests and ministers who speak their language(s) to minister to their communities...

From the perspective of Asian priests and religious, though they would not speak out publicly, many have quietly experienced deep frustration in their ministry in the U.S. They express a sense of isolation and loneliness, and a lack of support from the diocese...

A caution was raised by some diocesan staff personnel about difficulties encountered with some Asian priests in terms of ecclesiology. In some instances, these priests have not experienced the evolution of Vatican II — its directions and practices — and there are resultant conflicts within parishes.

While, in general, the Asians' understanding of Church comes out of a very traditional experience of the Catholic Church as noted above, this is not the case across the board...

> *A Catholic Response to the Asian Presence* (Washington, D.C.: National Catholic Education Association, 1990), xi–xii. Reprinted with permission.

140. Recommendations to the Catholic Church at National and Local Levels from National Hearings of Asian Catholic Communities in the United States, 1990

The hearings concluded with a series of recommendations. Of special note is the call for an Asian bishop — the old longing of previous immigrant groups.

The major call was for acknowledgment of the voice of Asian communities within the church in the United States through the following actions:

- A National Convocation of representatives of Asian Catholic communities in the U.S.;

- The naming of an Asian Bishop in the U.S.;

- A National Pastoral Letter on the Asian Presence in the U.S.

In addition, the respondents at the hearings offered many recommendations to Church ministers and educators. The following represent those most often cited as needs:

1. Welcoming committees within parishes;

2. "Centers" where liturgies, etc., can take place in native language;

3. Counseling for parents to assist them in dealing with cultural conflicts with children;

4. Leadership training for Asians, especially youth;

5. Language training for teachers, priests, and ministers;

6. Knowledge of and sensitivity to special Asian feasts and celebrations . . .

7. After-school programs for children of parents who work . . .

8. Training in cultural sensitivity for clergy, educators, and ministers;

9. Adult education programs for parents, especially ESL [English as a Second Language] classes;

10. Financial assistance to enable children to attend Catholic schools;

11. Ethnic studies in Catholic schools; curricular adaptations to reflect Eastern traditions, cultures;

12. Recruitment of Asian teachers and catechists;

13. Training of laity to be catechists and ministers . . .

14. Cultural awareness and language training in seminaries;

15. National Directory of catechetical materials available in various languages;

16. Acceptance of Asian peoples on parish and diocesan policy-making bodies.

A Catholic Response to the Asian Presence (Washington, D.C.: National Catholic Education Association, 1990), xvii. Reprinted with permission.

Part 6

NEW MODELS AND CONCERNS

Introduction

Many Catholics in the United States believed their church had reached its zenith in 1960 with the election of an Irish-American Catholic, John F. Kennedy, as president of the United States. To them, the election laid to rest the historic fears of the church's adversaries that a faithful Catholic could not be accepted as a loyal American. In fact Catholics by the millions had shown their loyalty with active military service in World War II. Their devotion to American values was reinforced in the public mind by their staunch anti-Communism during the subsequent Cold War. In that era, the American Catholic community welcomed Catholic refugees or "displaced persons" from central and eastern Europe who had fled Communism. By the late 1950s, they welcomed additional Catholic refugees fleeing from Cuba in the wake of Fidel Castro's imposition of Communism there. Thus, American Catholics, sharing in the country's postwar prosperity, gloried in their increasing economic success and their newfound acceptance by the American culture.

Catholics' momentary contentment was short-lived, however, as the events of the 1960s rocked American Catholics out of their reverie. Three major developments dramatically altered the accustomed patterns of American Catholic life. First, the Catholic Church initiated dramatic changes to its internal life with the reforms of Vatican II. Second, the social order was rent by the continual protests of the civil rights and antiwar movements and the counterculture that challenged traditional sources of authority. Third, and most important for this study, a new era of mass immigration began in response to the Immigration Act of 1965. These developments profoundly reshaped the U.S. Catholic Church.

The renewal of mass immigration at a time of such profound social and ecclesial change stimulated new models for ministering to immigrants. For most of the history of the U.S. Catholic Church, American Catholic leaders believed their church's main role was to assist immigrants to be good citizens as well as faithful Catholics. In other words, the church was to assist the Americanization of immigrants. This confidence in American life came under sharp attack during the 1960s as protest after protest associated the United States with the evils of racism, war, and imperialism. The suggestion to "Americanize" someone seemed incomprehensible. In addition, the various civil and ethnic rights movements called for greater respect and consideration to be given to minority cultures and peoples. Old-fashioned Americanization was no longer in vogue.

At the same time, Vatican II proclaimed a new understanding of the church as the "people of God" and placed the church at the service of the world. Accordingly, the church's approach to evangelization incorporated a respect for the social and spiritual aspects of ethnic cultures as expressed in their religious practices, traditions, and celebrations. A new model of ministry had emerged. It did so in time for the arrival of a new wave of refugees in the 1970s from Vietnam, Laos, Cambodia, El Salvador, Nicaragua, and elsewhere. The concluding documents reflect the church's varied responses to these new demands.

141. Cultural Pluralism as New Paradigm, 1985

Following the Immigration Act of 1965, immigration to the San Francisco Bay Area increased dramatically. The new immigrants came from quite different places of origin compared to earlier immigration. The bulk of immigrants now came from Asia and Latin America. In response to the new immigrants the Archdiocese of San Francisco created the Secretariat of Ethnic and Cultural Affairs in 1980 "to provide ministry, advocacy, and coordination" to the various ethnic groups. Significantly, the secretariat's attitude toward the immigrants represented a departure from previous ministry — the Americanization model of assimilation was discarded for cultural pluralism. The following document from the secretariat's resource book entitled Light of Nations, *edited by Father Anthony McGuire, advocates cultural pluralism.*

Ethnicity and culture are not static but dynamic realities which are constantly in the process of adaptation flowing from immigration, interfacing with other cultures, changing from one generation to the next. The history of the United States is the history of the acculturation of ethnic groups. There are different understandings of the acculturation process: *assimilation* to the dominant culture, the *melting pot,* and the *orchestra.*

[After briefly describing assimilation and the melting pot, the document continues:] Horace Kallen uses the figure of *orchestra:* "The American way is the way of orchestration. As in the orchestra, the different instruments, each with its own characteristic timbre and theme, contribute distinct and recognizable parts to the composition, so in the life and culture of a nation, the different regional, ethnic, occupational, religious and other communities compound their different activities to make up the national spirit. The national spirit is constituted by this union of the different..."

Of all these symbols, *the one to be operative in the Secretariat of Ethnic and Cultural Affairs is the model of orchestration* ... [I]n the mix of ethnic groups, it is important not to suppress cultural expressions and manifestations which are the heart of the ethnic group's identity in the name of uniformity, but rather through respect and dialogue to allow the normal process of integration of cultures to take its course ...

[A] statement published by the United States Catholic Conference on *Cultural Pluralism in the United States* [1980] declares, "In theory and practice, the Church has insisted on the freedom of all peoples to remain faithful to their cultural heritage, their particular language, and their traditions. At the same time recognizing the reality that culture is ever subject to development, that it is not something static but dynamic, the Church has favored the normal process of integration of cultures — sometimes described as acculturation distinguished from assimilation and from the extreme of exaggerated nationalism."

The tension is summed up in the great seal of the United States: *E. Pluribus Unum.* The two parts of the seal deserve equal attention: *E. Pluribus* and *Unum.* To exaggerate pluralism *Pluribus* without working toward the *Unum* causes factionalism. To insist on the *Unum* (uniformity) without respecting identities among the *Pluribus* is a form of cultural oppression.

As Pope John Paul II said, ... "the pluralism of national identities, all of these are compatible with the unity of society."

> Father Anthony McGuire, ed., *Light of Nations: A Resource Directory for Ministry to Ethnic Groups* (San Francisco: Archdiocese of San Francisco, 1985), A-7–A-8. Printed with permission.

142. *Chinese Pastoral Plan: Archdiocese of San Francisco,* 1992

The San Francisco Office of Chinese Catholic Ministry took the outlook of the secretariat (see previous document) and attempted to implement it. What follows is a section of the Chinese Pastoral Plan *for the Archdiocese of San Francisco.*

Development Plan for Pastoral Ministers

This is an area of great difficulty for all concerned. On the one hand, most of the members of the Chinese community have a desire to preserve the best of their culture in terms of values, tradition and faith. Fortunately, most of the people who choose to work with the Chinese community appreciate Chinese culture. Still, it is imperative that we work to eradicate the ignorance that breeds prejudice even among some Chinese, who in their efforts to assimilate may have disassociated themselves from their Chinese background altogether.

Consequently it becomes our task as members of the [O]ffice of Chinese Catholic Ministry to develop a plan that will (1) allow us to share with Priests,

Sisters, Brothers and Lay Leadership the rich and varied traditions of the Chinese culture, and (2) encourage all members of the Archdiocese to rejoice in our diversity as we gain strength and grow. We must find a way to nurture tolerance while we avoid cultural ethnic "ghettoization..."

We, in the Archdiocese of San Francisco, are an immigrant church. Whereas most of our American forebears came across the Atlantic or crossed our southern border, the present reality is that most immigrants are from the Pacific Basin. We need to be open and welcoming, recalling the terrible prejudices inflicted upon those who preceded us...

The hope is that with patience, prayer and the willingness to learn about the values, beauty and richness of what the Chinese community has to offer, the Chinese Catholic Community will take its rightful place in the Councils of the Church...

We need Chinese pastoral ministers who can speak the Chinese language and understand the culture, customs and traditions of their own people. It is also important to educate non-Chinese pastoral ministers, who will minister to the Chinese, so they will serve the Chinese communities more effectively.

Courses in Chinese cultural history and languages should be offered at St. Patrick's Seminary, at the Religious Education Institute, priest and religious formation days, etc...

> *Chinese Pastoral Plan: Archdiocese of San Francisco* (1992). Reprinted with
> permission.

143. Kerry Tremain, "Welcoming the New Americans: The Same Love," 1999

Since World War II the church has had to confront the problems of assisting refugees. Unfortunately, the flow of refugees has increased in the past twenty-five years. It has placed tremendous stress on Catholic Charities throughout the United States. The following comes from the newsletter of Catholic Charities of the Diocese of Oakland.

In war normal human relations, the patterns of love and interdependency that we take for granted, are blown apart...

Most of the refugees who seek Catholic Charities' services have been through a war. The Vietnam war. Wars in Bosnia, Afghanistan or Ethiopia — the places that supply the ghastly images we see at the tailend of the news broadcast.

The Mien (or Hmong) people who fought on the side of the United States in Southeast Asia are one such group. During the fighting in Laos, Mien families could not stay in their villages, which could be raided by the enemy and everyone killed. Instead, the women and children would travel with the fighting men. In the military camps however, they were a liability to the fighters...The women and children were also a military target — they were easier to pick off — and young children were subject to malnutrition and disease. Many, many died. Kristen Pursley, of the English Action Center in Richmond, says that it is common that the parents she counsels have lost three or more children...

Many refugees suffer from Post-Traumatic Stress Disorder (PTSD)...In denying a disability waiver to one of Kristen's clients, a middle-age Laotian mother with chronic depression, an INS official claimed she didn't have PTSD because "he knew a lot of vets" and she wasn't like them.

The Veteran[s] Administration's National Center for PTSD takes a some-what less-subjective approach. The symptoms they've identified include re-peated nightmares, flashbacks, pessimism about the future and expectation of early death, and emotional numbness...

Families have difficulty coping with members who experience PTSD. They may grow discouraged, angry, and distant...

Refugees to the United States carry with them these memories as they step off the plane into a new land, a land of plenty, a land without mines exploding or bullets flying, but one in which a different language is spoken and whose cultural customs are usually radically different from the villages of home...

For thousands of immigrants, Catholic Charities has been the life saver, providing emergency shelter and food, classes in English, job training and placement. It is a crucial first step, but far from the last...

> *Charity: Newsletter of Catholic Charities of the East Bay* (March/April 1999): 1.
> Reprinted with permission.

144. Laotian Catholic Refugees in the United States, 1993

Father Louis Leduc describes the difficult experience endured by Laotian refu-gees in an interview with Migration World, *a publication of the Center for Migration Studies in Staten Island, New York.*

Father Louis S. Leduc, a priest of the Paris Foreign Missionary Society, spent nearly 30 years as a missionary in Thailand and Laos. In 1984 he began ser-vice to the Laotian community of St. George Church, Fort Worth, Texas. The following year Father Leduc accompanied the Most Rev. Pierre Bach, former Bishop of Thakek, Laos, on an extensive pastoral visit to Laotian Catholic communities in the United States and Canada. Bishop Bach and Father Leduc...endeavored to link Laotian refugee faith communities most in need to their local parishes and dioceses. Also in 1985, Father Leduc was a founding member of the Laotian Mission Team, a preaching program in the Laotian language, aimed at leading people to a renewal and deeper com-mitment to Jesus Christ, the Church and the life of the Church as it is lived in the local community. Among the locations in which the Mission

Team ministered to Laotian refugees were Bridgeport, CT; Columbus, OH; Rochester, MN; San Diego and Richmond, CA; Seattle, WA; Philadelphia and Scranton, PA; Lowell, Lynn and Roxbury, MA; Des Moines, IA; Fort Smith, AR; Fort Worth, TX; Honolulu, HI; Portland, OR; Nashville, TN; and Vancouver, BC.

Father Leduc directs the Laotian Pastoral Center in Fort Worth, TX...

Q. Are refugees in general and Laotian refugees in particular made to feel welcome in the local church?

A. Generally speaking, it is impossible to talk about all refugees. Please bear in mind that all of them have some things in common. They are refugees for many reasons. There is starvation, religious, political or social persecutions. All of them have suffered violence and all of them are in the same intolerable situation. They have been forced to abandon their homeland, their relations, their homes, all their properties and their loved ones.

Where do I find them? Very often I find them on the outskirts of the cities — dejected, in bad housing, among illegal migrants, in the midst of violence, fear, dirtiness and sadness. They are at the bottom of society...

I can find some Laotian Catholics absolutely lost in this country. They search in vain among our hundreds of temples and churches for a helping hand and someone who will introduce them to the Church, the rectory and the priest. But unfortunately, many do not care...

By temperament and faith, I am ordinarily optimistic, but my position and the situation of the refugees and the reactions of many Catholics leaves me sorrowful...

Q. Where do the Lao come from? What are some characteristics of their country of origin and their religious orientation?

A. They come from Laos, a small country (91,494 sq. miles), located in Southeast Asia...The Lao population is relatively small, with fewer than 4 million inhabitants, composed of many ethnic groups. The two major groups are the Lowland Lao — the largest single group, and the Highland Lao — made up of a variety of ethnic groups, the largest of which are the Hmong who have a distinct language and culture.

Theravada Buddhism, the religion of the state, is adhered to by 90 percent of the population. Animism is still present among various tribes. Christians represent only about one percent of the population. Buddhism affects the moral, social, and cultural life of the Laotians. Daily life in the village revolves around the pagoda as the center and the heart of the village. Buddhist monks traditionally have filled roles as teachers, counselors, healers, and community leaders...

Q. How have the events of their migration affected Lao refugees?

A. It is important to remember the traumatic sufferings endured by the Lao before coming to America. They had to walk for days and nights to reach the Mekong River and cross it amid the bullets of the communists.

Their difficult life in the refugee camps in Thailand left an indelible mark. When they finally arrived in the United States many were disillusioned. Prior events were unforgettable and had an irreversible effect which destroyed the peace and the convictions in the hearts of these refugees.

When they arrived, they were totally lost, physically and morally. One of the refugees has said, "You know, only my body is here. The rest of me, including my soul and my thoughts, are still back there." Each refugee comes with different feelings and from very different backgrounds... When relocated in the United States, almost all refugees go through a period of exile shock. This realization that they are cut off from their family and the old way of life...

The Lao remain greatly interested in events occurring in their native country. They hope against hope to return some day...

Their homesickness is especially prevalent during the Lao New Year, the Feast of Water and other significant occasions such as births, marriages or deaths...

Q. What is the relationship of Laotian refugees to the Church?

A. Here too we find a wide range of situations ranging from abandonment to full integration. Generally speaking, clergy are not sufficiently aware of the problems facing Asiatic refugees. Contact between clergy and the newcomers is very difficult because the Lao people are timid and shy. There is a language barrier on both sides so neither the Lao nor American clergy know how to reach each other.

The Lao are in the habit of going to the rectory any time to talk to the priest. They ask that their child, born two days before, be baptized the next day. They decide the marriage of their children according to their local Lao customs and inform the priest two weeks in advance. They are lost when it comes to the regulations of the church in the United States. Not understanding English, they find attending Sunday Mass to be boring. They have an English-Lao prayerbook and they can pray in their own language, but they feel bad that they cannot participate with English-speaking congregations. Where there is a sufficiently large Lao community (20 to 50 families), the parish priest celebrates a special monthly Mass for them, usually on Sunday afternoon. The priest celebrates in English, of course, but the readings and songs are in the Laotian language...

In certain parishes Lao are more or less integrated into the church. In these instances there are religious sisters or lay persons to sponsor them and take care of them. These Lao do not have major problems about attending church and can contact the priest through their sponsors. In several places, even without the presence of a Laotian-speaking priest, our Lao Catholics are really "at home" in the local church...

All things considered, however, the majority of Lao refugees remain far from being fully integrated into the local church. With a few exceptions, they remain strangers in the church.

One cannot forget that Lao people are from mission territories where they were members of a subsidized church and they in turn were assisted by the church.

The missionaries helped them to face all kinds of problems: disease, poverty, education of their children, assistance to the whole family. In America, instead, they must assist the church by participating in Sunday collections. To reach the priest, when they have no sponsor to assist them, they have to call the parish office to make an appointment. When the secretary asks them to spell their name, which is generally long, they hang up and await the next visit of the Laotian-speaking priest, which may be quite a while, to have a child baptized or a child registered for religious education classes. The Catholic Church in the United States lacks the personnel to provide adequate pastoral care for Lao refugees and it is an illusion to think that some former missionaries who speak Lao will come. The problem has to be faced and solved right here in America...

...Above all, it is important to explain [to the Lao] the relationship between faith and life. They cannot become Catholics alone, apart from a caring, receptive community. We need to help them to find their place among us. We have to receive them with a new kind of thinking and wisdom as brothers and sisters in Christ and members of his church, recognizing their differences from us as being complementary. We need to help them retain their Laotian identity as members of the Catholic Church. When the Lao refugee feels that he or she is accepted as a brother or sister, they are finally at home, free from fear, in the church.

Migration World 21, no. 1 (1993). Printed with permission of the Center for Migration Studies.

145. Robert W. McChesney, "The Mother Teresa of Immigration Detention," 1999

The following document, written by Jesuit Father Robert W. McChesney, chaplain at the San Pedro Immigration and Naturalization Service Detention Center and Los Angeles director of the Jesuit Refugee Service Immigration Detention Program, describes a growing problem with the new immigration — detainees. As in other immigrant communities, laypeople have become central to effective ministry.

The other detainees in Pod 6 at the immigration detention center in San Pedro, Calif., call her "Mother Teresa." El Salvador-born Ana Amalia Guzman Molina arrived at the Immigration and Naturalization Service lock-up...on March 20, 1998. Back home she had worked as an accountant and had studied at the Jesuit university in San Salvador...Amalia's husband, José, is also detained at San Pedro, in another unit. José's father was shot in the back of the head in an assassination attempt... Fortunately, he survived.

Eventually the couple and their three children fled to the United States, where they petitioned for asylum in one of the immigration courts operated by the U.S. Department of Justice at the detention center. Their claim is complicated by financial debts left behind when they fled during the chaos of war. Last fall the immigration judge ruled against them, and they wait patiently... while their case is reviewed on appeal.

...I.N.S. detainees represent the fastest-growing segment of the nation's exploding prison population. The I.N.S. calls it "administrative detention" or even "administrative processing,..."

Amalia wastes no time while she waits, in evangelical alertness, along with up to 100 other female detainees in their cramped unit. The anticipation of Emmanuel, God With Us, is never far from her consciousness. For many of the other women Amalia is, in fact, a tangible sign of God's care for them in their present predicament.

The Jesuit Refugee Service seeks to empower and minister through those it serves, aware that detainees themselves are the primary resource. Amalia, a natural leader, is bilingual, educated and a devout Catholic. She serves as J.R.S. liaison for religious services in Pod 6 — a fellow apostle. We regularly consult on the needs of the unit. The hours of access for outside religious providers are quite limited, and with few exceptions the phenomenon of immigration detention has caught the Catholic Church by surprise; so Catholic detainees often depend upon God to raise up leaders from within their places of incarceration.

The working of divine providence is particularly evident right now at San Pedro in Pod 6. On a typical day Amalia will gather other interested detainees at 6:00 P.M. for Bible studies and faith sharing. Pod security officers announce over an internal speaker system that the "Catholic study group" is about to begin. Then, before lights out at 10 P.M., Amalia brings the women together again to pray the rosary. J.R.S. supplies a variety of devotional articles, Bibles and study materials, and I bless them at the weekly Eucharist. Presently the study group is working its way through the Gospel of Mark. "This is our church, our parish," Amalia explains in a matter-of-fact tone...

Recently Amalia noticed that a new Chinese arrival did not join the Chinese Protestants for prayer, but made the Sign of the Cross reverently next to her bed before retiring. She established (through another detainee as interpreter) that the Chinese woman was a Roman Catholic...

Amalia introduced me to the Chinese woman at the first opportunity, and I listened to her tearful account. Six months pregnant with her second child, she was forced to have an abortion by Chinese authorities. At that point she fled with her husband in search of political asylum, and was detained at San Pedro. The young woman reveres traditional Catholic symbols — last month she rejoiced in the gift of a Marian holy card and smiled movingly at the opportunity to hold the small standing crucifix I place on the picnic-table altar during religious services...

...[W]hat a blessing upon the Catholic Church in the United States is [Amalia], this faith-filled, determined apostle of the Lord. May she be reunited with her family soon.

America, April 24, 1999, 14–15. Reprinted with permission.

OF RELATED INTEREST

Other volumes in the American Catholic Identities Series,
Christopher J. Kauffmann, General Editor

*An indispensable resource of original documents
relating to the social and political history of American Catholics
from the Spanish, French, and English colonial beginnings to the present.*

*Absolutely must be in the library of every student of American Catholicism...
a marvelous resource for the classroom... brings alive the whole
panorama of Catholics struggling with and finding identity.*

Public Voices: Catholics in the American Context
Steven M. Avella and Elizabeth McKeown, editors
ISBN 1-57075-266-4

Catholics find their voice in the new republic, moving from outsiders to
insiders, adapting to their new homeland, staying loyal to the Catholic
vision.

The Frontier and Catholic Identities
Anne M. Butler, Michael E. Engh, SJ, and Thomas W. Spalding, CFX, editors
ISBN 1-57075-269-9

The Catholic experience in the epic adventure of expanding frontiers and
settling in a vast continent.

Prayer and Practice in the American Catholic Community
Joseph Chinnici, OFM, and Angelyn Dries, OSF
ISBN 1-57075-342-3

Grappling with the fusion and maintenance of spiritual practices and
prayer from a host of European traditions in the new land.

¡Presente! Latino Catholics from Colonial Origins to the Present
Timothy Matovina and Gerald E. Poyo, editors
ISBN 1-57075-328-8

Latinos preserve their Catholic traditions in the emerging culture, struggling to gain the attention of an often indifferent, sometimes hostile
church.

Creative Fidelity: U. S. Catholic Intellectual Identities

R. Scott Appleby, Patricia Byren, William Portier, editors
ISBN 1-57075-349-0

> Over against the Protestant ascendancy, American Catholics make a distinctive voice heard in the American intellectual landscape.

Gender Identities in American Catholicism

Paula Kane, James Kenneally, Karen Kennelly, CSJ, editors
ISBN 1-57075-350-4

> Women and men rub up against gender-defined roles inherited from ancient cultures and struggle to create a more egalitarian Catholic community within the larger culture.

The Crossing of Two Roads: Being Catholic and Native in the United States

Marie Therese Archambault, OSF, Mark Theil, and Christopher Vecsey, editors
ISBN 1-57075-352-0

> Native American Catholics and their quest to retain traditional identities while joining in the religious faith of those who have taken over their land.

"Stamped with the Image of God": African-Americans as God's Image in Black

Cyprian Davis, OSB, and Jamie Phelps, OP, editors
ISBN 1-57075-351-2

> African Americans experience an ambiguous welcome from their white fellow Catholics and seek a way to be both black and Catholic.

Please support your local bookstore, or call 1-800-258-5838

For a free catalogue, please write us at

Orbis Books, Box 302
Maryknoll NY 10545-0302

or visit our website at www.maryknoll.com.

Thank you for reading Orbis Books.

ORBIS BOOKS

Maryknoll, New York 10545